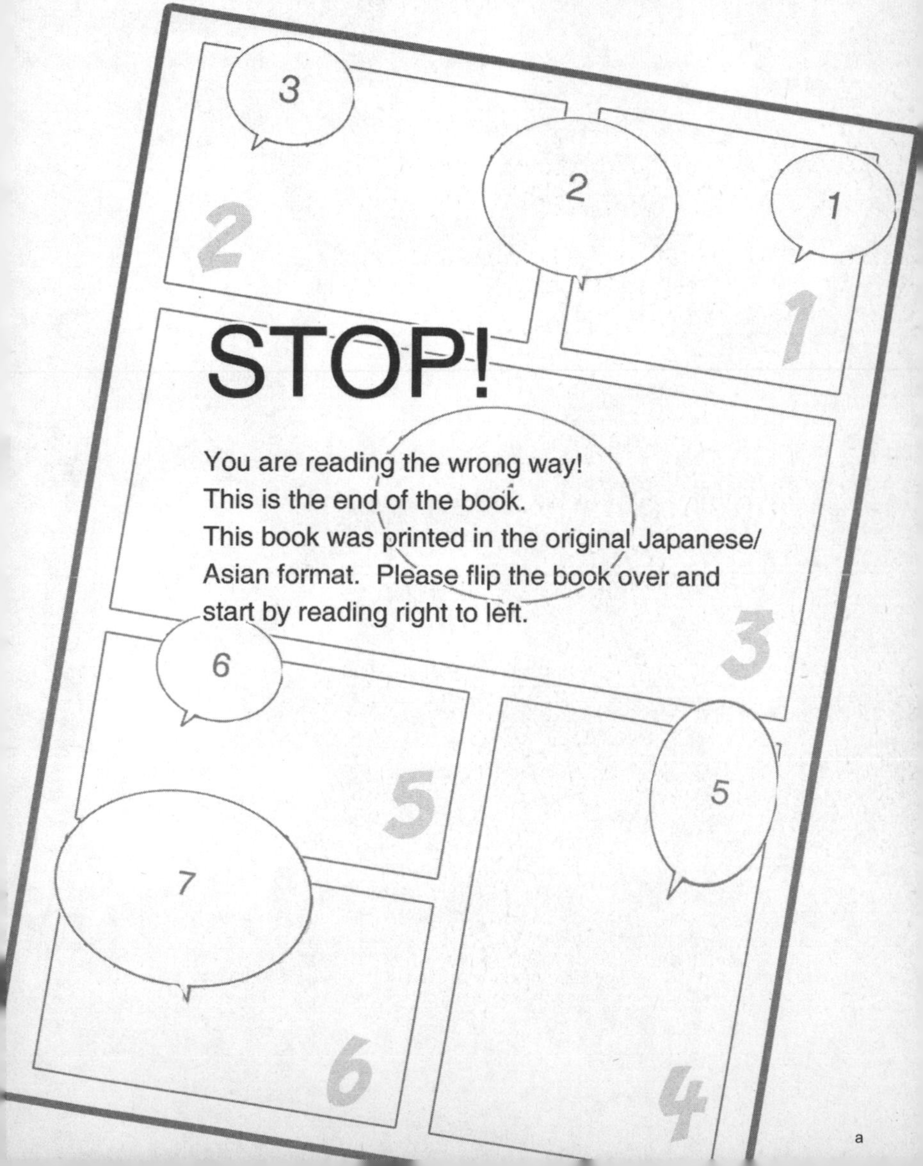

STOP!

You are reading the wrong way!
This is the end of the book.
This book was printed in the original Japanese/
Asian format. Please flip the book over and
start by reading right to left.

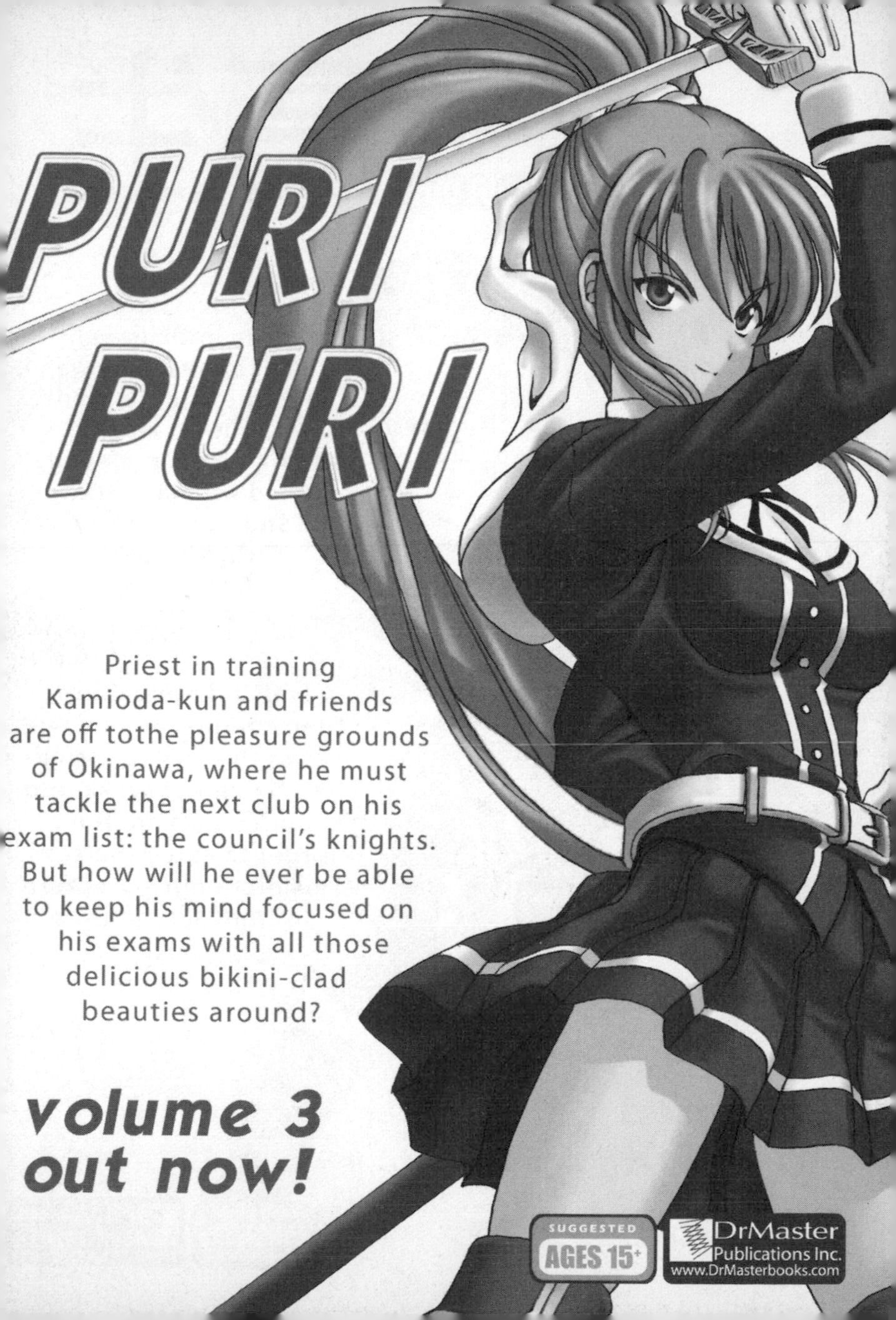
PURI PURI
Priest in training Kamioda-kun and friends are off tothe pleasure grounds of Okinawa, where he must tackle the next club on his exam list: the council's knights. But how will he ever be able to keep his mind focused on his exams with all those delicious bikini-clad beauties around?
volume 3 out now!
SUGGESTED
AGES 15+
DrMaster Publications Inc.
www.DrMasterbooks.com

女子高生
High School Girls
© Towa Oshima

We're in Okinawa!
What awaits us as we
venture into the land
of exotica, Japan's
southernmost prefecture
filled with mysteries
old and new? Romance?
Forbidden love?
Adventure?

Emi and Kouda face
their toughest challenge
yet as they try to assimi-
late Nao and Sayaka into
our club! And don't
forget to catch the con-
clusion to our adventure
in *High School Girls
vol. 9*, available
this March!

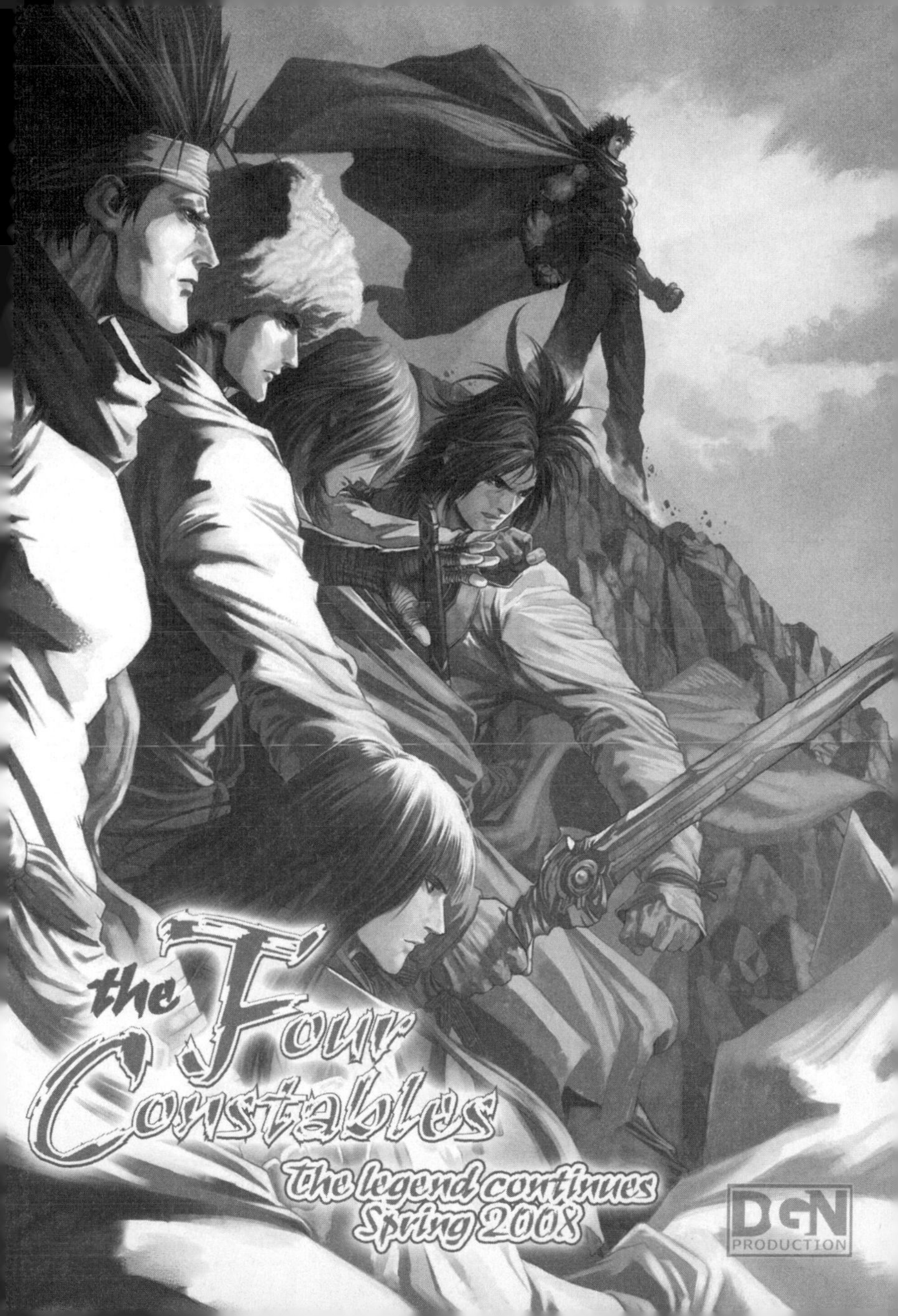
the Four Constables
The legend continues
Spring 2008
DGN PRODUCTION

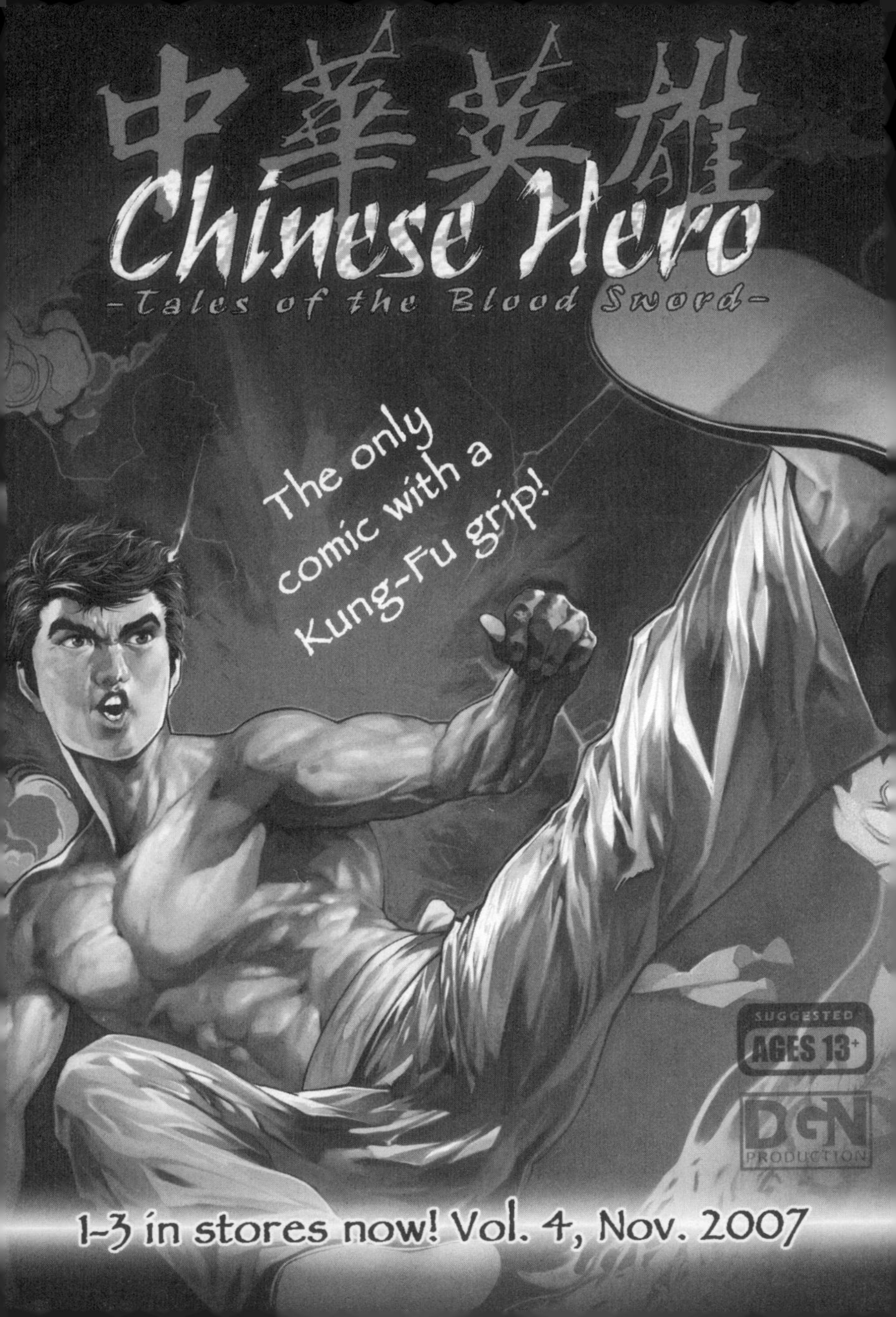

中華英雄
Chinese Hero
-Tales of the Blood Sword-
The only comic with a Kung-Fu grip!
SUGGESTED AGES 13+
DGN PRODUCTION
1-3 in stores now! Vol. 4, Nov. 2007

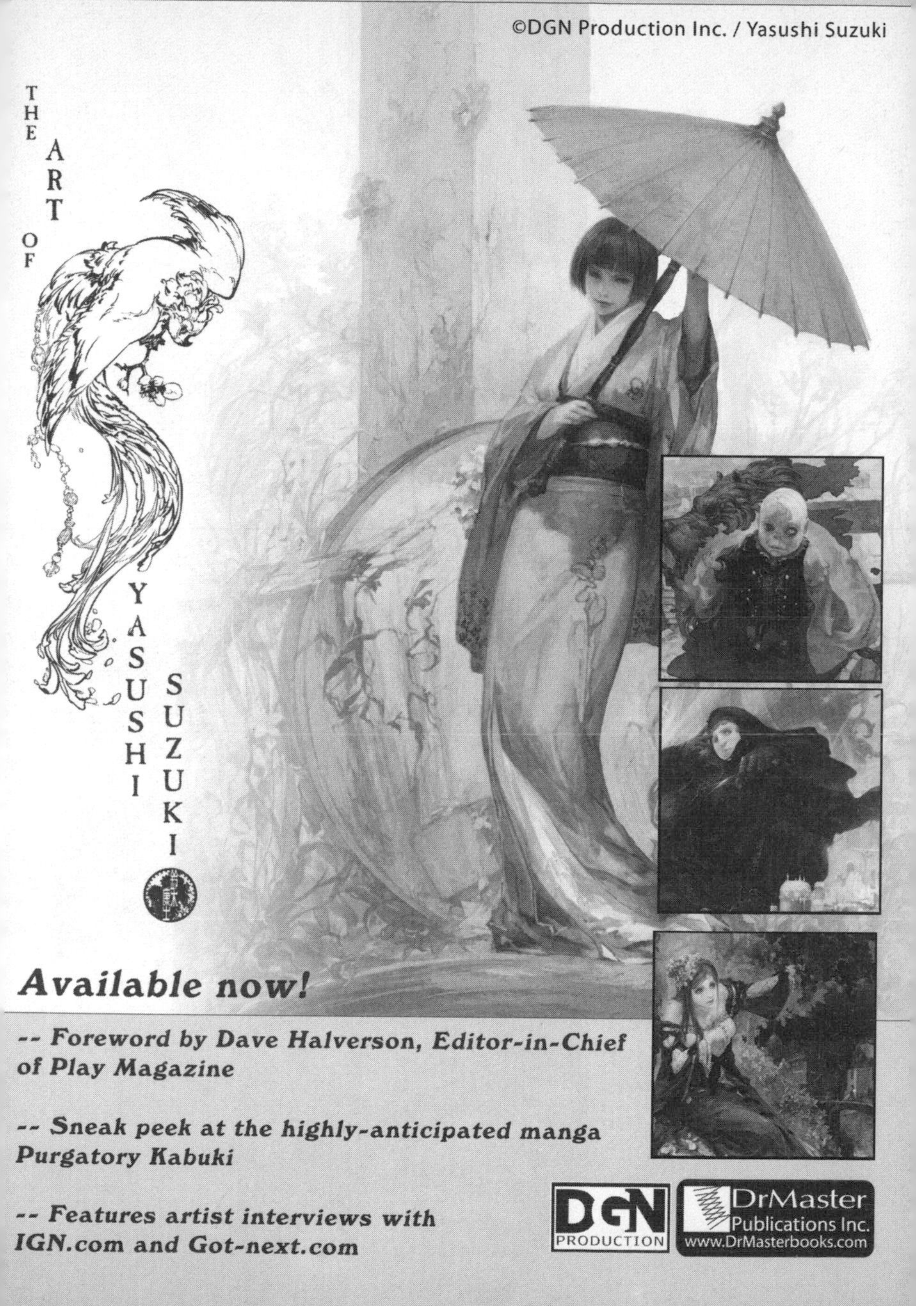
©DGN Production Inc. / Yasushi Suzuki
THE ART OF YASUSHI SUZUKI
Available now!
-- Foreword by Dave Halverson, Editor-in-Chief of Play Magazine
-- Sneak peek at the highly-anticipated manga Purgatory Kabuki
-- Features artist interviews with IGN.com and Got-next.com
DGN PRODUCTION
DrMaster Publications Inc.
www.DrMasterbooks.com

METRO SURVIVE

AVAILABLE FEB. 2008

YŪKI FUJISAWA

PURGATORY KABUKI

DrMaster Publications Inc.
www.DrMasterbooks.com

DARK✝EDGE

evil returns volume 7
Spring 2008

DrMaster
Publications Inc.
www.DrMasterbooks.com

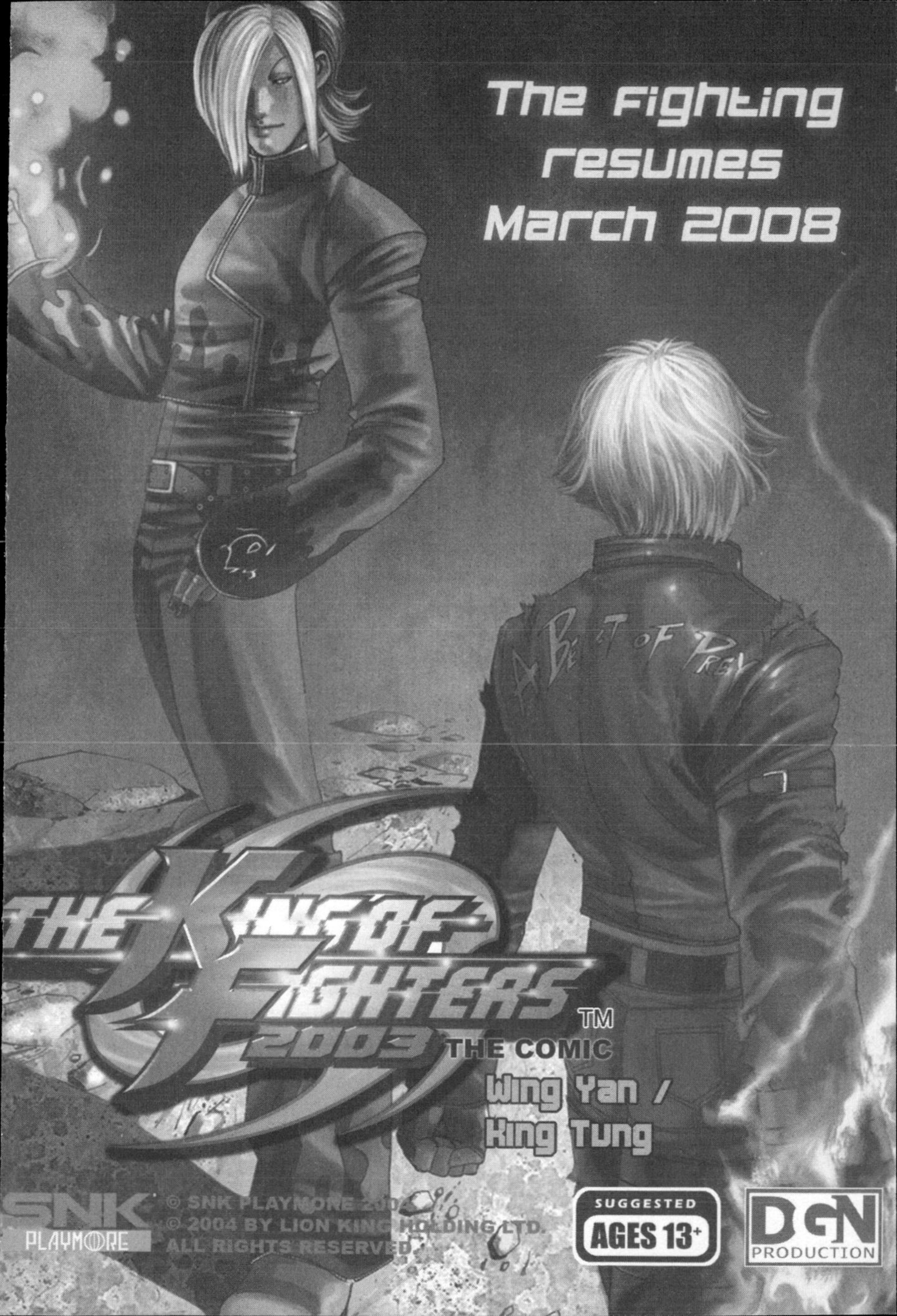
The fighting resumes March 2008
A BEAST OF PREY
THE KING OF FIGHTERS 2003 ™
THE COMIC
Wing Yan /
King Tung
SNK PLAYMORE
© SNK PLAYMORE 2004
© 2004 BY LION KING HOLDING LTD.
ALL RIGHTS RESERVED
SUGGESTED AGES 13+
DGN PRODUCTION

AFTERWORD

AT THE END OF SERIALIZATION...
BY KEIKO OYAMA

THE FIVE YEARS I'VE WORKED ON THIS PIECE SEEMED TO HAVE PASSED BY QUICKLY, THOUGH. IT WAS STILL LONG. IT FEELS LIKE AN ERA HAS ENDED IN THE HISTORY OF MANGA. THROUGH AN ERA OF ONE BILLION GOURMETS TO ONE BILLION FAKE CHEFS, IRON WOK JAN HAS SEEN IT ALL! IT REALLY IS SOMETHING, WHEN YOU THINK ABOUT IT.

I'VE HAD SUDDEN CHEST PAINS AND INEXPLICABLE MILD FEVER THROUGHOUT THE COURSE OF THIS WORK AND I FREQUENTLY COMPLAINED ABOUT MY PHYSICAL DISCOMFORT TO THE EDITOR IN CHARGE. BUT, WHEN I MET WITH THE PEOPLE FROM SAIJYO PRODUCTION STUDIO AT THE NEW YEAR'S PARTY, I THINK I FIGURED THE CAUSE OF THIS. I SAW THEIR COLD EYES, EVERYWHERE – EVERYWHERE I LOOK. "IS THIS THE OYAMA SENSEI WHO ASKS YOU TO REDRAW THE PAGES OVER AND OVER?" AND I SEE THEM HOLDING A VOODOO DOLL AND A LONG, SHARP NAIL IN THEIR HAND! SCARY! I SNUCK OUT OF THE PARTY SITE RIGHT AFTER THAT.

NOW THAT THE SERIALIZATION IS OVER, I NO LONGER HAVE THE SUDDEN CHEST PAINS AND INEXPLICABLE MILD FEVER, BUT SOMEHOW, I FEEL VERY NOSTALGIC ABOUT THE CHEST PAINS AND MILD FEVER... WHAT THE HELL DOES THIS MEAN?! JAN, KIRIKO, TELL ME WHY!!

IRON WOK JAN! VOL. 27 THE END (SERIES CONCLUDED)

DrMaster
Publications Inc.
www.DrMasterbooks.com

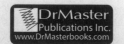

IRON WOK JAN!

Author / Shinji Saijyo

Translator / Toshikazu Hosaka

Editor / Benjamin Stone

Supervising Editor / Matthew Scrivner

Production Artist / Michael Sandborn

Production Manager / Bryce Gunkel

V.P. of Operations / Yuki Chung

President / Jennifer Chen

DrMaster Publications, Inc.
4044 Clipper Ct.
Fremont, CA 94538
www.DrMasterbooks.com

First Edition: December 2007
ISBN: 978-1-59796-050-2

IRON WOK JAN VOLUME 27

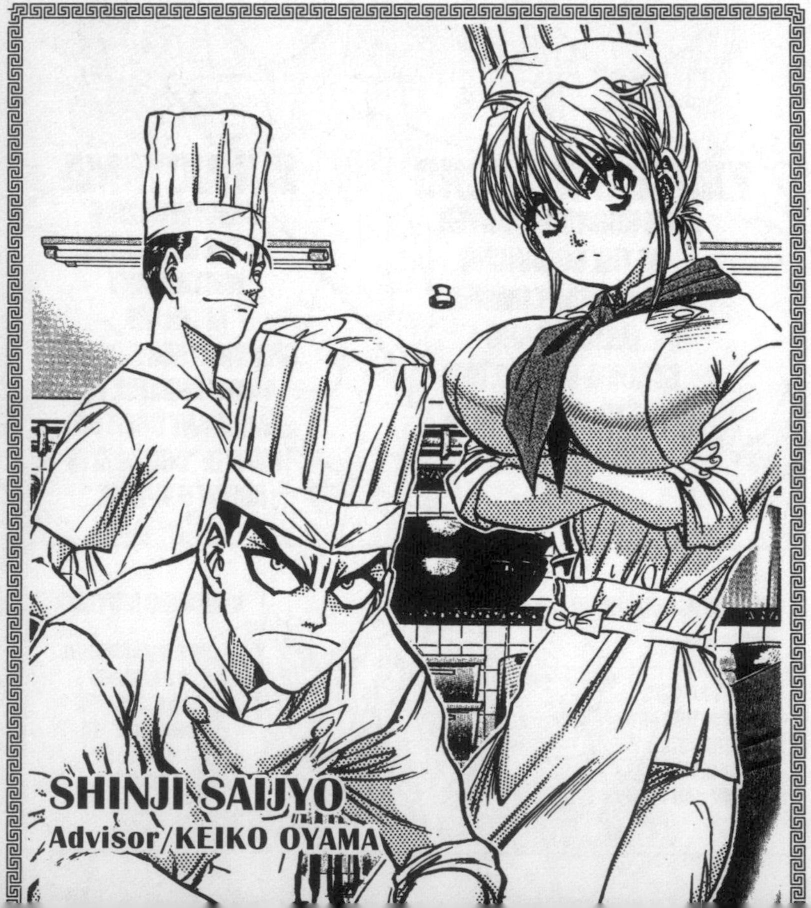
SHINJI SAIJYO
Advisor/KEIKO OYAMA

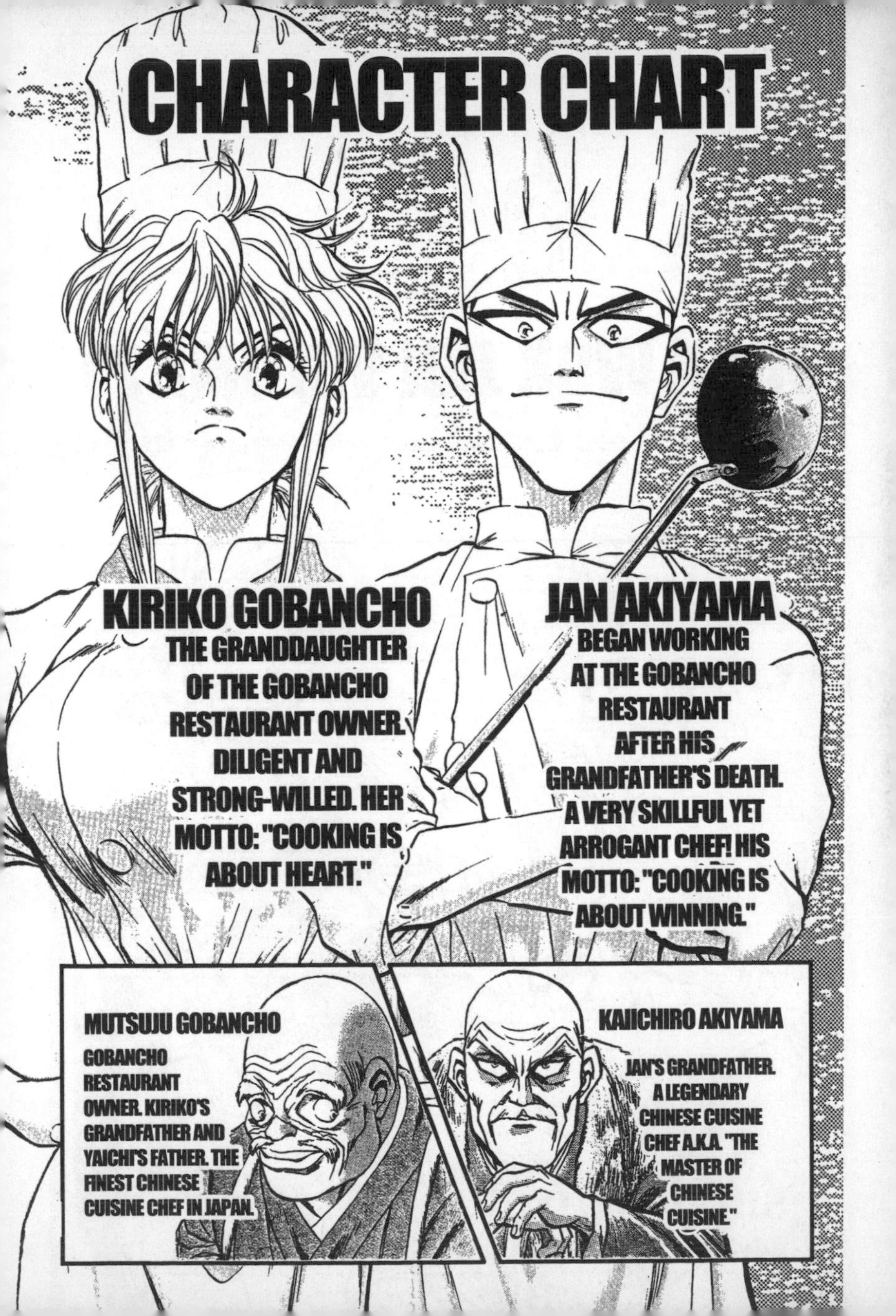
CHARACTER CHART
JAN AKIYAMA
BEGAN WORKING AT THE GOBANCHO RESTAURANT AFTER HIS GRANDFATHER'S DEATH. A VERY SKILLFUL YET ARROGANT CHEF! HIS MOTTO: "COOKING IS ABOUT WINNING."
KIRIKO GOBANCHO
THE GRANDDAUGHTER OF THE GOBANCHO RESTAURANT OWNER. DILIGENT AND STRONG-WILLED. HER MOTTO: "COOKING IS ABOUT HEART."
KAIICHIRO AKIYAMA
JAN'S GRANDFATHER. A LEGENDARY CHINESE CUISINE CHEF A.K.A. "THE MASTER OF CHINESE CUISINE."
MUTSUJU GOBANCHO
GOBANCHO RESTAURANT OWNER. KIRIKO'S GRANDFATHER AND YAICHI'S FATHER. THE FINEST CHINESE CUISINE CHEF IN JAPAN.

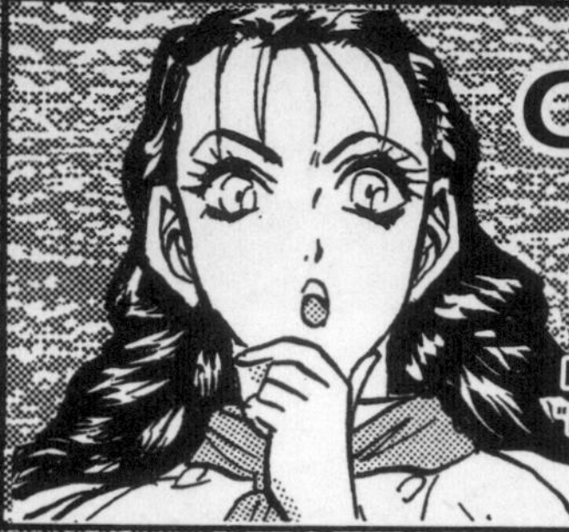

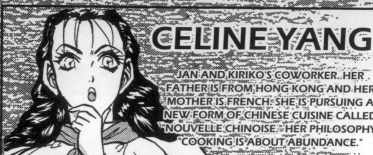

CELINE YANG

JAN AND KIRIKO'S COWORKER. HER FATHER IS FROM HONG KONG AND HER MOTHER IS FRENCH. SHE IS PURSUING A NEW FORM OF CHINESE CUISINE CALLED "NOUVELLE CHINOISE." HER PHILOSOPHY: "COOKING IS ABOUT ABUNDANCE."

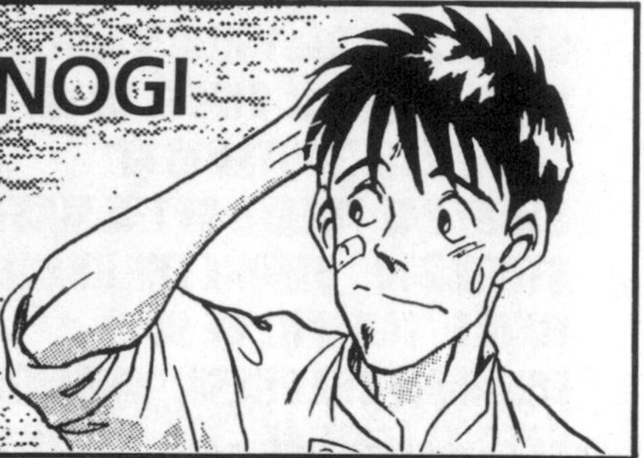

TAKAO OKONOGI

GOBANCHO RESTAURANT TRAINEE WHO CONSTANTLY SCREWS UP BUT IS THE ONLY PERSON JAN OPENS UP TO.

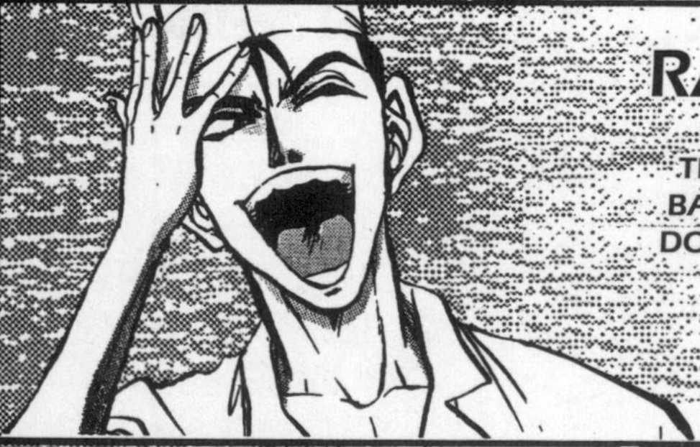

RANSEI KOH

THE SUCCESSOR TO THE BAI LAN WANG WHICH IS DOMINATING THE WORLD OF CHINESE CUISINE IN ALL OF ASIA.

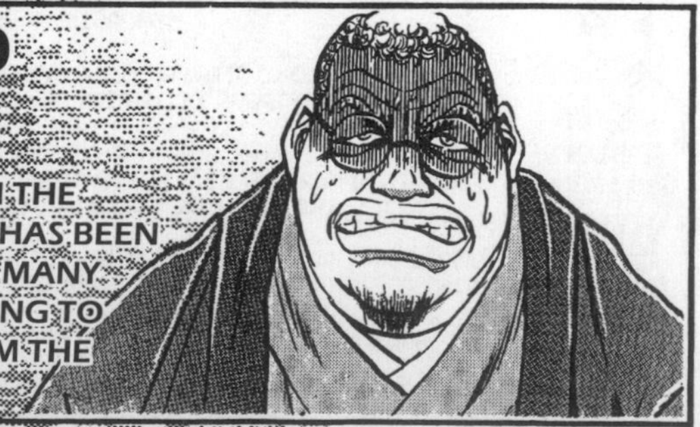

NICHIDO OTANI

A FOOD CRITIC WITH THE TONGUE OF A GOD. HAS BEEN HUMILIATED BY JAN MANY TIMES AND IS PLOTTING TO ELIMINATE JAN FROM THE COOKING WORLD.

IRON WOK JAN!

VOLUME 27 TABLE OF CONTENTS

STORY 243: "IT'S ALL CHAOS!" --- 7

STORY 244: "MUTSUJU'S ABILITY!" --- 27

STORY 245: "I'LL GIVE IT TO YA!" --- 47

STORY 246: "MUTSUJU X!" --- 67

STORY 247: "DEATH OF THE MASTER!" --- 87

STORY 248: "BEFORE THE GRAVE...!" ---107

FINALE: "JAN WILL BE JAN!" ---127

FRESH OFF THE PRESS: "SHOCKING ENDING" ---157

SPECIAL FEATURE – MR. SAIJYO'S DEBUT WORK:
"MYSTERY ALLIANCE" ---165

SYNOPSIS

IT IS THE SECOND ANNUAL YOUNG CHINESE CHEF COOK-OFF.
THE FINAL ROUND THEME IS OSTRICH, MEAT FOR THE 21ST CENTURY.

JAN PREPARED A "MAGIC BOX" THAT TURNED THE LEAN RED OSTRICH
FLESH INTO MARBLED MEAT. HE HAD ACTUALLY INFESTED THE BOX
WITH FLIES WHICH THEN LAID MAGGOTS ON THE MEAT!

EVEN OTANI HADN'T BEEN PREPARED FOR SUCH A HORRIFIC DISH,
BUT AS HE GOT UP TO PUNCH JAN, SOMETHING STRANGE HAPPENED--
JAN HIT THE FLOOR HARD! SOMEBODY--OR SOMETHING--
HAD DELIVERED A FLYING KICK, RIGHT INTO HIS FACE!

THIS IS A WORK OF FICTION.

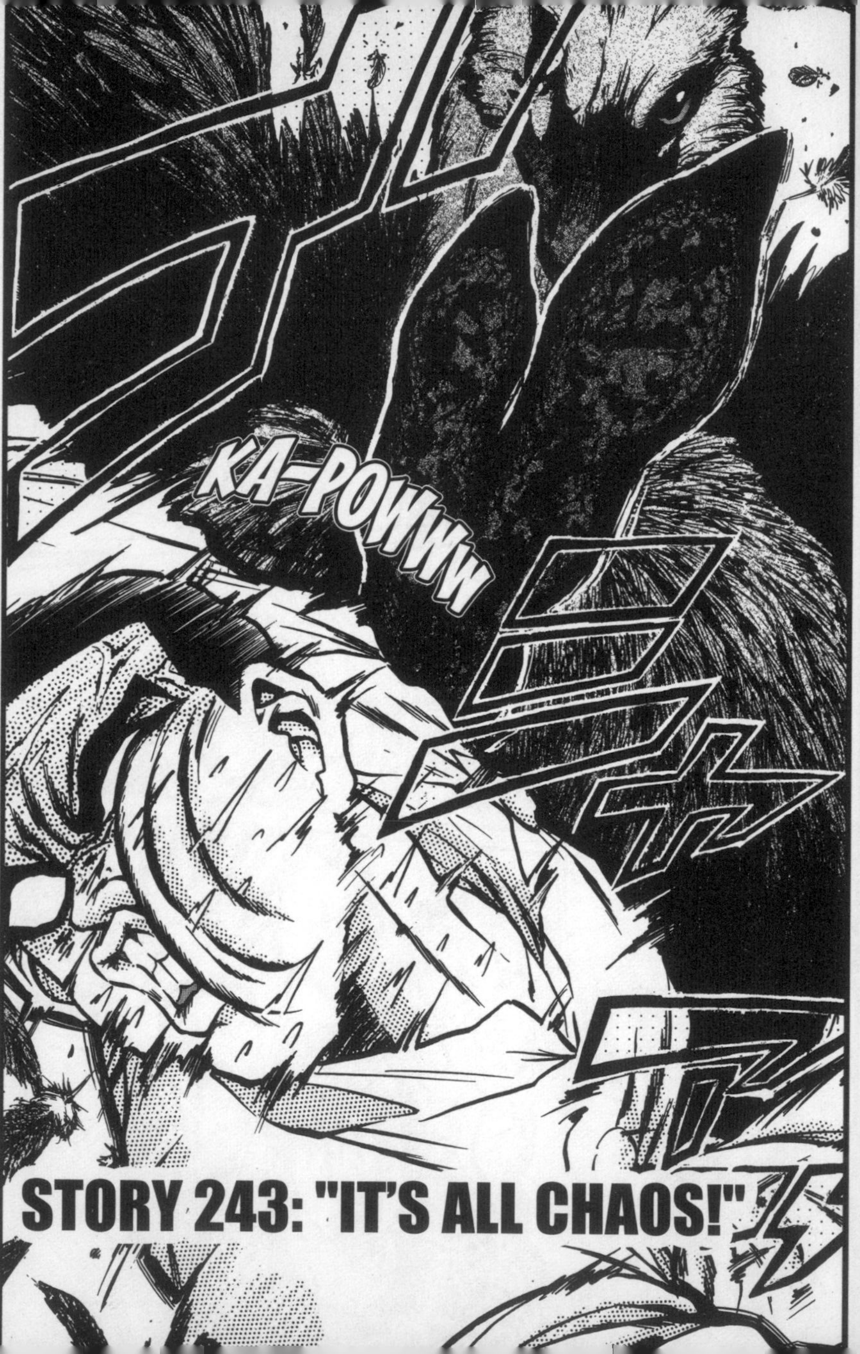
KA-POWWW
STORY 243: "IT'S ALL CHAOS!"

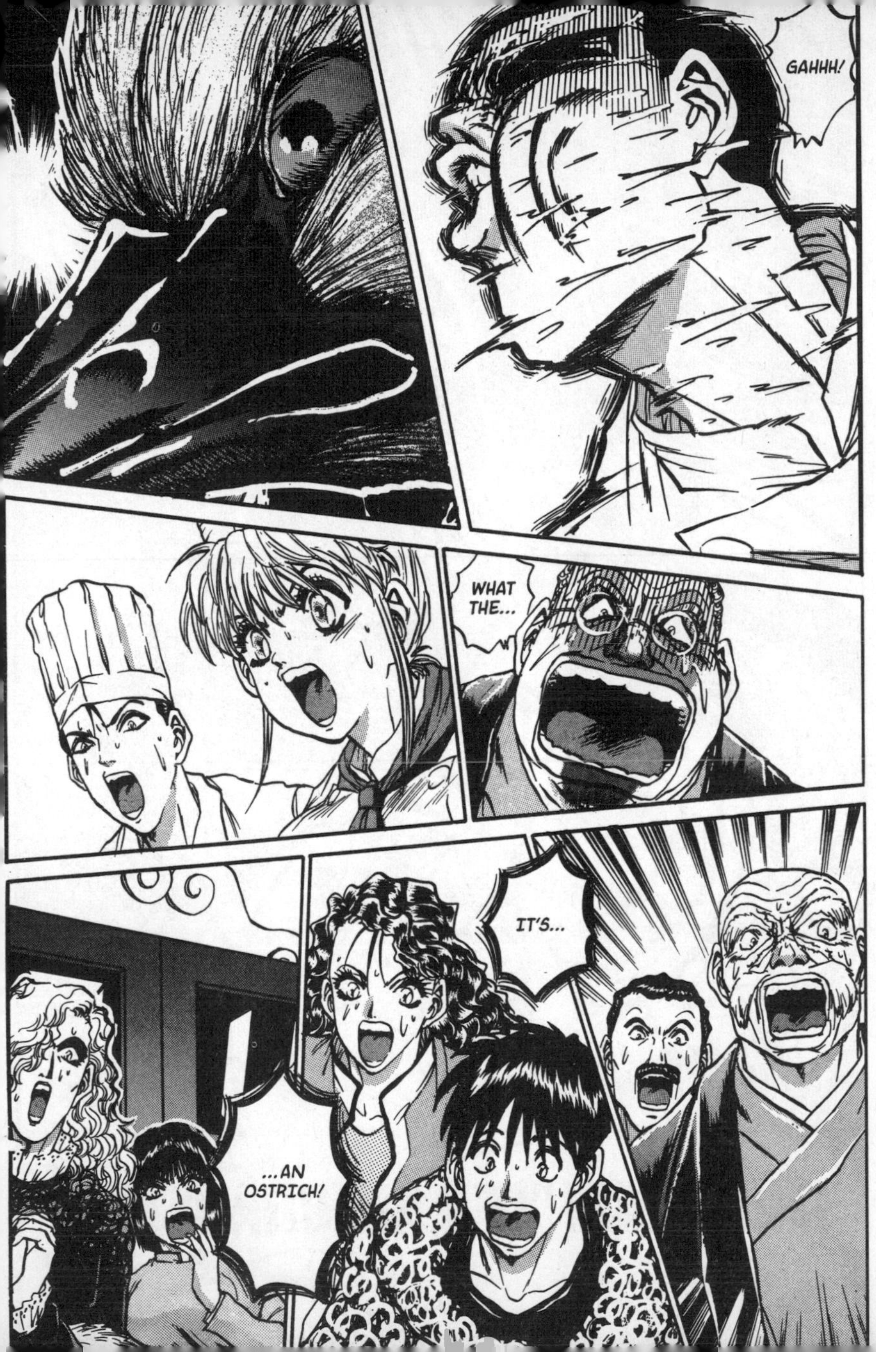
GAHHH!
WHAT THE...
IT'S...
...AN OSTRICH!

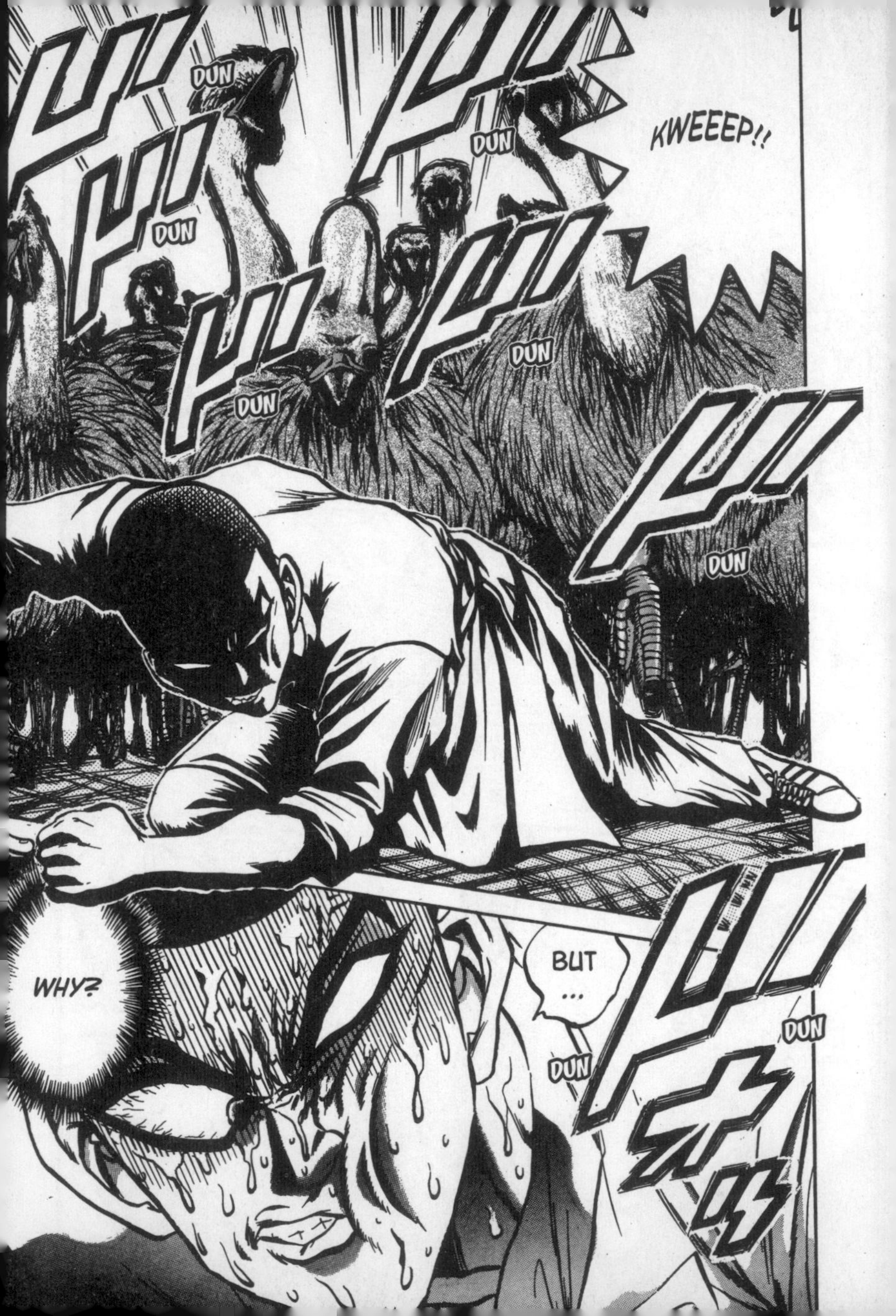
KWEEEP!!
DUN
DUN
DUN
DUN
DUN
DUN
DUN
BUT ...
DUN
WHY?

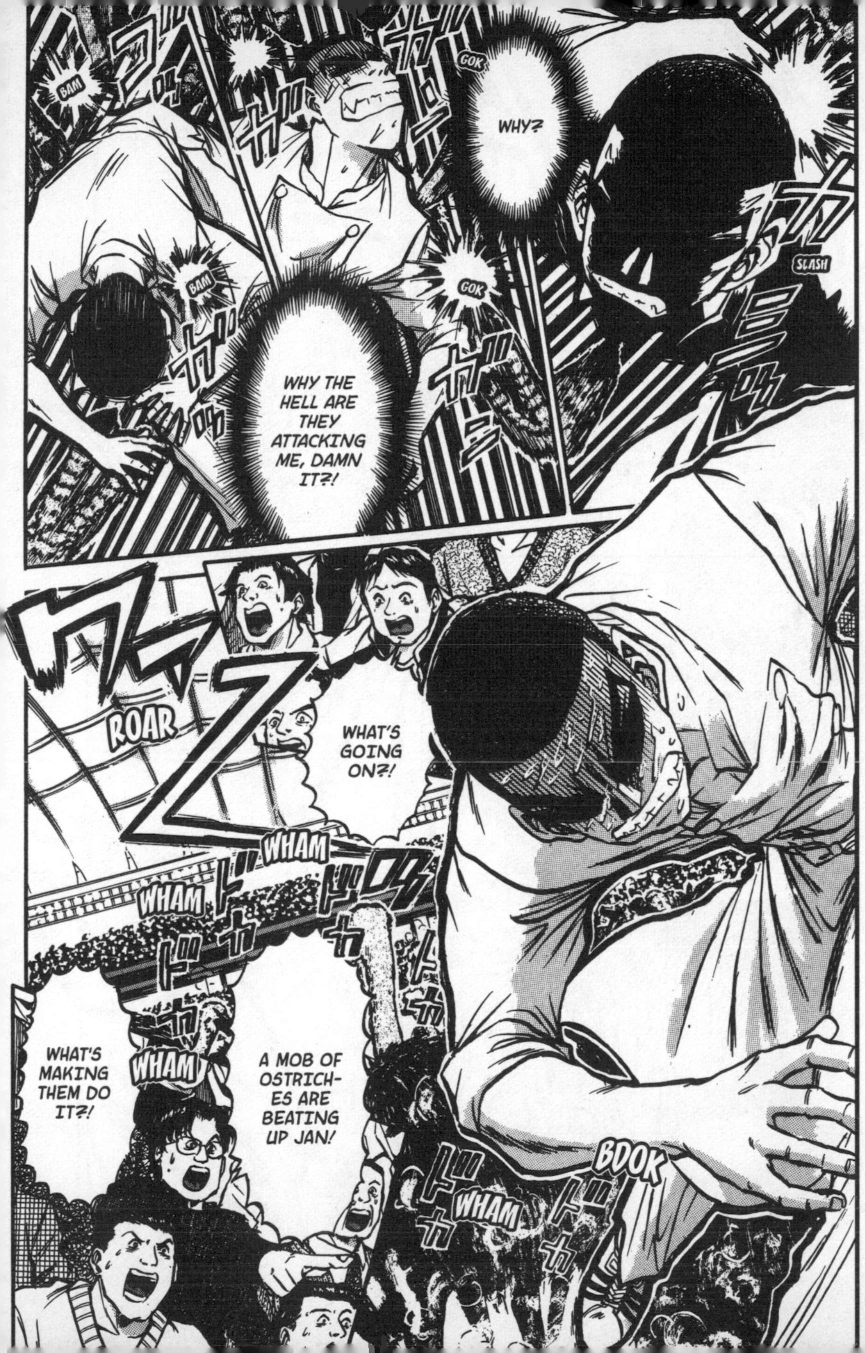
GOK
WHY?
SLASH
GOK
BAM
BAM
WHY THE HELL ARE THEY ATTACKING ME, DAMN IT?!
BDOK
WHAM
ROAR
WHAT'S GOING ON?!
WHAM
WHAM
A MOB OF OSTRICH-ES ARE BEATING UP JAN!
WHAT'S MAKING THEM DO IT?!
WHAM

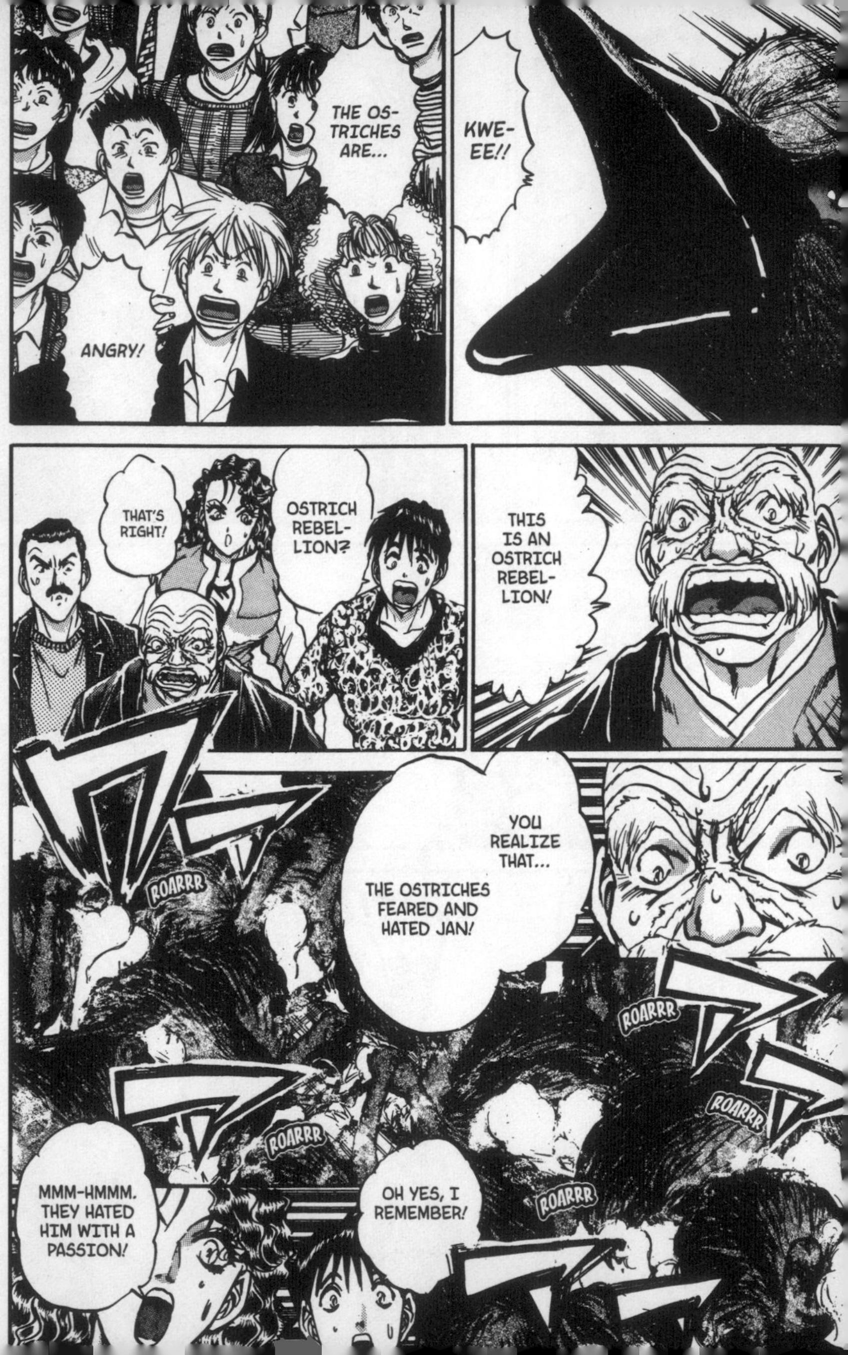
KWEE-EE!!
THE OS-TRICHES ARE...
ANGRY!
THIS IS AN OSTRICH REBEL-LION!
OSTRICH REBEL-LION?
THAT'S RIGHT!
YOU REALIZE THAT...
THE OSTRICHES FEARED AND HATED JAN!
ROARRR
ROARRR
ROARRR
ROARRR
ROARRR
OH YES, I REMEMBER!
MMM-HMMM. THEY HATED HIM WITH A PASSION!

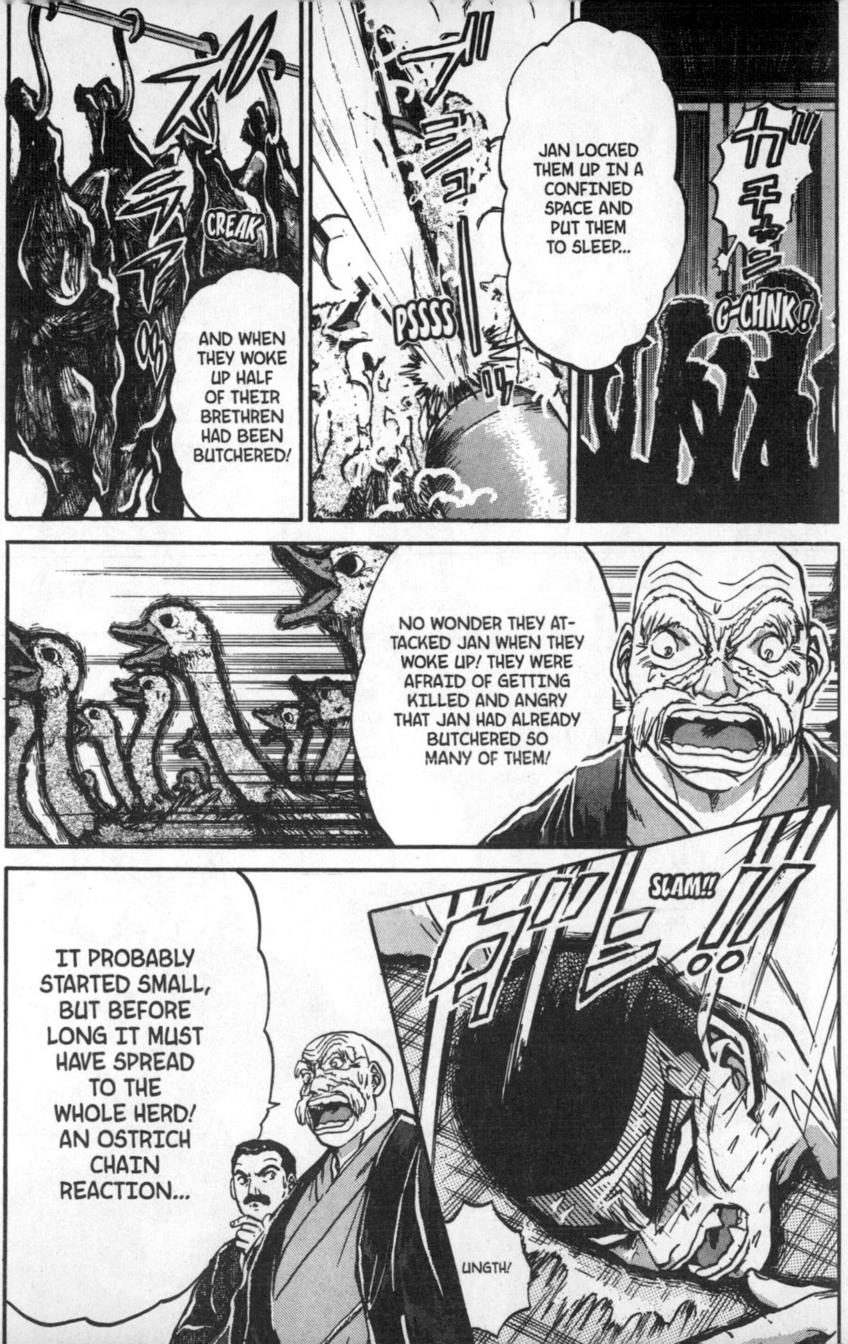

JAN LOCKED THEM UP IN A CONFINED SPACE AND PUT THEM TO SLEEP...
G-CHNK!
PSSSS
CREAK
AND WHEN THEY WOKE UP HALF OF THEIR BRETHREN HAD BEEN BUTCHERED!
NO WONDER THEY ATTACKED JAN WHEN THEY WOKE UP! THEY WERE AFRAID OF GETTING KILLED AND ANGRY THAT JAN HAD ALREADY BUTCHERED SO MANY OF THEM!
SLAM!!
UNGTH!
IT PROBABLY STARTED SMALL, BUT BEFORE LONG IT MUST HAVE SPREAD TO THE WHOLE HERD! AN OSTRICH CHAIN REACTION...

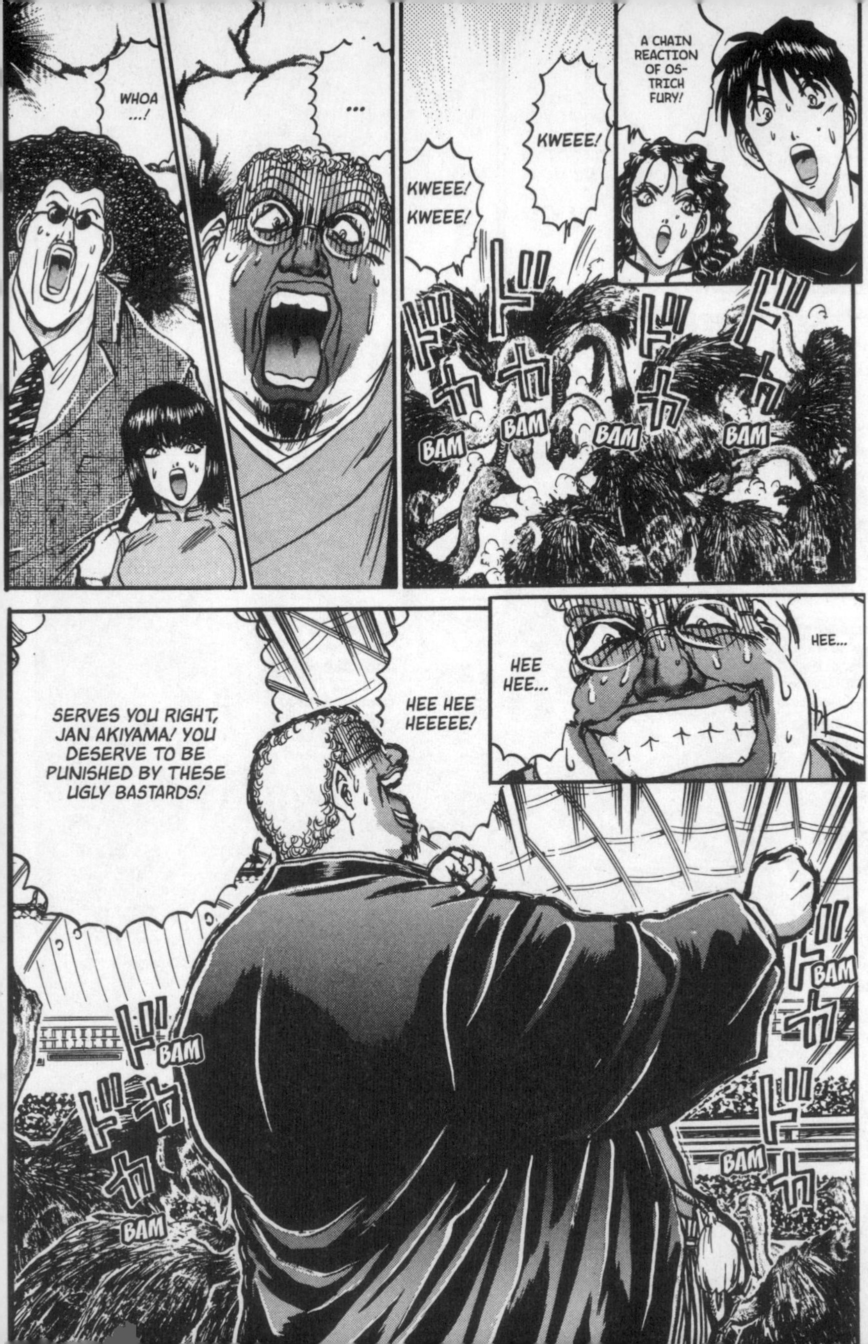
A CHAIN REACTION OF OS-TRICH FURY!
KWEEE!
KWEEE! KWEEE!
BAM
BAM
BAM
BAM
...
WHOA ...!
HEE...
HEE HEE...
HEE HEE HEEEEE!
SERVES YOU RIGHT, JAN AKIYAMA! YOU DESERVE TO BE PUNISHED BY THESE UGLY BASTARDS!
BAM
BAM
BAM
BAM

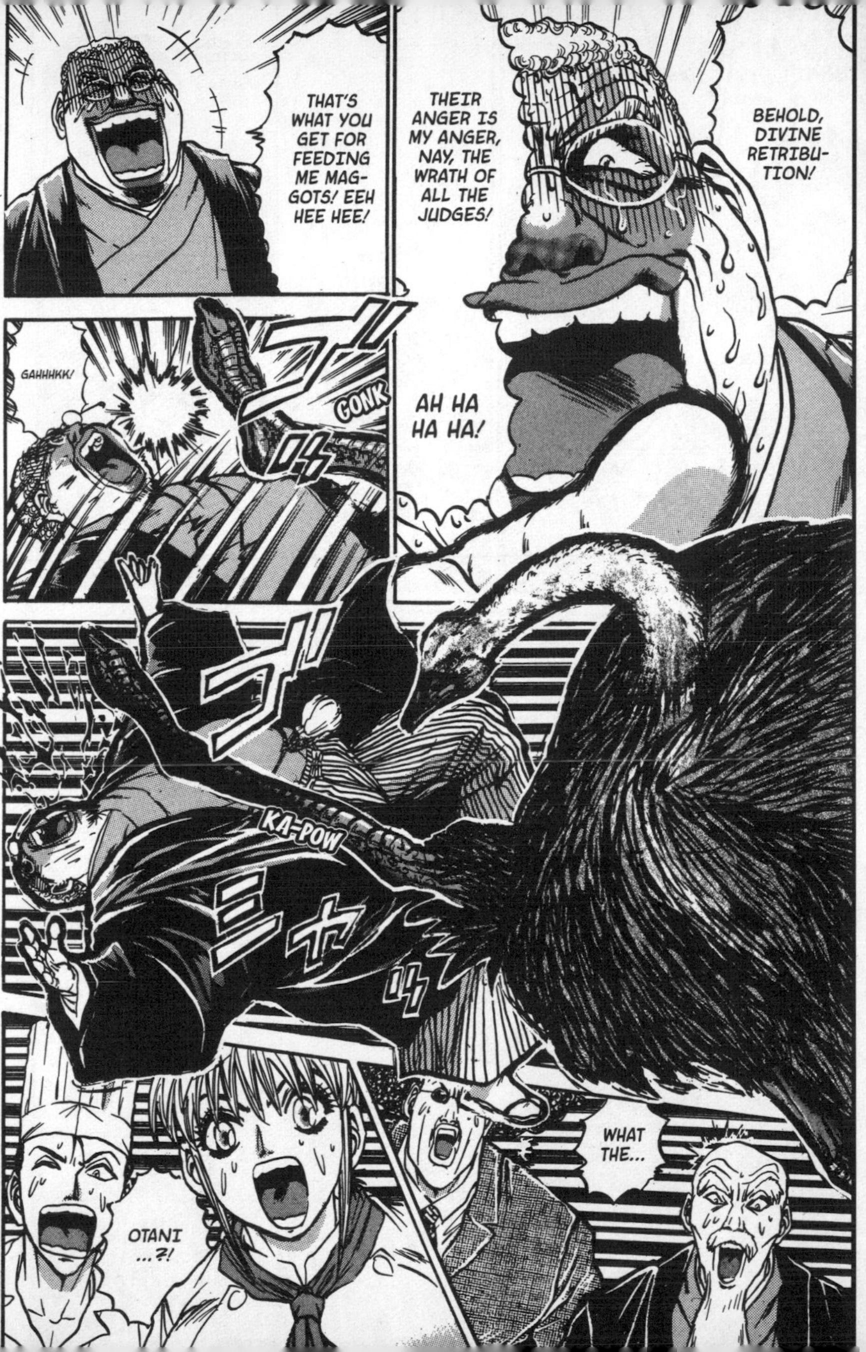
BEHOLD, DIVINE RETRIBUTION!
THEIR ANGER IS MY ANGER, NAY, THE WRATH OF ALL THE JUDGES!
AH HA HA HA!
THAT'S WHAT YOU GET FOR FEEDING ME MAGGOTS! EEH HEE HEE!
GONK
GAHHHKK!
KA-POW
WHAT THE...
OTANI ...?!

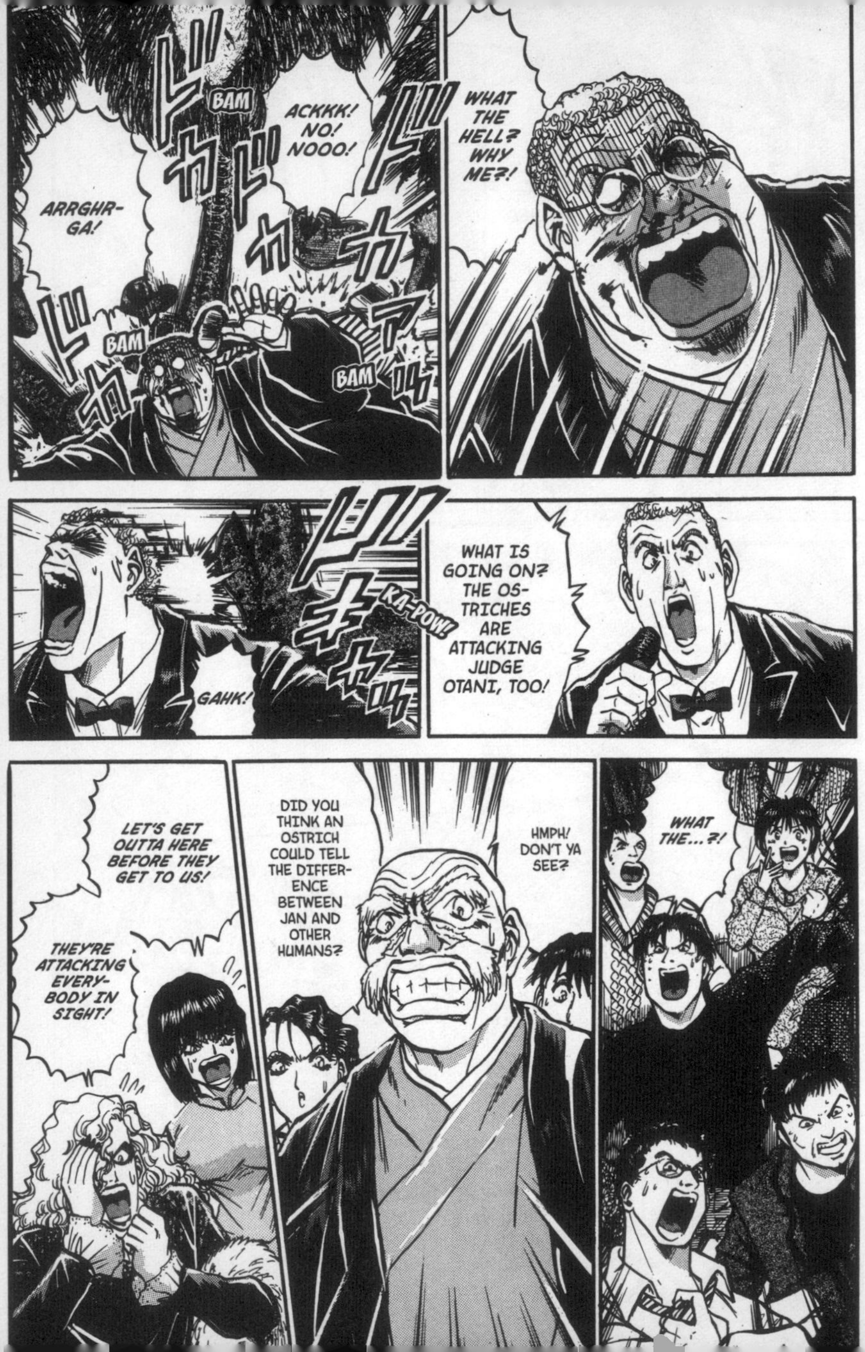
WHAT THE HELL?! WHY ME?!
ACKKK! NO! NOOO!
BAM
ARRGHR-GA!
BAM
BAM
WHAT IS GOING ON? THE OS-TRICHES ARE ATTACKING JUDGE OTANI, TOO!
KA-POW!
GAHK!
WHAT THE...?!
HMPH! DON'T YA SEE?
DID YOU THINK AN OSTRICH COULD TELL THE DIFFER-ENCE BETWEEN JAN AND OTHER HUMANS?
LET'S GET OUTTA HERE BEFORE THEY GET TO US!
THEY'RE ATTACKING EVERY-BODY IN SIGHT!

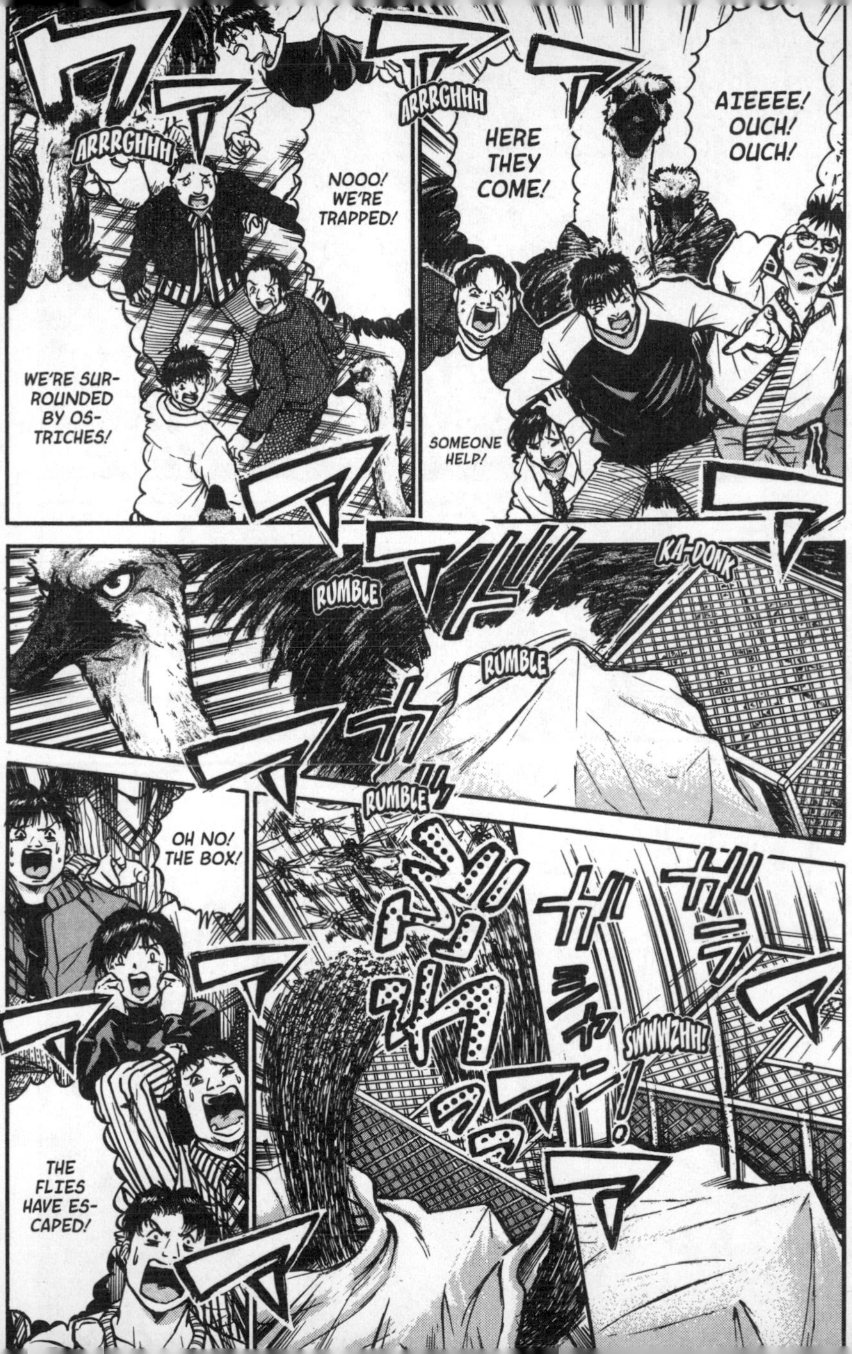
AIEEEE! OUCH! OUCH!
HERE THEY COME!
ARRRGHHH
SOMEONE HELP!
ARRRGHHH
NOOO! WE'RE TRAPPED!
WE'RE SURROUNDED BY OSTRICHES!
KA-DONK
RUMBLE
RUMBLE
SWWWZHH!
RUMBLE
OH NO! THE BOX!
THE FLIES HAVE ESCAPED!

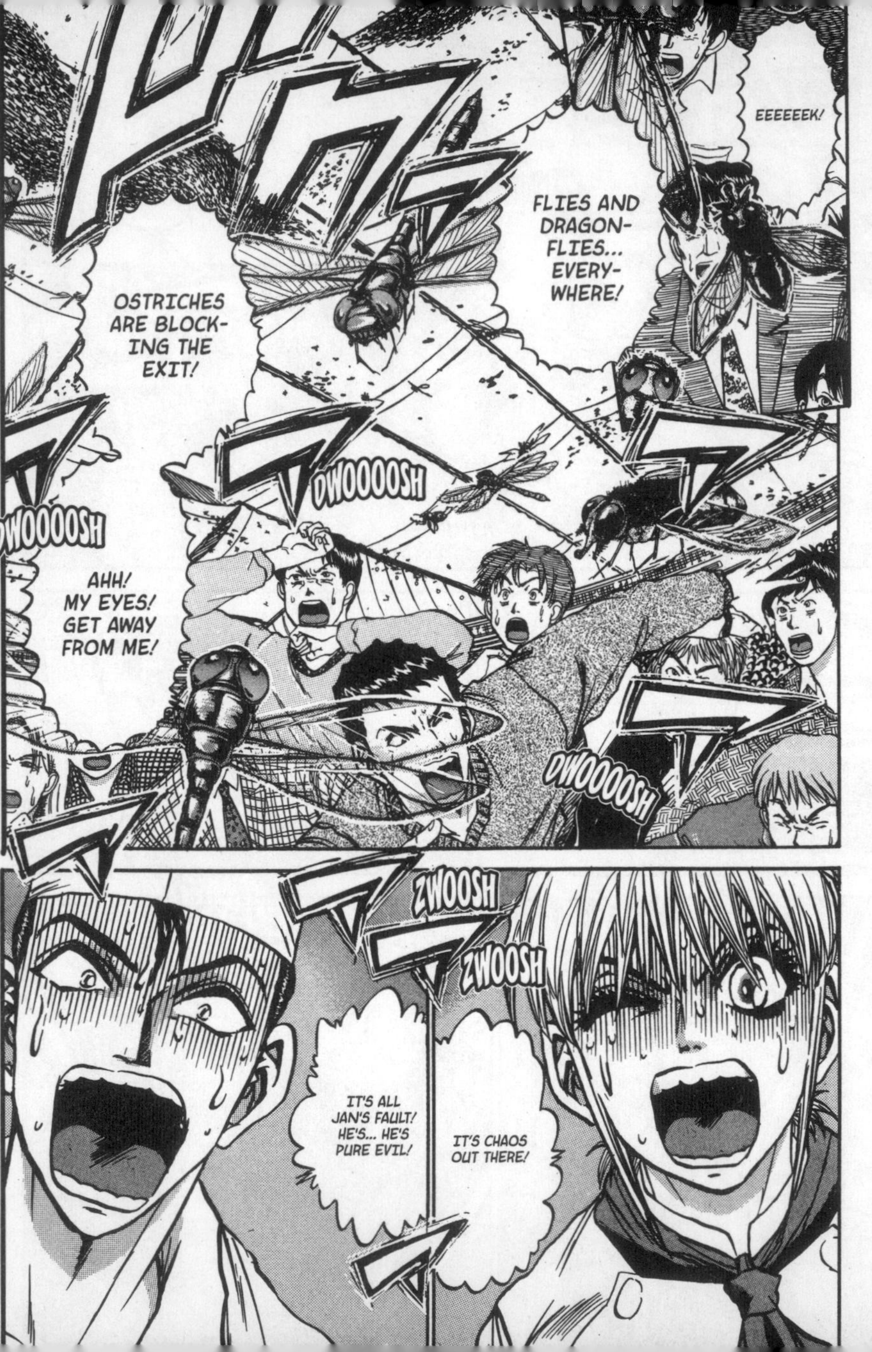
EEEEEEK!
FLIES AND DRAGON-FLIES... EVERY-WHERE!
OSTRICHES ARE BLOCK-ING THE EXIT!
DWOOOOSH
DWOOOOSH
DWOOOOSH
AHH! MY EYES! GET AWAY FROM ME!
ZWOOSH
ZWOOSH
IT'S CHAOS OUT THERE!
IT'S ALL JAN'S FAULT! HE'S... HE'S PURE EVIL!

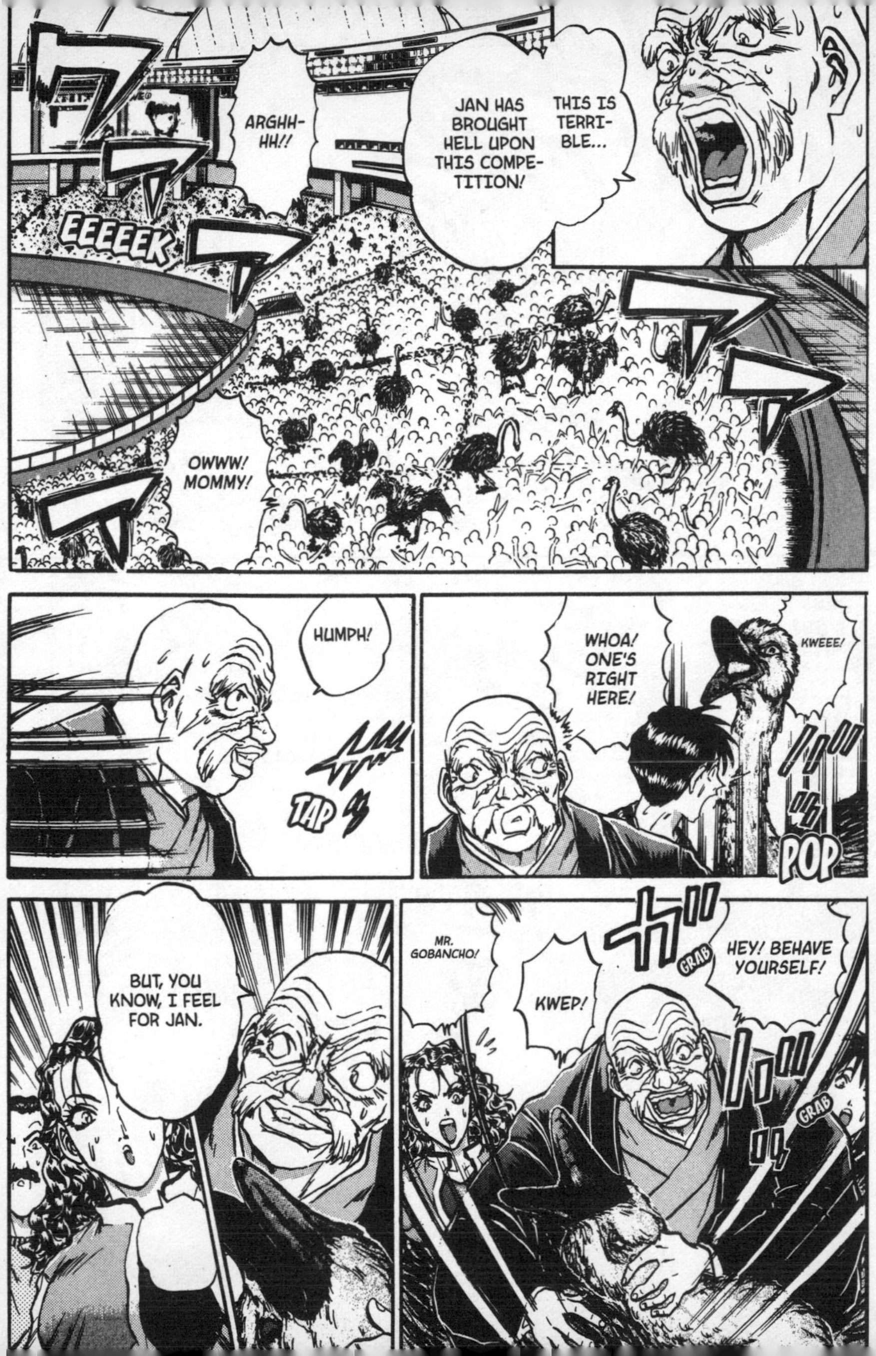
THIS IS TERRIBLE...
JAN HAS BROUGHT HELL UPON THIS COMPETITION!
ARGHHH!!
EEEEEK
OWWW! MOMMY!
KWEEE!
WHOA! ONE'S RIGHT HERE!
POP
HUMPH!
TAP
HEY! BEHAVE YOURSELF!
GRAB
KWEP!
MR. GOBANCHO!
GRAB
BUT, YOU KNOW, I FEEL FOR JAN.

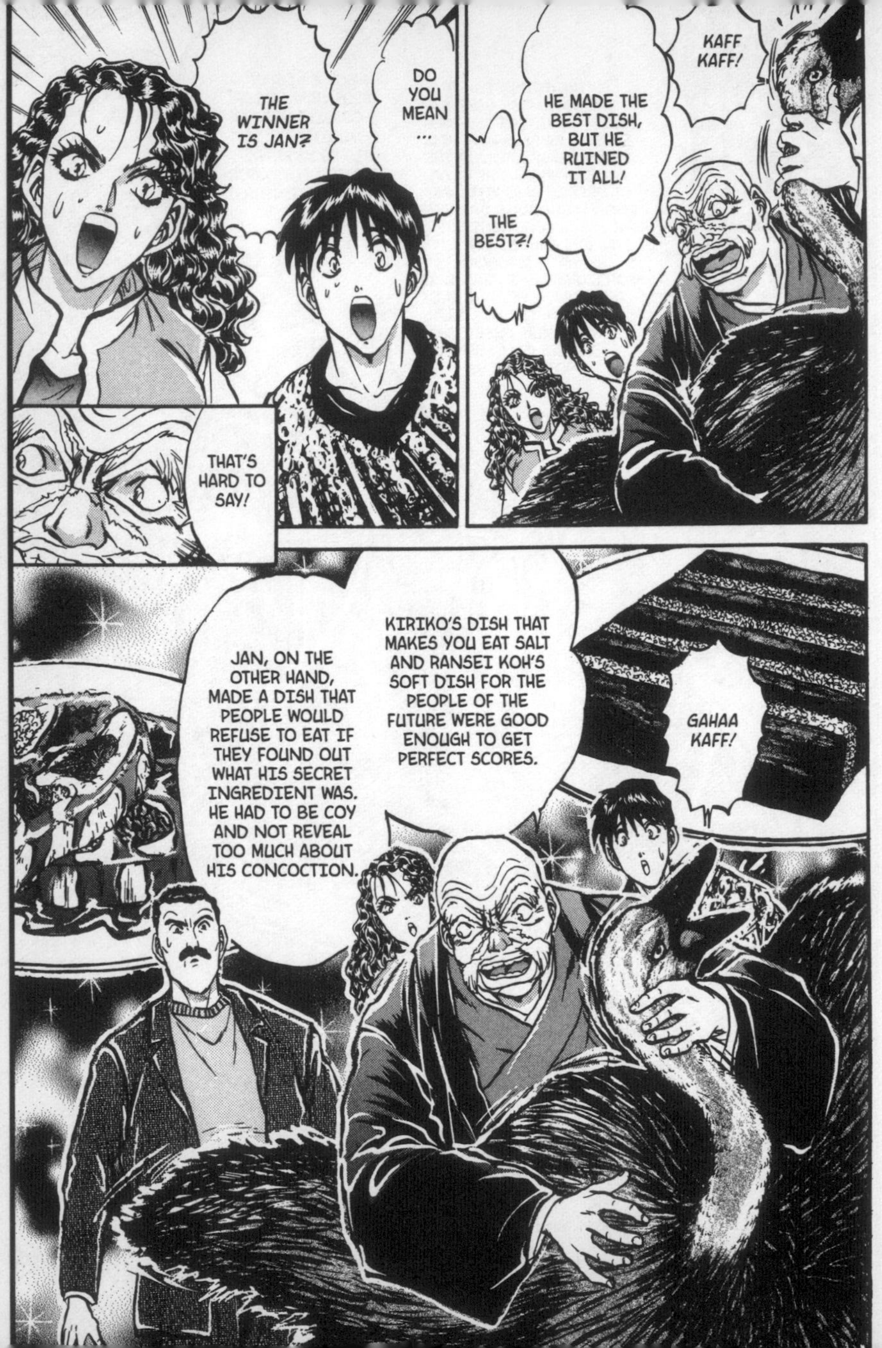
KAFF KAFF!
HE MADE THE BEST DISH, BUT HE RUINED IT ALL!
THE BEST?!
DO YOU MEAN ...
THE WINNER IS JAN?
THAT'S HARD TO SAY!
GAHAA KAFF!
KIRIKO'S DISH THAT MAKES YOU EAT SALT AND RANSEI KOH'S SOFT DISH FOR THE PEOPLE OF THE FUTURE WERE GOOD ENOUGH TO GET PERFECT SCORES.
JAN, ON THE OTHER HAND, MADE A DISH THAT PEOPLE WOULD REFUSE TO EAT IF THEY FOUND OUT WHAT HIS SECRET INGREDIENT WAS. HE HAD TO BE COY AND NOT REVEAL TOO MUCH ABOUT HIS CONCOCTION.

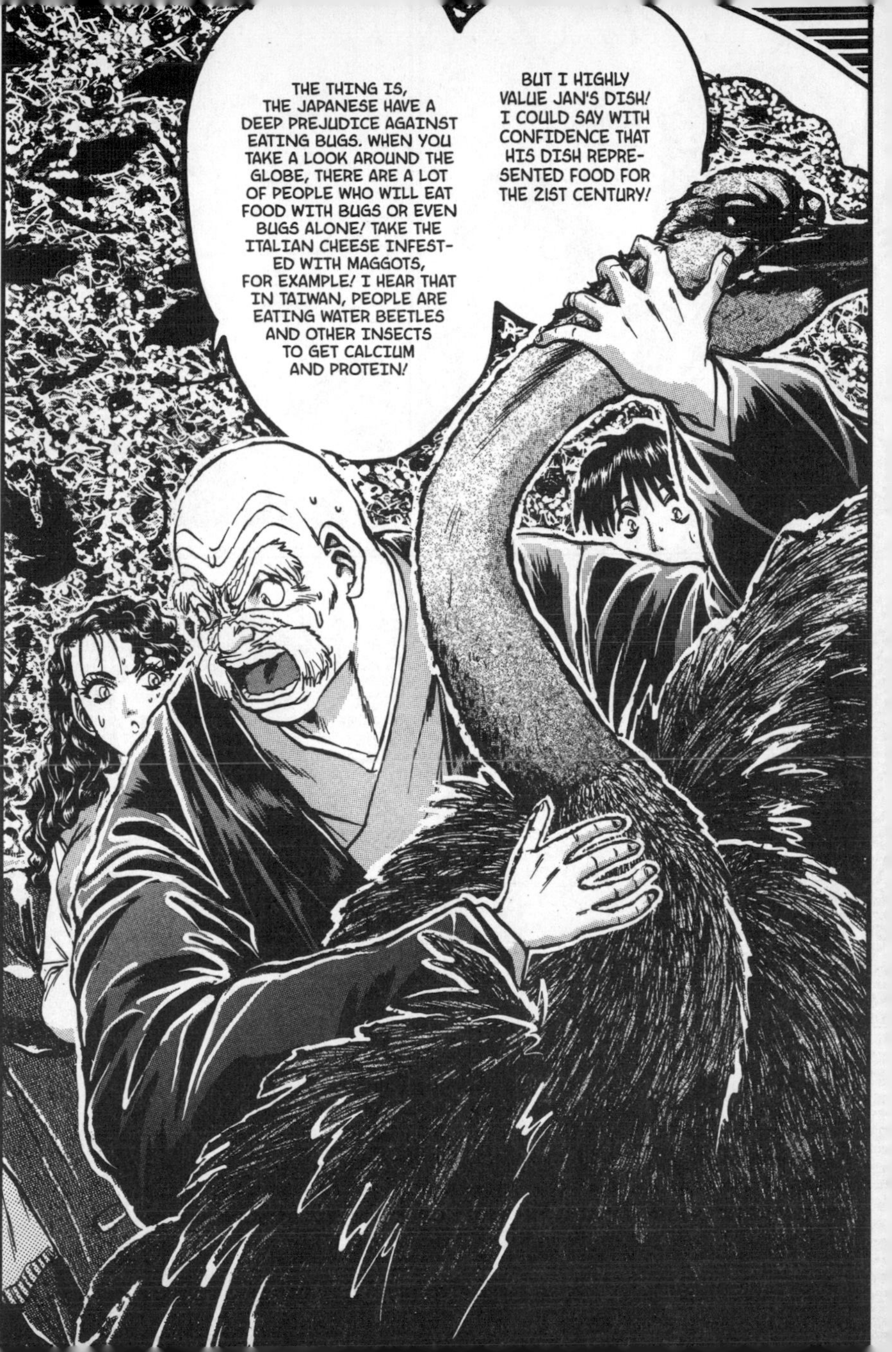
THE THING IS, THE JAPANESE HAVE A DEEP PREJUDICE AGAINST EATING BUGS. WHEN YOU TAKE A LOOK AROUND THE GLOBE, THERE ARE A LOT OF PEOPLE WHO WILL EAT FOOD WITH BUGS OR EVEN BUGS ALONE! TAKE THE ITALIAN CHEESE INFEST-ED WITH MAGGOTS, FOR EXAMPLE! I HEAR THAT IN TAIWAN, PEOPLE ARE EATING WATER BEETLES AND OTHER INSECTS TO GET CALCIUM AND PROTEIN!
BUT I HIGHLY VALUE JAN'S DISH! I COULD SAY WITH CONFIDENCE THAT HIS DISH REPRE-SENTED FOOD FOR THE 21ST CENTURY!

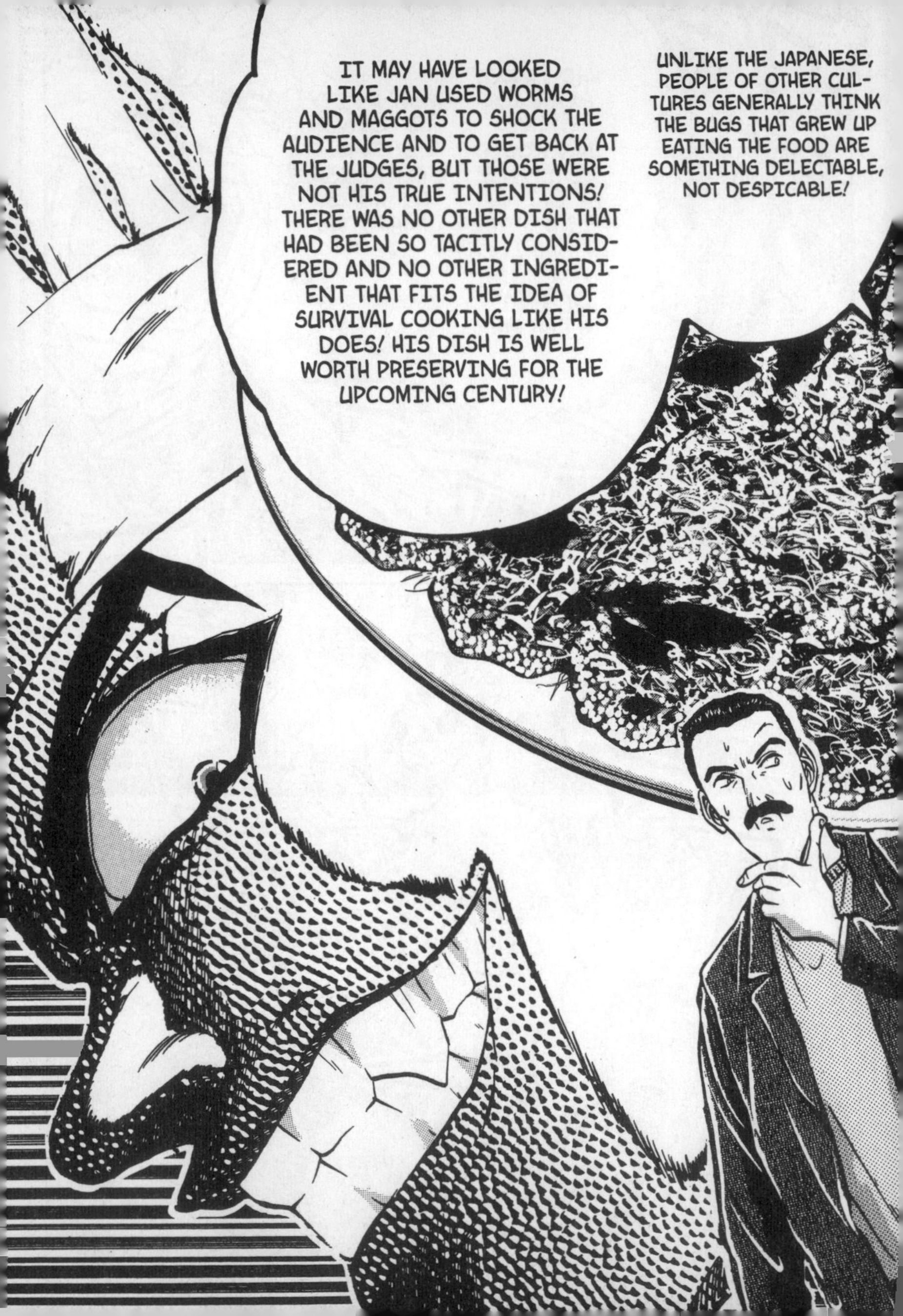
UNLIKE THE JAPANESE, PEOPLE OF OTHER CUL-TURES GENERALLY THINK THE BUGS THAT GREW UP EATING THE FOOD ARE SOMETHING DELECTABLE, NOT DESPICABLE!
IT MAY HAVE LOOKED LIKE JAN USED WORMS AND MAGGOTS TO SHOCK THE AUDIENCE AND TO GET BACK AT THE JUDGES, BUT THOSE WERE NOT HIS TRUE INTENTIONS! THERE WAS NO OTHER DISH THAT HAD BEEN SO TACITLY CONSID-ERED AND NO OTHER INGREDI-ENT THAT FITS THE IDEA OF SURVIVAL COOKING LIKE HIS DOES! HIS DISH IS WELL WORTH PRESERVING FOR THE UPCOMING CENTURY!

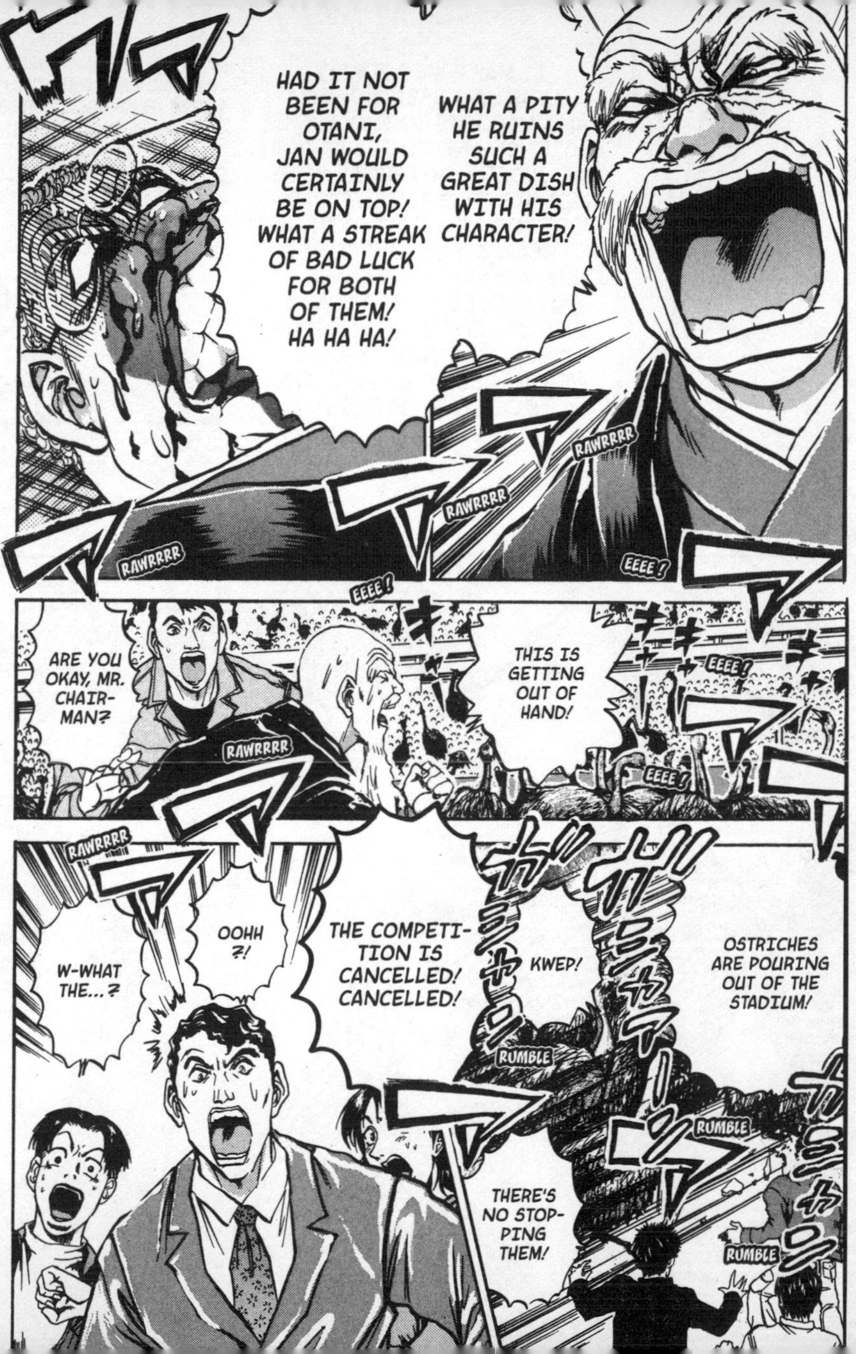
WHAT A PITY HE RUINS SUCH A GREAT DISH WITH HIS CHARACTER!
HAD IT NOT BEEN FOR OTANI, JAN WOULD CERTAINLY BE ON TOP! WHAT A STREAK OF BAD LUCK FOR BOTH OF THEM! HA HA HA!
RAWRRRR
RAWRRRR
RAWRRRR
EEEE!
EEEE!
EEEE!
THIS IS GETTING OUT OF HAND!
EEEE!
RAWRRRR
ARE YOU OKAY, MR. CHAIRMAN?
RAWRRRR
OSTRICHES ARE POURING OUT OF THE STADIUM!
RUMBLE
RUMBLE
THERE'S NO STOPPING THEM!
RUMBLE
KWEP!
THE COMPETITION IS CANCELLED! CANCELLED!
OOHH?!
W-WHAT THE...?

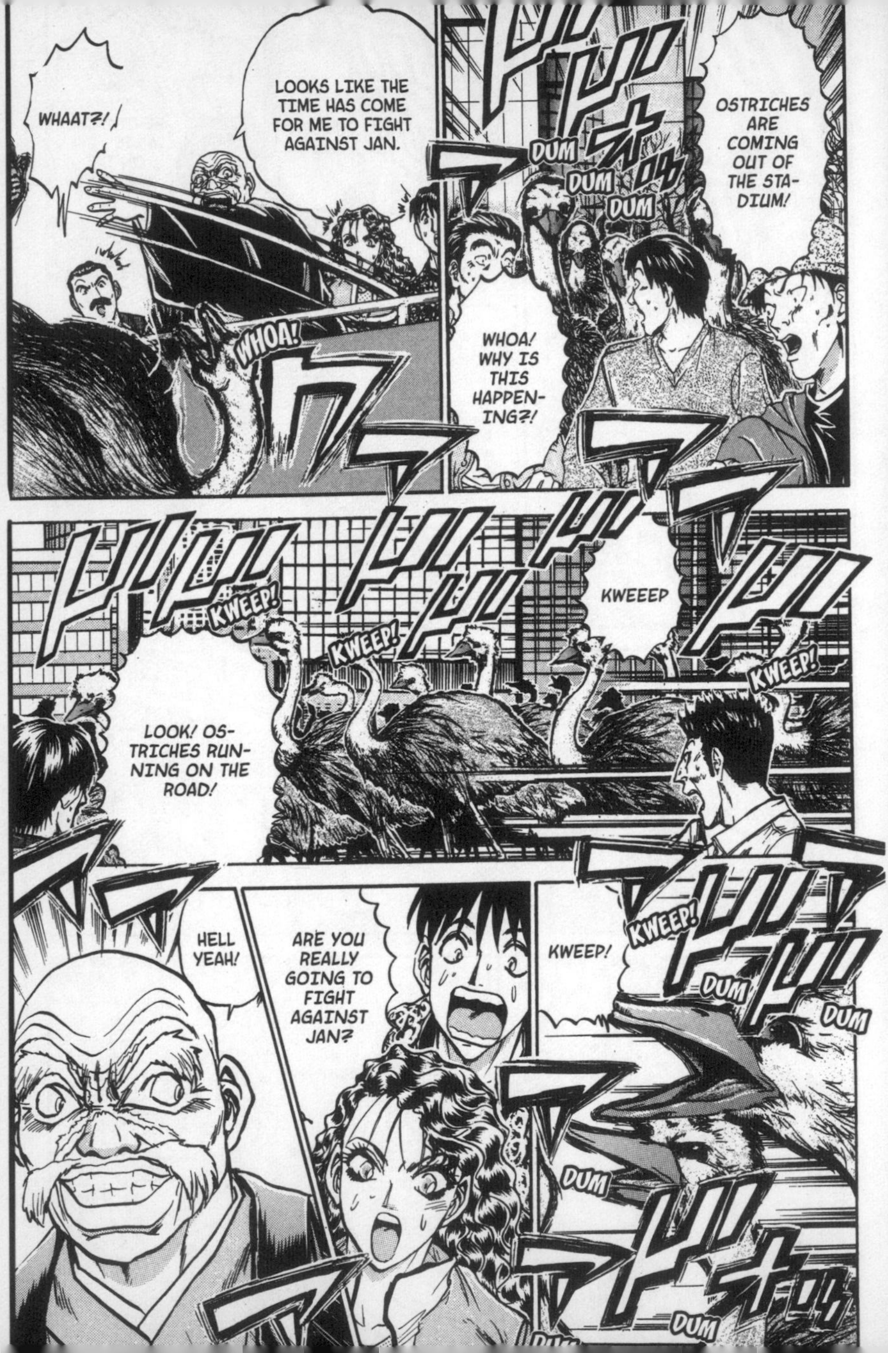
OSTRICHES ARE COMING OUT OF THE STA-DIUM!
DUM
DUM
DUM
WHOA! WHY IS THIS HAPPEN-ING?!
LOOKS LIKE THE TIME HAS COME FOR ME TO FIGHT AGAINST JAN.
WHAAT?!
WHOA!
KWEEP!
KWEEEP
KWEEP!
KWEEP!
LOOK! OS-TRICHES RUN-NING ON THE ROAD!
KWEEP!
KWEEP!
DUM
DUM
DUM
DUM
ARE YOU REALLY GOING TO FIGHT AGAINST JAN?
HELL YEAH!

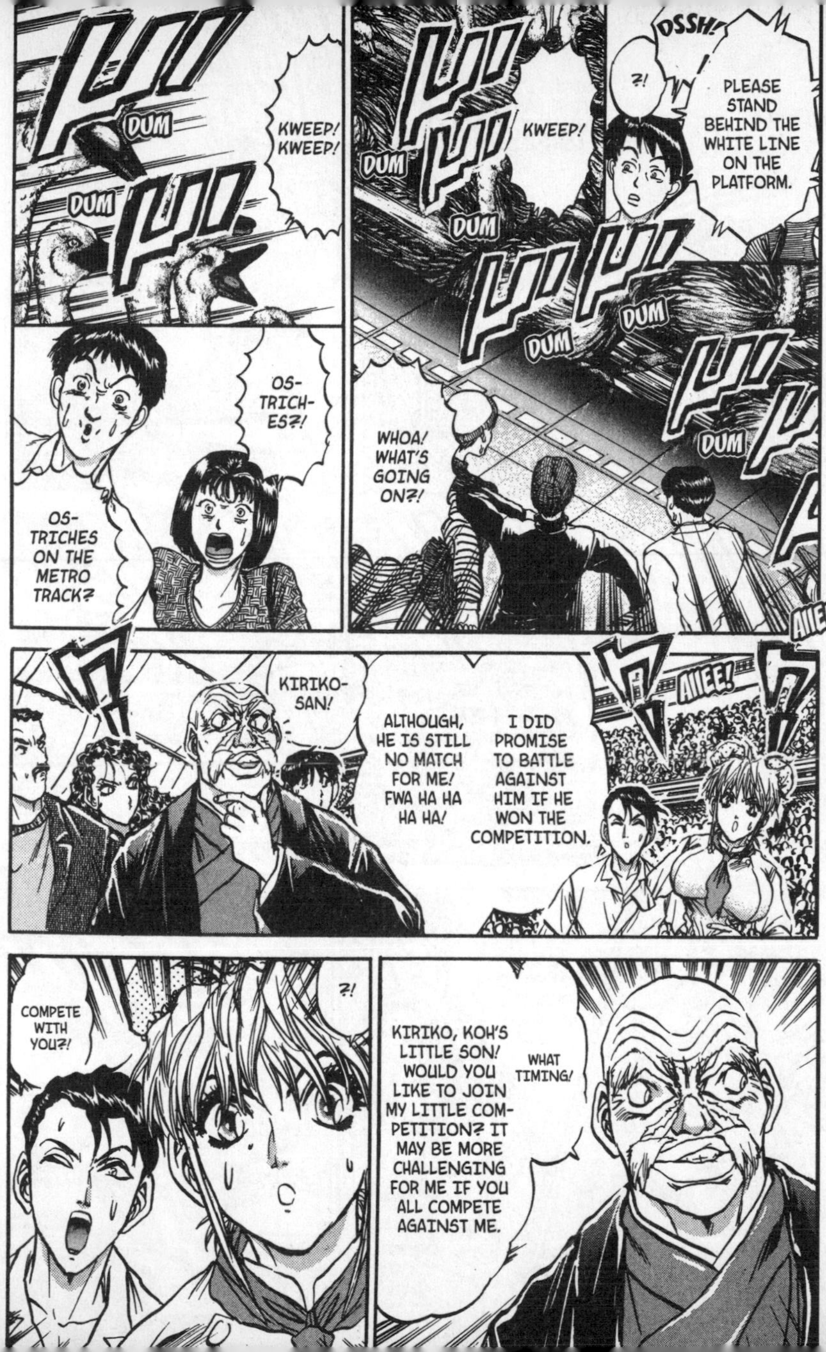
DSSH!
?!
PLEASE STAND BEHIND THE WHITE LINE ON THE PLATFORM.
KWEEP!
DUM
DUM
DUM
DUM
DUM
WHOA! WHAT'S GOING ON?!
KWEEP! KWEEP!
DUM
DUM
OS-TRICH-ES?!
OS-TRICHES ON THE METRO TRACK?
AIIEE!
AIIEE!
I DID PROMISE TO BATTLE AGAINST HIM IF HE WON THE COMPETITION.
ALTHOUGH, HE IS STILL NO MATCH FOR ME! FWA HA HA HA HA!
KIRIKO-SAN!
KIRIKO, KOH'S LITTLE SON! WOULD YOU LIKE TO JOIN MY LITTLE COM-PETITION? IT MAY BE MORE CHALLENGING FOR ME IF YOU ALL COMPETE AGAINST ME.
WHAT TIMING!
?!
COMPETE WITH YOU?!

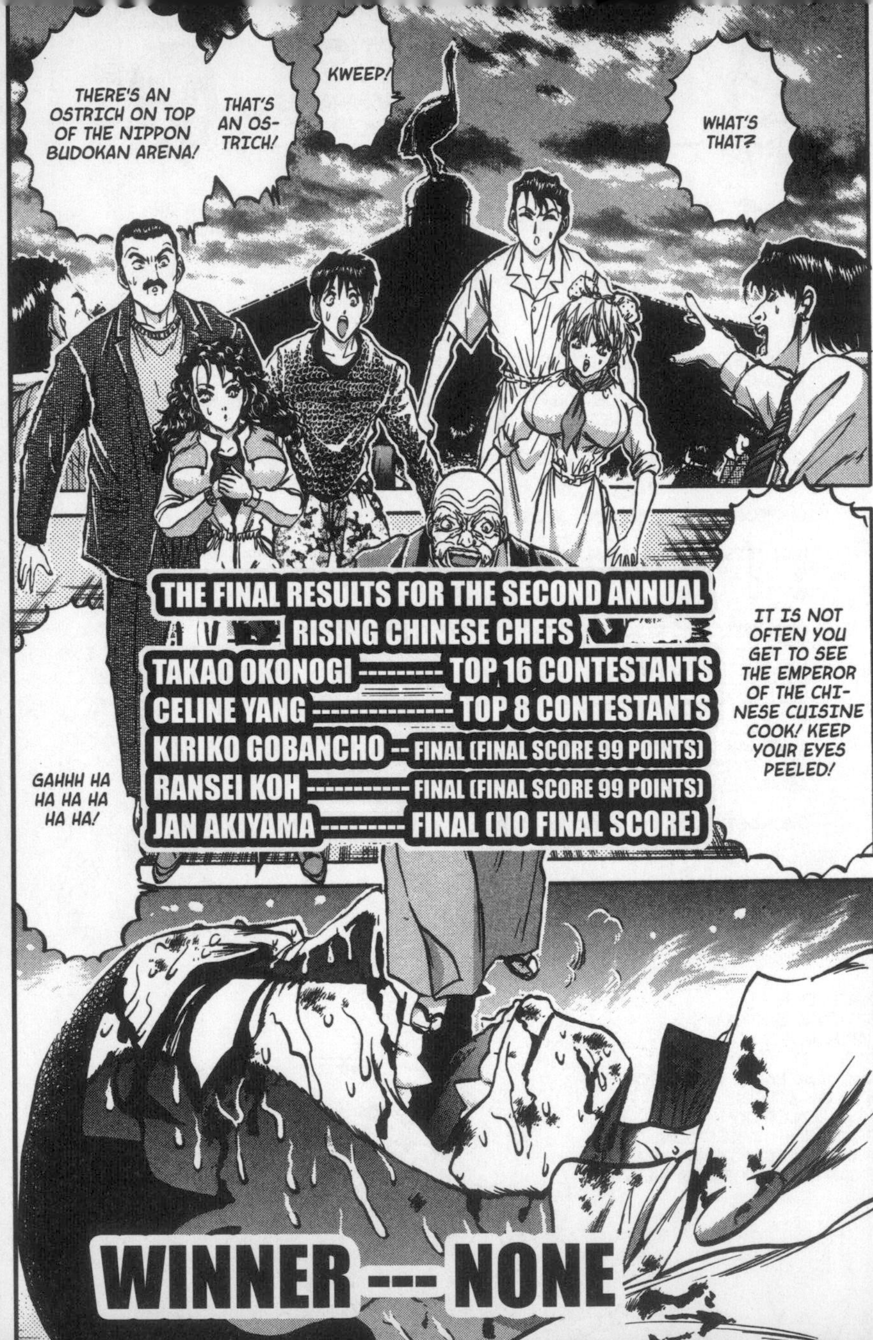

WHAT'S THAT?
KWEEP!
THAT'S AN OS-TRICH!
THERE'S AN OSTRICH ON TOP OF THE NIPPON BUDOKAN ARENA!
IT IS NOT OFTEN YOU GET TO SEE THE EMPEROR OF THE CHI-NESE CUISINE COOK! KEEP YOUR EYES PEELED!
THE FINAL RESULTS FOR THE SECOND ANNUAL RISING CHINESE CHEFS
TAKAO OKONOGI --------- TOP 16 CONTESTANTS
CELINE YANG --------------- TOP 8 CONTESTANTS
KIRIKO GOBANCHO -- FINAL (FINAL SCORE 99 POINTS)
RANSEI KOH ----------- FINAL (FINAL SCORE 99 POINTS)
JAN AKIYAMA --------- FINAL (NO FINAL SCORE)
GAHHH HA HA HA HA HA HA!
WINNER --- NONE

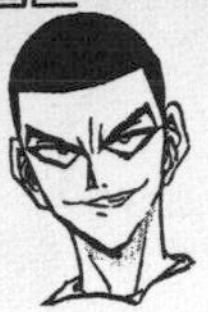

JAN AND OKONOGI'S

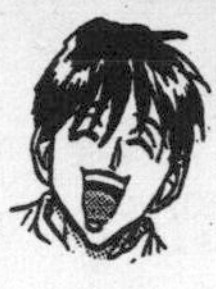

XIE NI LU SUN (GREEN ASPARAGUS WITH CRAB MEAT SAUCE)

JAN: HEY, OKONOGI! READY TO TRAIN LIKE A SPARTAN? I'M GONNA START WITH XIE NI LU SUN. CANNED CRAB MEAT IS A LITTLE EXPENSIVE, BUT IT'S EASY TO COOK WITH, SO YOU SHOULD LEARN THIS. ARE YOU READY?

OKONOGI: W-WAIT! I HAVE A SUGGESTION!

JAN: WHAT IS IT?

OKONOGI: WE'VE MADE A LOT OF DISHES TOGETHER, BUT THIS BEING THE LAST VOLUME AND ALL, I THOUGHT WE COULD PICK THE ONES WE STRONGLY RECOMMEND AND GO OVER THEM. YOU KNOW, LIKE THE "BEST OF JAN AND OKONOGI" OR "JAN AND OKONOGI: GREATEST HITS..."

JAN: AH, IS THAT RIGHT? YOU JUST DON'T WANT TO LEARN ANY MORE RECIPES, DO YOU?

OKONOGI: OF COURSE I DO, JAN. I... UMM...

JAN: *SIGH*... HEY, LISTEN. THE READERS WANT TO SEE NEW RECIPES AND MOST OF ALL, I'M DOING THIS FOR YOU, OKONOGI! DON'T BE LOOKING FOR AN EASY WAY OUT!

OKONOGI: ...ALL RIGHT, ALL RIGHT. I GET IT. LET'S GET STARTED. BOOHOO...

JAN: THIS IS GONNA BE A PIECE OF CAKE. FIRST, CUT OFF AN INCH FROM THE BOTTOM OF SOME ASPARAGUS, REMOVE THE TOUGH SKIN AROUND THE BASE AND CUT THEM INTO 2 INCH PIECES. BOIL THEM AL DENTE AND DRAIN. THEN, SAUTEE THEM QUICKLY IN OIL AND KEEP THEM WARM. HEAT SOUP, SAKE, AND CRAB MEAT IN A POT. WHEN IT STARTS TO BOIL, ADD GINGER EXTRACT AND SEASON TO TASTE. ADD CORNSTARCH MIXED IN WATER TO THICKEN THE SAUCE. POUR THEM OVER THE ASPARAGUS AND VOILA, IT'S DONE!

OKONOGI: OOOH, IT'S GOOOOD! I'M REALLY GLAD YOU TAUGHT ME THIS, JAN!

INGREDIENTS

- ASPARAGUS: 300 GRAMS
- CRAB MEAT: 1 CAN
- SOUP: 1 CUP
- GINGER EXTRACT: 1 TABLESPOON
- OIL: 2 TABLESPOON
- SAKE: 1 TABLESPOON
- CORNSTARCH: 1 TABLESPOON

* MAKE SURE TO PUT THE JUICE FROM THE CAN OF CRAB MEAT IN THE SOUP!

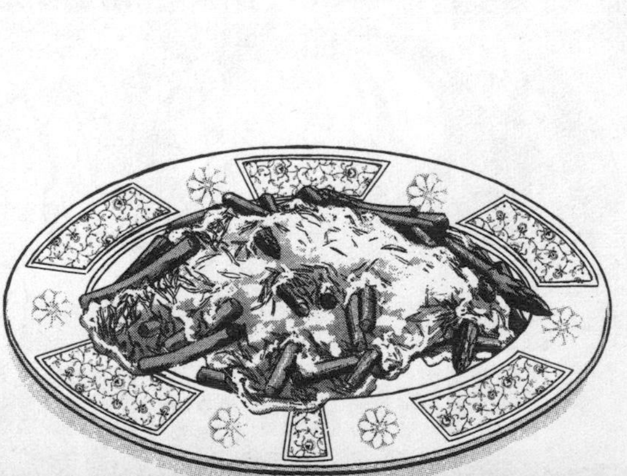

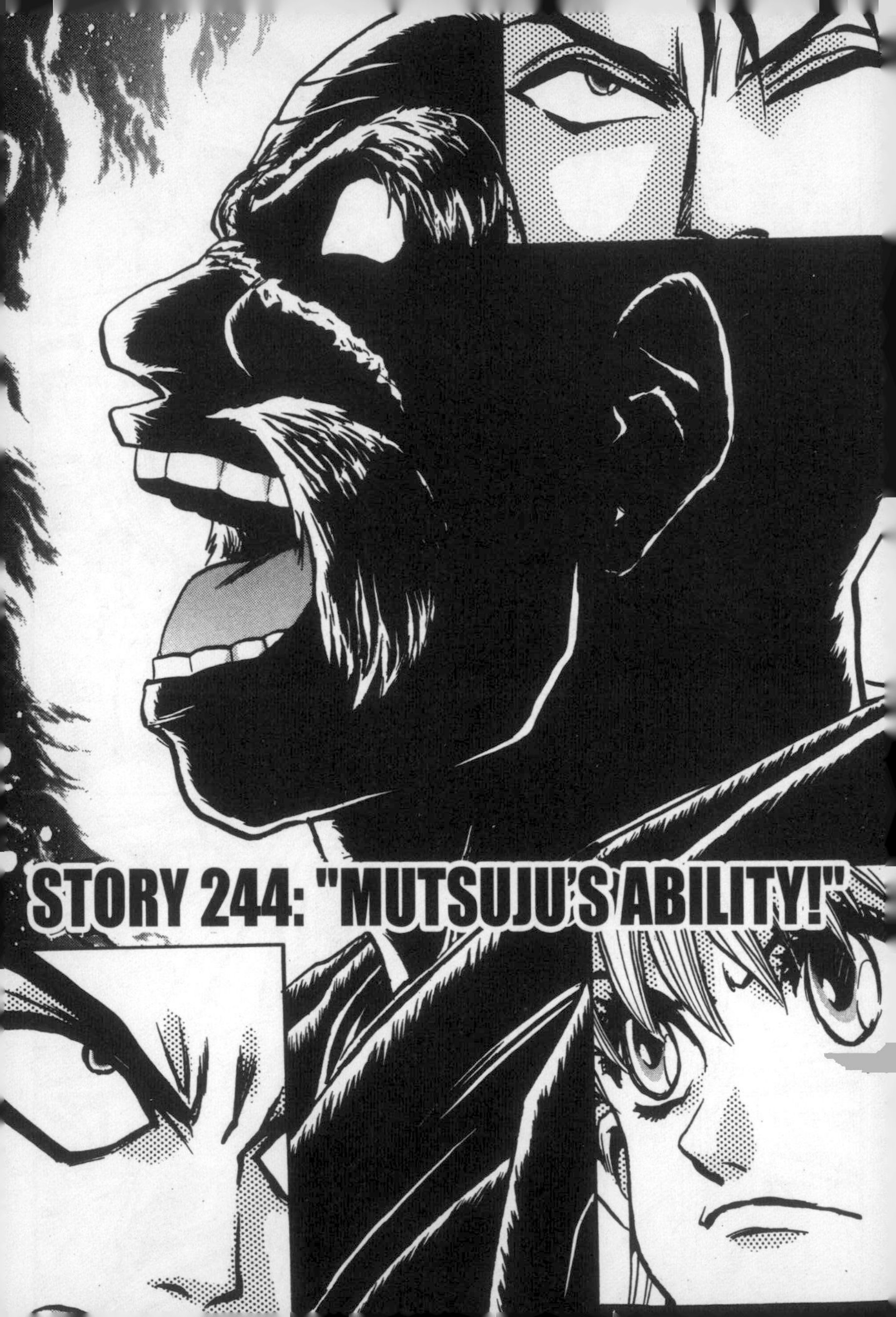
STORY 244: "MUTSUJU'S ABILITY!"

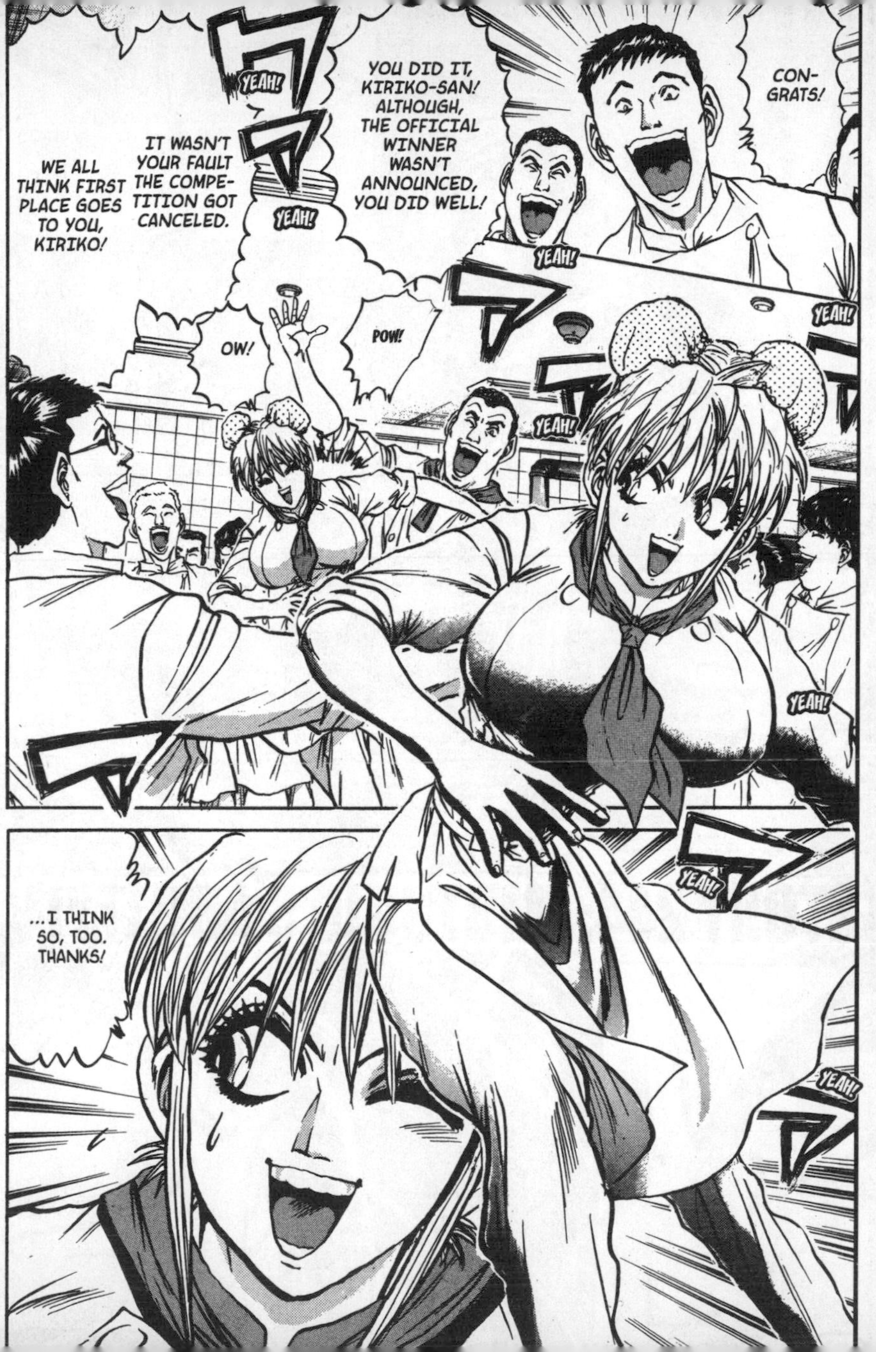
CON-GRATS!
YOU DID IT, KIRIKO-SAN! ALTHOUGH, THE OFFICIAL WINNER WASN'T ANNOUNCED, YOU DID WELL!
YEAH!
YEAH!
IT WASN'T YOUR FAULT THE COMPETITION GOT CANCELED.
WE ALL THINK FIRST PLACE GOES TO YOU, KIRIKO!
YEAH!
YEAH!
POW!
OW!
YEAH!
YEAH!
YEAH!
YEAH!
...I THINK SO, TOO. THANKS!

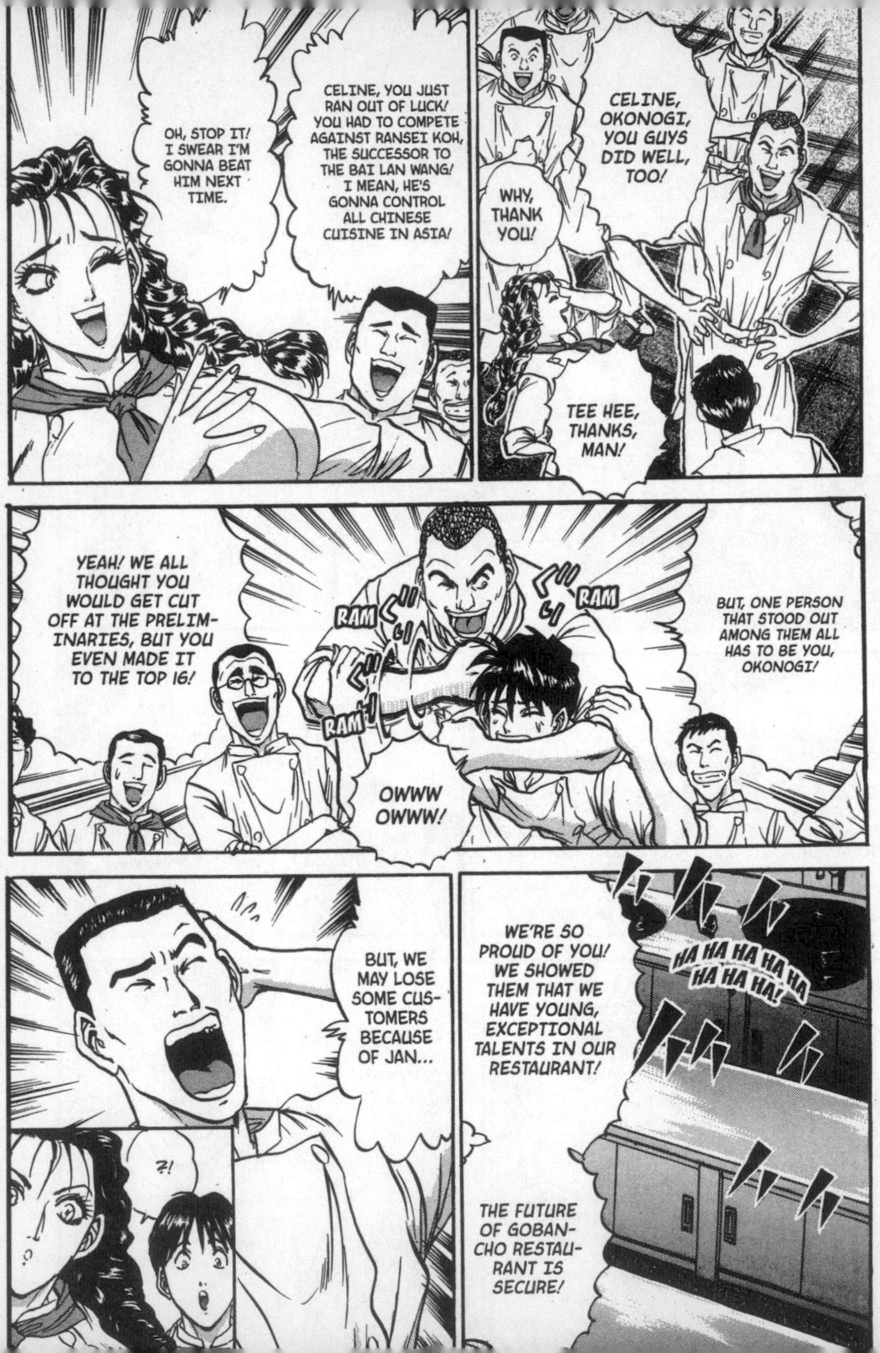
CELINE, OKONOGI, YOU GUYS DID WELL, TOO!
WHY, THANK YOU!
TEE HEE, THANKS, MAN!
CELINE, YOU JUST RAN OUT OF LUCK! YOU HAD TO COMPETE AGAINST RANSEI KOH, THE SUCCESSOR TO THE BAI LAN WANG! I MEAN, HE'S GONNA CONTROL ALL CHINESE CUISINE IN ASIA!
OH, STOP IT! I SWEAR I'M GONNA BEAT HIM NEXT TIME.
BUT, ONE PERSON THAT STOOD OUT AMONG THEM ALL HAS TO BE YOU, OKONOGI!
RAM
RAM
RAM
YEAH! WE ALL THOUGHT YOU WOULD GET CUT OFF AT THE PRELIMINARIES, BUT YOU EVEN MADE IT TO THE TOP 16!
OWWW OWWW!
HA HA HA HA HA HA HA HA!
WE'RE SO PROUD OF YOU! WE SHOWED THEM THAT WE HAVE YOUNG, EXCEPTIONAL TALENTS IN OUR RESTAURANT!
THE FUTURE OF GOBANCHO RESTAURANT IS SECURE!
BUT, WE MAY LOSE SOME CUSTOMERS BECAUSE OF JAN...
?!

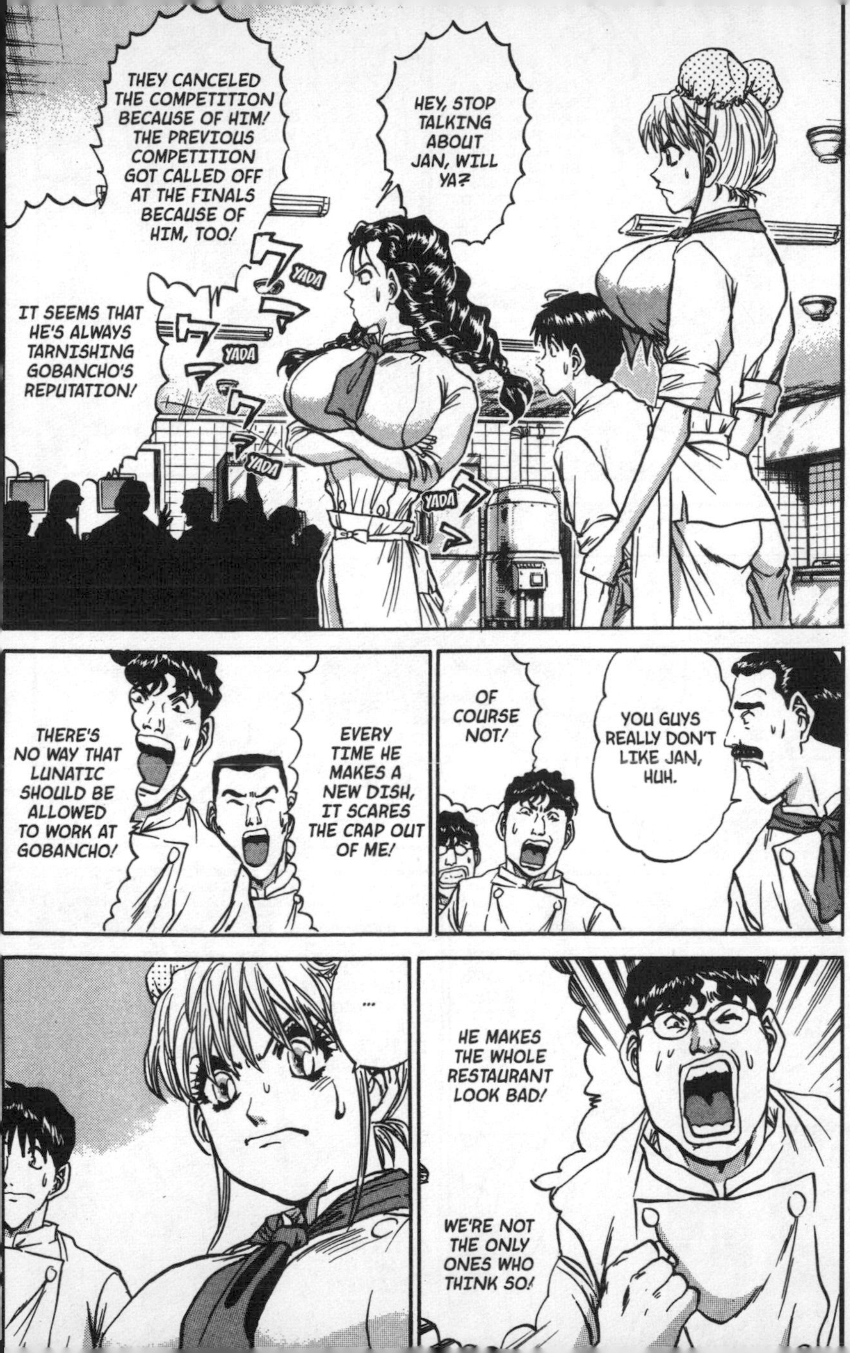
HEY, STOP TALKING ABOUT JAN, WILL YA?
THEY CANCELED THE COMPETITION BECAUSE OF HIM! THE PREVIOUS COMPETITION GOT CALLED OFF AT THE FINALS BECAUSE OF HIM, TOO!
YADA
IT SEEMS THAT HE'S ALWAYS TARNISHING GOBANCHO'S REPUTATION!
YADA
YADA
YADA
YOU GUYS REALLY DON'T LIKE JAN, HUH.
OF COURSE NOT!
EVERY TIME HE MAKES A NEW DISH, IT SCARES THE CRAP OUT OF ME!
THERE'S NO WAY THAT LUNATIC SHOULD BE ALLOWED TO WORK AT GOBANCHO!
HE MAKES THE WHOLE RESTAURANT LOOK BAD!
WE'RE NOT THE ONLY ONES WHO THINK SO!
...

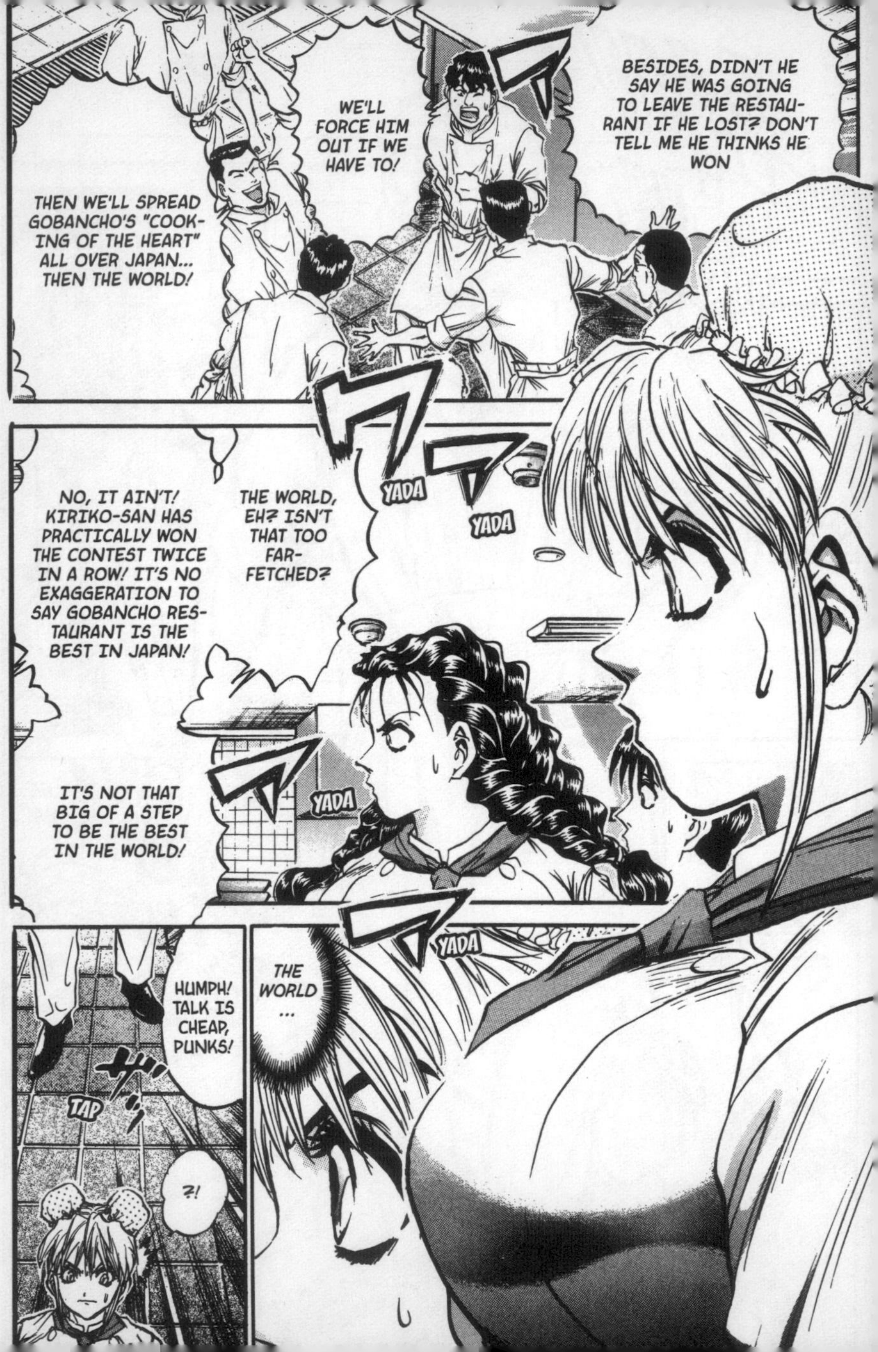
BESIDES, DIDN'T HE SAY HE WAS GOING TO LEAVE THE RESTAURANT IF HE LOST? DON'T TELL ME HE THINKS HE WON
WE'LL FORCE HIM OUT IF WE HAVE TO!
THEN WE'LL SPREAD GOBANCHO'S "COOKING OF THE HEART" ALL OVER JAPAN... THEN THE WORLD!
YADA
YADA
THE WORLD, EH? ISN'T THAT TOO FAR-FETCHED?
NO, IT AIN'T! KIRIKO-SAN HAS PRACTICALLY WON THE CONTEST TWICE IN A ROW! IT'S NO EXAGGERATION TO SAY GOBANCHO RESTAURANT IS THE BEST IN JAPAN!
YADA
IT'S NOT THAT BIG OF A STEP TO BE THE BEST IN THE WORLD!
YADA
THE WORLD ...
HUMPH! TALK IS CHEAP, PUNKS!
TAP
?!

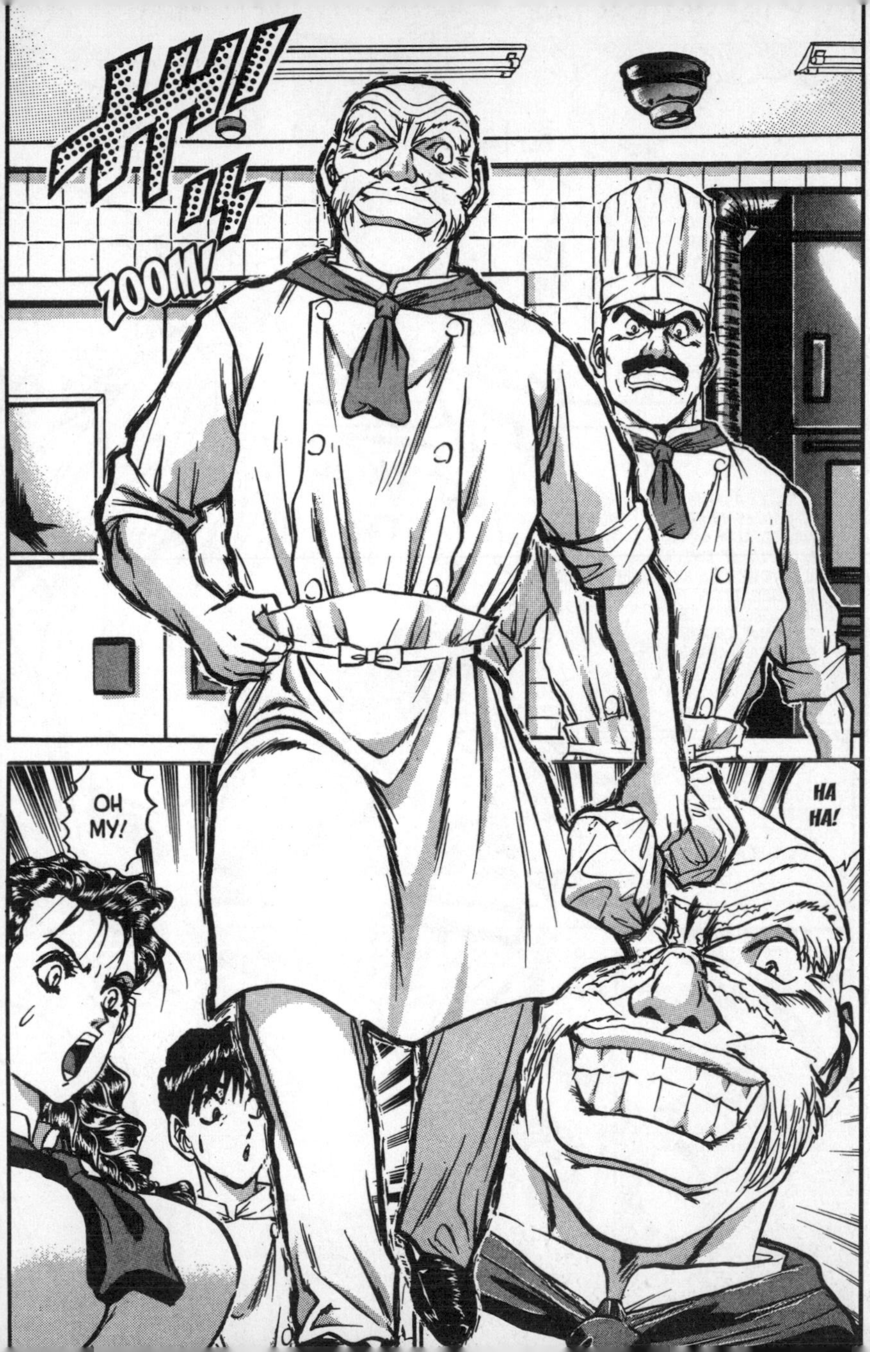
ZOOM!
HA HA!
OH MY!

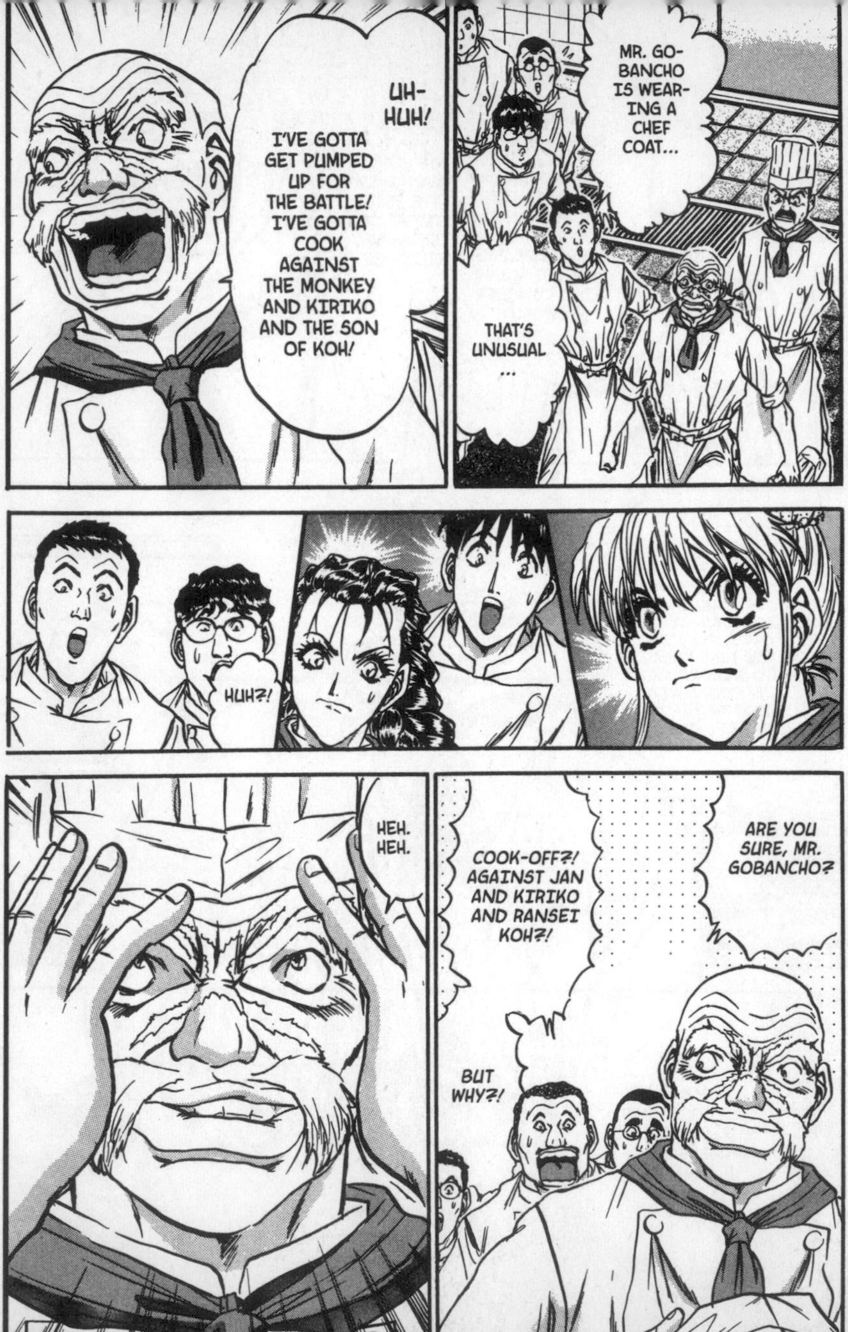
MR. GO-BANCHO IS WEAR-ING A CHEF COAT...
THAT'S UNUSUAL ...
UH-HUH!
I'VE GOTTA GET PUMPED UP FOR THE BATTLE! I'VE GOTTA COOK AGAINST THE MONKEY AND KIRIKO AND THE SON OF KOH!
HUH?!
ARE YOU SURE, MR. GOBANCHO?
COOK-OFF?! AGAINST JAN AND KIRIKO AND RANSEI KOH?!
BUT WHY?!
HEH. HEH.

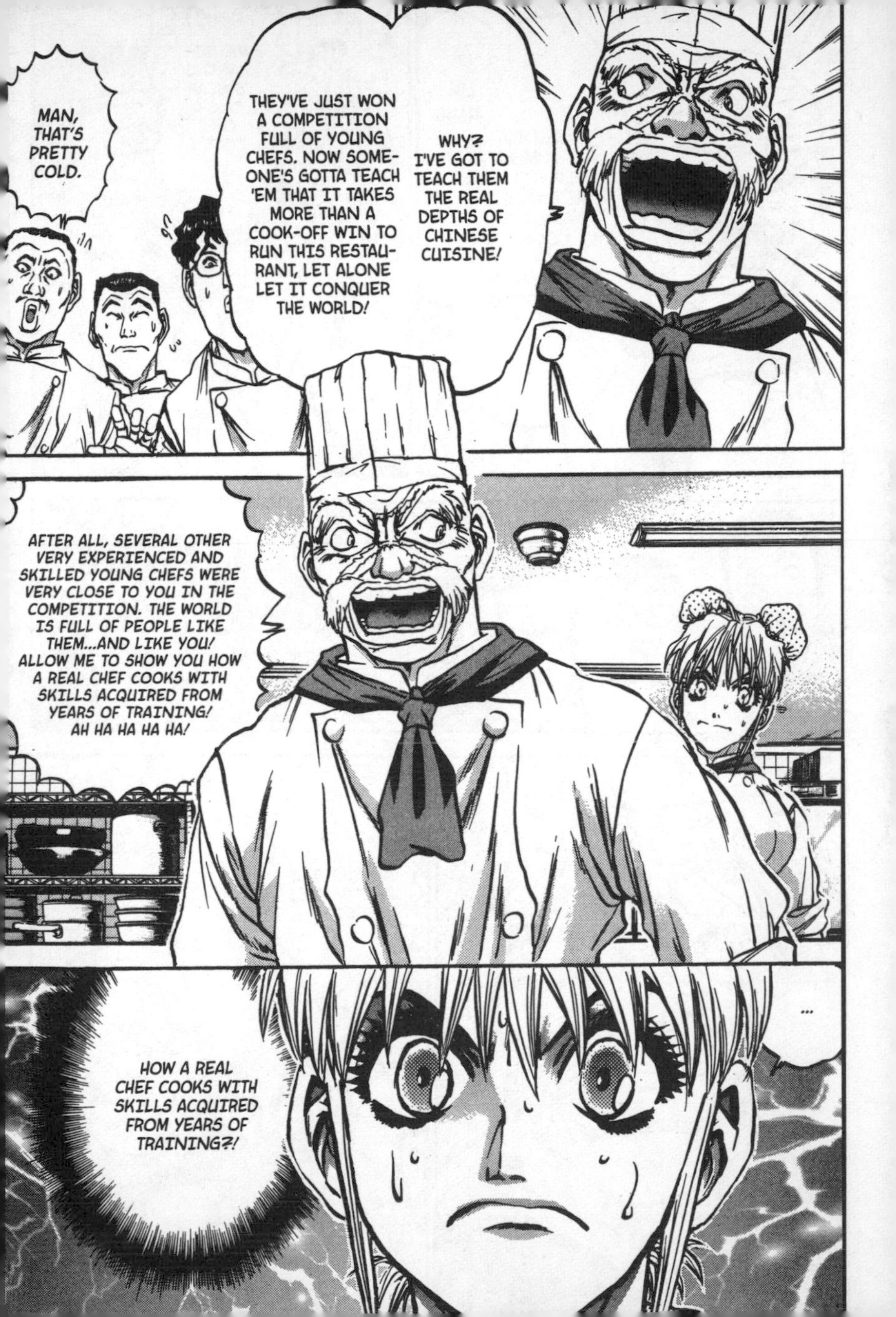
WHY? I'VE GOT TO TEACH THEM THE REAL DEPTHS OF CHINESE CUISINE!
THEY'VE JUST WON A COMPETITION FULL OF YOUNG CHEFS. NOW SOME-ONE'S GOTTA TEACH 'EM THAT IT TAKES MORE THAN A COOK-OFF WIN TO RUN THIS RESTAU-RANT, LET ALONE LET IT CONQUER THE WORLD!
MAN, THAT'S PRETTY COLD.
AFTER ALL, SEVERAL OTHER VERY EXPERIENCED AND SKILLED YOUNG CHEFS WERE VERY CLOSE TO YOU IN THE COMPETITION. THE WORLD IS FULL OF PEOPLE LIKE THEM...AND LIKE YOU! ALLOW ME TO SHOW YOU HOW A REAL CHEF COOKS WITH SKILLS ACQUIRED FROM YEARS OF TRAINING! AH HA HA HA HA!
...
HOW A REAL CHEF COOKS WITH SKILLS ACQUIRED FROM YEARS OF TRAINING?!

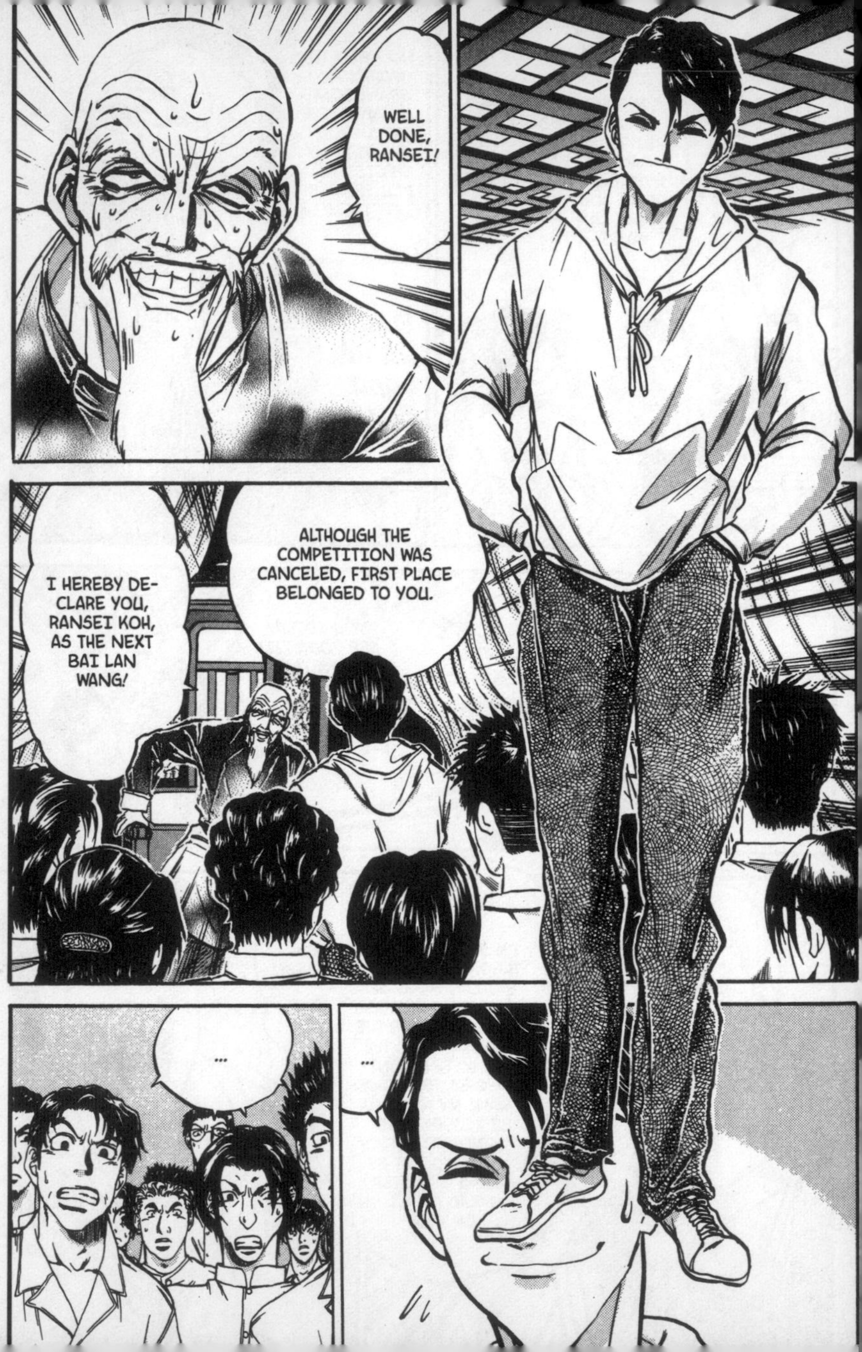
WELL DONE, RANSEI!
ALTHOUGH THE COMPETITION WAS CANCELED, FIRST PLACE BELONGED TO YOU.
I HEREBY DE-CLARE YOU, RANSEI KOH, AS THE NEXT BAI LAN WANG!
...
...

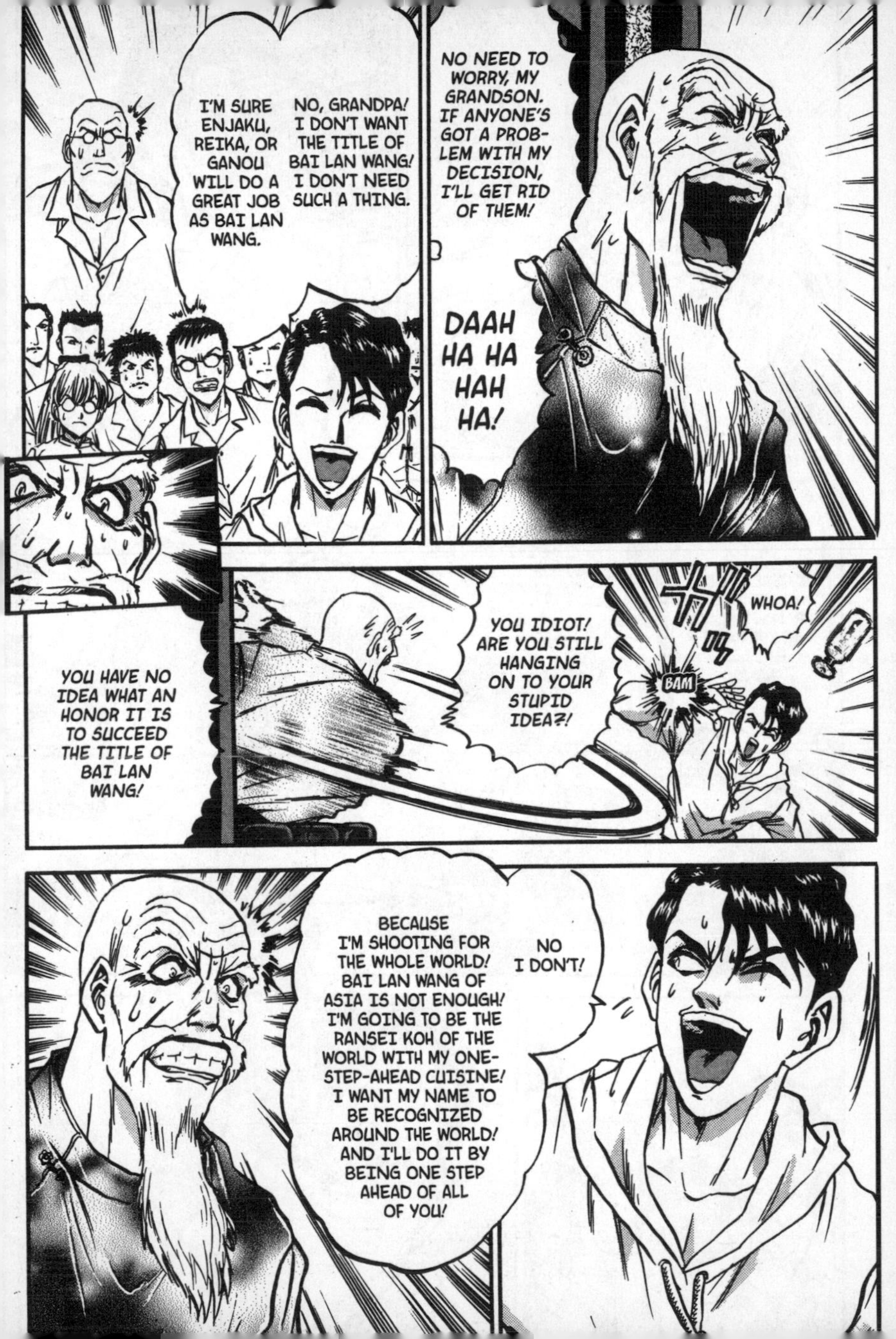
NO NEED TO WORRY, MY GRANDSON. IF ANYONE'S GOT A PROBLEM WITH MY DECISION, I'LL GET RID OF THEM!
DAAH HA HA HAH HA!
NO, GRANDPA! I DON'T WANT THE TITLE OF BAI LAN WANG! I DON'T NEED SUCH A THING.
I'M SURE ENJAKU, REIKA, OR GANOU WILL DO A GREAT JOB AS BAI LAN WANG.
WHOA!
BAM
YOU IDIOT! ARE YOU STILL HANGING ON TO YOUR STUPID IDEA?!
YOU HAVE NO IDEA WHAT AN HONOR IT IS TO SUCCEED THE TITLE OF BAI LAN WANG!
NO I DON'T!
BECAUSE I'M SHOOTING FOR THE WHOLE WORLD! BAI LAN WANG OF ASIA IS NOT ENOUGH! I'M GOING TO BE THE RANSEI KOH OF THE WORLD WITH MY ONE-STEP-AHEAD CUISINE! I WANT MY NAME TO BE RECOGNIZED AROUND THE WORLD! AND I'LL DO IT BY BEING ONE STEP AHEAD OF ALL OF YOU!

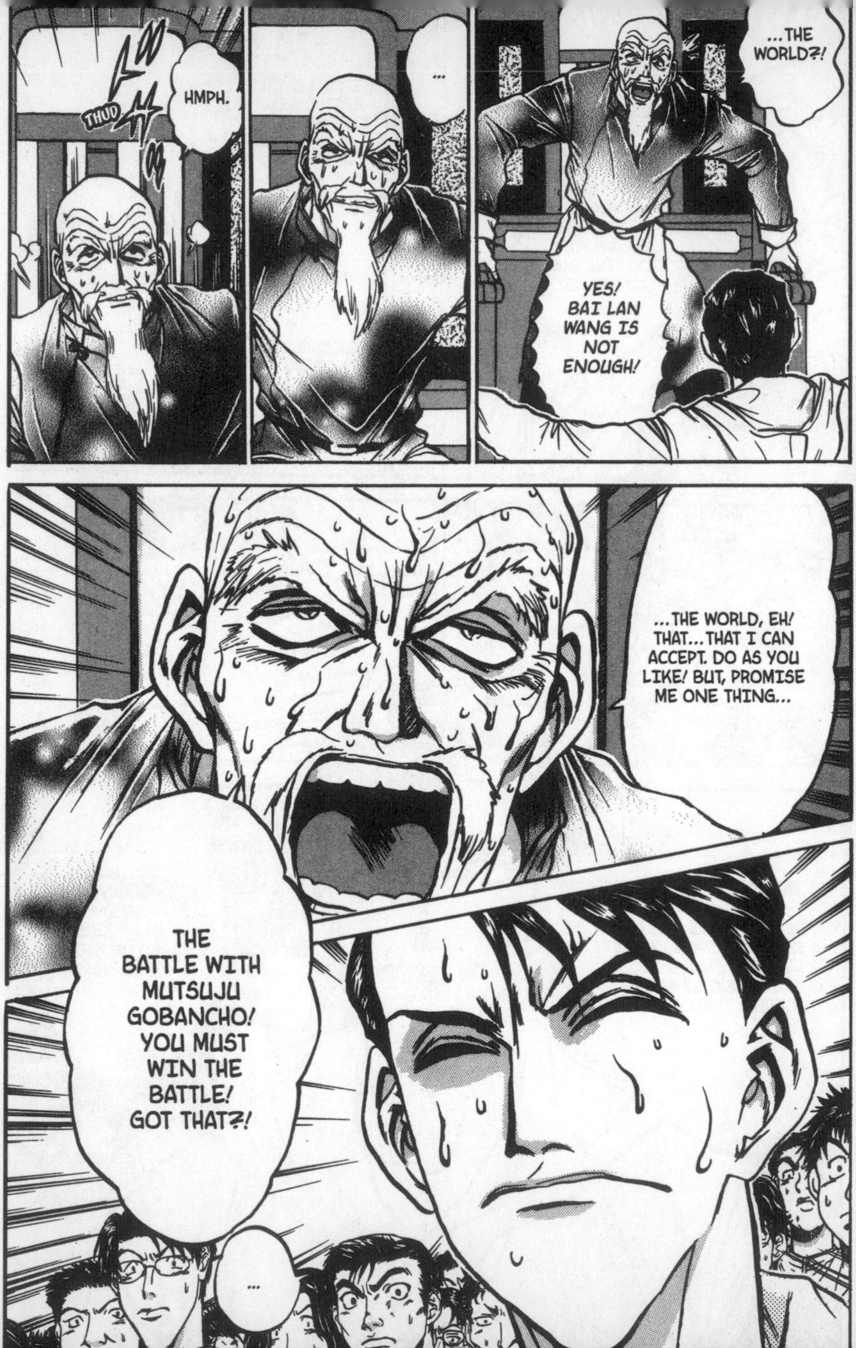
...THE WORLD?!
YES! BAI LAN WANG IS NOT ENOUGH!
...
HMPH.
THUD
...THE WORLD, EH! THAT...THAT I CAN ACCEPT. DO AS YOU LIKE! BUT, PROMISE ME ONE THING...
THE BATTLE WITH MUTSUJU GOBANCHO! YOU MUST WIN THE BATTLE! GOT THAT?!
...

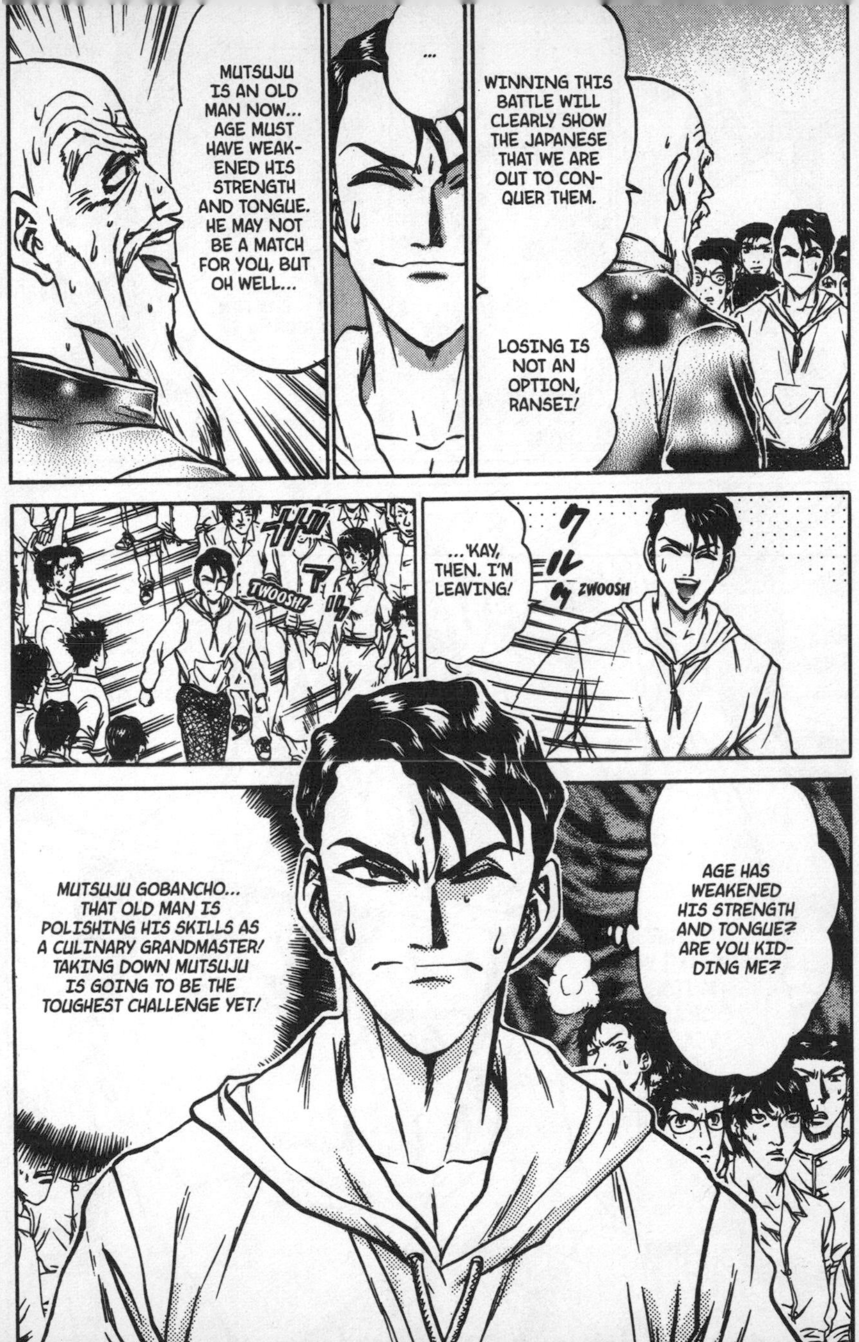
WINNING THIS BATTLE WILL CLEARLY SHOW THE JAPANESE THAT WE ARE OUT TO CON-QUER THEM.
LOSING IS NOT AN OPTION, RANSEI!
...
MUTSUJU IS AN OLD MAN NOW... AGE MUST HAVE WEAK-ENED HIS STRENGTH AND TONGUE. HE MAY NOT BE A MATCH FOR YOU, BUT OH WELL...
...'KAY, THEN. I'M LEAVING!
ZWOOSH
TWOOSH!
AGE HAS WEAKENED HIS STRENGTH AND TONGUE? ARE YOU KID-DING ME?
MUTSUJU GOBANCHO... THAT OLD MAN IS POLISHING HIS SKILLS AS A CULINARY GRANDMASTER! TAKING DOWN MUTSUJU IS GOING TO BE THE TOUGHEST CHALLENGE YET!

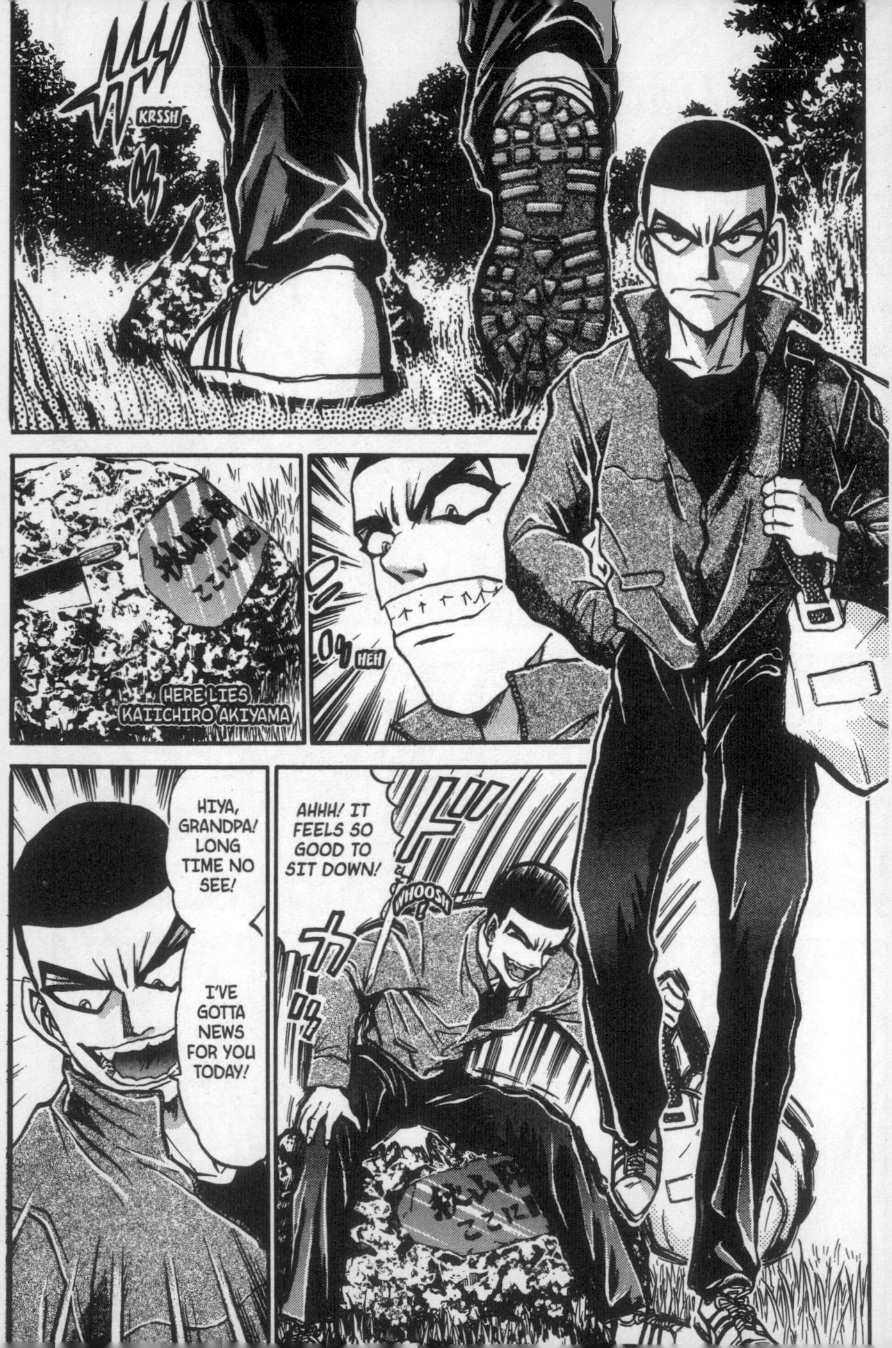
KRSSH
HEH
HERE LIES KAIICHIRO AKIYAMA
AHHH! IT FEELS SO GOOD TO SIT DOWN!
WHOOSH
HIYA, GRANDPA! LONG TIME NO SEE!
I'VE GOTTA NEWS FOR YOU TODAY!

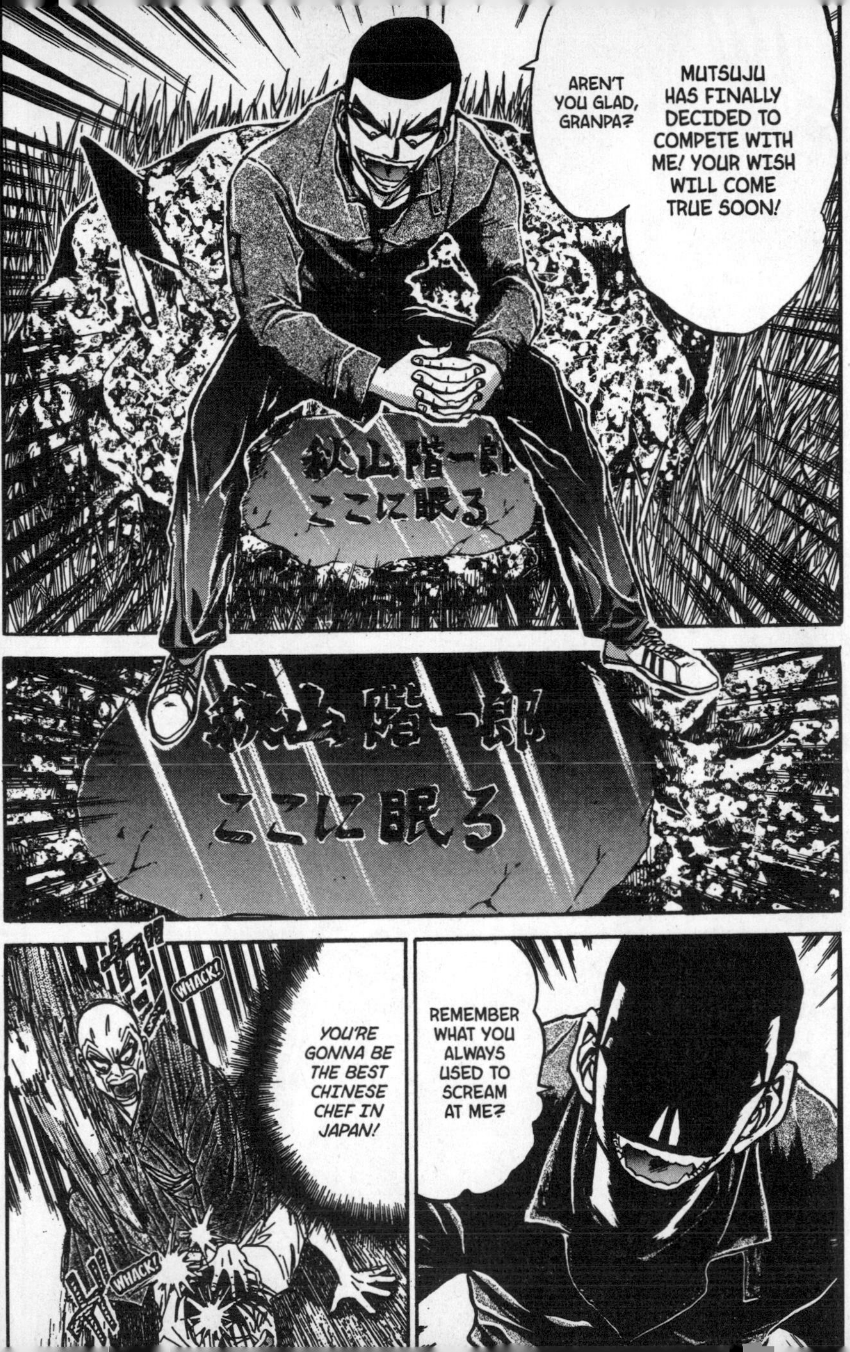
MUTSUJU HAS FINALLY DECIDED TO COMPETE WITH ME! YOUR WISH WILL COME TRUE SOON!
AREN'T YOU GLAD, GRANPA?
秋山階一郎
ここに眠る
秋山階一郎
ここに眠る
REMEMBER WHAT YOU ALWAYS USED TO SCREAM AT ME?
YOU'RE GONNA BE THE BEST CHINESE CHEF IN JAPAN!
WHACK!
WHACK!

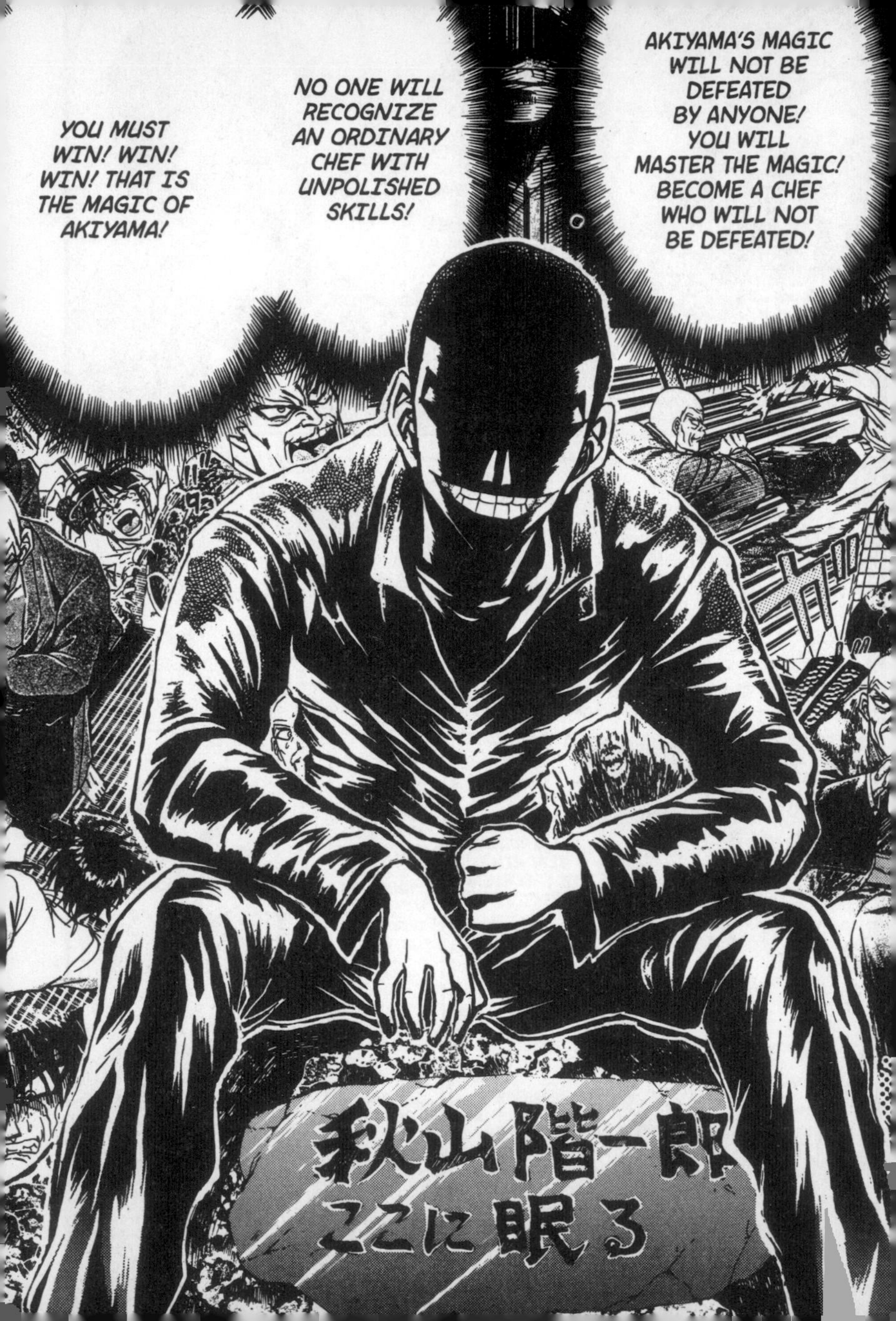
AKIYAMA'S MAGIC WILL NOT BE DEFEATED BY ANYONE! YOU WILL MASTER THE MAGIC! BECOME A CHEF WHO WILL NOT BE DEFEATED!
NO ONE WILL RECOGNIZE AN ORDINARY CHEF WITH UNPOLISHED SKILLS!
YOU MUST WIN! WIN! WIN! THAT IS THE MAGIC OF AKIYAMA!
秋山階一郎
ここに眠る

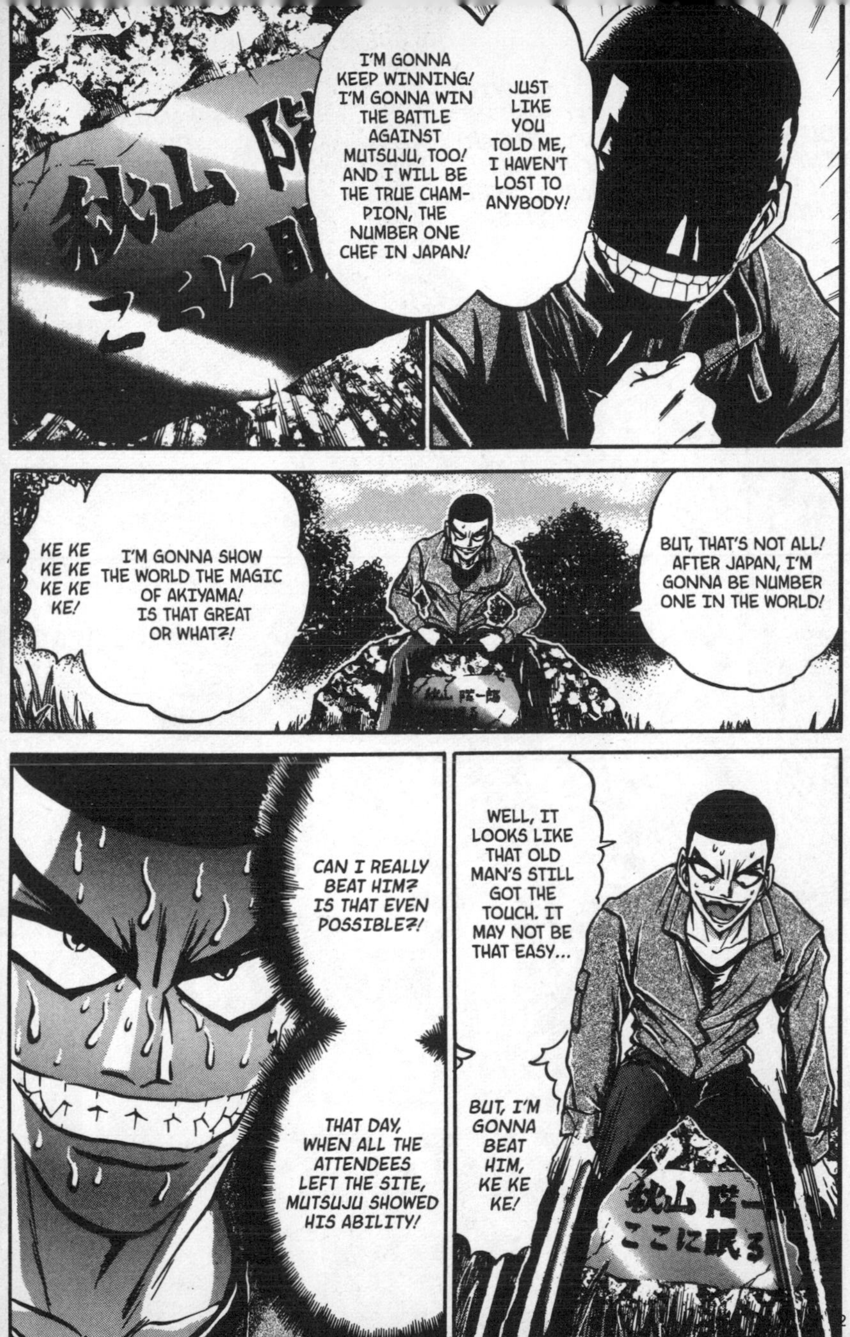
JUST LIKE YOU TOLD ME, I HAVEN'T LOST TO ANYBODY!
I'M GONNA KEEP WINNING! I'M GONNA WIN THE BATTLE AGAINST MUTSUJU, TOO! AND I WILL BE THE TRUE CHAMPION, THE NUMBER ONE CHEF IN JAPAN!
BUT, THAT'S NOT ALL! AFTER JAPAN, I'M GONNA BE NUMBER ONE IN THE WORLD!
I'M GONNA SHOW THE WORLD THE MAGIC OF AKIYAMA! IS THAT GREAT OR WHAT?!
KE KE KE KE KE KE KE!
WELL, IT LOOKS LIKE THAT OLD MAN'S STILL GOT THE TOUCH. IT MAY NOT BE THAT EASY...
BUT, I'M GONNA BEAT HIM, KE KE KE!
秋山 階一
ここに眠る
CAN I REALLY BEAT HIM? IS THAT EVEN POSSIBLE?!
THAT DAY, WHEN ALL THE ATTENDEES LEFT THE SITE, MUTSUJU SHOWED HIS ABILITY!

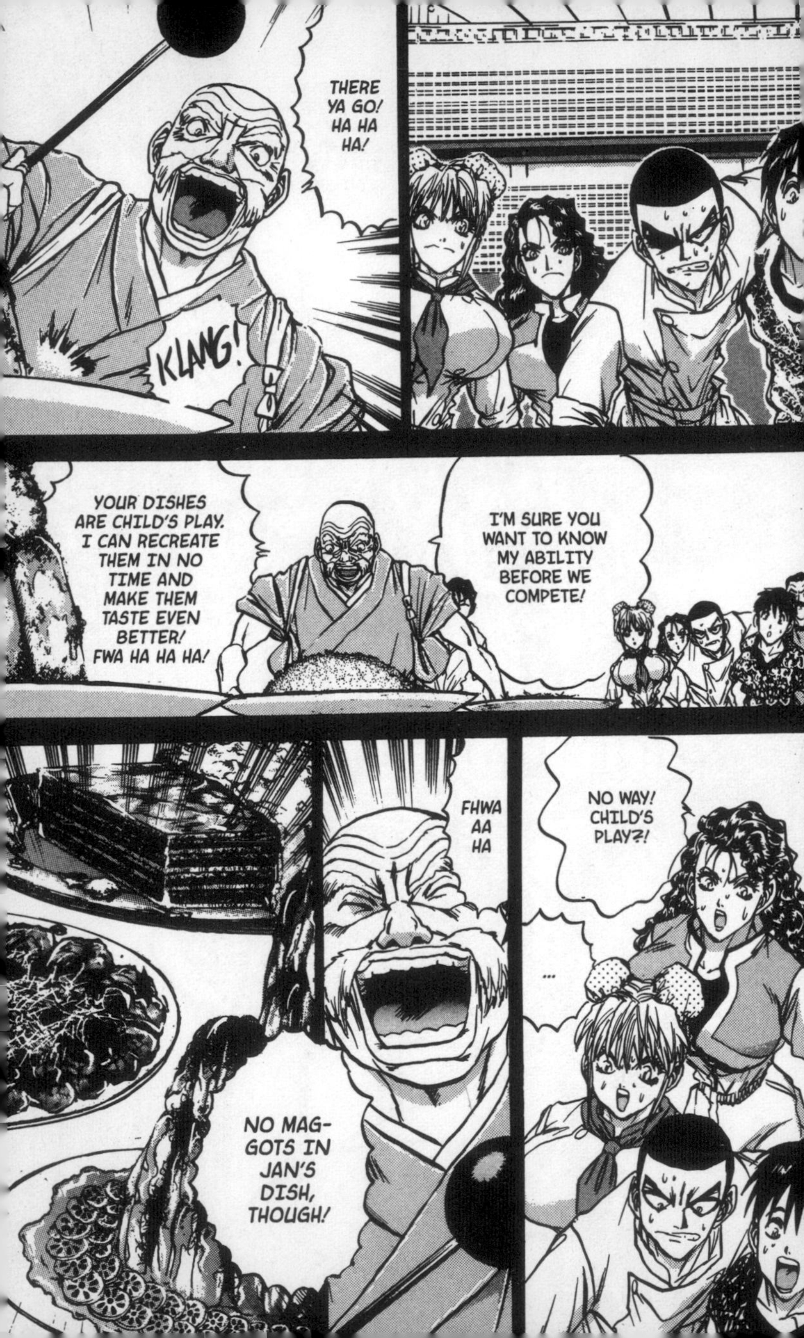
THERE YA GO! HA HA HA!
KLANG!
I'M SURE YOU WANT TO KNOW MY ABILITY BEFORE WE COMPETE!
YOUR DISHES ARE CHILD'S PLAY. I CAN RECREATE THEM IN NO TIME AND MAKE THEM TASTE EVEN BETTER! FWA HA HA HA!
NO WAY! CHILD'S PLAY?!
...
FHWA AA HA
NO MAG-GOTS IN JAN'S DISH, THOUGH!

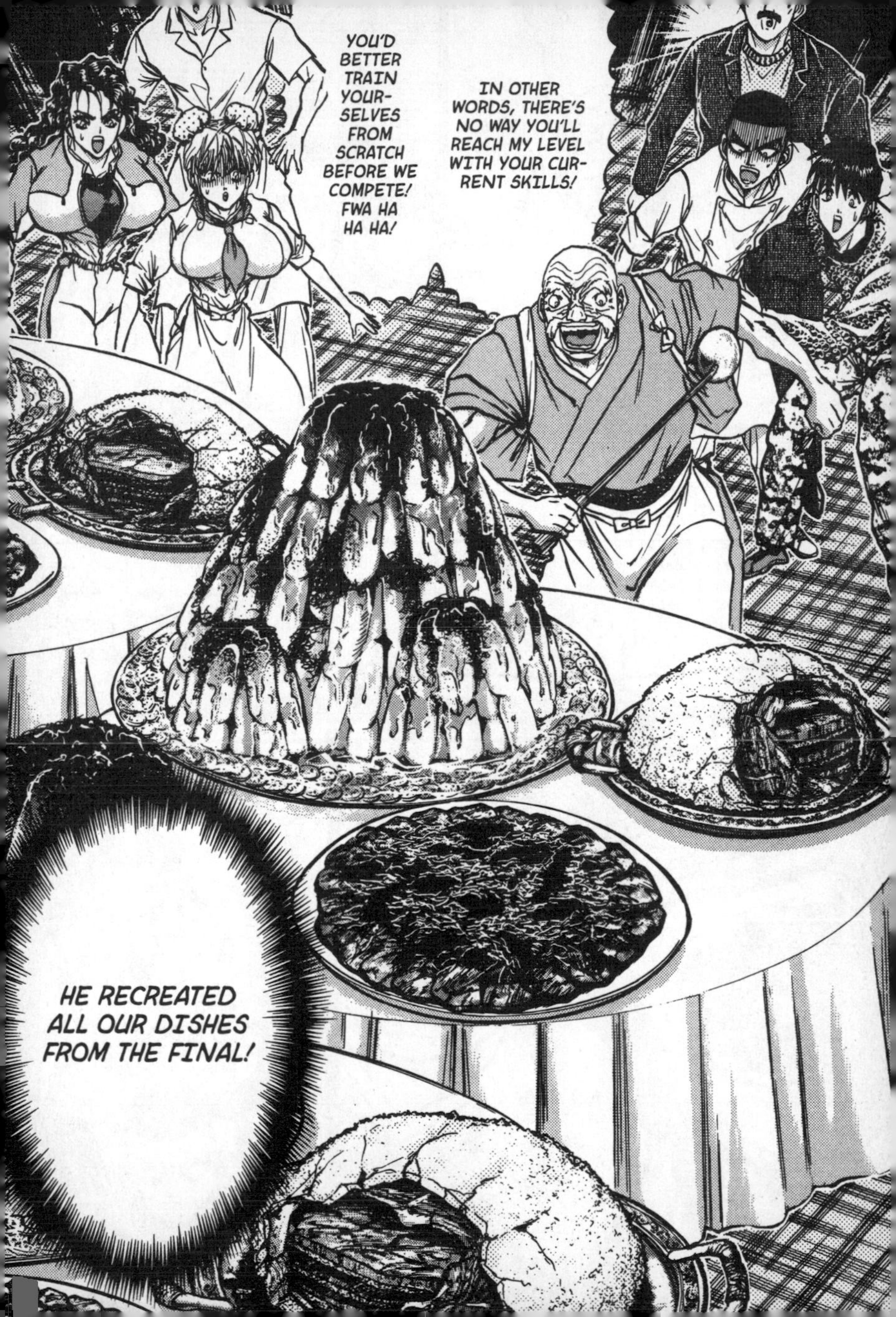
IN OTHER WORDS, THERE'S NO WAY YOU'LL REACH MY LEVEL WITH YOUR CURRENT SKILLS!
YOU'D BETTER TRAIN YOURSELVES FROM SCRATCH BEFORE WE COMPETE! FWA HA HA HA!
HE RECREATED ALL OUR DISHES FROM THE FINAL!

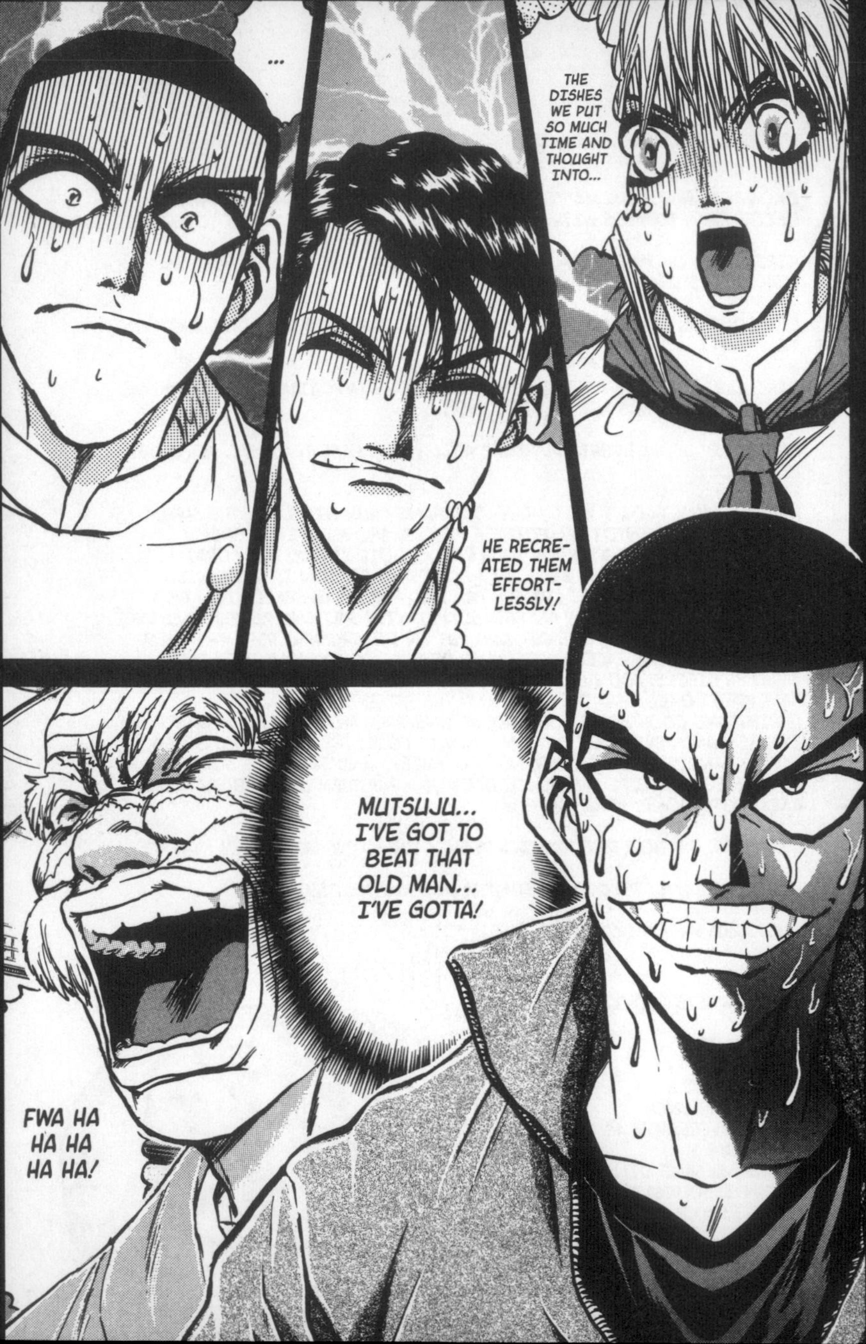
THE DISHES WE PUT SO MUCH TIME AND THOUGHT INTO...
HE RECREATED THEM EFFORTLESSLY!
...
MUTSUJU... I'VE GOT TO BEAT THAT OLD MAN... I'VE GOTTA!
FWA HA HA HA HA HA!

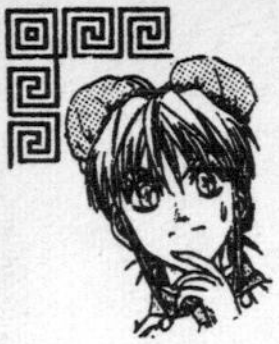

KIRIKO AND OKONOGI'S

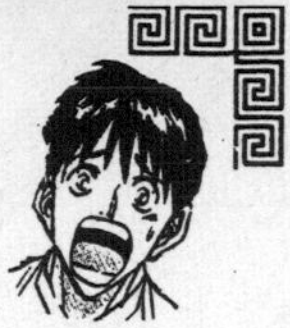

JIA CHANG CHUN BING (SPRING ROLL VARIATION)

OKONOGI: WHAT'S THE MATTER WITH JAN, FOR CHRIST'S SAKE! HE KNOWS BETTER THAN TO MESS WITH ME WHEN THERE'S A TV SHOW I WANT TO WATCH!

KIRIKO: OH, OKONOGI! I'M SO IMPRESSED! JAN JUST TOLD ME YOU ARE REALLY INTO LEARNING NEW RECIPES!

OKONOGI: AU CONTRAIRE, I'M GOING HOME. I WANNA WATCH THIS SHOW ON TV...

KIRIKO: OH, REALLY? SO, WATCHING TV IS MORE IMPORTANT THAN COOKING, HUH? I GUESS I WAS WRONG ABOUT YOU...

OKONOGI: ... ALL RIGHT, ALL RIGHT. WILL YOU PLEASE TEACH ME, KIRIKO? BOO HOO...

KIRIKO: OKAY, THEN. I WILL MAKE JIA CHANG CHUN BING. CUT THE SHRIMP AND THE CHIVES INTO 1 CENTIMETER PIECES, AND MINCE THE GREEN ONION. CRUSH THE TOFU WITH YOUR HANDS, BOIL IT, AND THEN DRAIN IT IN A COLANDER. MIX THE EGGS IN A BOWL AND SEASON IT WITH SALT, PEPPER, AND SESAME OIL. OIL THE PAN AND FRY THE GREEN ONION AND COOK THE SHRIMP HALFWAY AND SEASON IT WITH SALT AND PEPPER AND TAKE IT OUT. ADD A LITTLE MORE OIL AND PUT IN THE CRUSHED TOFU. FRY THEM TO GET RID OF THE EXCESS WATER AND BE SURE TO CRUMBLE THEM INTO SMALLER PIECES. ADD THE EGG MIXTURE AND WHEN THE EGG IS MORE THAN HALF WAY COOKED, ADD THE CHIVE AND THE FRIED GREEN ONION AND SHRIMP AND COOK SOME MORE. ADD CORNSTARCH MIXED WITH WATER TO THICKEN AND POUR THEM OUT ON A PAN TO COOL. THEN, YOU JUST SPREAD SOME PEANUT BUTTER ON SPRING ROLL SHEETS AND SPRINKLE SOME SUGAR, PUT THE EGG MIXTURE IN THE MIDDLE AND WRAP THEM UP. FRY BOTH SIDES AND YOU'RE DONE! HERE YOU GO!

OKONOGI: OH, THIS IS GOOD! ALL RIGHTY, I'M GOING HOME NOW, KIRIKO.

KIRIKO: CELINE! I'M DONE WITH HIM. HE'S ALL YOURS!!

OKONOGI: WHAAAAT?!!

INGREDIENTS:
- SPRING ROLL SHEETS (MINI): 15 SHEETS
- TOFU: 2
- PRAWN: 100 GRAMS
- EGG: 2 OR 3
- GREEN ONION: 1 STALK
- CHINESE CHIVE: 1 BUNCH
- PEANUT BUTTER (CREAMY): AS NEEDED
- SALT: 1 TEASPOON
- SUGAR, PEPPER, SESAME OIL: SEASON TO TASTE
- CORNSTARCH DISSOLVED IN WATER: AS NEEDED
- OIL: 3-5 TABLESPOON
- GLUE FOR THE SPRING ROLL: 1 TABLESPOON FLOUR MIXED WITH 1/4 CUP WATER

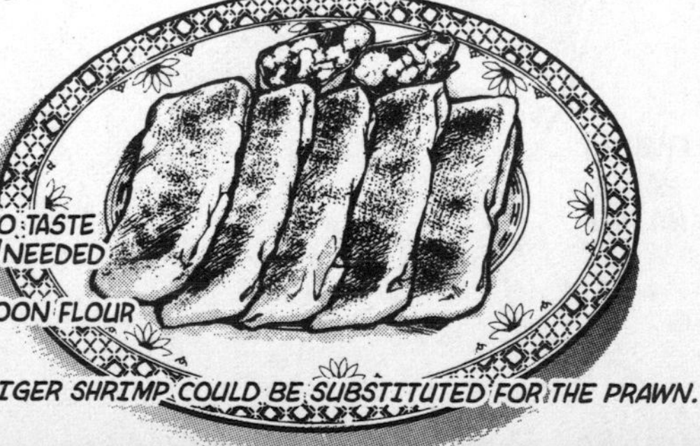

*TIGER SHRIMP COULD BE SUBSTITUTED FOR THE PRAWN.

STORY 245 "I'LL GIVE IT TO YA!"

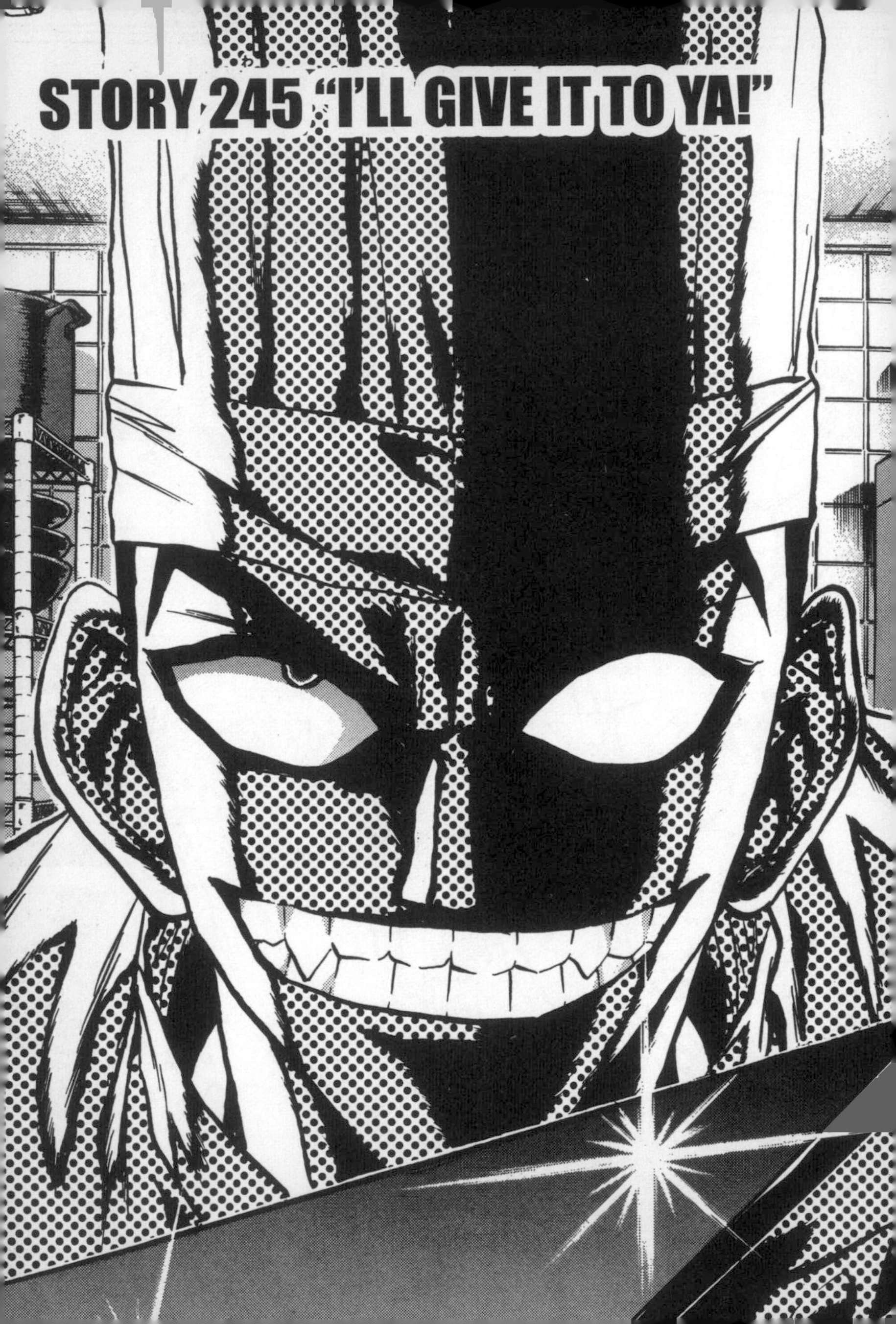

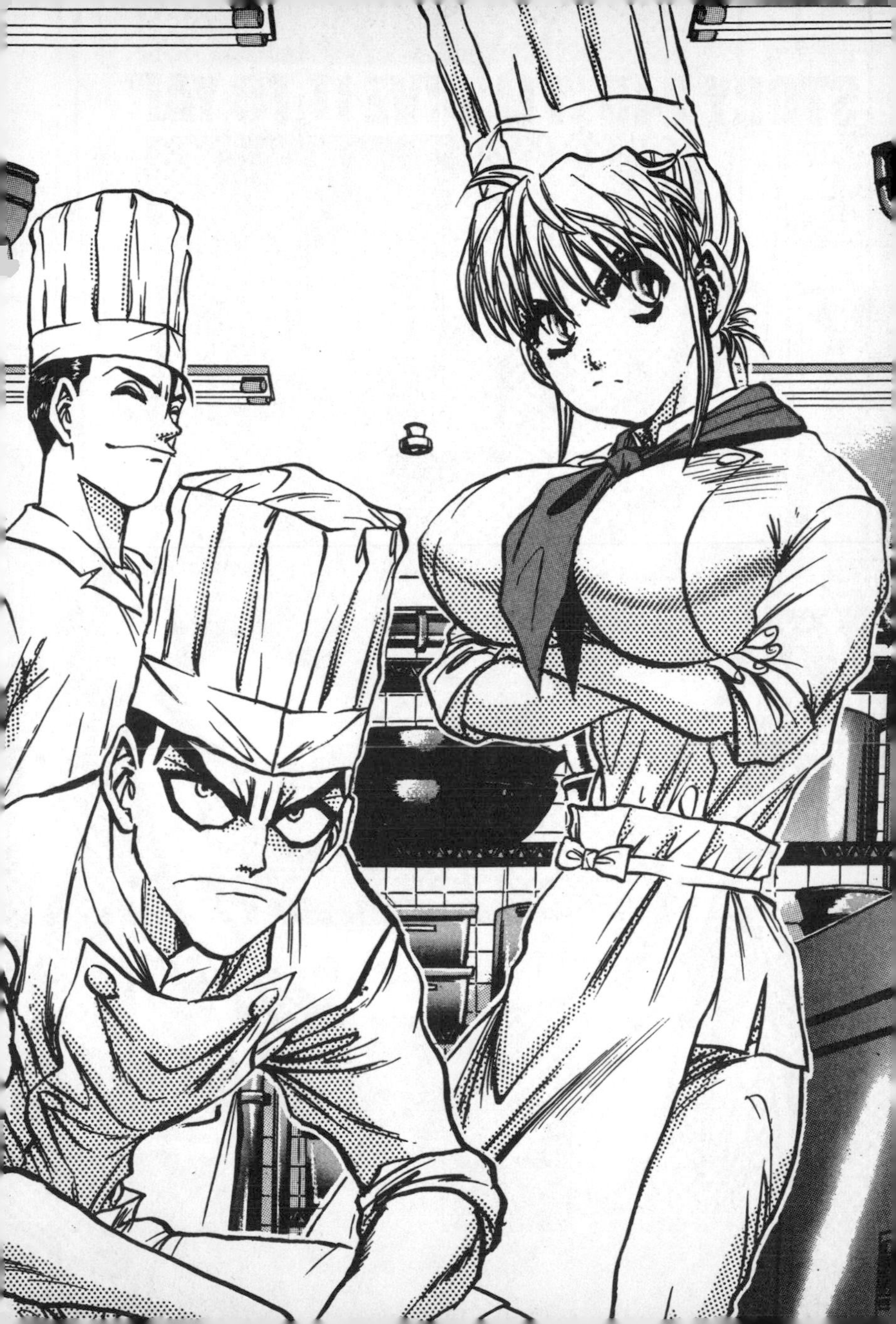

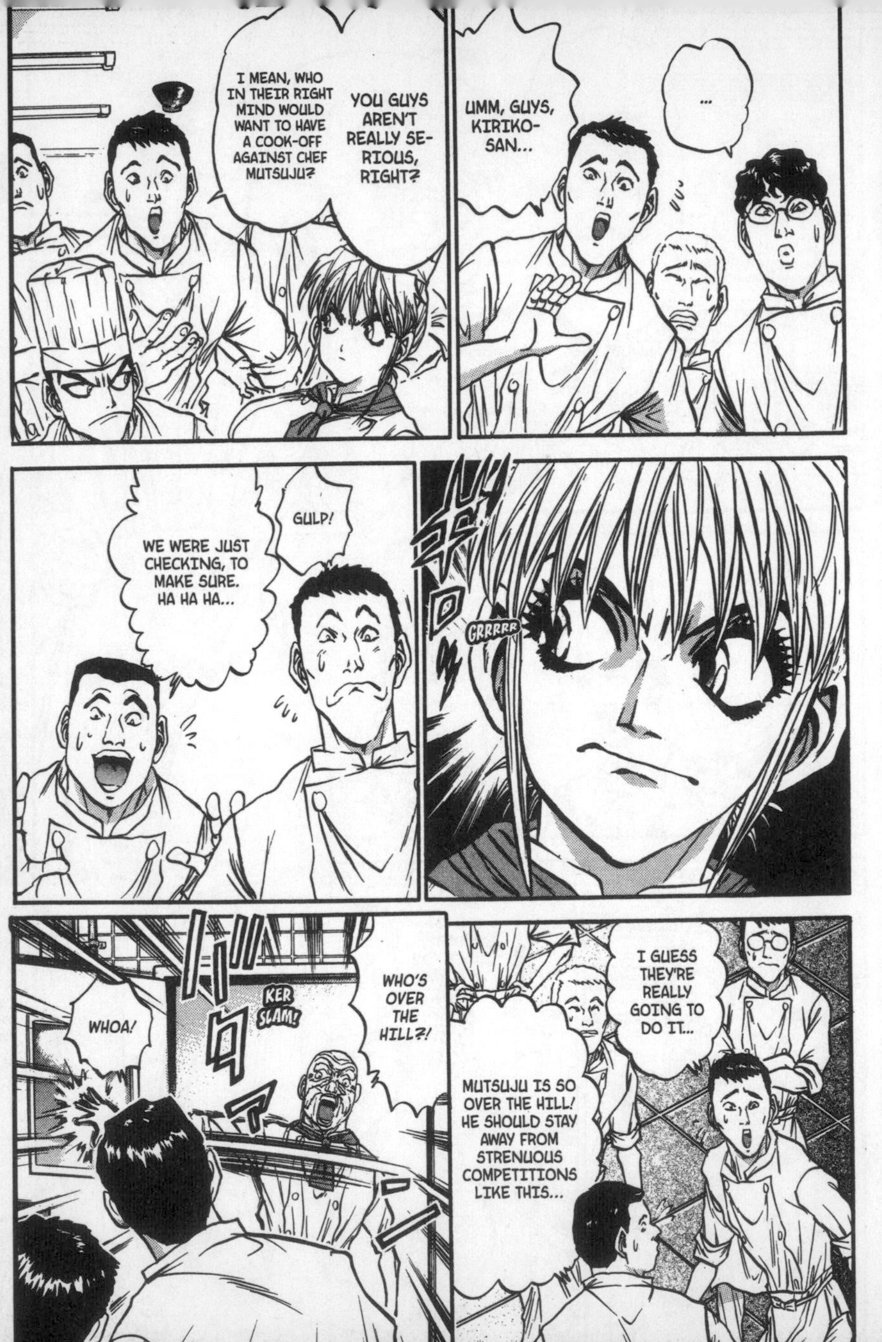
...
UMM, GUYS, KIRIKO-SAN...
YOU GUYS AREN'T REALLY SE-RIOUS, RIGHT?
I MEAN, WHO IN THEIR RIGHT MIND WOULD WANT TO HAVE A COOK-OFF AGAINST CHEF MUTSUJU?
GRRRRR
GULP!
WE WERE JUST CHECKING, TO MAKE SURE. HA HA HA...
I GUESS THEY'RE REALLY GOING TO DO IT...
MUTSUJU IS SO OVER THE HILL! HE SHOULD STAY AWAY FROM STRENUOUS COMPETITIONS LIKE THIS...
WHO'S OVER THE HILL?!
KER SLAM!
WHOA!

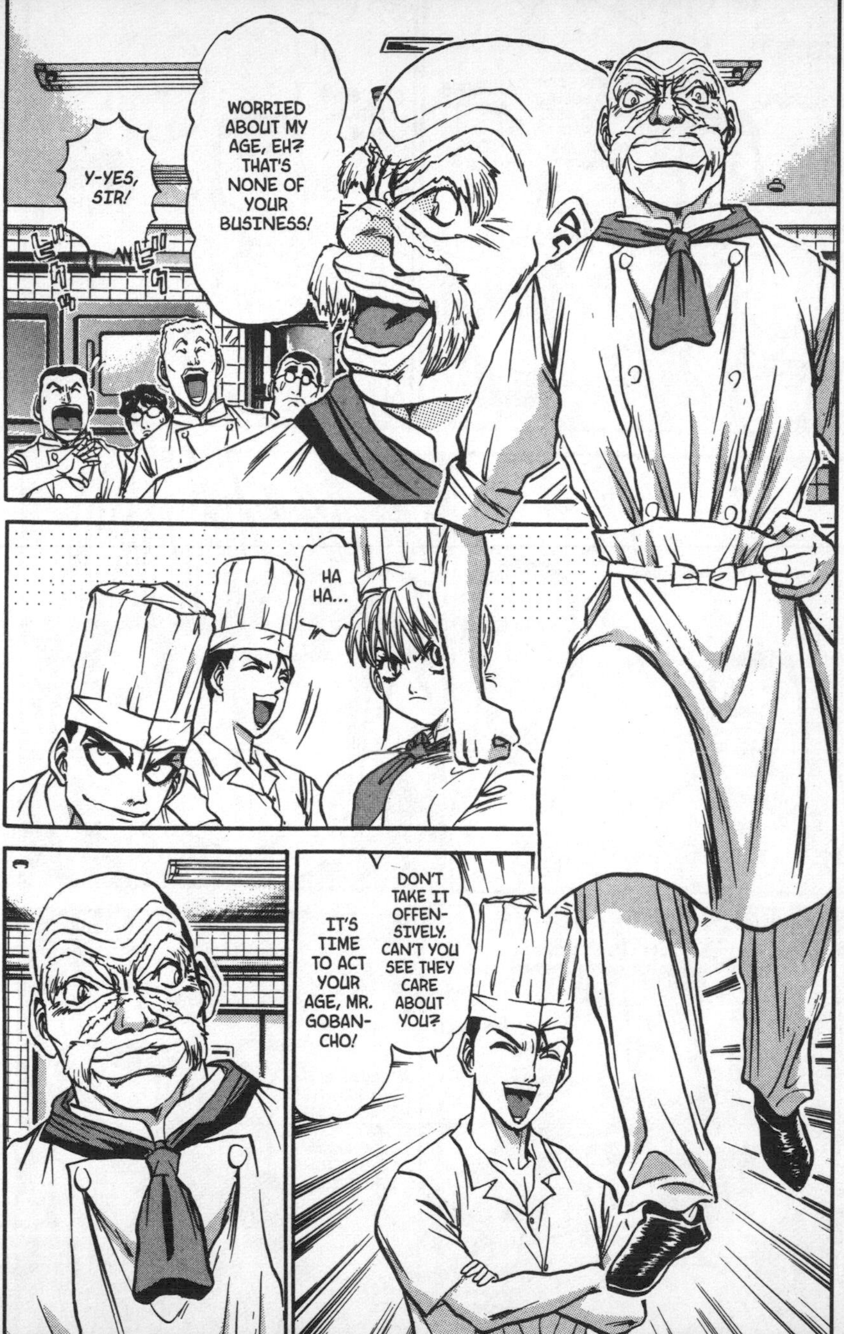
WORRIED ABOUT MY AGE, EH? THAT'S NONE OF YOUR BUSINESS!
Y-YES, SIR!
HA HA...
DON'T TAKE IT OFFENSIVELY. CAN'T YOU SEE THEY CARE ABOUT YOU?
IT'S TIME TO ACT YOUR AGE, MR. GOBANCHO!

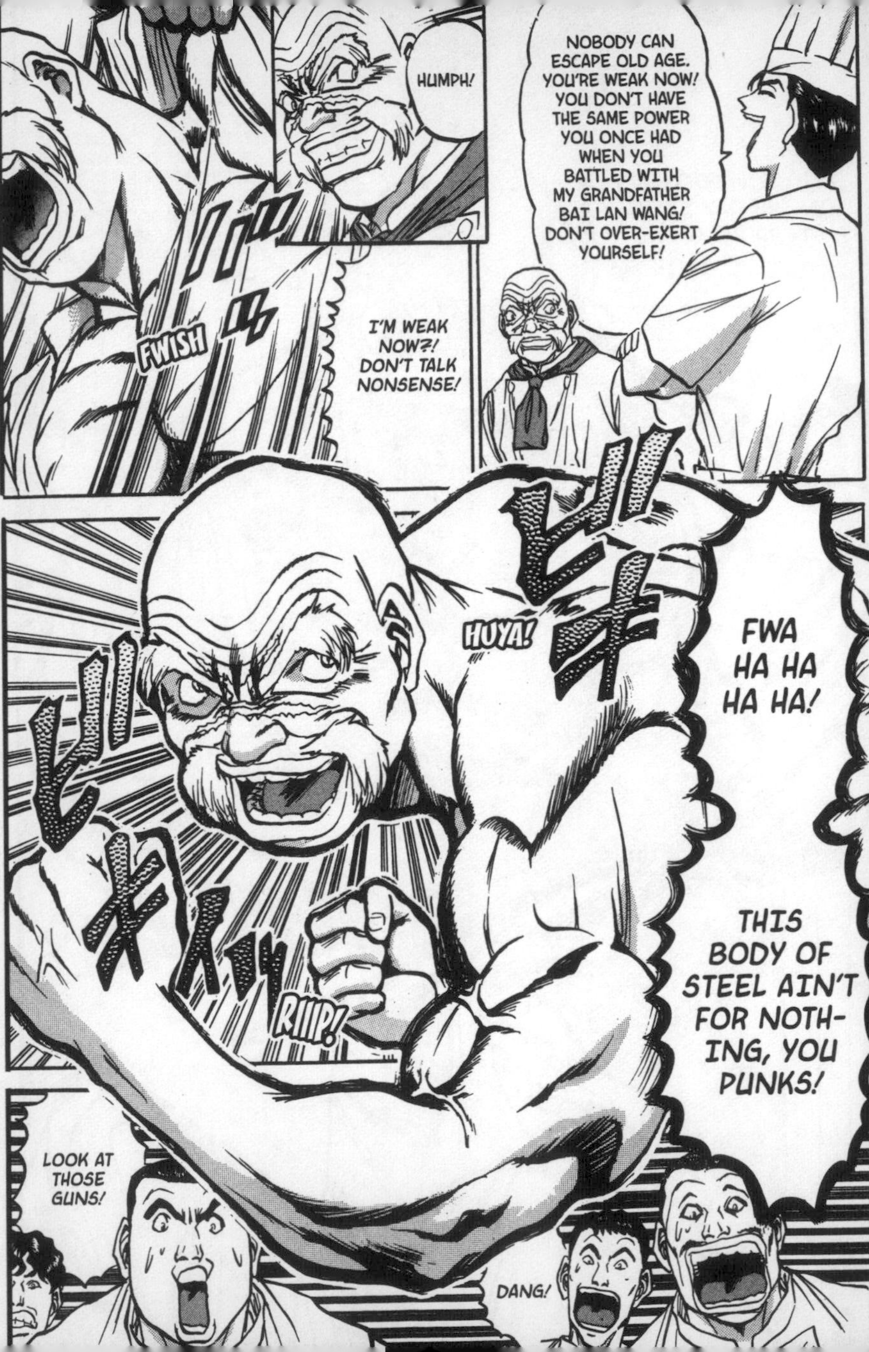
NOBODY CAN ESCAPE OLD AGE. YOU'RE WEAK NOW! YOU DON'T HAVE THE SAME POWER YOU ONCE HAD WHEN YOU BATTLED WITH MY GRANDFATHER BAI LAN WANG! DON'T OVER-EXERT YOURSELF!
HUMPH!
I'M WEAK NOW?! DON'T TALK NONSENSE!
FWISH
FWA HA HA HA HA!
THIS BODY OF STEEL AIN'T FOR NOTH-ING, YOU PUNKS!
HUYA!
RIIP!
DANG!
LOOK AT THOSE GUNS!

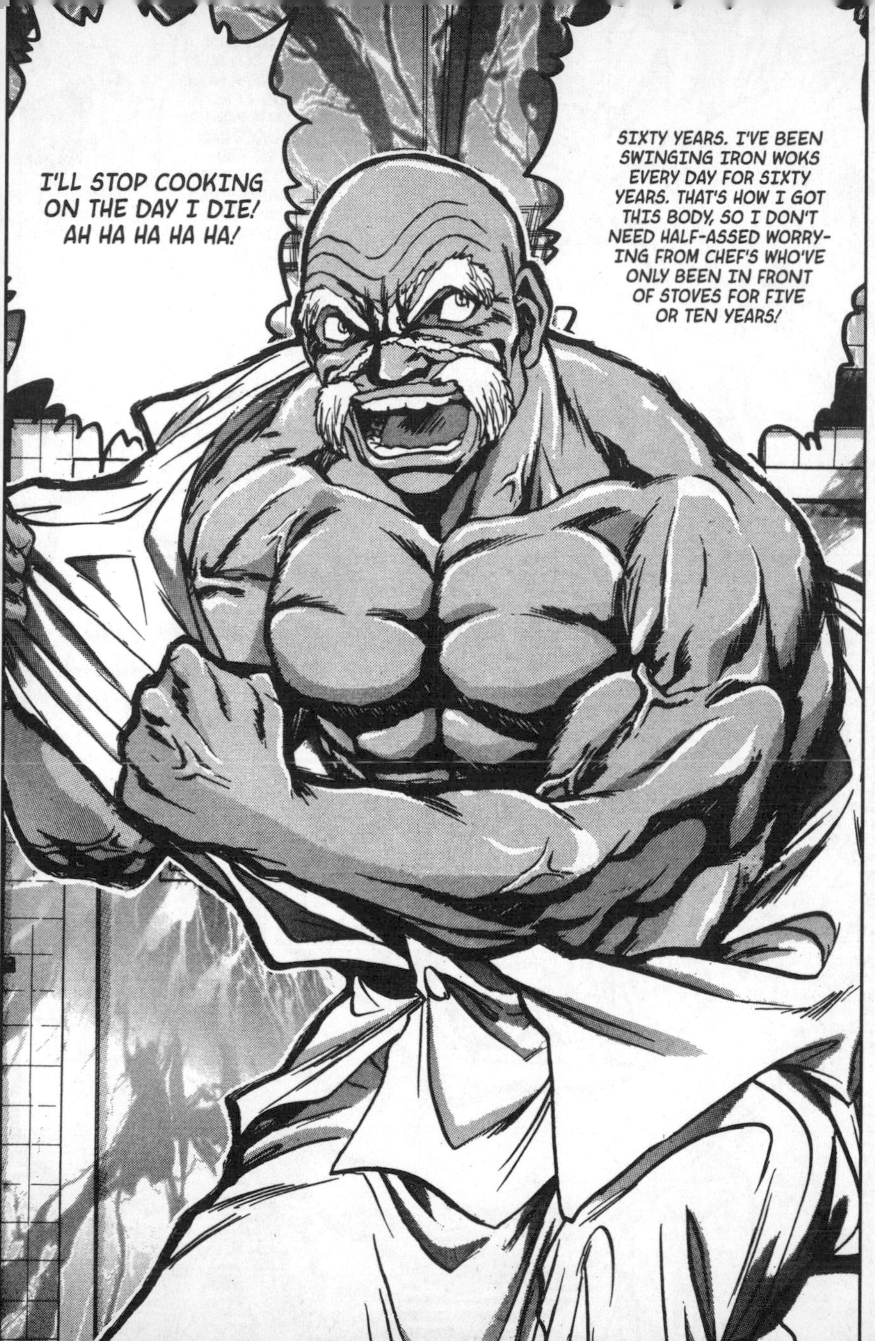
SIXTY YEARS. I'VE BEEN SWINGING IRON WOKS EVERY DAY FOR SIXTY YEARS. THAT'S HOW I GOT THIS BODY, SO I DON'T NEED HALF-ASSED WORRY-ING FROM CHEF'S WHO'VE ONLY BEEN IN FRONT OF STOVES FOR FIVE OR TEN YEARS!
I'LL STOP COOKING ON THE DAY I DIE! AH HA HA HA HA!

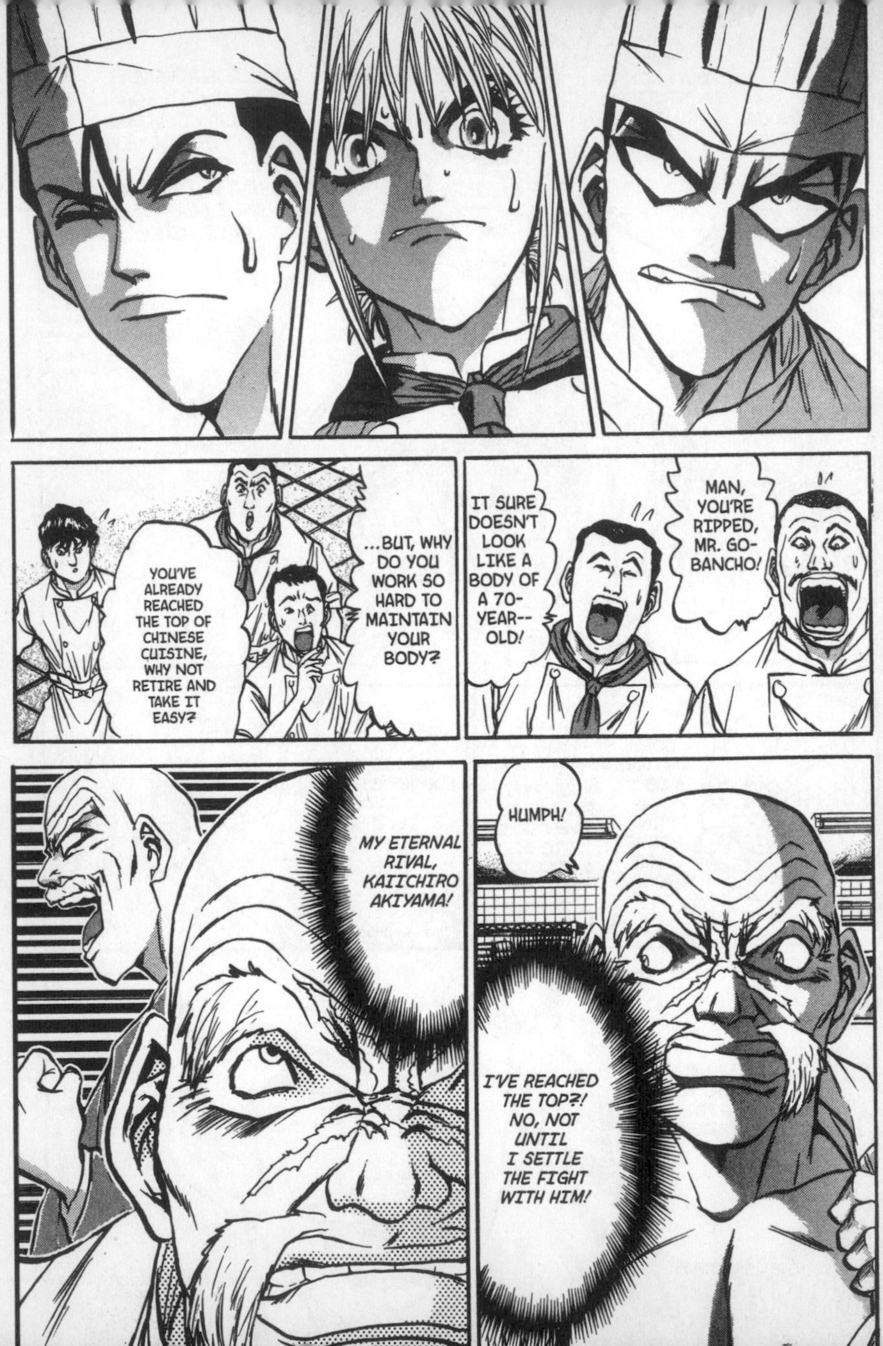
MAN, YOU'RE RIPPED, MR. GO-BANCHO!
IT SURE DOESN'T LOOK LIKE A BODY OF A 70-YEAR--OLD!
...BUT, WHY DO YOU WORK SO HARD TO MAINTAIN YOUR BODY?
YOU'VE ALREADY REACHED THE TOP OF CHINESE CUISINE, WHY NOT RETIRE AND TAKE IT EASY?
HUMPH!
I'VE REACHED THE TOP?! NO, NOT UNTIL I SETTLE THE FIGHT WITH HIM!
MY ETERNAL RIVAL, KAIICHIRO AKIYAMA!

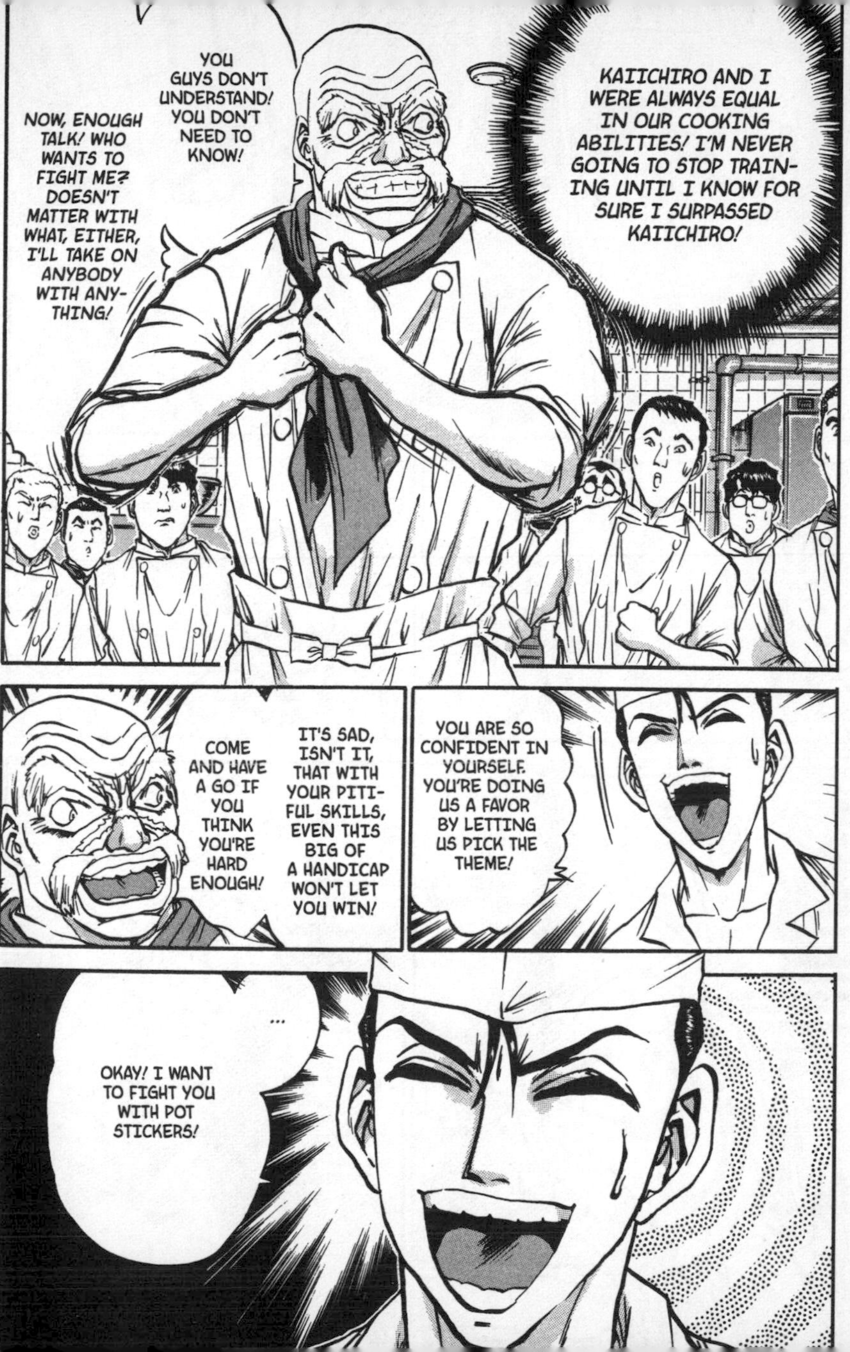
KAIICHIRO AND I WERE ALWAYS EQUAL IN OUR COOKING ABILITIES! I'M NEVER GOING TO STOP TRAIN-ING UNTIL I KNOW FOR SURE I SURPASSED KAIICHIRO!
YOU GUYS DON'T UNDERSTAND! YOU DON'T NEED TO KNOW!
NOW, ENOUGH TALK! WHO WANTS TO FIGHT ME? DOESN'T MATTER WITH WHAT, EITHER, I'LL TAKE ON ANYBODY WITH ANY-THING!
YOU ARE SO CONFIDENT IN YOURSELF. YOU'RE DOING US A FAVOR BY LETTING US PICK THE THEME!
IT'S SAD, ISN'T IT, THAT WITH YOUR PITI-FUL SKILLS, EVEN THIS BIG OF A HANDICAP WON'T LET YOU WIN!
COME AND HAVE A GO IF YOU THINK YOU'RE HARD ENOUGH!
...
OKAY! I WANT TO FIGHT YOU WITH POT STICKERS!

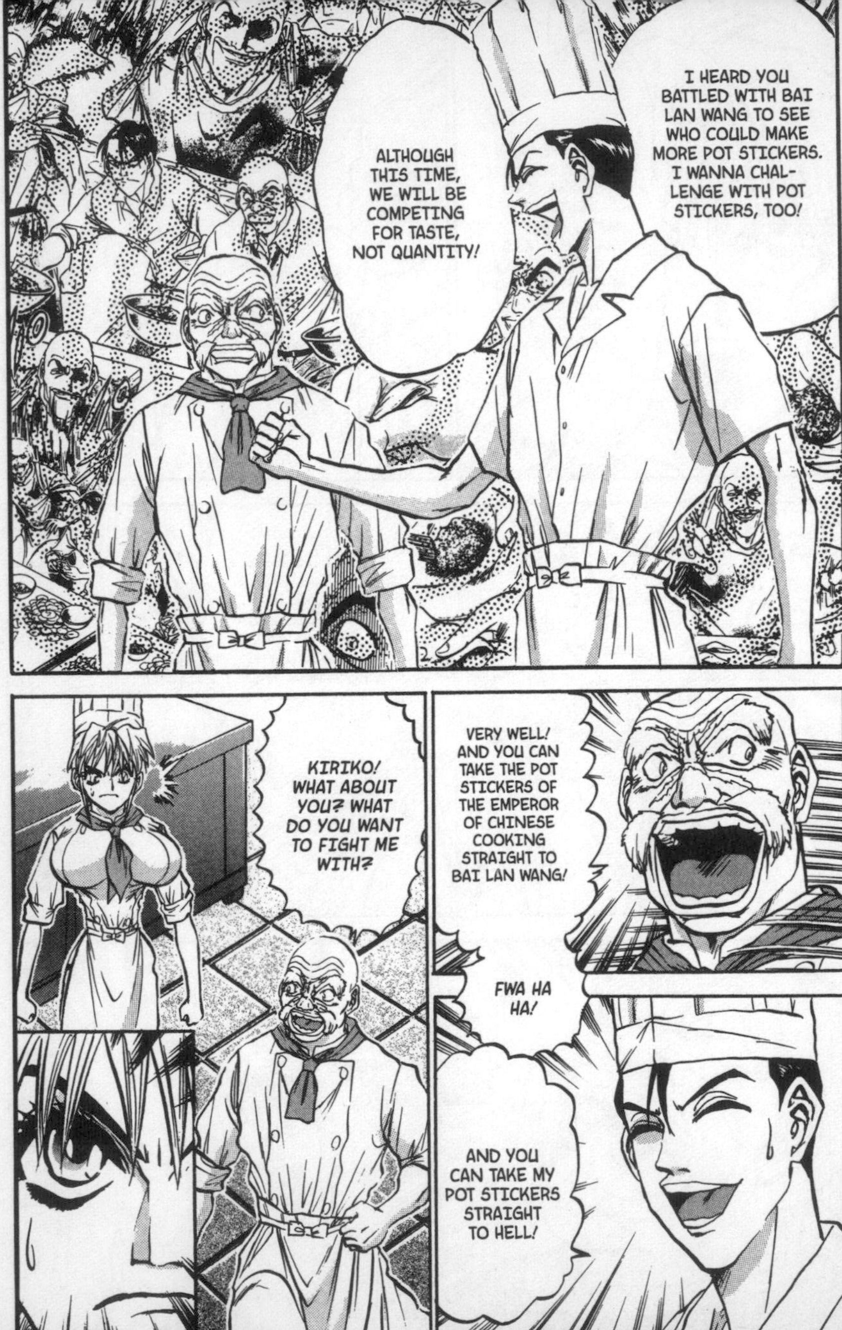
I HEARD YOU BATTLED WITH BAI LAN WANG TO SEE WHO COULD MAKE MORE POT STICKERS. I WANNA CHALLENGE WITH POT STICKERS, TOO!
ALTHOUGH THIS TIME, WE WILL BE COMPETING FOR TASTE, NOT QUANTITY!
VERY WELL! AND YOU CAN TAKE THE POT STICKERS OF THE EMPEROR OF CHINESE COOKING STRAIGHT TO BAI LAN WANG!
FWA HA HA!
AND YOU CAN TAKE MY POT STICKERS STRAIGHT TO HELL!
KIRIKO! WHAT ABOUT YOU? WHAT DO YOU WANT TO FIGHT ME WITH?

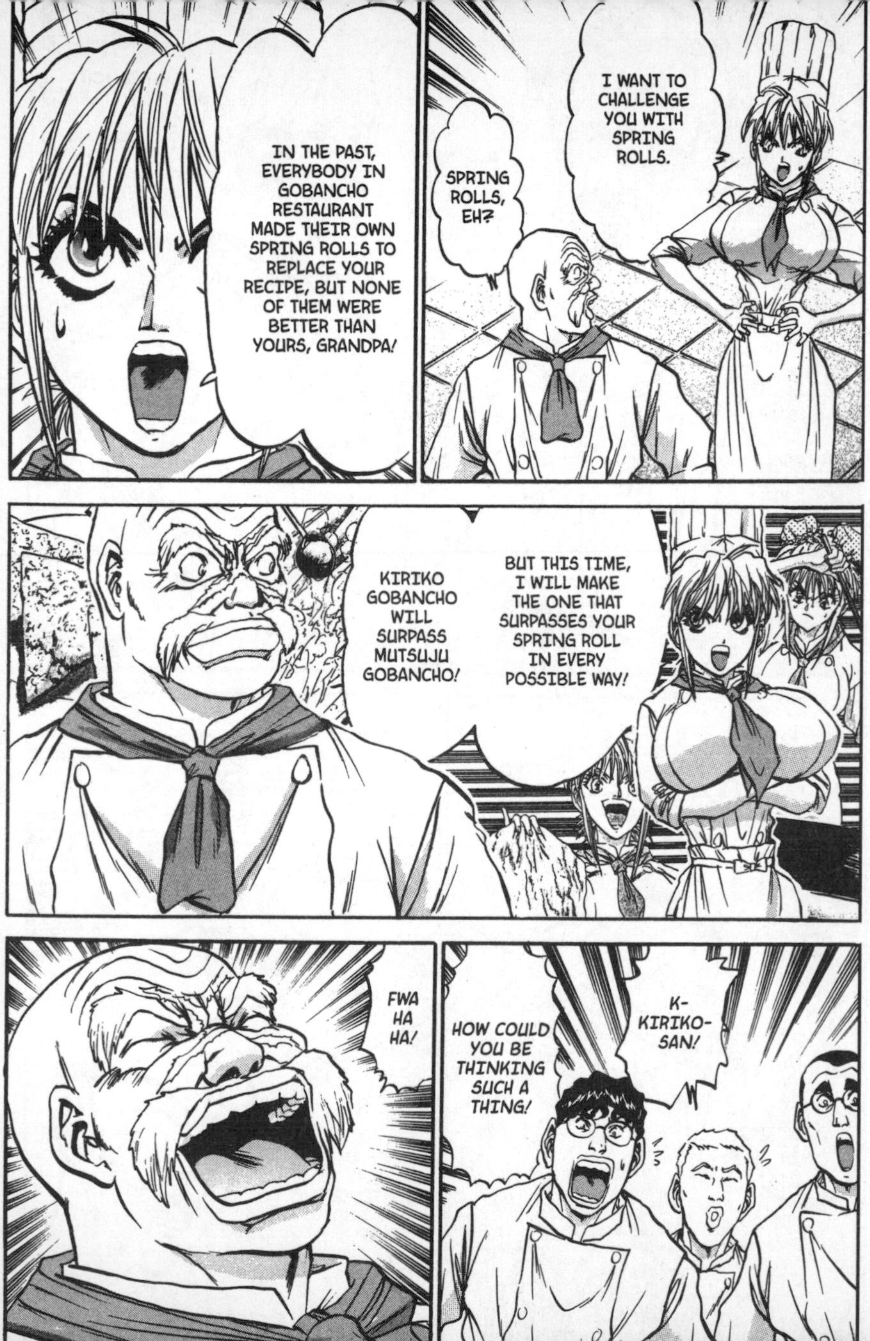
I WANT TO CHALLENGE YOU WITH SPRING ROLLS.
SPRING ROLLS, EH?
IN THE PAST, EVERYBODY IN GOBANCHO RESTAURANT MADE THEIR OWN SPRING ROLLS TO REPLACE YOUR RECIPE, BUT NONE OF THEM WERE BETTER THAN YOURS, GRANDPA!
BUT THIS TIME, I WILL MAKE THE ONE THAT SURPASSES YOUR SPRING ROLL IN EVERY POSSIBLE WAY!
KIRIKO GOBANCHO WILL SURPASS MUTSUJU GOBANCHO!
K-KIRIKO-SAN!
HOW COULD YOU BE THINKING SUCH A THING!
FWA HA HA!

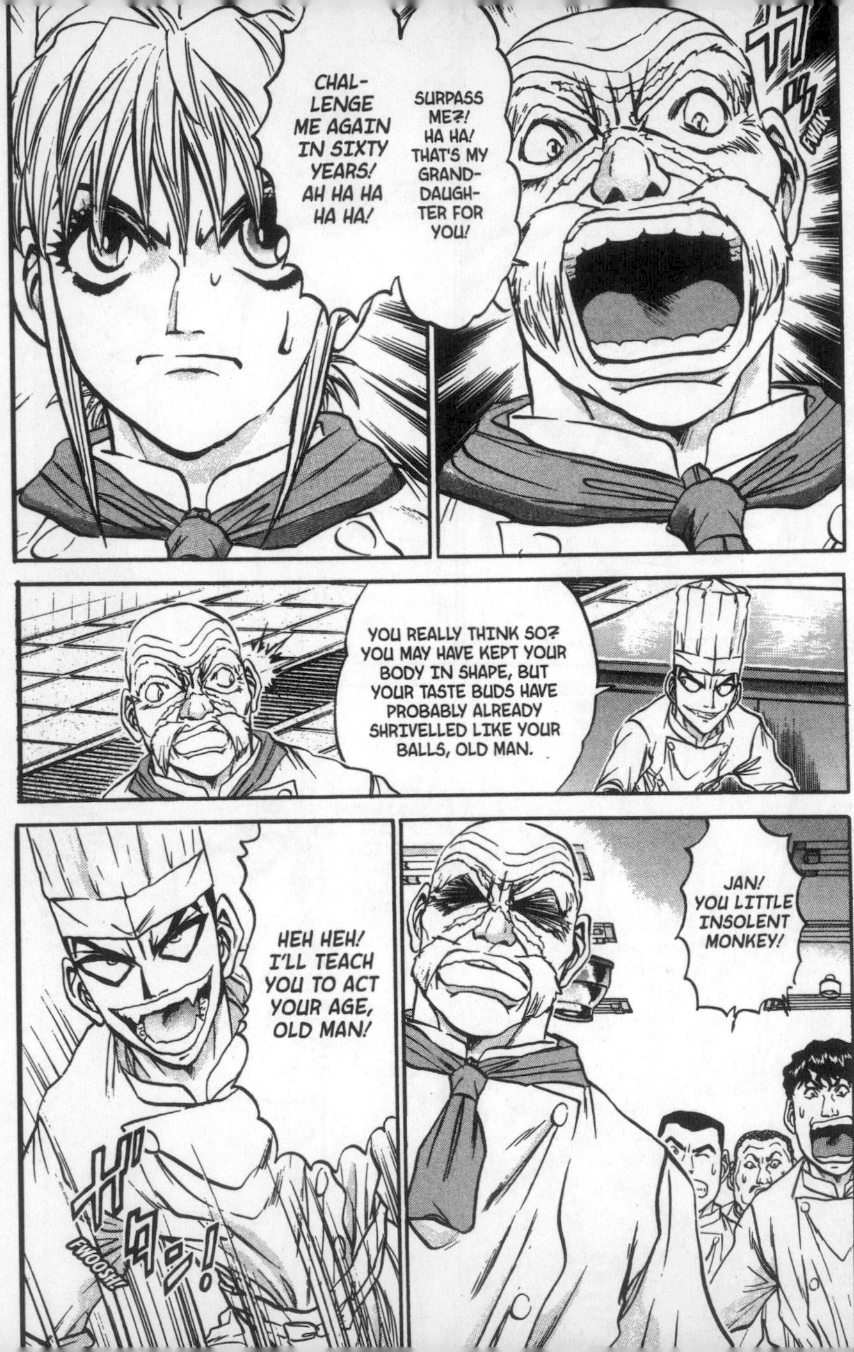
GWAK
SURPASS ME?! HA HA! THAT'S MY GRAND-DAUGHTER FOR YOU!
CHAL-LENGE ME AGAIN IN SIXTY YEARS! AH HA HA HA HA!
YOU REALLY THINK SO? YOU MAY HAVE KEPT YOUR BODY IN SHAPE, BUT YOUR TASTE BUDS HAVE PROBABLY ALREADY SHRIVELLED LIKE YOUR BALLS, OLD MAN.
JAN! YOU LITTLE INSOLENT MONKEY!
HEH HEH! I'LL TEACH YOU TO ACT YOUR AGE, OLD MAN!
FWOOSH!!

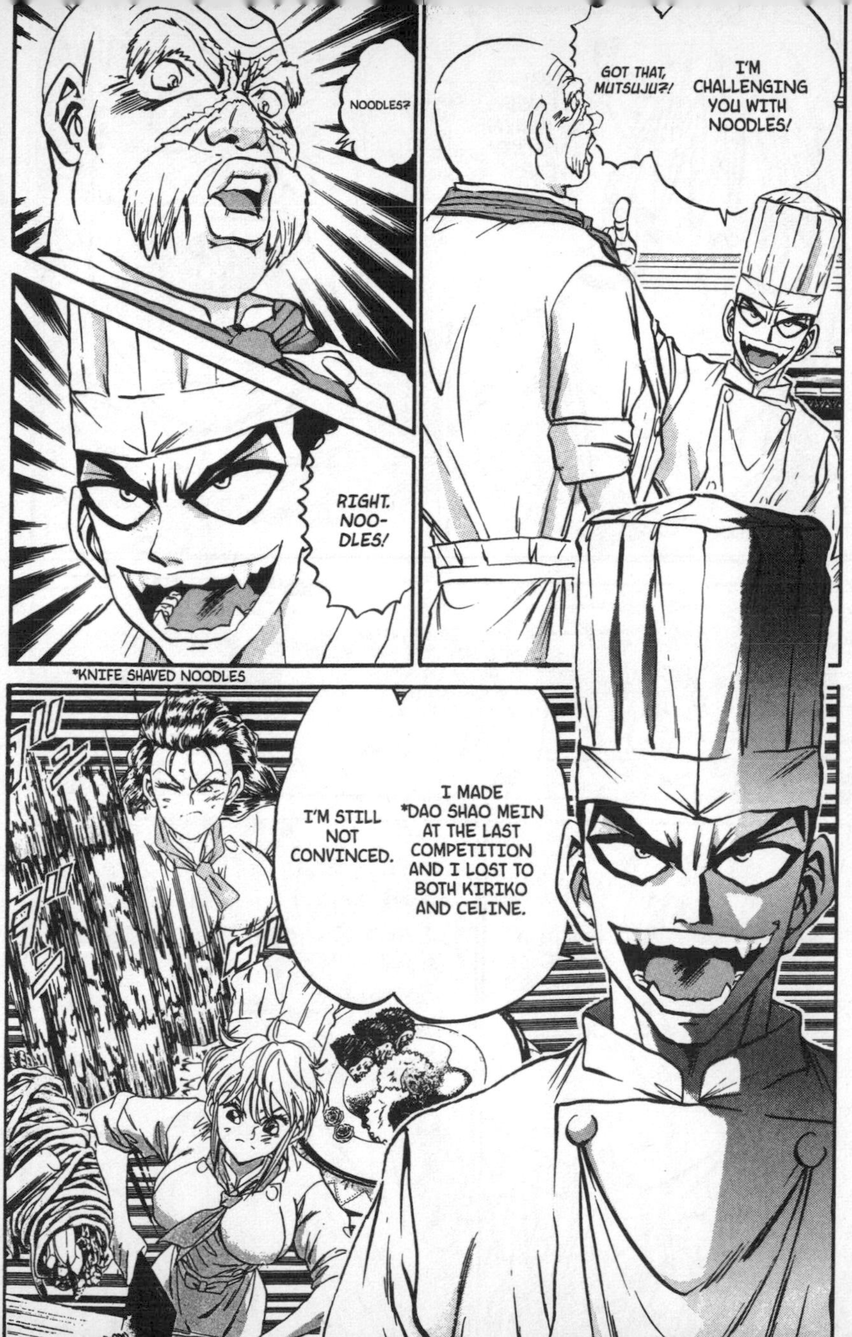
I'M CHALLENGING YOU WITH NOODLES!
GOT THAT, MUTSUJU?!
NOODLES?
RIGHT. NOO-DLES!
I MADE *DAO SHAO MEIN AT THE LAST COMPETITION AND I LOST TO BOTH KIRIKO AND CELINE.
I'M STILL NOT CONVINCED.
*KNIFE SHAVED NOODLES

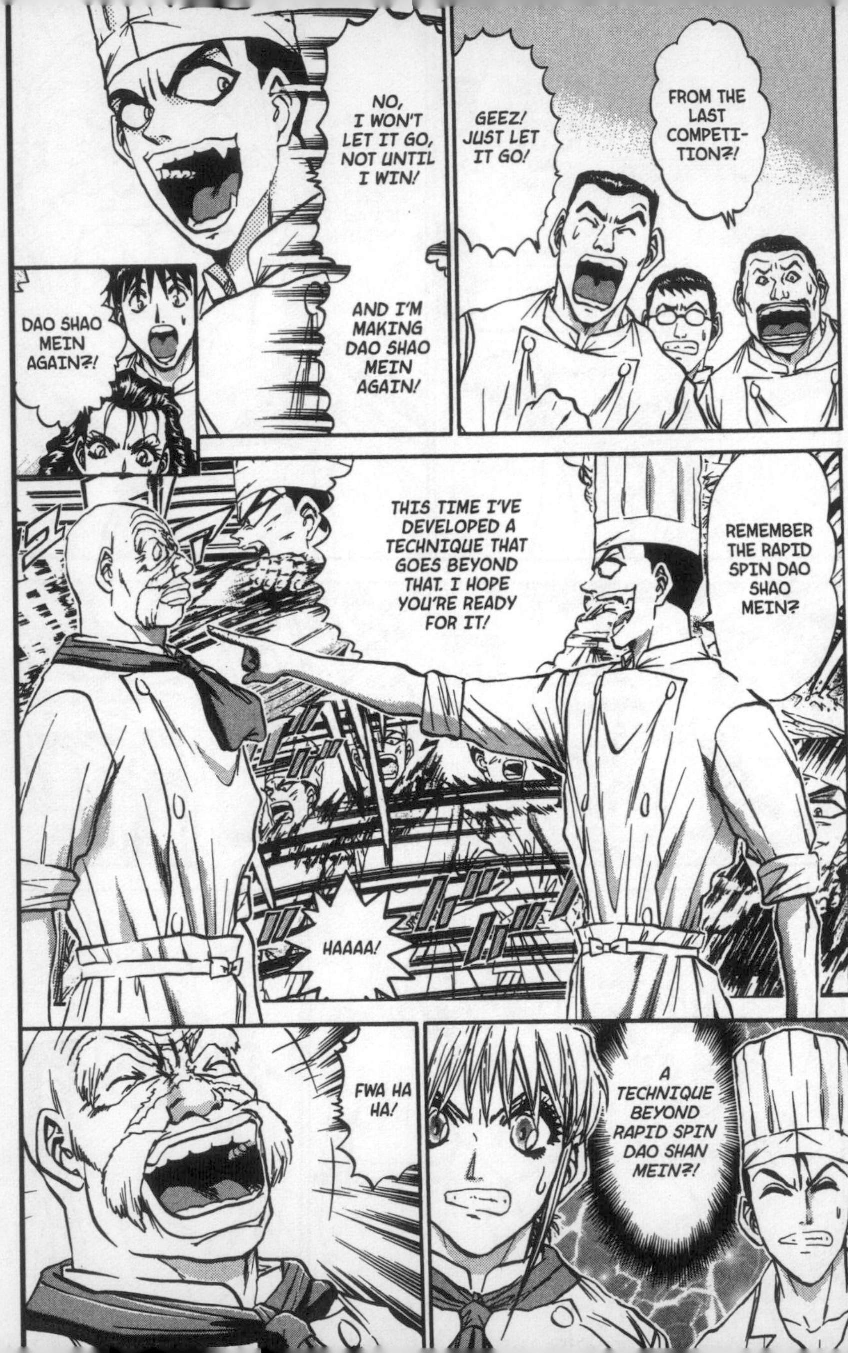
FROM THE LAST COMPETITION?!
GEEZ! JUST LET IT GO!
NO, I WON'T LET IT GO, NOT UNTIL I WIN!
AND I'M MAKING DAO SHAO MEIN AGAIN!
DAO SHAO MEIN AGAIN?!
REMEMBER THE RAPID SPIN DAO SHAO MEIN?
THIS TIME I'VE DEVELOPED A TECHNIQUE THAT GOES BEYOND THAT. I HOPE YOU'RE READY FOR IT!
HAAAA!
A TECHNIQUE BEYOND RAPID SPIN DAO SHAN MEIN?!
FWA HA HA!

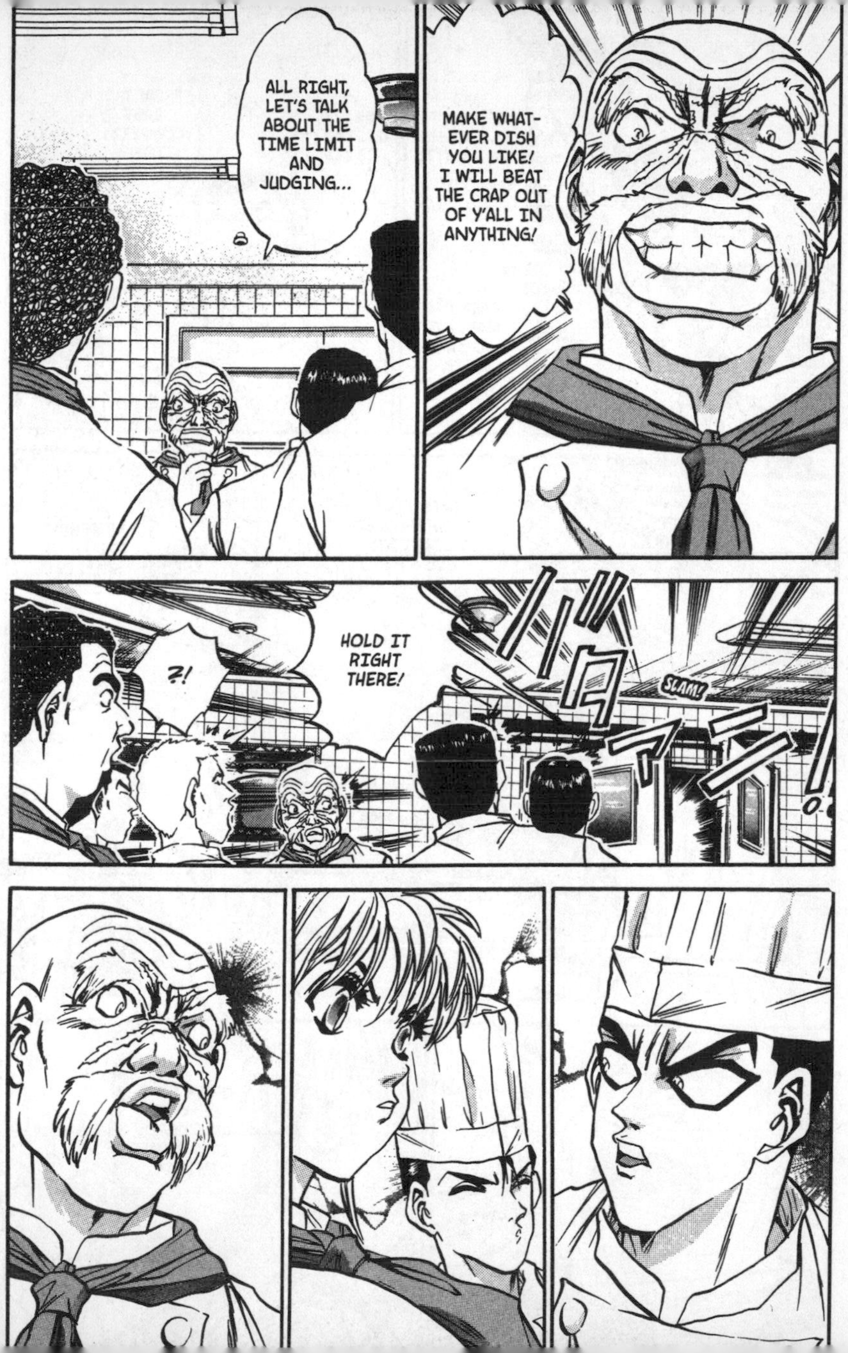
MAKE WHAT-EVER DISH YOU LIKE! I WILL BEAT THE CRAP OUT OF Y'ALL IN ANYTHING!
ALL RIGHT, LET'S TALK ABOUT THE TIME LIMIT AND JUDGING...
SLAM!
HOLD IT RIGHT THERE!
?!

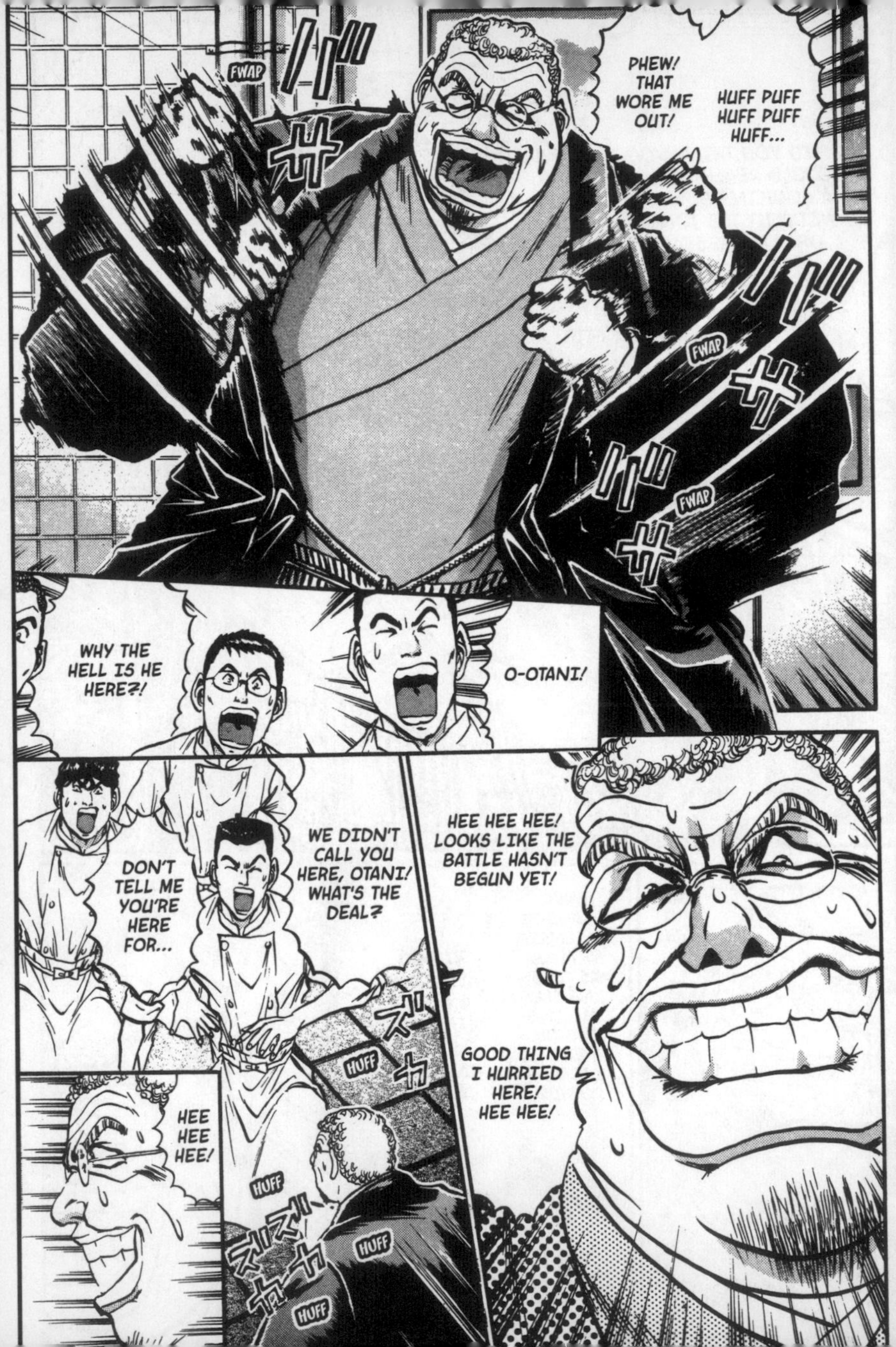
HUFF PUFF HUFF PUFF HUFF...
PHEW! THAT WORE ME OUT!
FWAP
FWAP
FWAP
O-OTANI!
WHY THE HELL IS HE HERE?!
HEE HEE HEE! LOOKS LIKE THE BATTLE HASN'T BEGUN YET!
GOOD THING I HURRIED HERE! HEE HEE!
WE DIDN'T CALL YOU HERE, OTANI! WHAT'S THE DEAL?
DON'T TELL ME YOU'RE HERE FOR...
HUFF
HUFF
HUFF
HUFF
HEE HEE HEE!

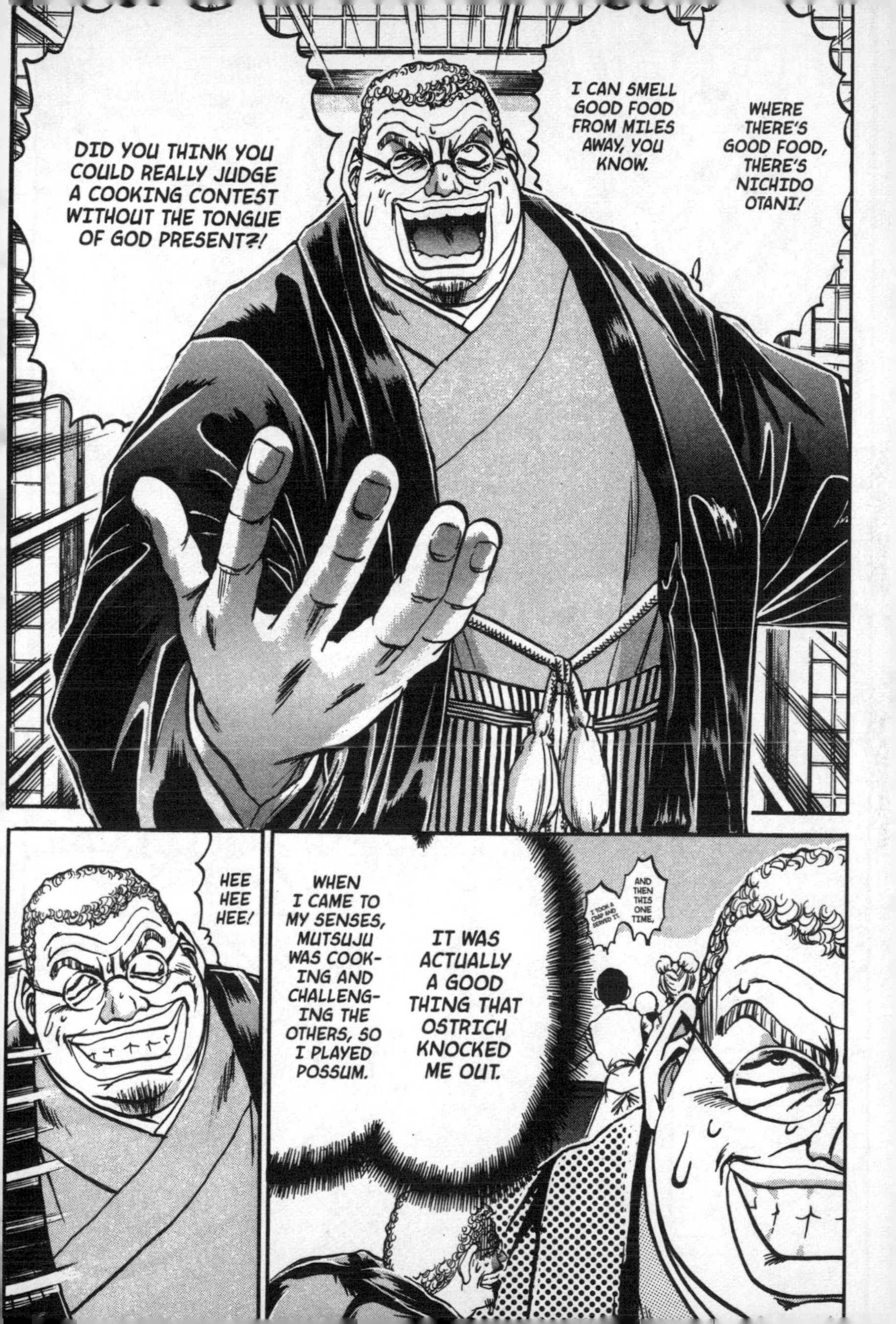
WHERE THERE'S GOOD FOOD, THERE'S NICHIDO OTANI!
I CAN SMELL GOOD FOOD FROM MILES AWAY, YOU KNOW.
DID YOU THINK YOU COULD REALLY JUDGE A COOKING CONTEST WITHOUT THE TONGUE OF GOD PRESENT?!
AND THEN THIS ONE TIME,
I TOOK A CRAP AND SERVED IT.
IT WAS ACTUALLY A GOOD THING THAT OSTRICH KNOCKED ME OUT.
WHEN I CAME TO MY SENSES, MUTSUJU WAS COOKING AND CHALLENGING THE OTHERS, SO I PLAYED POSSUM.
HEE HEE HEE!

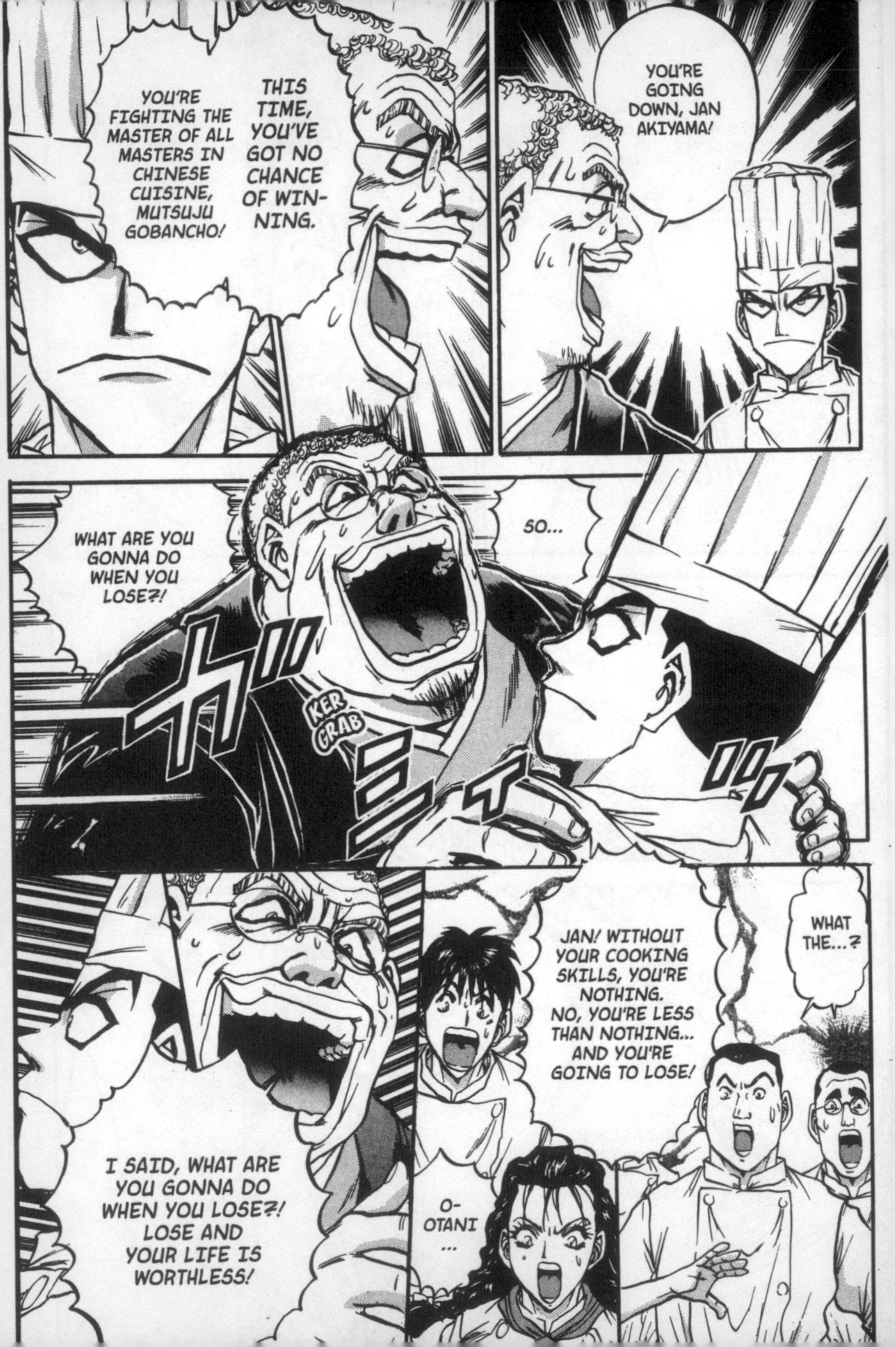
YOU'RE GOING DOWN, JAN AKIYAMA!
THIS TIME, YOU'VE GOT NO CHANCE OF WIN-NING.
YOU'RE FIGHTING THE MASTER OF ALL MASTERS IN CHINESE CUISINE, MUTSUJU GOBANCHO!
SO...
WHAT ARE YOU GONNA DO WHEN YOU LOSE?!
KER GRAB
WHAT THE...?
JAN! WITHOUT YOUR COOKING SKILLS, YOU'RE NOTHING. NO, YOU'RE LESS THAN NOTHING... AND YOU'RE GOING TO LOSE!
O-OTANI ...
I SAID, WHAT ARE YOU GONNA DO WHEN YOU LOSE?! LOSE AND YOUR LIFE IS WORTHLESS!

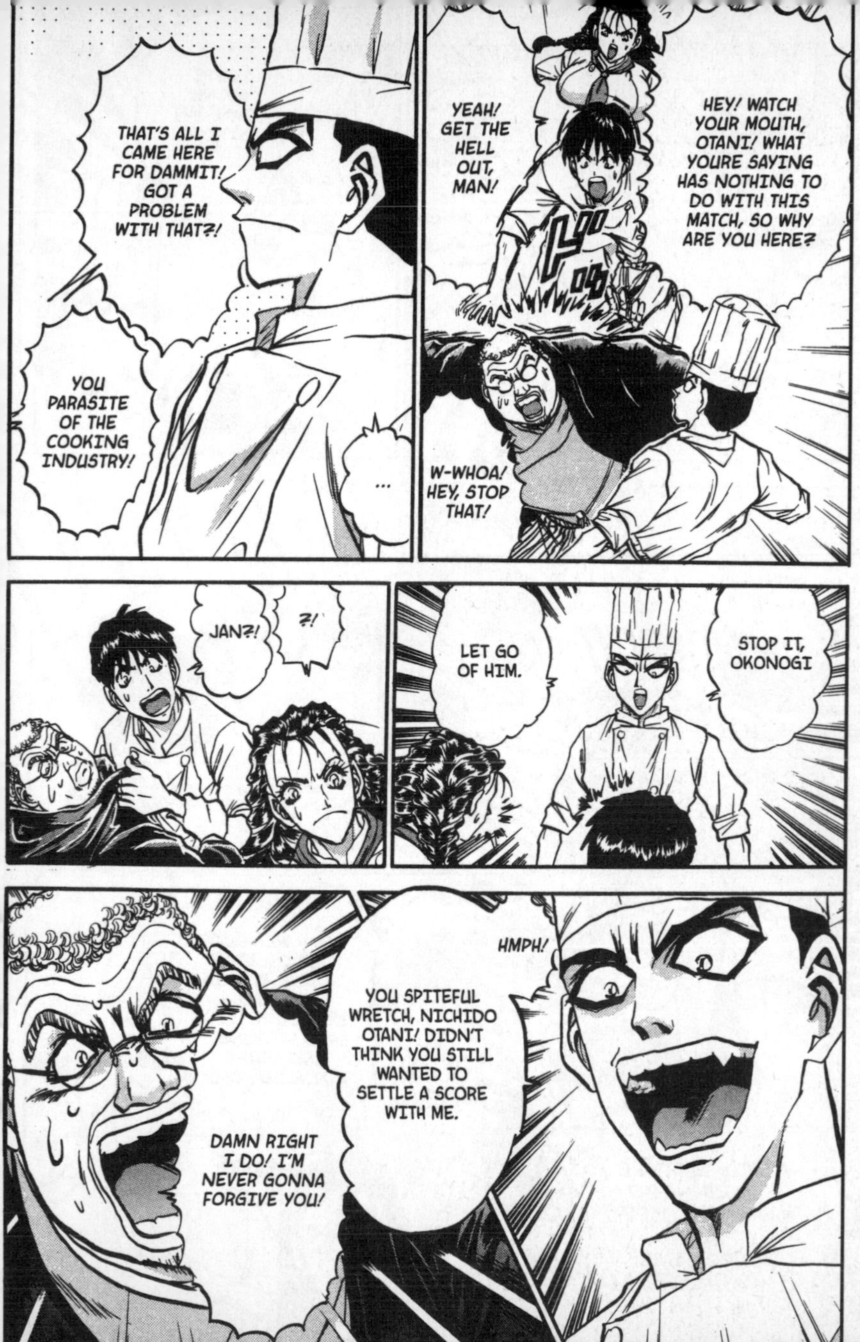
HEY! WATCH YOUR MOUTH, OTANI! WHAT YOURE SAYING HAS NOTHING TO DO WITH THIS MATCH, SO WHY ARE YOU HERE?
YEAH! GET THE HELL OUT, MAN!
W-WHOA! HEY, STOP THAT!
THAT'S ALL I CAME HERE FOR DAMMIT! GOT A PROBLEM WITH THAT?!
YOU PARASITE OF THE COOKING INDUSTRY!
...
STOP IT, OKONOGI
LET GO OF HIM.
?!
JAN?!
HMPH!
YOU SPITEFUL WRETCH, NICHIDO OTANI! DIDN'T THINK YOU STILL WANTED TO SETTLE A SCORE WITH ME.
DAMN RIGHT I DO! I'M NEVER GONNA FORGIVE YOU!

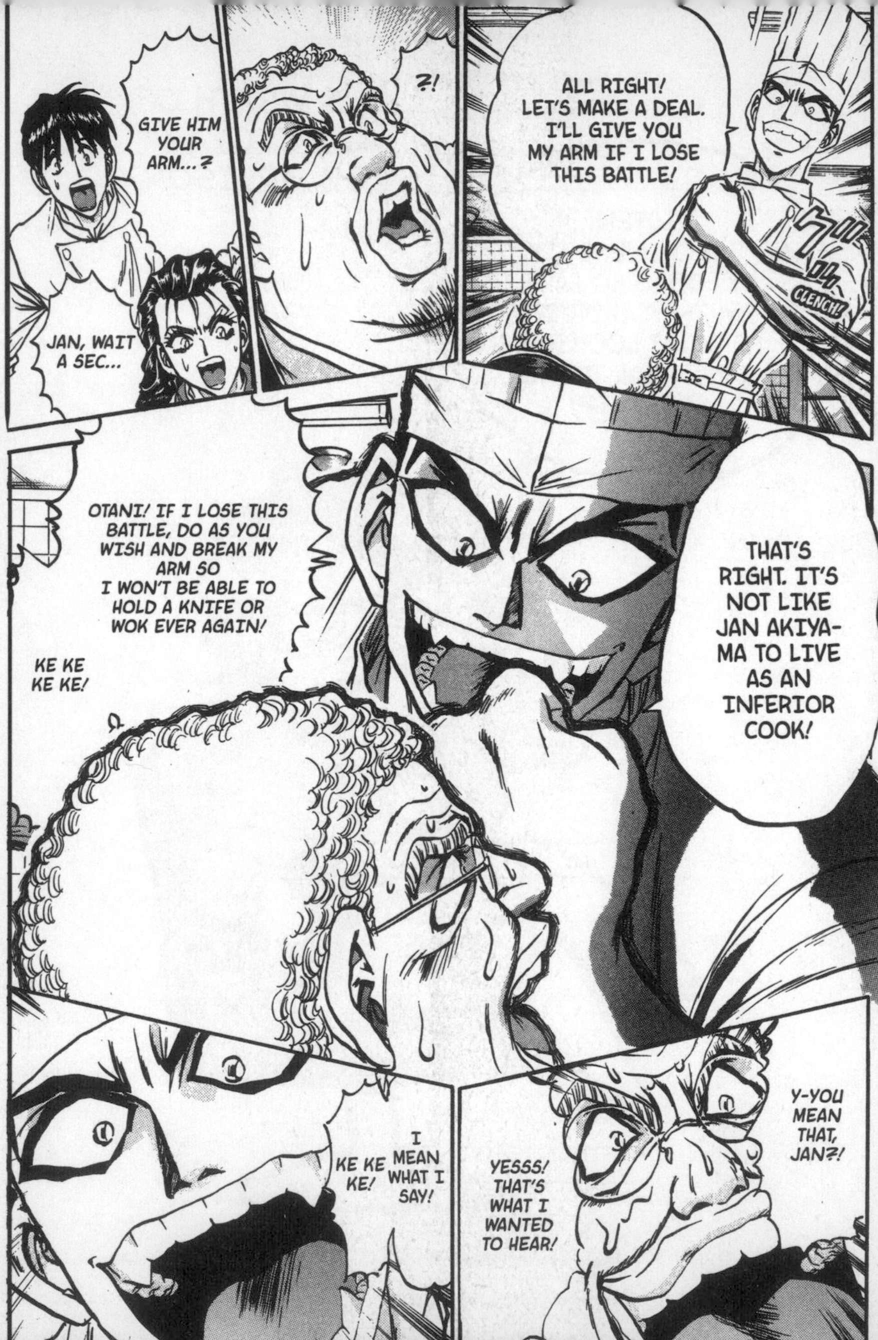
ALL RIGHT! LET'S MAKE A DEAL. I'LL GIVE YOU MY ARM IF I LOSE THIS BATTLE!
CLENCH!
?!
GIVE HIM YOUR ARM...?
JAN, WAIT A SEC...
THAT'S RIGHT. IT'S NOT LIKE JAN AKIYAMA TO LIVE AS AN INFERIOR COOK!
OTANI! IF I LOSE THIS BATTLE, DO AS YOU WISH AND BREAK MY ARM SO I WON'T BE ABLE TO HOLD A KNIFE OR WOK EVER AGAIN!
KE KE KE KE!
Y-YOU MEAN THAT, JAN?!
YESSS! THAT'S WHAT I WANTED TO HEAR!
I MEAN WHAT I SAY!
KE KE KE!

THE WRATH OF KEIKO OYAMA (THE ADVISOR)

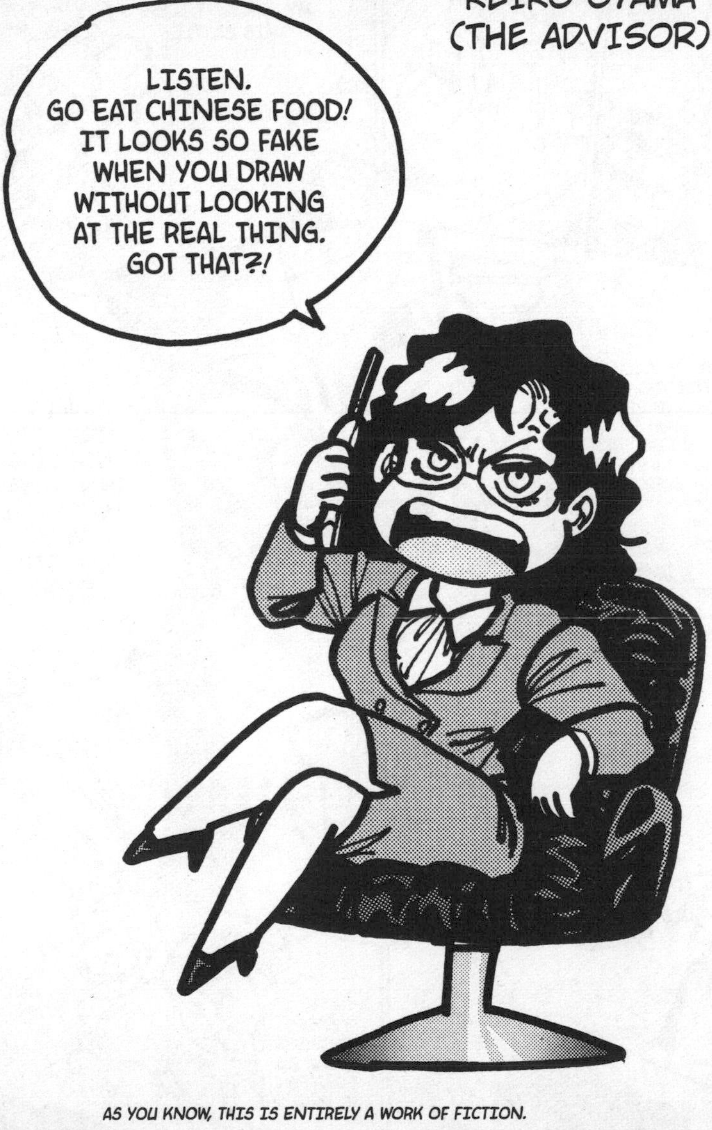
LISTEN. GO EAT CHINESE FOOD! IT LOOKS SO FAKE WHEN YOU DRAW WITHOUT LOOKING AT THE REAL THING. GOT THAT?!

AS YOU KNOW, THIS IS ENTIRELY A WORK OF FICTION.

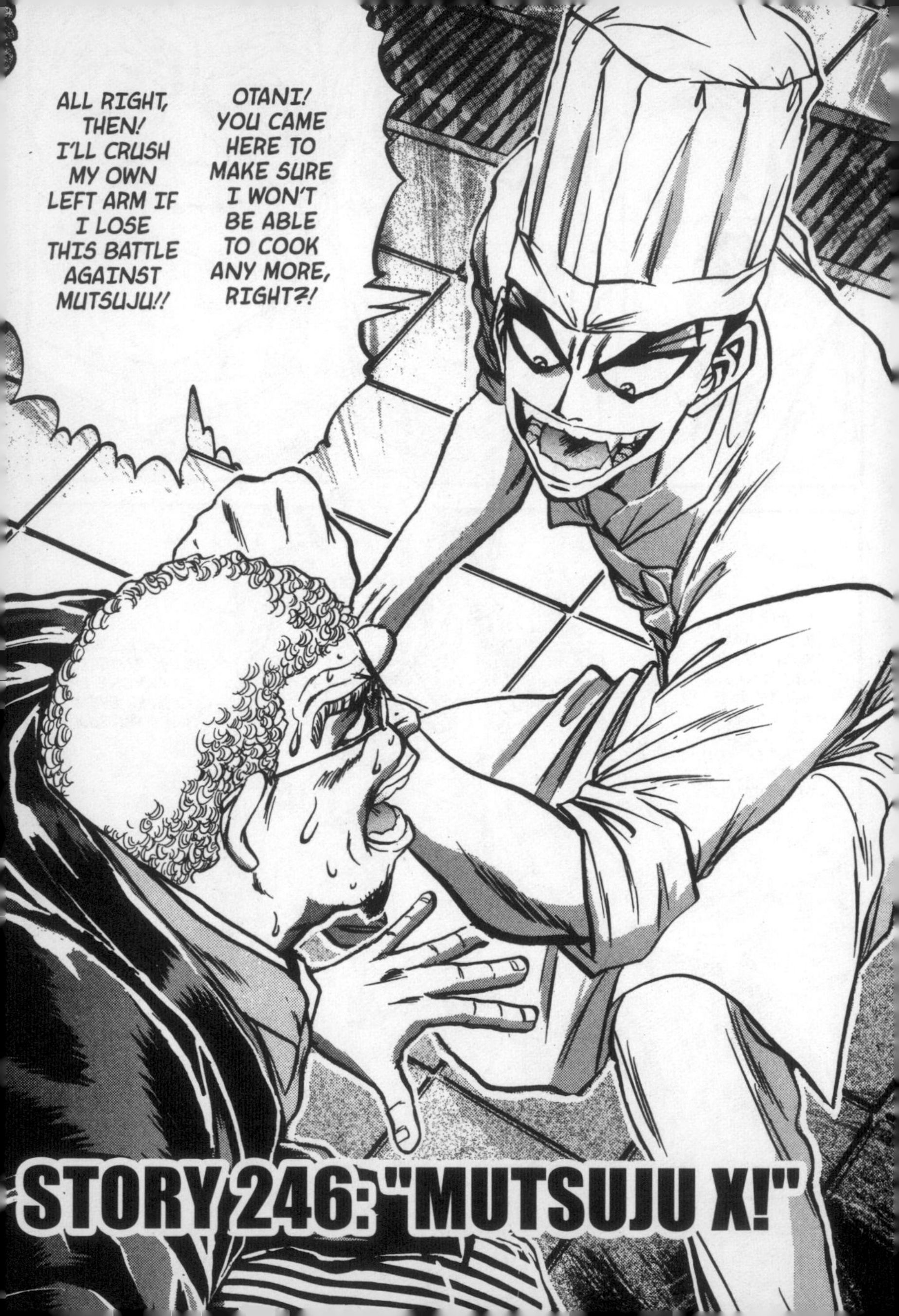
OTANI! YOU CAME HERE TO MAKE SURE I WON'T BE ABLE TO COOK ANY MORE, RIGHT?!
ALL RIGHT, THEN! I'LL CRUSH MY OWN LEFT ARM IF I LOSE THIS BATTLE AGAINST MUTSUJU!!
STORY 246: "MUTSUJU X!"

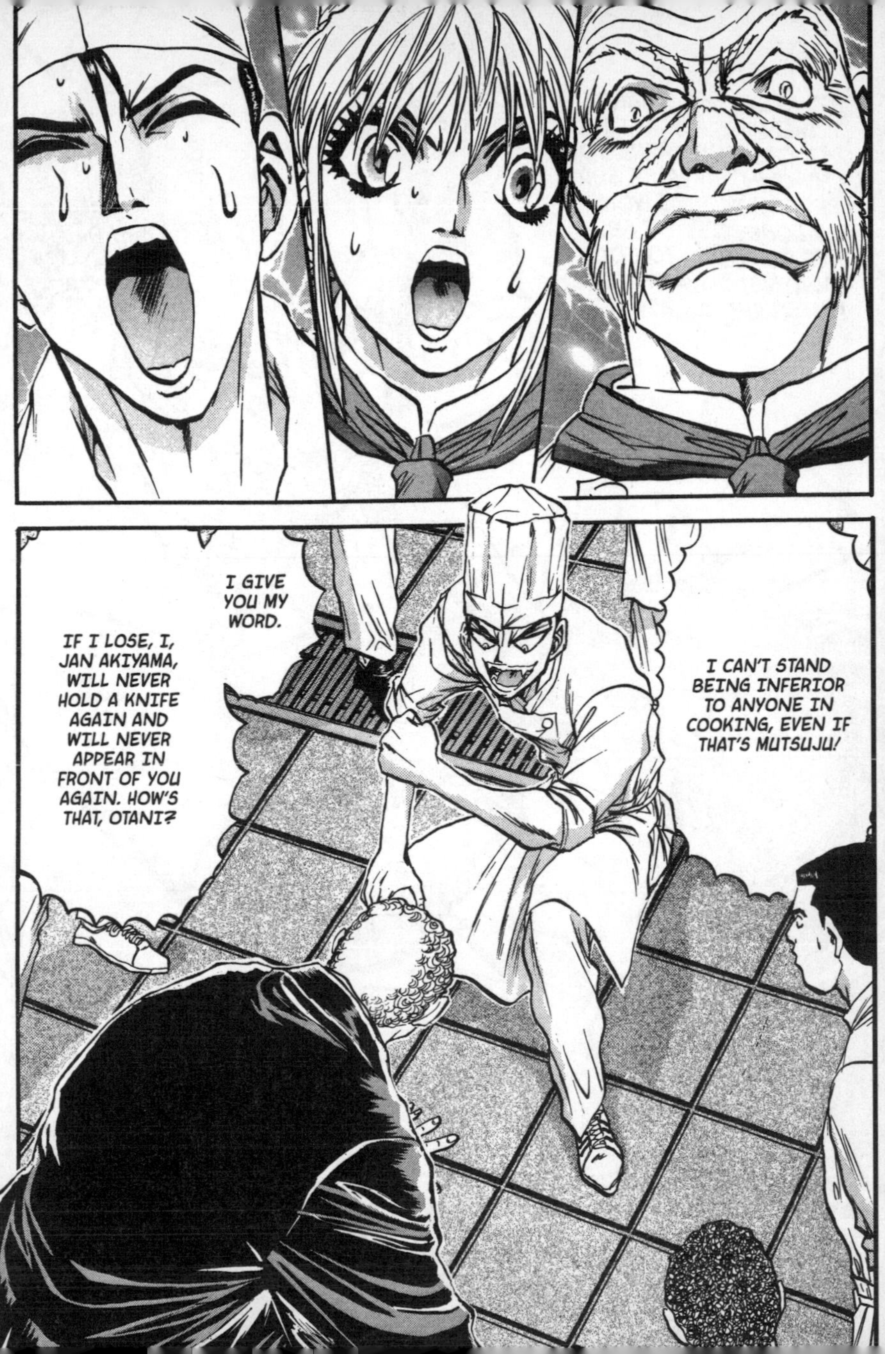
I CAN'T STAND BEING INFERIOR TO ANYONE IN COOKING, EVEN IF THAT'S MUTSUJU!
I GIVE YOU MY WORD.
IF I LOSE, I, JAN AKIYAMA, WILL NEVER HOLD A KNIFE AGAIN AND WILL NEVER APPEAR IN FRONT OF YOU AGAIN. HOW'S THAT, OTANI?

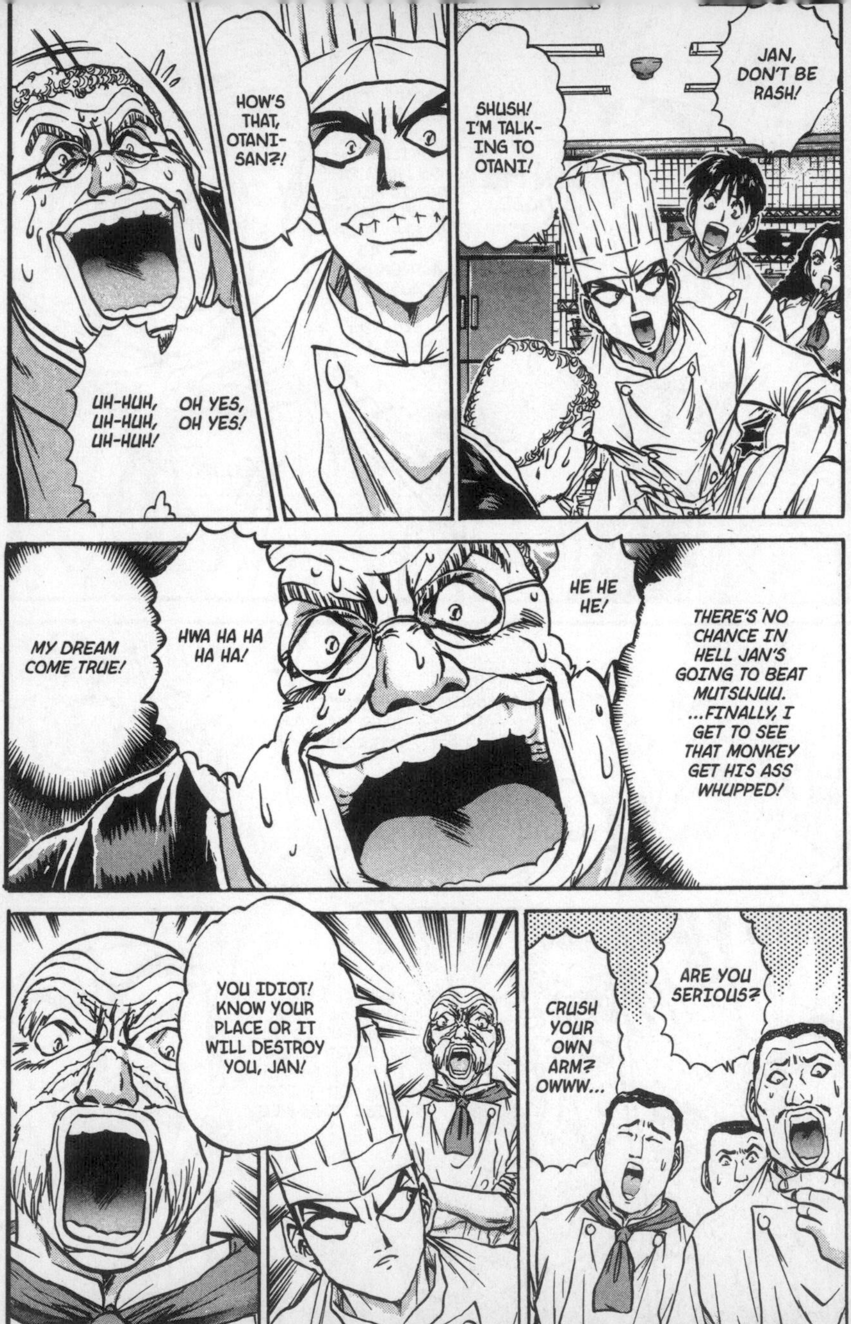
JAN, DON'T BE RASH!
SHUSH! I'M TALKING TO OTANI!
HOW'S THAT, OTANI-SAN?!
OH YES, OH YES!
UH-HUH, UH-HUH, UH-HUH!
THERE'S NO CHANCE IN HELL JAN'S GOING TO BEAT MUTSUJUU. ...FINALLY, I GET TO SEE THAT MONKEY GET HIS ASS WHUPPED!
HE HE HE!
HWA HA HA HA HA!
MY DREAM COME TRUE!
ARE YOU SERIOUS?
CRUSH YOUR OWN ARM? OWWW...
YOU IDIOT! KNOW YOUR PLACE OR IT WILL DESTROY YOU, JAN!

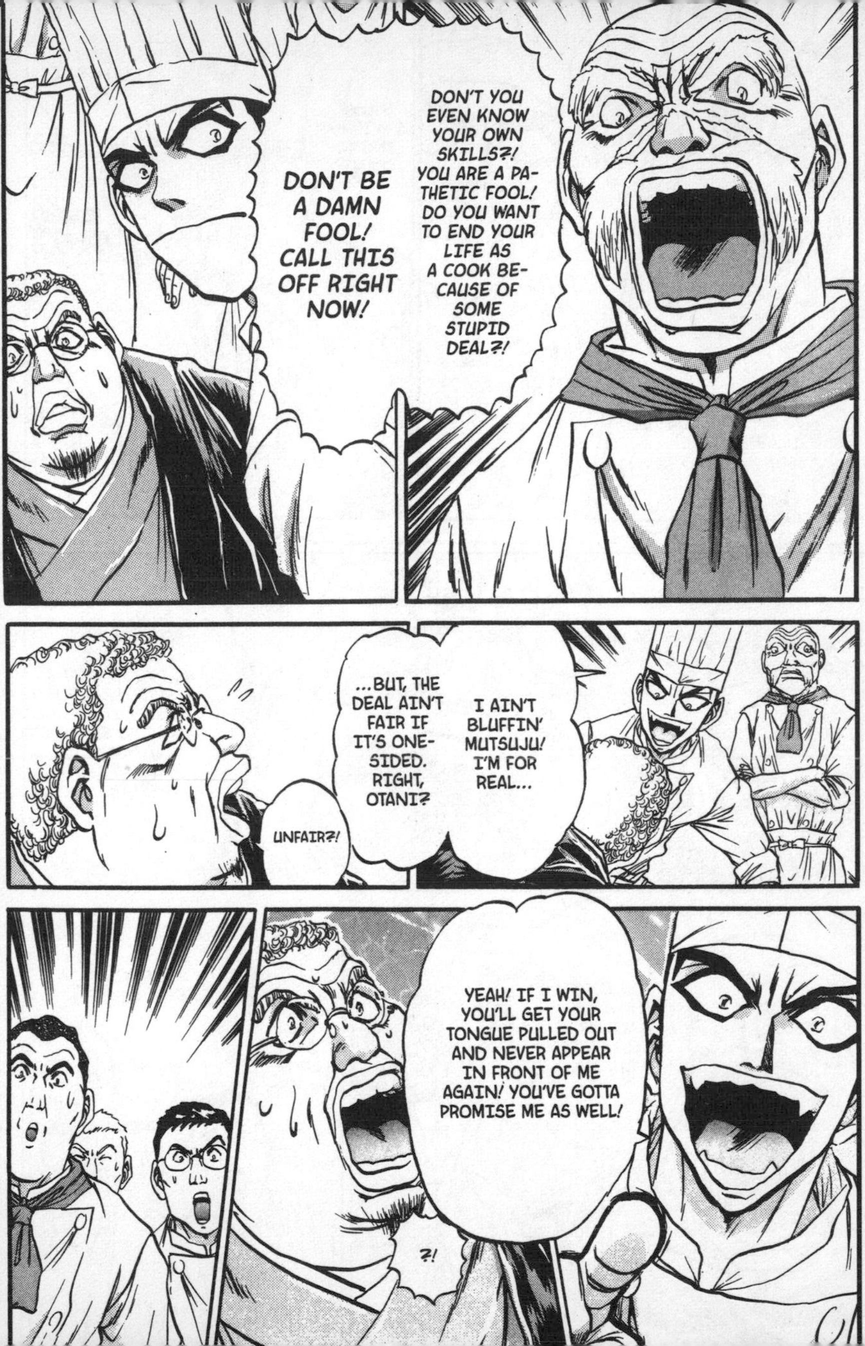

DON'T YOU EVEN KNOW YOUR OWN SKILLS?! YOU ARE A PA-THETIC FOOL! DO YOU WANT TO END YOUR LIFE AS A COOK BE-CAUSE OF SOME STUPID DEAL?!
DON'T BE A DAMN FOOL! CALL THIS OFF RIGHT NOW!
I AIN'T BLUFFIN' MUTSUJU! I'M FOR REAL...
...BUT, THE DEAL AIN'T FAIR IF IT'S ONE-SIDED. RIGHT, OTANI?
UNFAIR?!
YEAH! IF I WIN, YOU'LL GET YOUR TONGUE PULLED OUT AND NEVER APPEAR IN FRONT OF ME AGAIN! YOU'VE GOTTA PROMISE ME AS WELL!
?!
?!

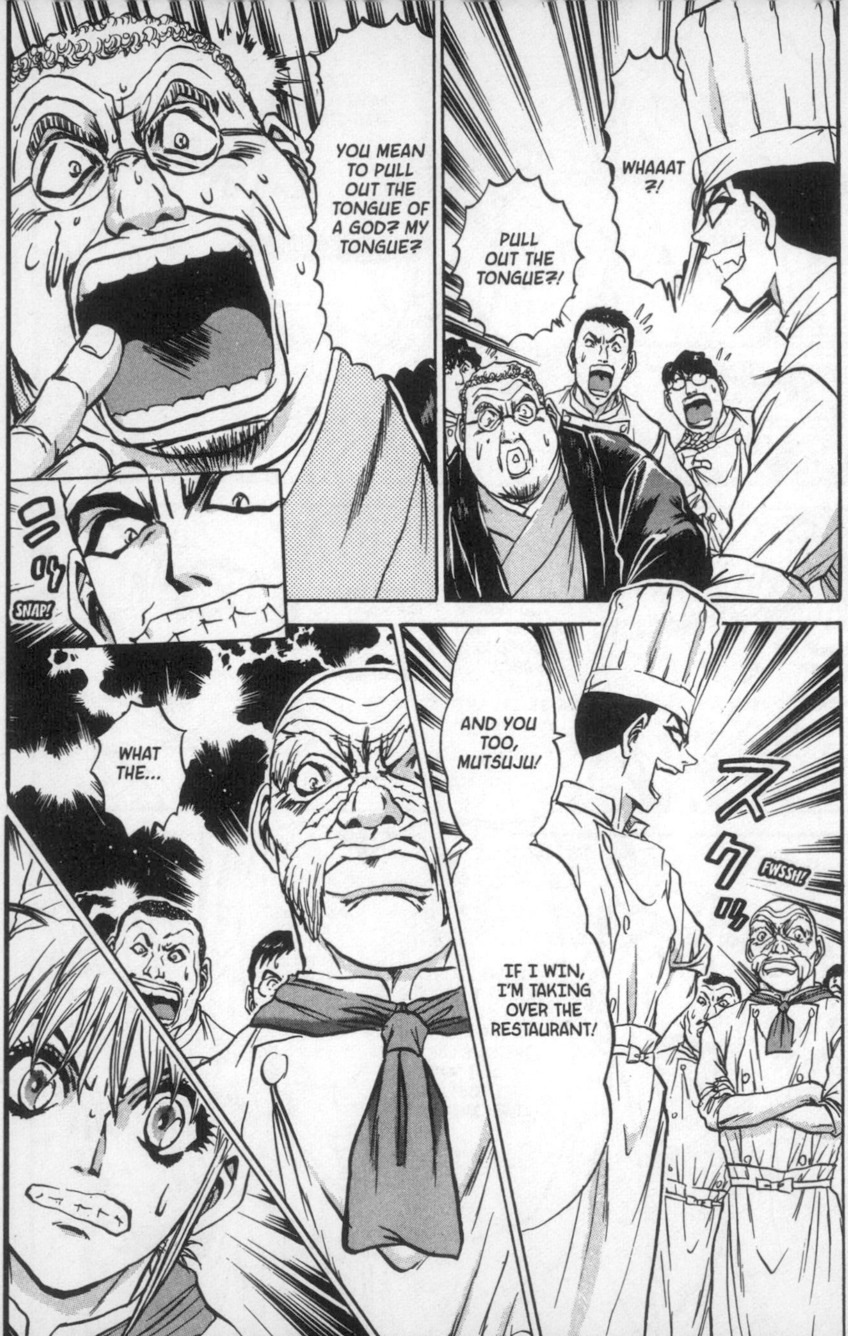
WHAAAT?!
PULL OUT THE TONGUE?!
YOU MEAN TO PULL OUT THE TONGUE OF A GOD? MY TONGUE?
SNAP!
AND YOU TOO, MUTSUJU!
FWSSH!
IF I WIN, I'M TAKING OVER THE RESTAURANT!
WHAT THE...

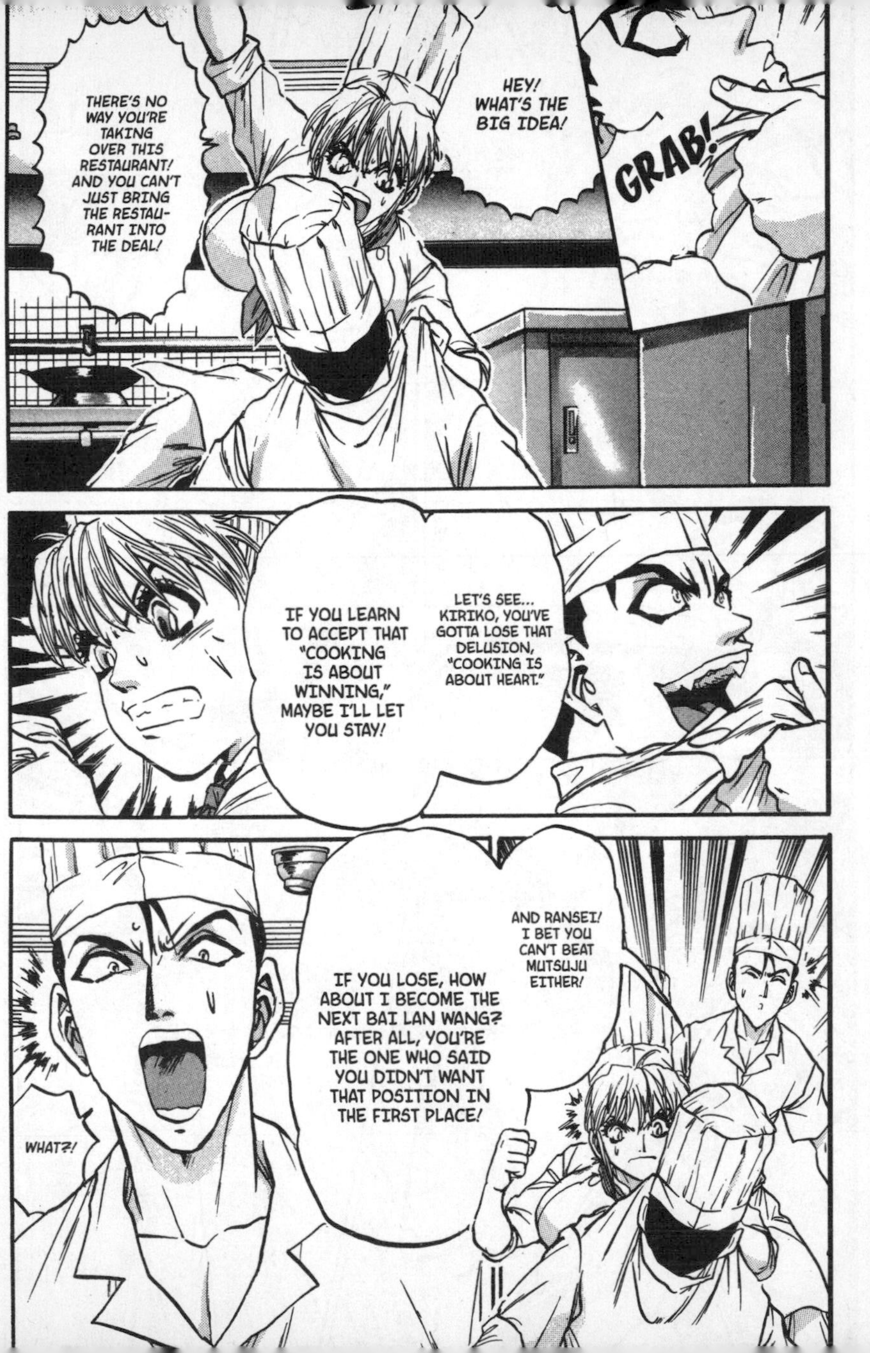
GRAB!
HEY! WHAT'S THE BIG IDEA!
THERE'S NO WAY YOU'RE TAKING OVER THIS RESTAURANT! AND YOU CAN'T JUST BRING THE RESTAU-RANT INTO THE DEAL!
LET'S SEE... KIRIKO, YOU'VE GOTTA LOSE THAT DELUSION, "COOKING IS ABOUT HEART."
IF YOU LEARN TO ACCEPT THAT "COOKING IS ABOUT WINNING," MAYBE I'LL LET YOU STAY!
AND RANSEI! I BET YOU CAN'T BEAT MUTSUJU EITHER!
IF YOU LOSE, HOW ABOUT I BECOME THE NEXT BAI LAN WANG? AFTER ALL, YOU'RE THE ONE WHO SAID YOU DIDN'T WANT THAT POSITION IN THE FIRST PLACE!
WHAT?!

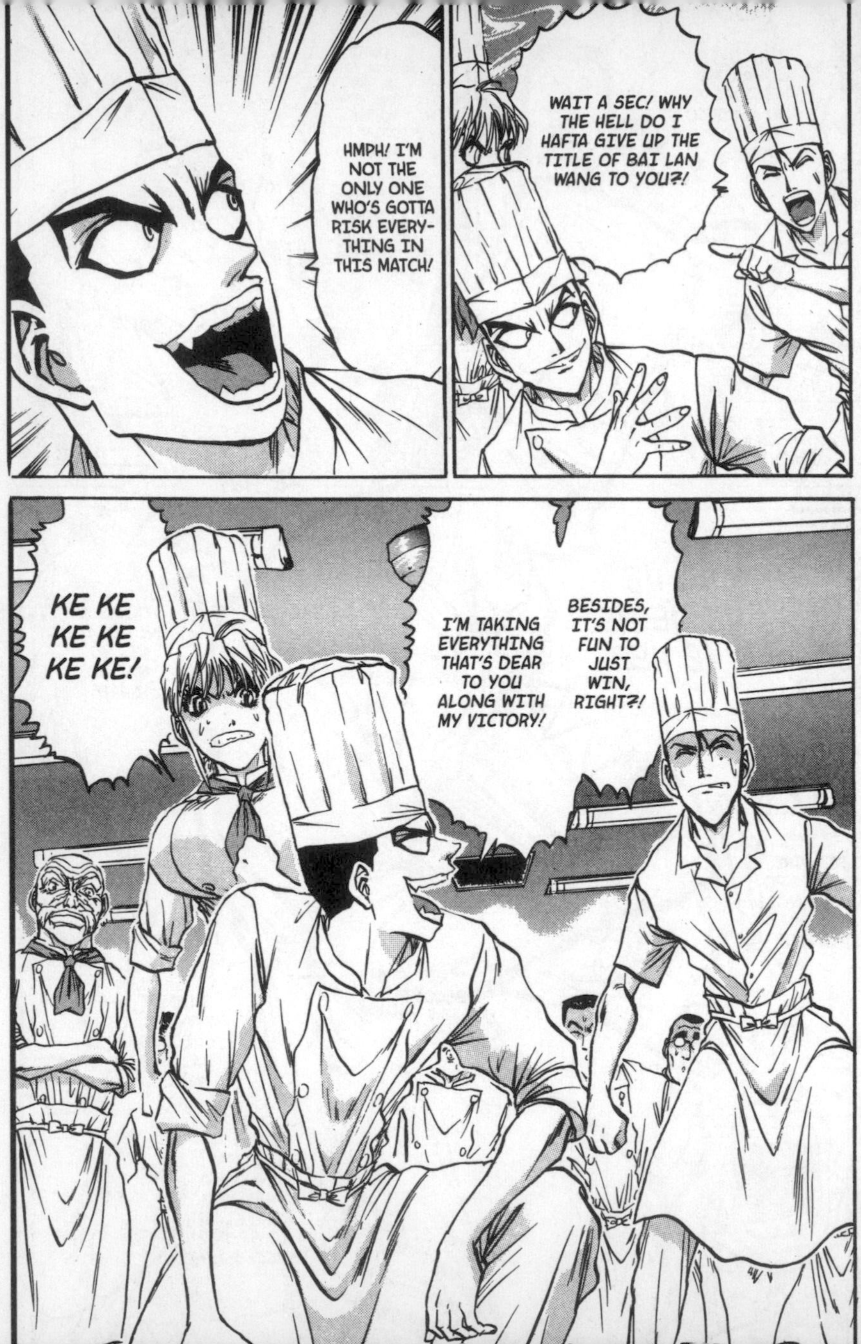
WAIT A SEC! WHY THE HELL DO I HAFTA GIVE UP THE TITLE OF BAI LAN WANG TO YOU?!
HMPH! I'M NOT THE ONLY ONE WHO'S GOTTA RISK EVERY-THING IN THIS MATCH!
BESIDES, IT'S NOT FUN TO JUST WIN, RIGHT?!
I'M TAKING EVERYTHING THAT'S DEAR TO YOU ALONG WITH MY VICTORY!
KE KE KE KE KE KE!

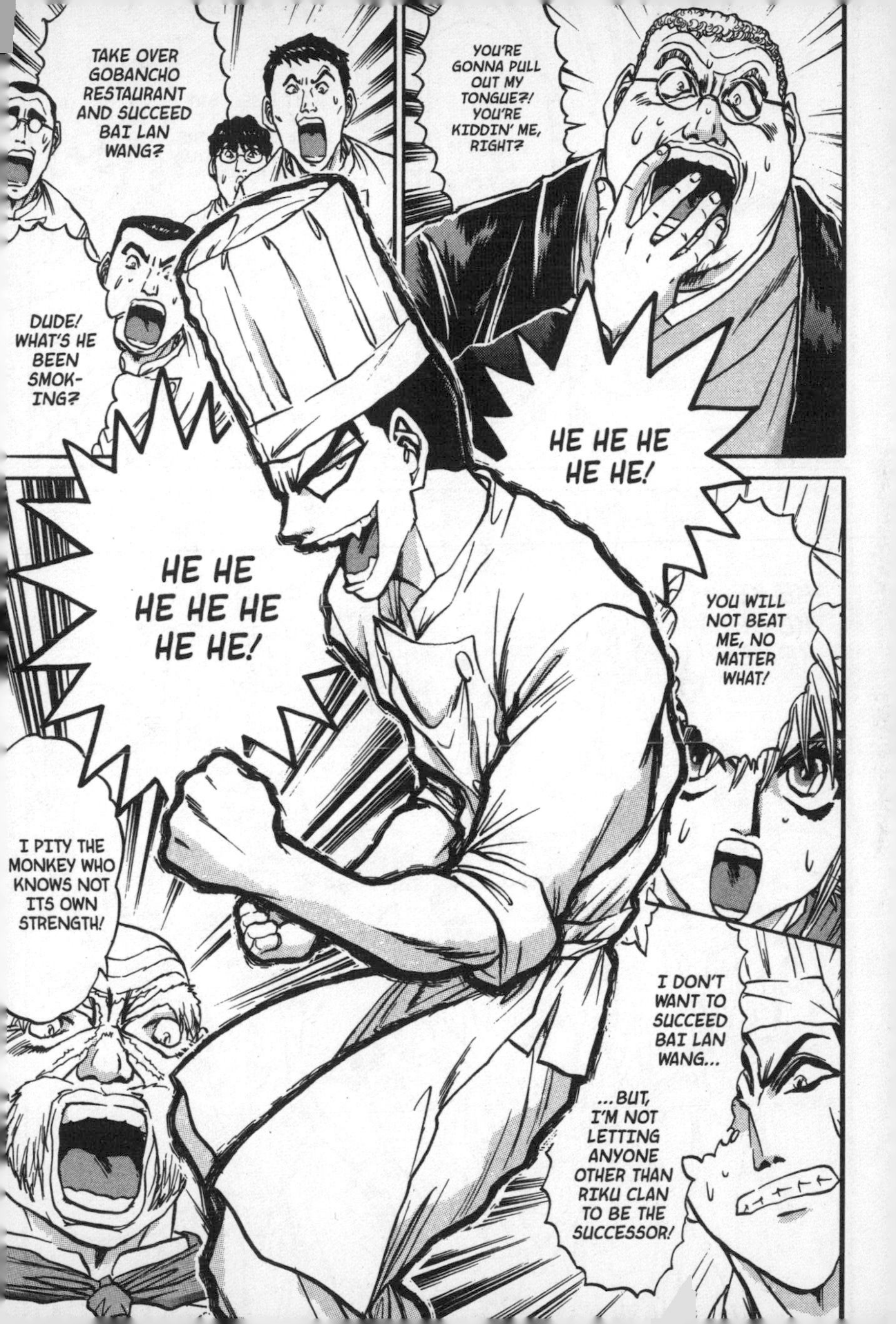
YOU'RE GONNA PULL OUT MY TONGUE?! YOU'RE KIDDIN' ME, RIGHT?
TAKE OVER GOBANCHO RESTAURANT AND SUCCEED BAI LAN WANG?
DUDE! WHAT'S HE BEEN SMOK-ING?
HE HE HE HE HE!
HE HE HE HE HE HE HE!
YOU WILL NOT BEAT ME, NO MATTER WHAT!
I DON'T WANT TO SUCCEED BAI LAN WANG...
...BUT, I'M NOT LETTING ANYONE OTHER THAN RIKU CLAN TO BE THE SUCCESSOR!
I PITY THE MONKEY WHO KNOWS NOT ITS OWN STRENGTH!

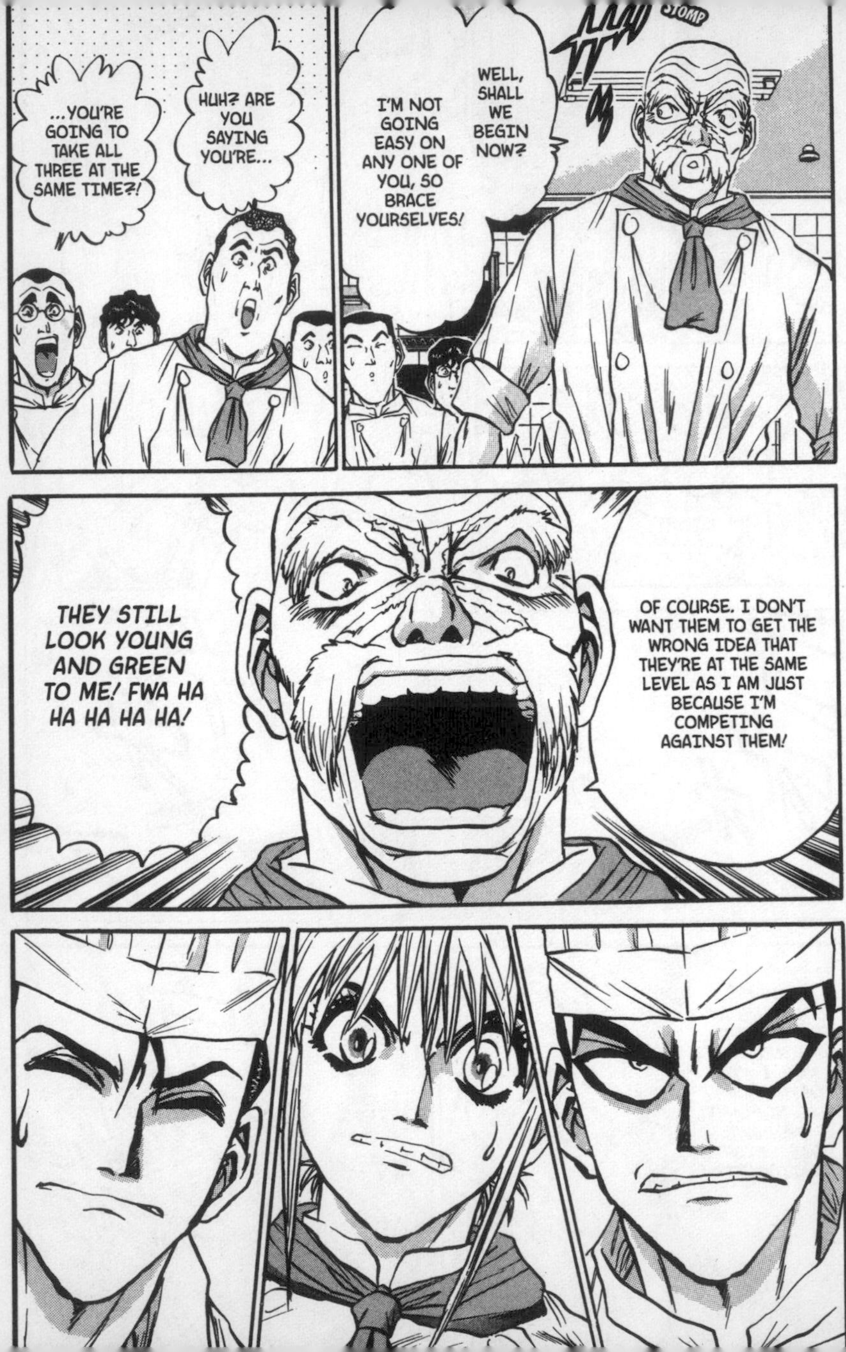
STOMP
WELL, SHALL WE BEGIN NOW?
I'M NOT GOING EASY ON ANY ONE OF YOU, SO BRACE YOURSELVES!
HUH? ARE YOU SAYING YOU'RE...
...YOU'RE GOING TO TAKE ALL THREE AT THE SAME TIME?!
OF COURSE. I DON'T WANT THEM TO GET THE WRONG IDEA THAT THEY'RE AT THE SAME LEVEL AS I AM JUST BECAUSE I'M COMPETING AGAINST THEM!
THEY STILL LOOK YOUNG AND GREEN TO ME! FWA HA HA HA HA HA!

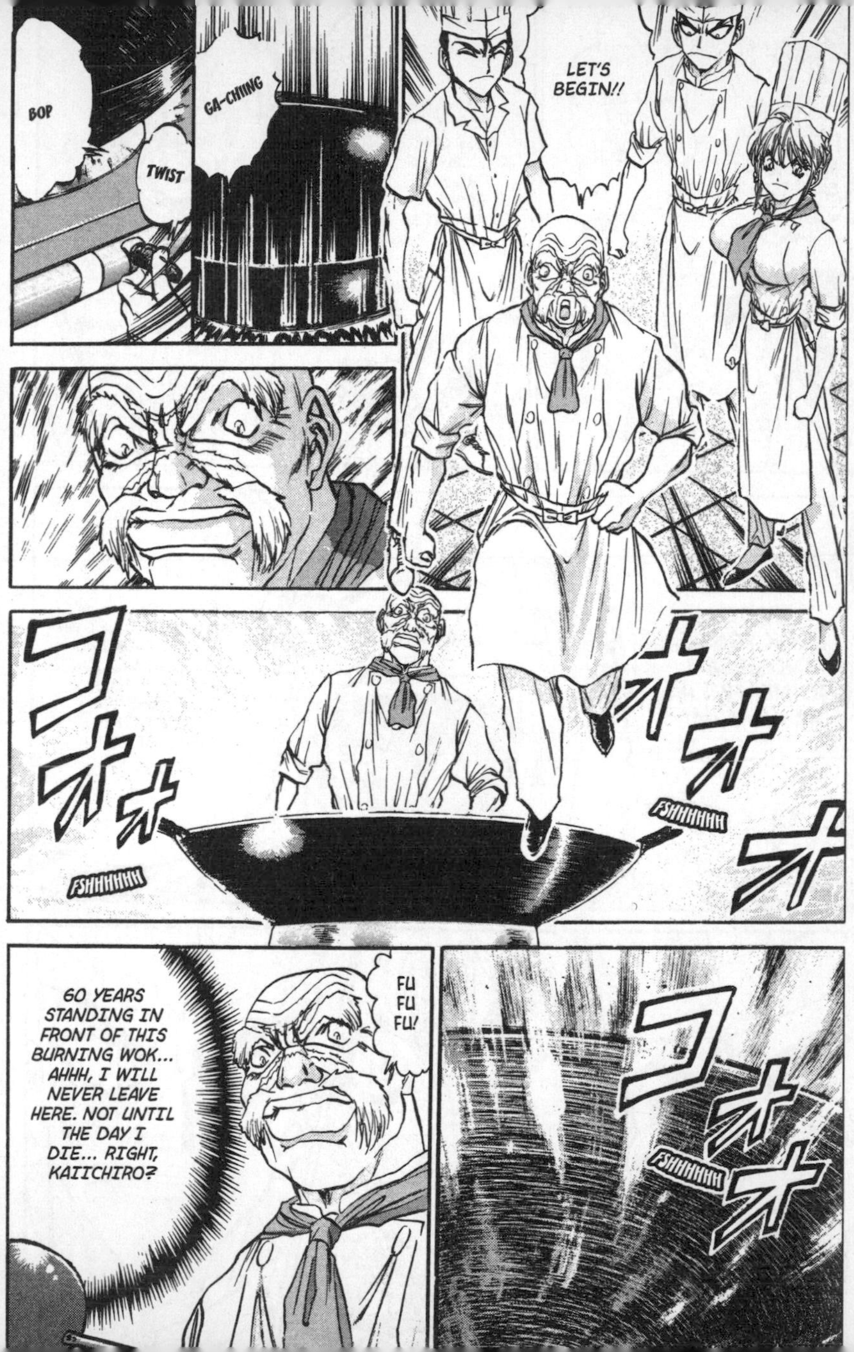
LET'S BEGIN!!
GA-CHING
TWIST
BOP
フォォォ
FSHHHHHH
フォォ
FSHHHHHH
フォォ
FSHHHHHH
FU FU FU!
60 YEARS STANDING IN FRONT OF THIS BURNING WOK... AHHH, I WILL NEVER LEAVE HERE. NOT UNTIL THE DAY I DIE... RIGHT, KAIICHIRO?

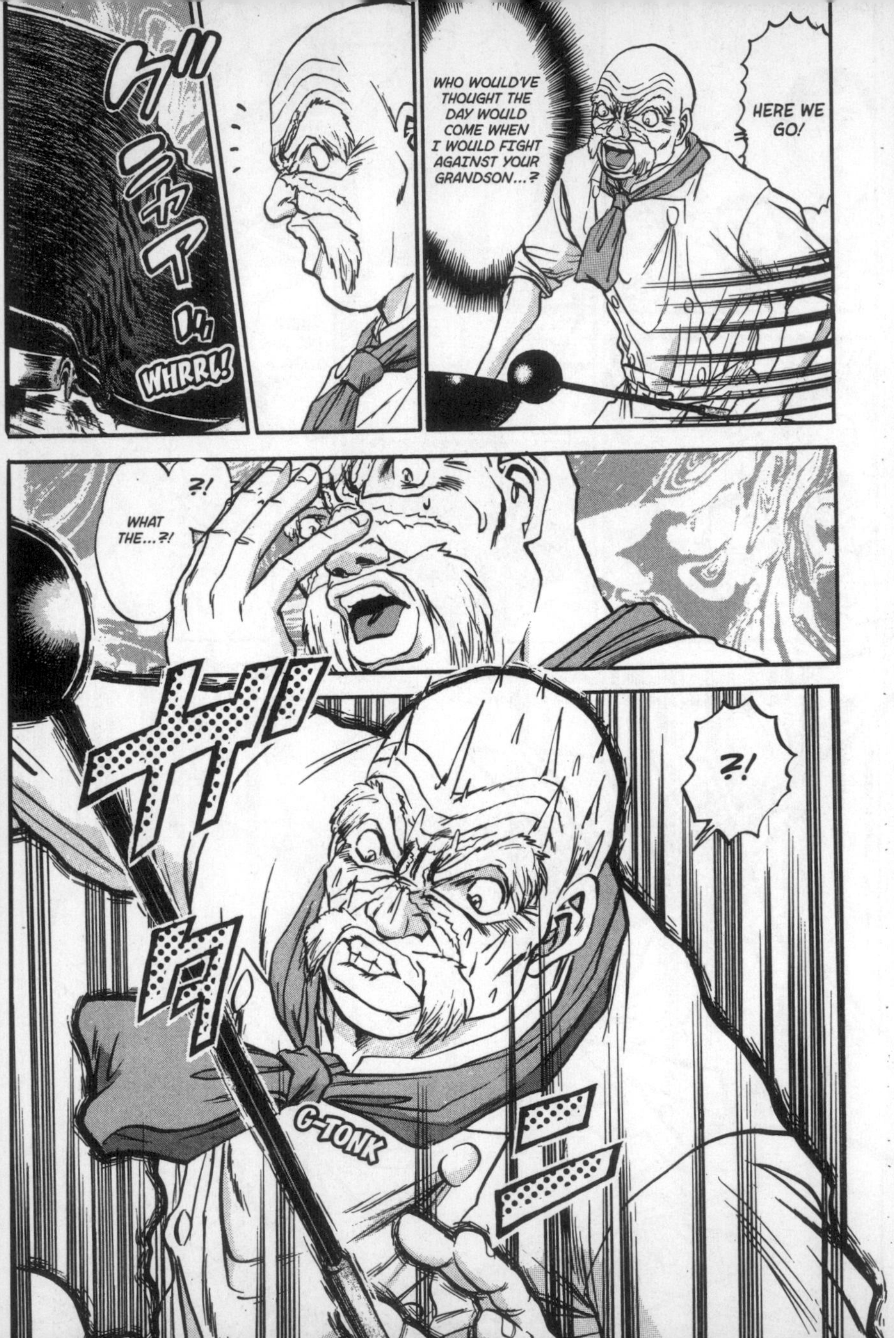
HERE WE GO!
WHO WOULD'VE THOUGHT THE DAY WOULD COME WHEN I WOULD FIGHT AGAINST YOUR GRANDSON...?
WHRRL!
?!
WHAT THE...?!
?!
G-TONK

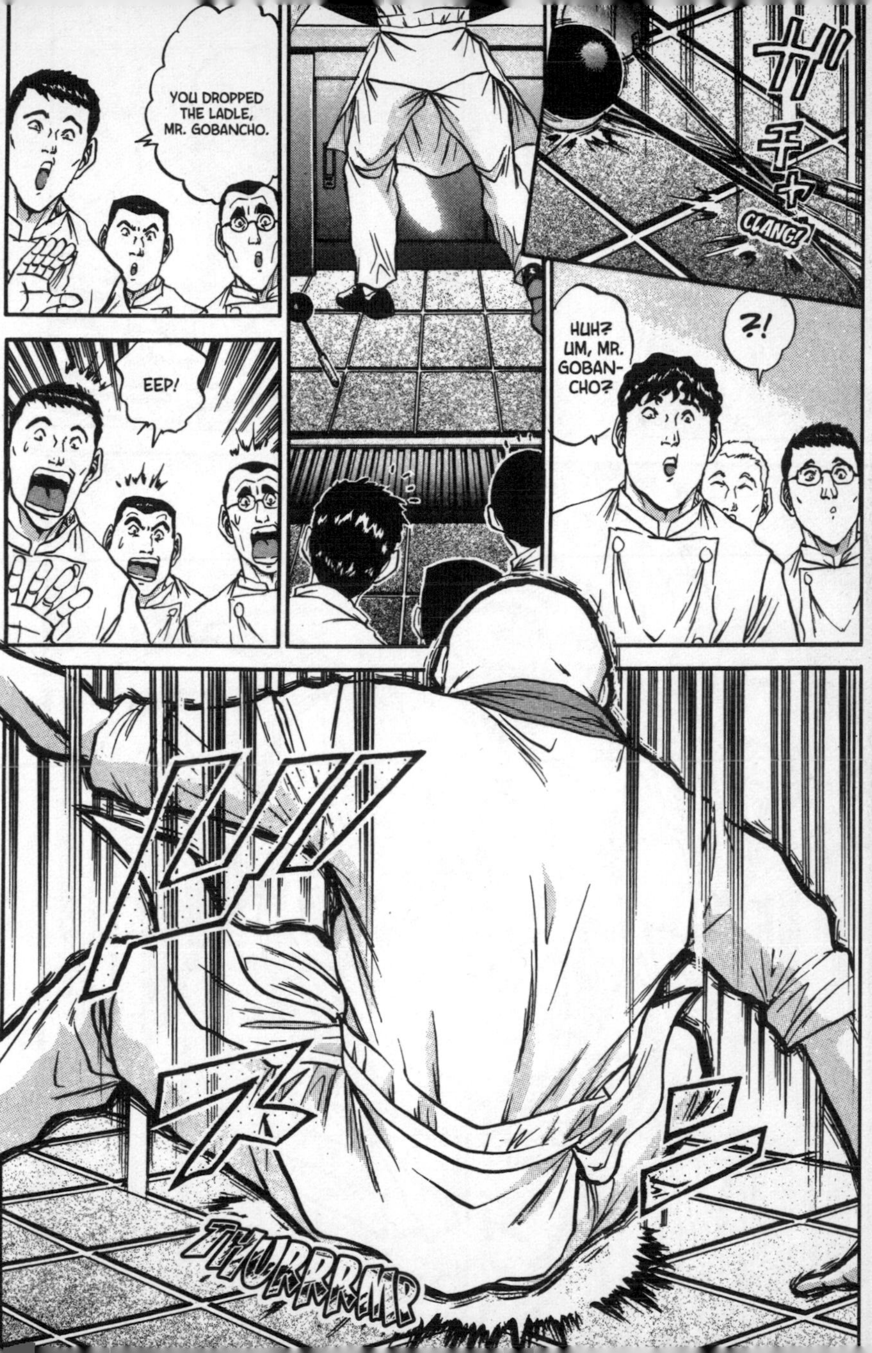
ガチャ
CLANG!
?!
HUH? UM, MR. GOBANCHO?
YOU DROPPED THE LADLE, MR. GOBANCHO.
EEP!
THURRRMP

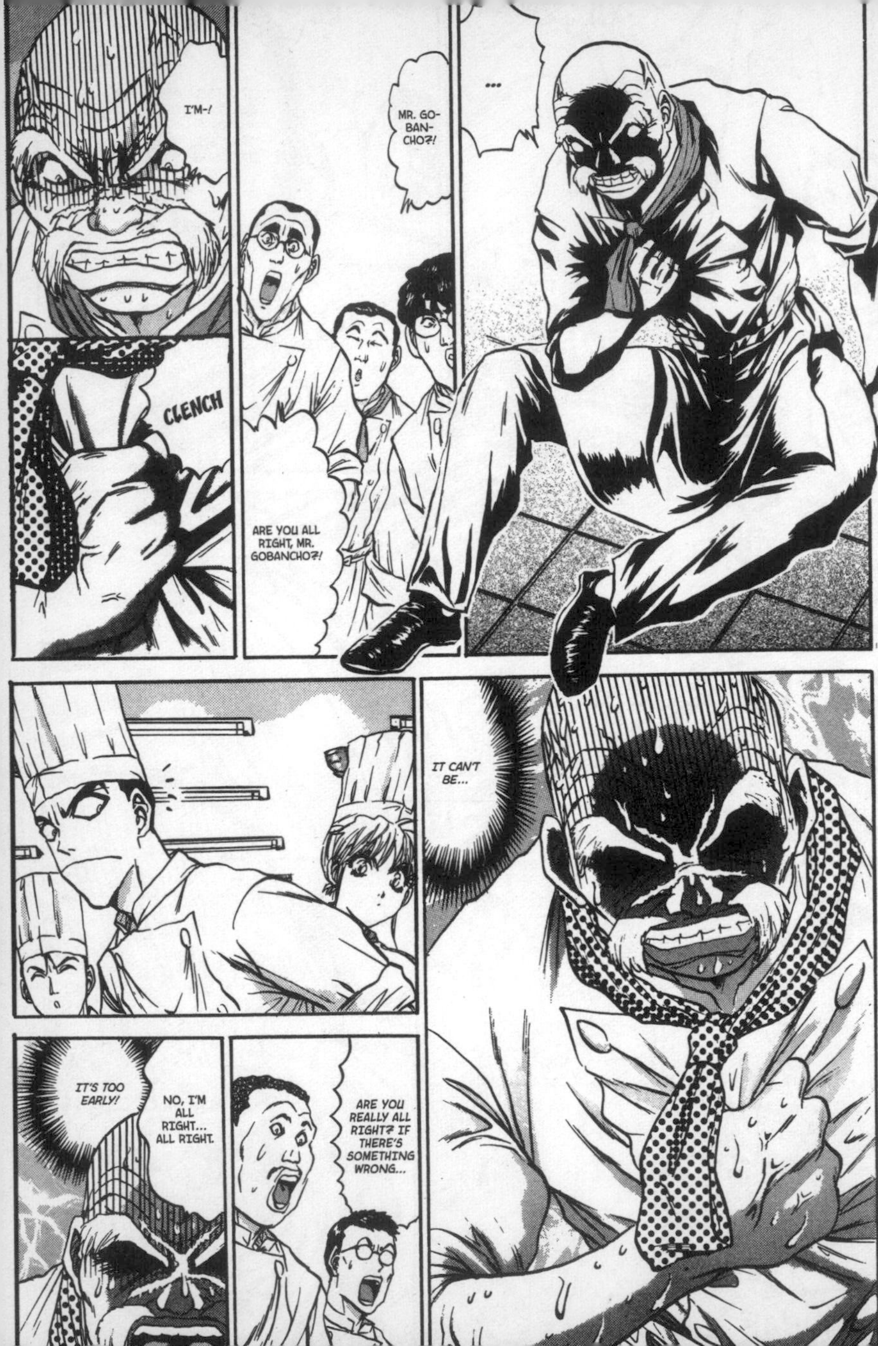
...
MR. GO-BAN-CHO?!
ARE YOU ALL RIGHT, MR. GOBANCHO?!
I'M-!
CLENCH
IT CAN'T BE...
ARE YOU REALLY ALL RIGHT? IF THERE'S SOMETHING WRONG...
NO, I'M ALL RIGHT... ALL RIGHT.
IT'S TOO EARLY!

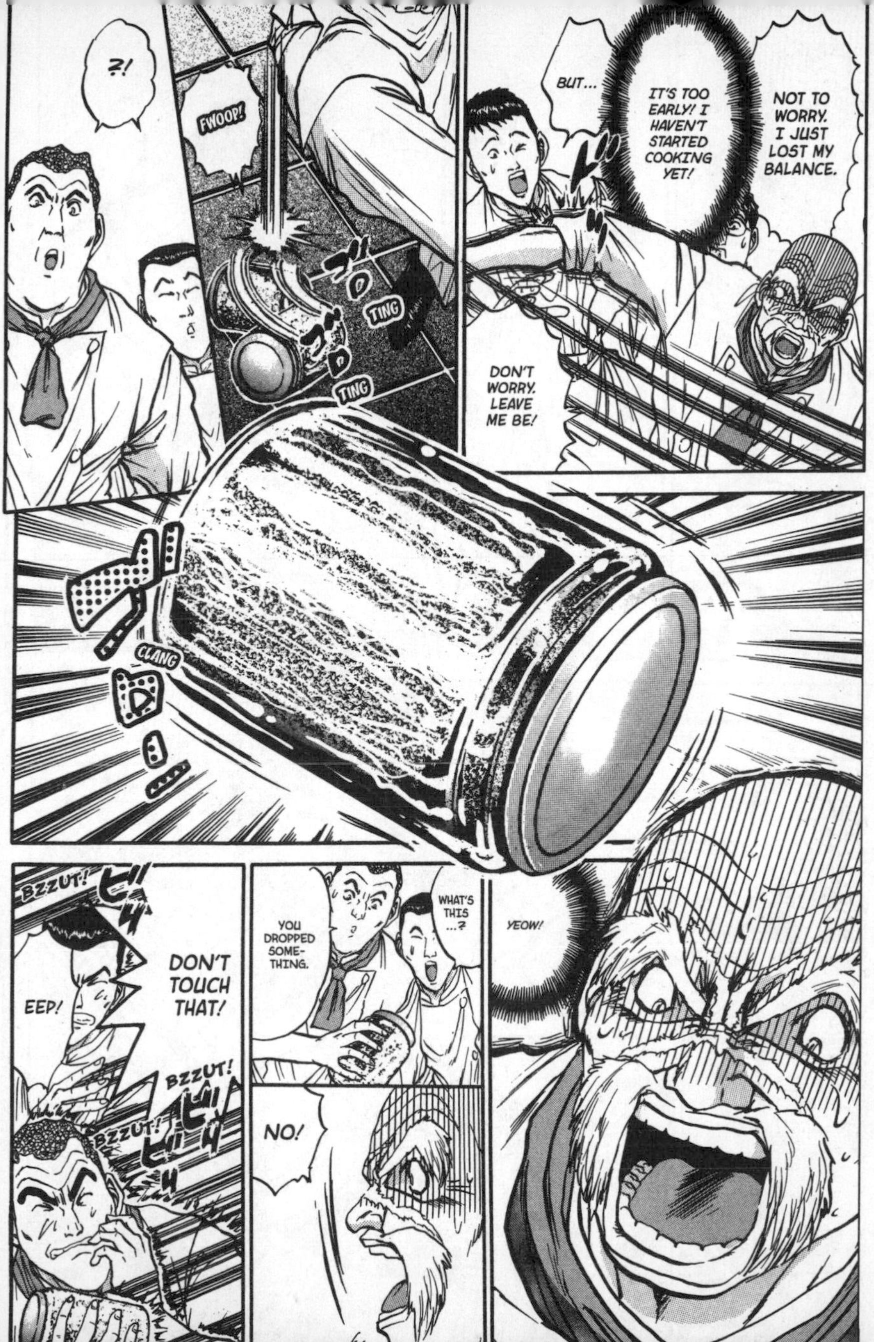
NOT TO WORRY. I JUST LOST MY BALANCE.
IT'S TOO EARLY! I HAVEN'T STARTED COOKING YET!
BUT...
DON'T WORRY. LEAVE ME BE!
FWOOP!
TING
TING
?!
CLANG
YEOW!
WHAT'S THIS ...?
YOU DROPPED SOME-THING.
NO!
BZZUT!
DON'T TOUCH THAT!
EEP!
BZZUT!
BZZUT!

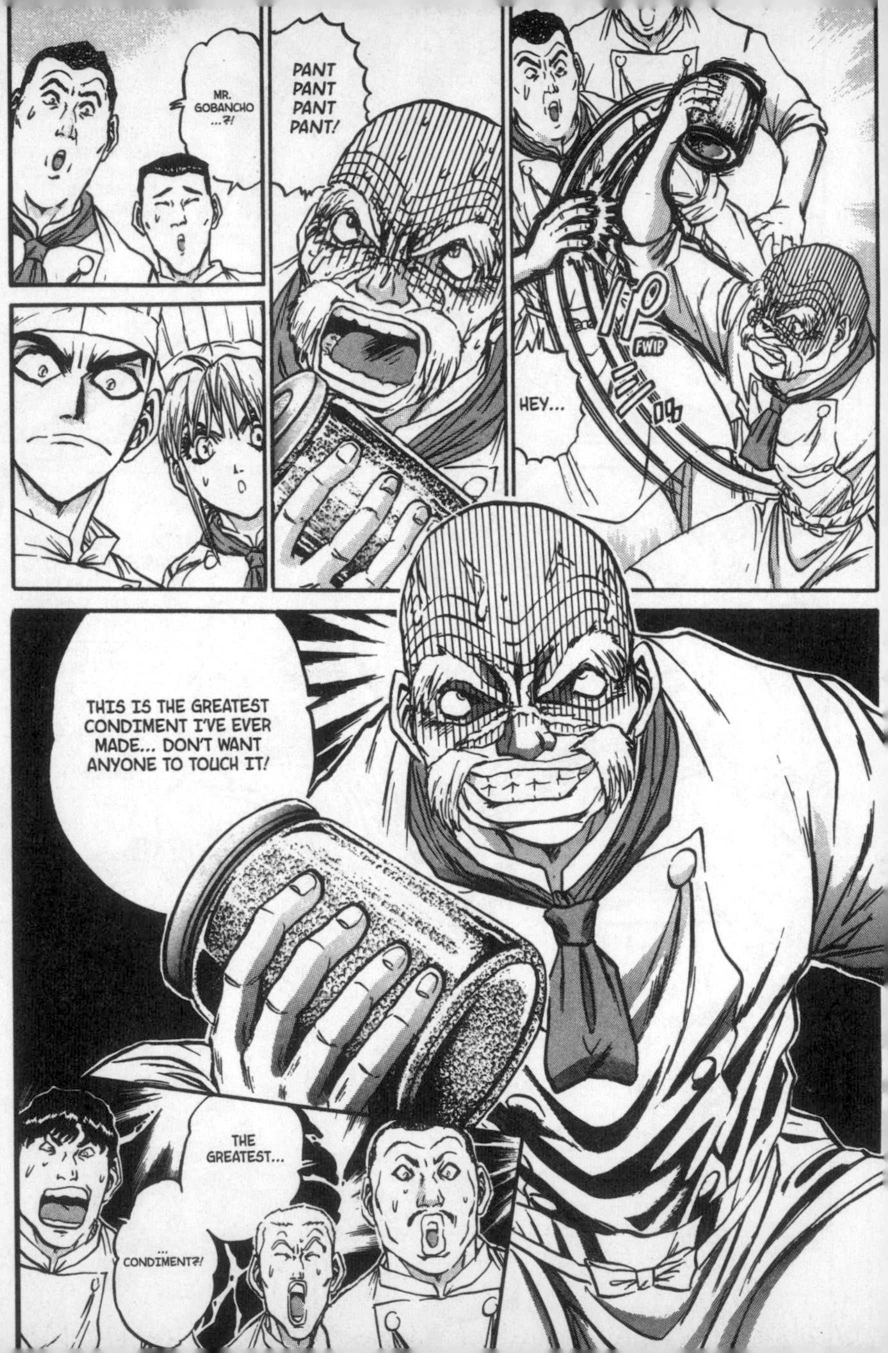
FWIP
HEY...
PANT PANT PANT PANT!
MR. GOBANCHO ...?!
THIS IS THE GREATEST CONDIMENT I'VE EVER MADE... DON'T WANT ANYONE TO TOUCH IT!
THE GREATEST...
...CONDIMENT?!

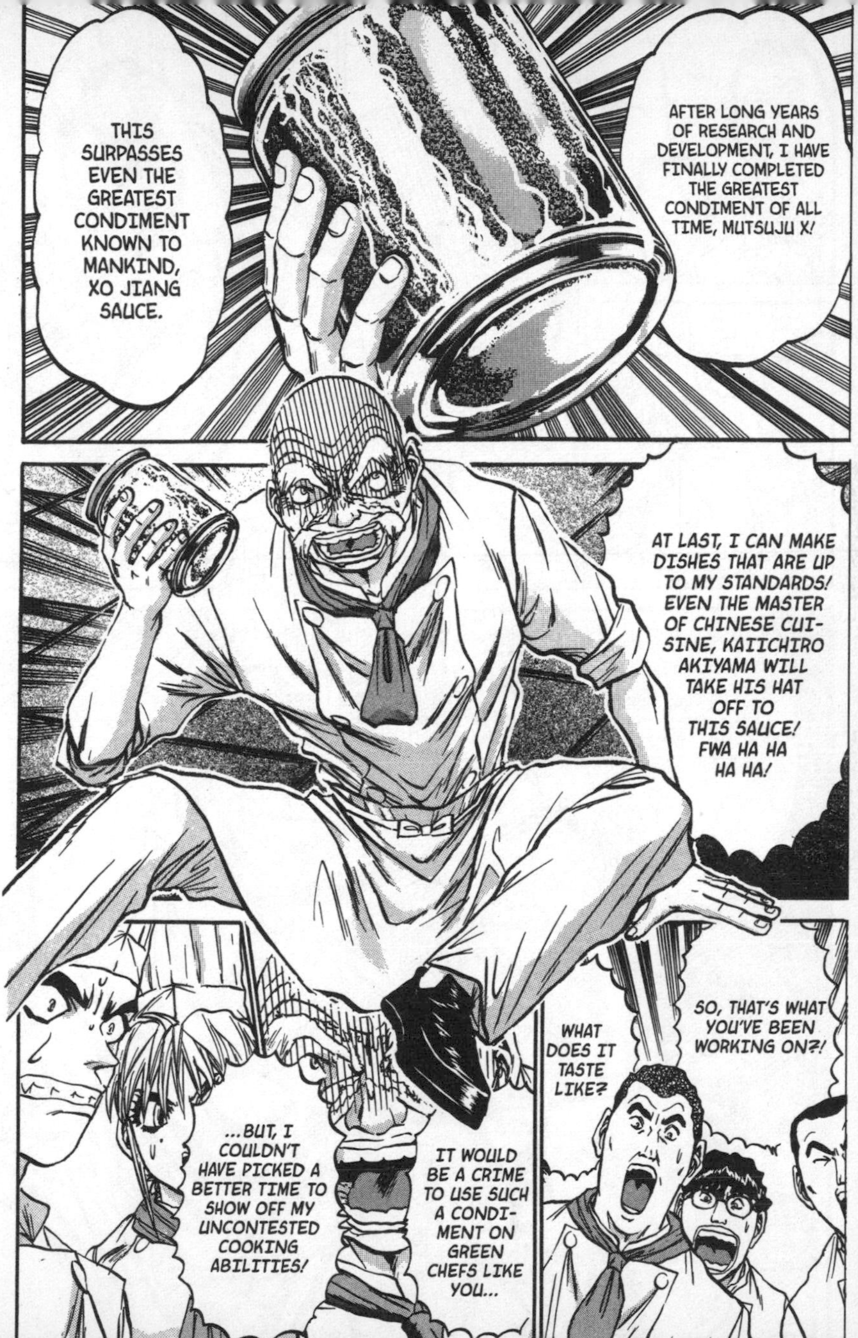
AFTER LONG YEARS OF RESEARCH AND DEVELOPMENT, I HAVE FINALLY COMPLETED THE GREATEST CONDIMENT OF ALL TIME, MUTSUJU X!
THIS SURPASSES EVEN THE GREATEST CONDIMENT KNOWN TO MANKIND, XO JIANG SAUCE.
AT LAST, I CAN MAKE DISHES THAT ARE UP TO MY STANDARDS! EVEN THE MASTER OF CHINESE CUI-SINE, KAIICHIRO AKIYAMA WILL TAKE HIS HAT OFF TO THIS SAUCE! FWA HA HA HA HA!
SO, THAT'S WHAT YOU'VE BEEN WORKING ON?!
WHAT DOES IT TASTE LIKE?
IT WOULD BE A CRIME TO USE SUCH A CONDI-MENT ON GREEN CHEFS LIKE YOU...
...BUT, I COULDN'T HAVE PICKED A BETTER TIME TO SHOW OFF MY UNCONTESTED COOKING ABILITIES!

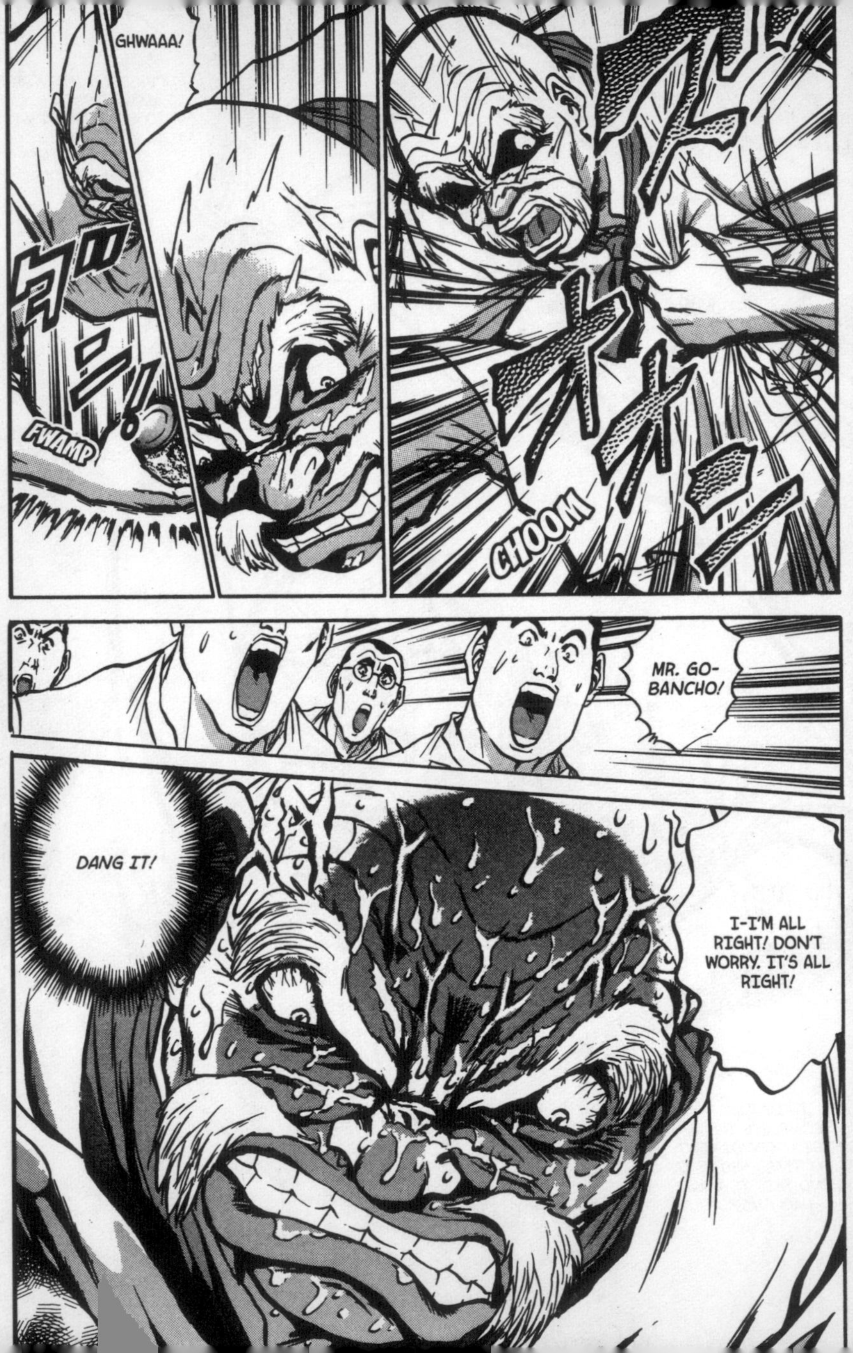

CHOOM
GHWAAA!
FWAMP
MR. GO-BANCHO!
I-I'M ALL RIGHT! DON'T WORRY. IT'S ALL RIGHT!
DANG IT!

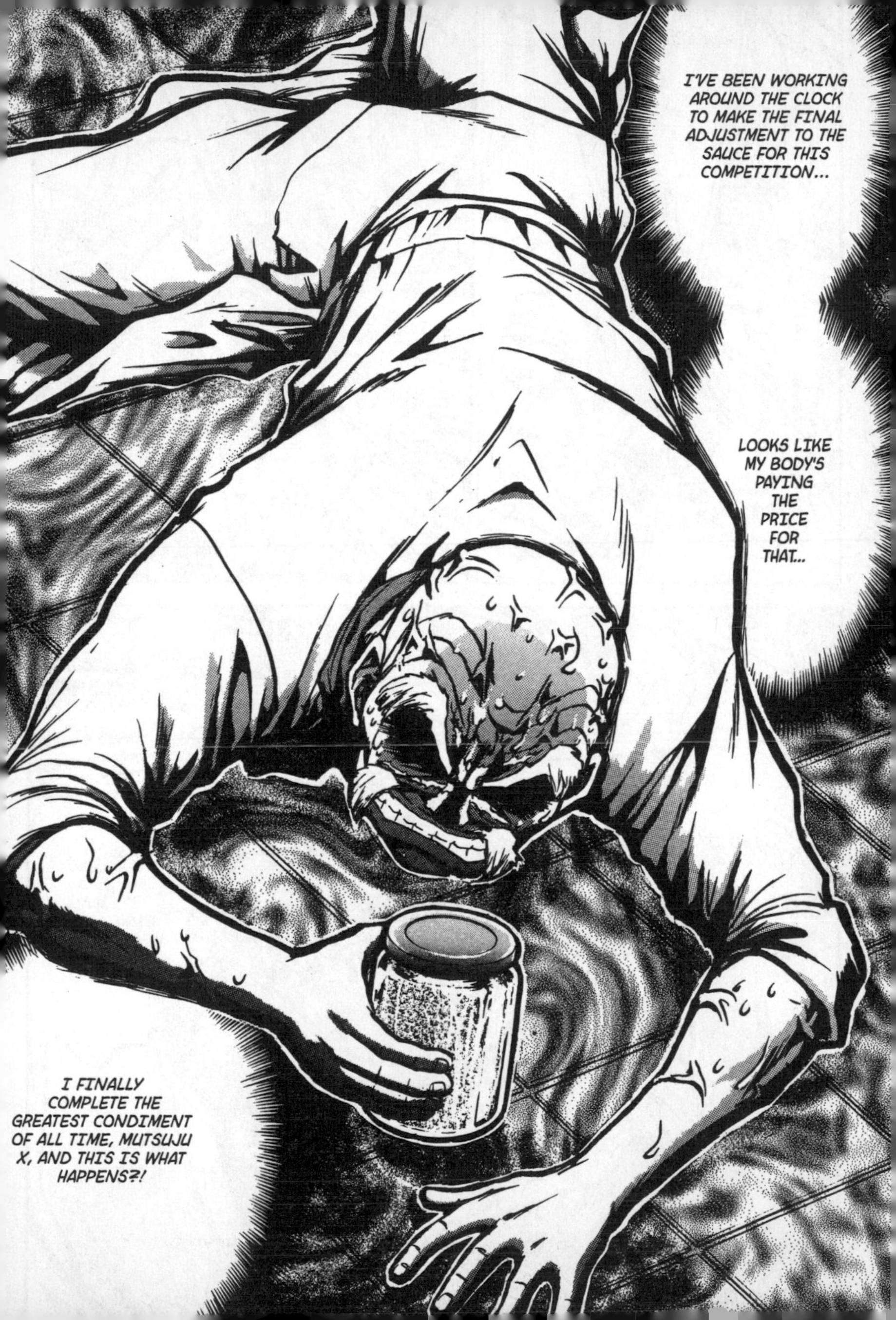
I'VE BEEN WORKING AROUND THE CLOCK TO MAKE THE FINAL ADJUSTMENT TO THE SAUCE FOR THIS COMPETITION...
LOOKS LIKE MY BODY'S PAYING THE PRICE FOR THAT...
I FINALLY COMPLETE THE GREATEST CONDIMENT OF ALL TIME, MUTSUJU X, AND THIS IS WHAT HAPPENS?!

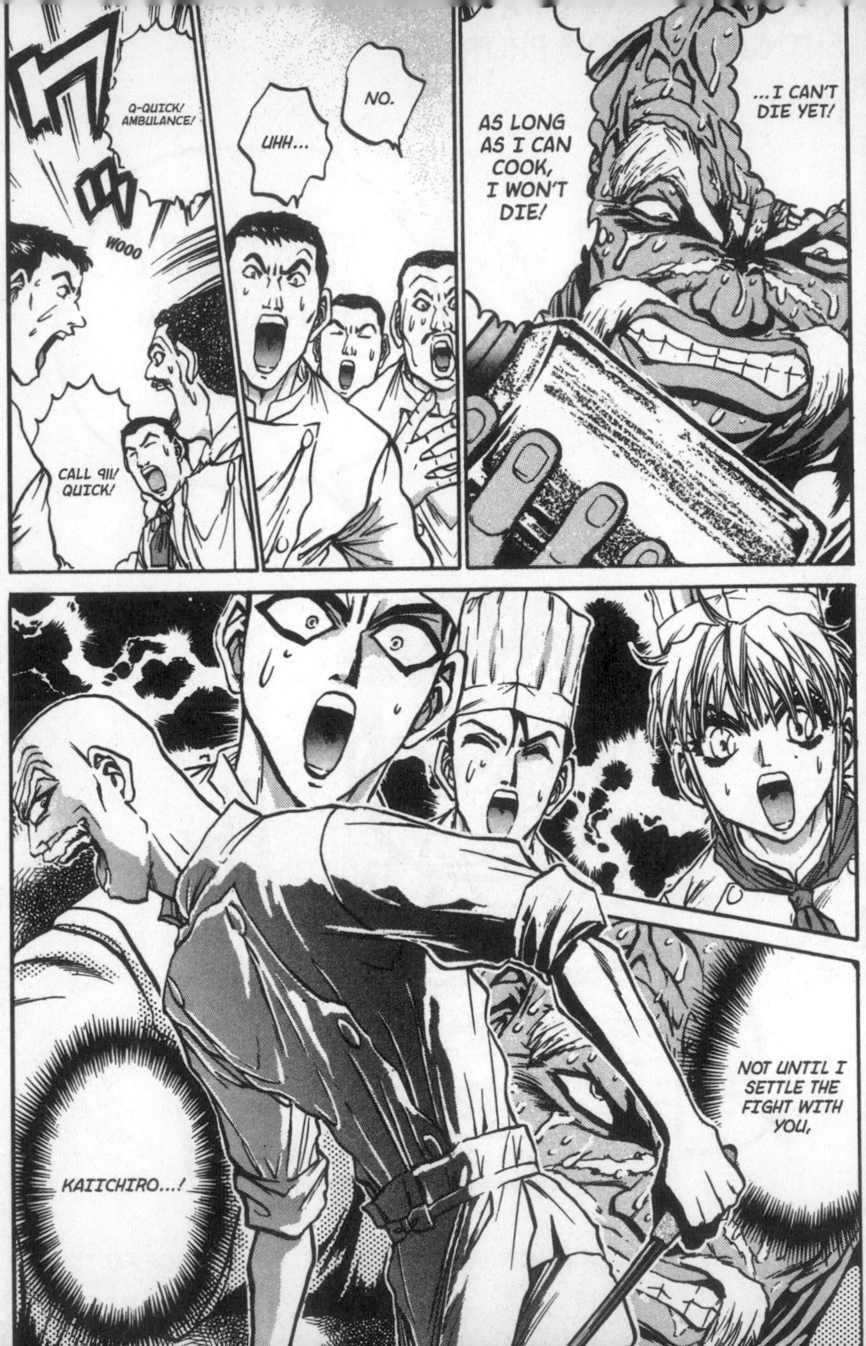
...I CAN'T DIE YET!
AS LONG AS I CAN COOK, I WON'T DIE!
NO.
UHH...
Q-QUICK! AMBULANCE!
WOOO
CALL 911! QUICK!
NOT UNTIL I SETTLE THE FIGHT WITH YOU,
KAIICHIRO...!

SHINJI SAIJYO'S PROTEST

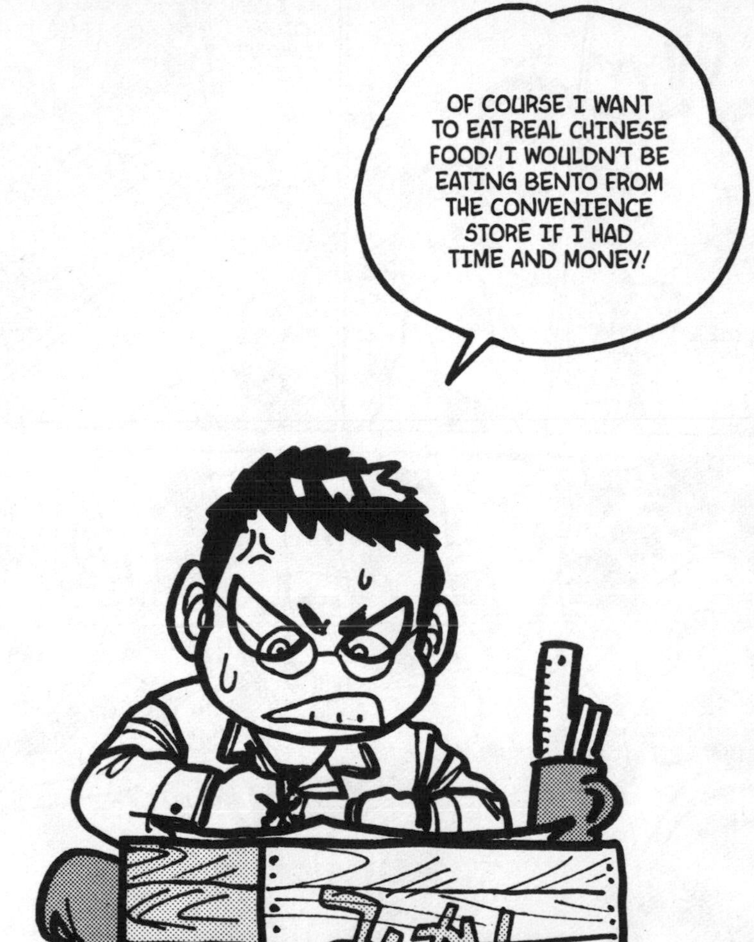
OF COURSE I WANT TO EAT REAL CHINESE FOOD! I WOULDN'T BE EATING BENTO FROM THE CONVENIENCE STORE IF I HAD TIME AND MONEY!
MANDARIN ORANGES

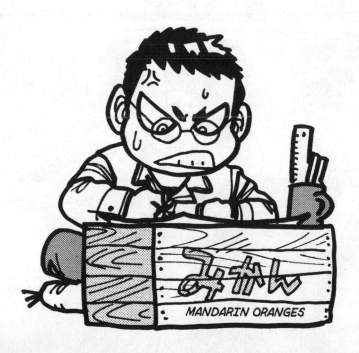

PLEASE NOTE THIS IS ENTIRELY A WORK OF FICTION.

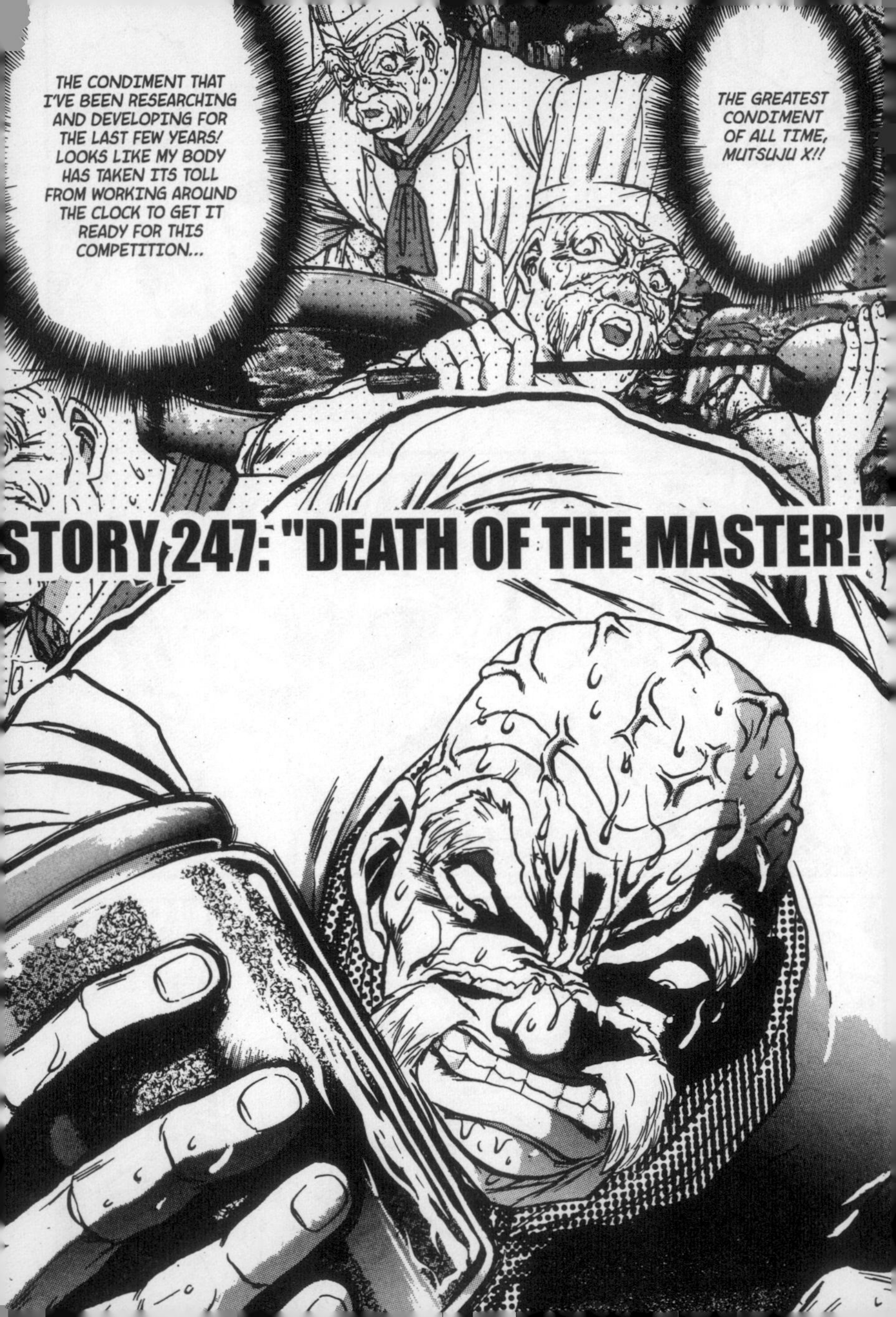
THE GREATEST CONDIMENT OF ALL TIME, MUTSUJU X!!
THE CONDIMENT THAT I'VE BEEN RESEARCHING AND DEVELOPING FOR THE LAST FEW YEARS! LOOKS LIKE MY BODY HAS TAKEN ITS TOLL FROM WORKING AROUND THE CLOCK TO GET IT READY FOR THIS COMPETITION...
STORY 247: "DEATH OF THE MASTER!"

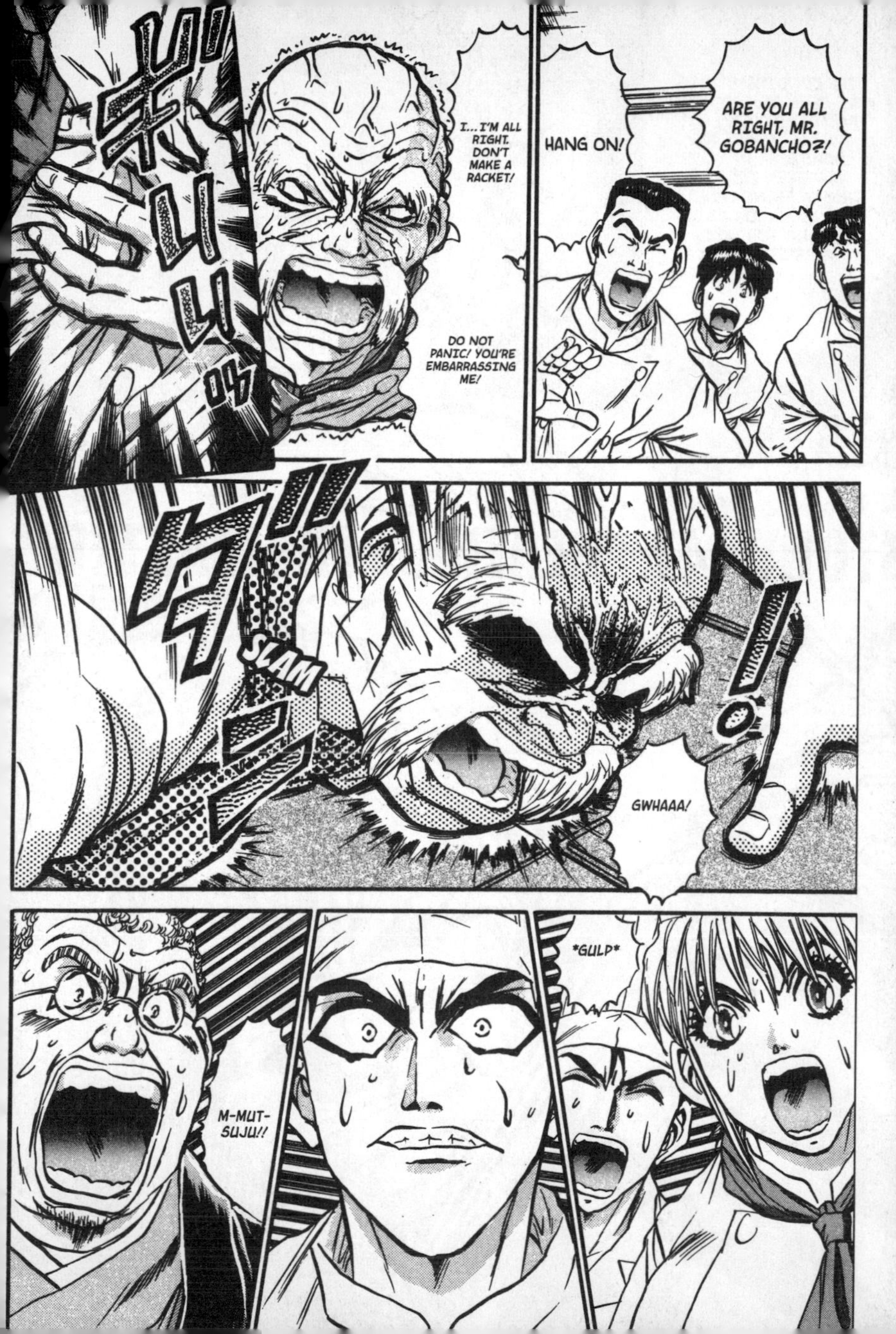
ARE YOU ALL RIGHT, MR. GOBANCHO?!
HANG ON!
I...I'M ALL RIGHT. DON'T MAKE A RACKET!
DO NOT PANIC! YOU'RE EMBARRASSING ME!
SLAM
GWHAAA!
GULP
M-MUT-SUJU!!

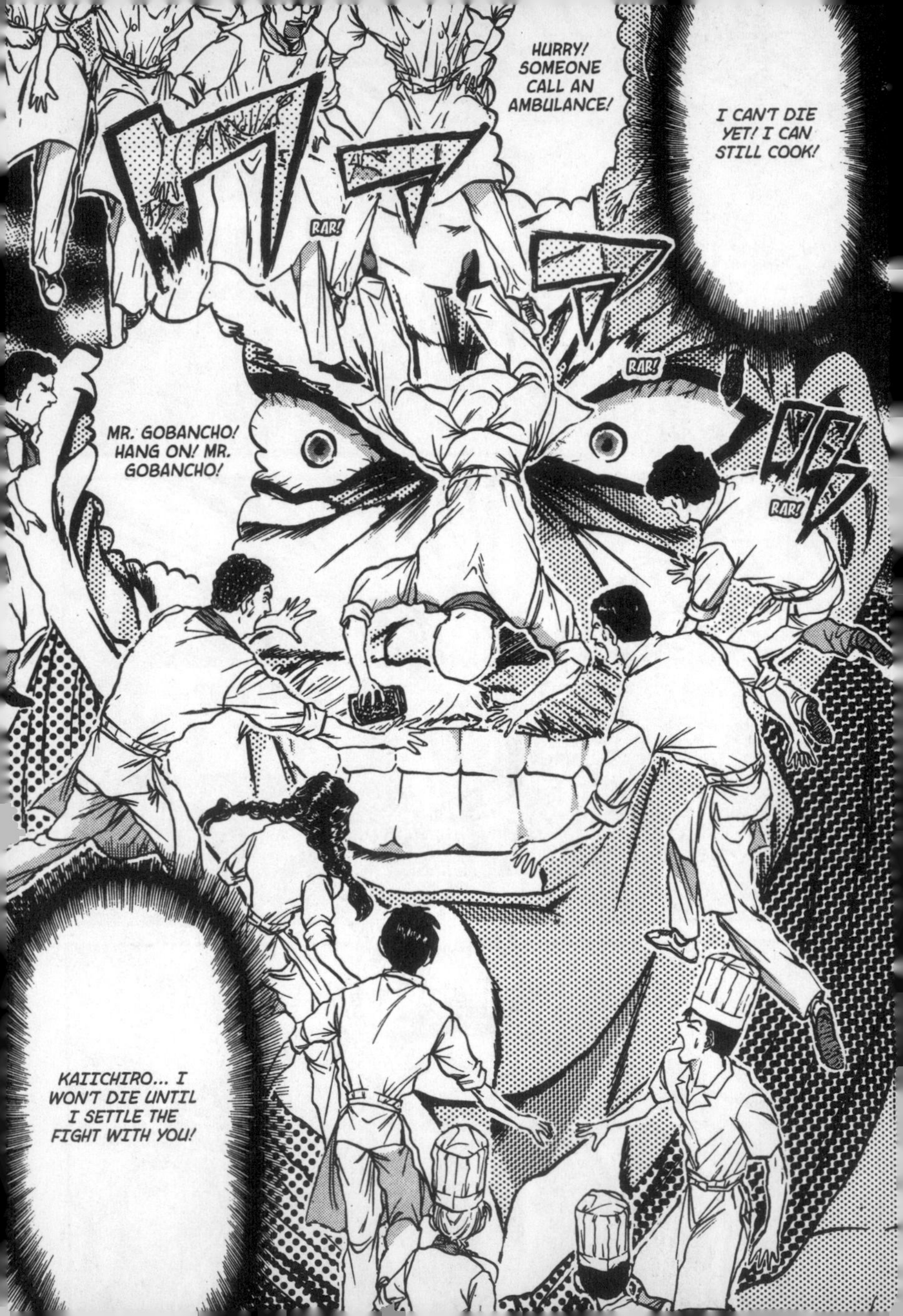
I CAN'T DIE YET! I CAN STILL COOK!
HURRY! SOMEONE CALL AN AMBULANCE!
RAR!
RAR!
RAR!
MR. GOBANCHO! HANG ON! MR. GOBANCHO!
KAIICHIRO... I WON'T DIE UNTIL I SETTLE THE FIGHT WITH YOU!

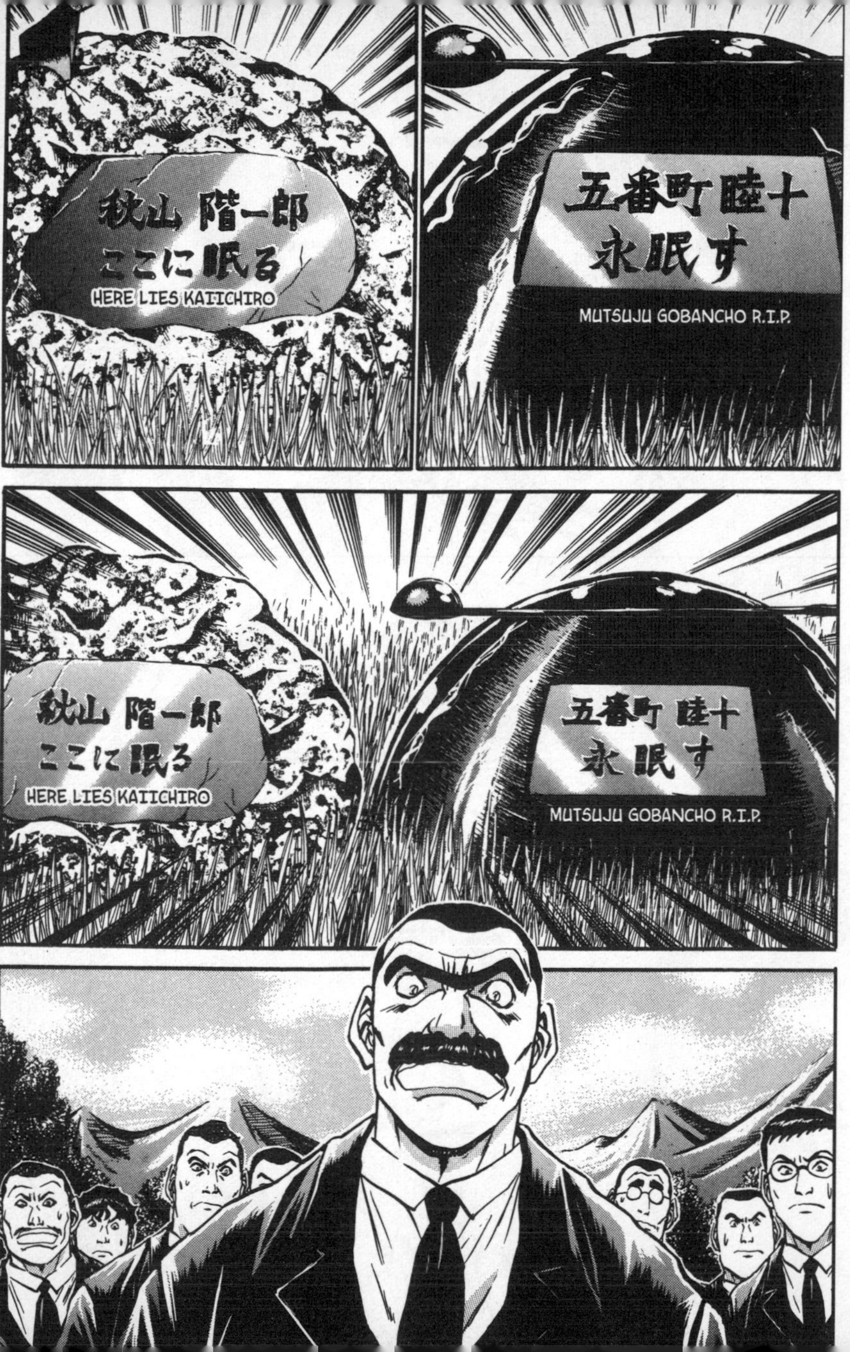
五番町 睦十
永眠す
MUTSUJU GOBANCHO R.I.P.
秋山 階一郎
ここに眠る
HERE LIES KAIICHIRO
五番町 睦十
永眠す
MUTSUJU GOBANCHO R.I.P.
秋山 階一郎
ここに眠る
HERE LIES KAIICHIRO

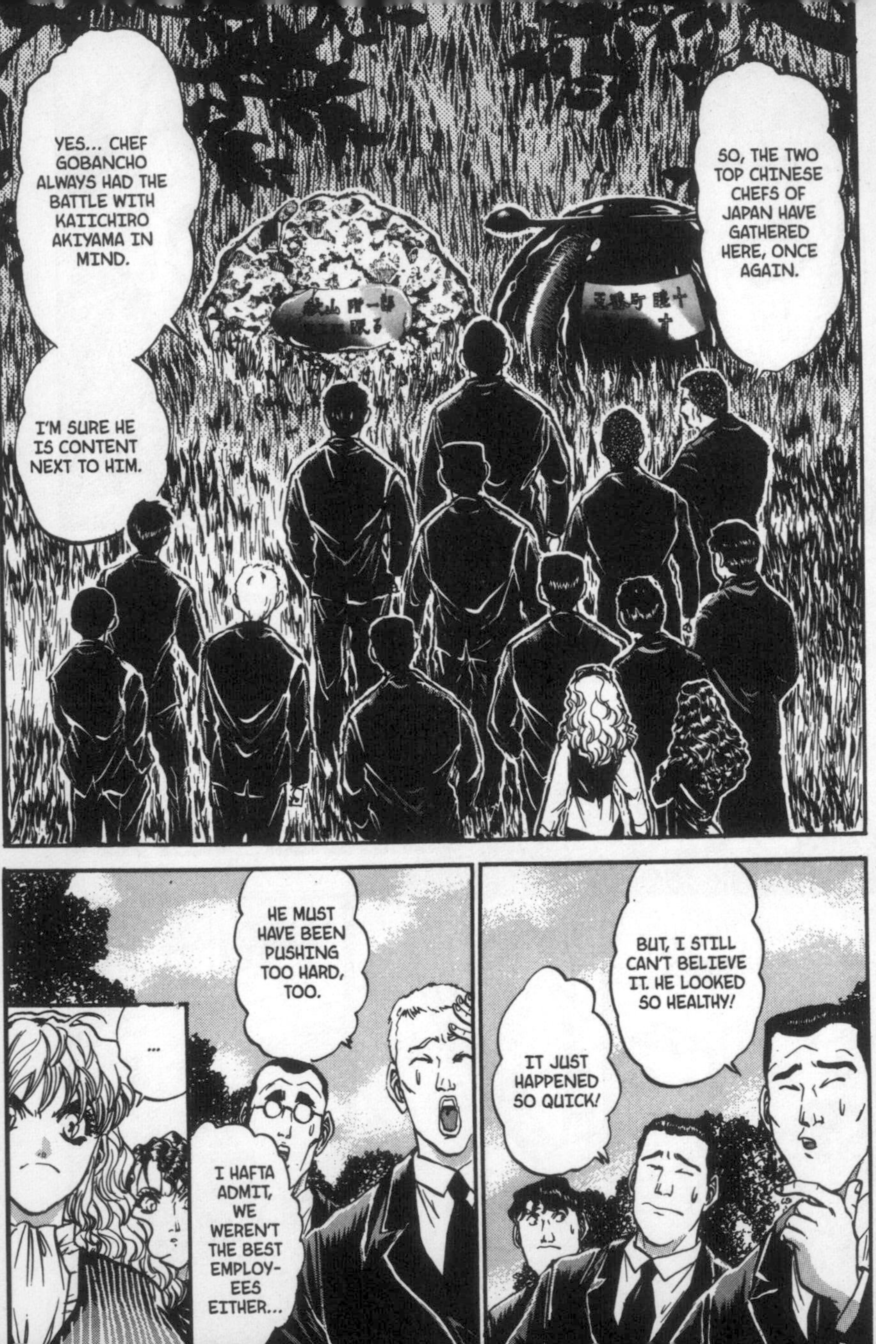
SO, THE TWO TOP CHINESE CHEFS OF JAPAN HAVE GATHERED HERE, ONCE AGAIN.
YES... CHEF GOBANCHO ALWAYS HAD THE BATTLE WITH KAIICHIRO AKIYAMA IN MIND.
I'M SURE HE IS CONTENT NEXT TO HIM.
BUT, I STILL CAN'T BELIEVE IT. HE LOOKED SO HEALTHY!
IT JUST HAPPENED SO QUICK!
HE MUST HAVE BEEN PUSHING TOO HARD, TOO.
I HAFTA ADMIT, WE WEREN'T THE BEST EMPLOY-EES EITHER...
...

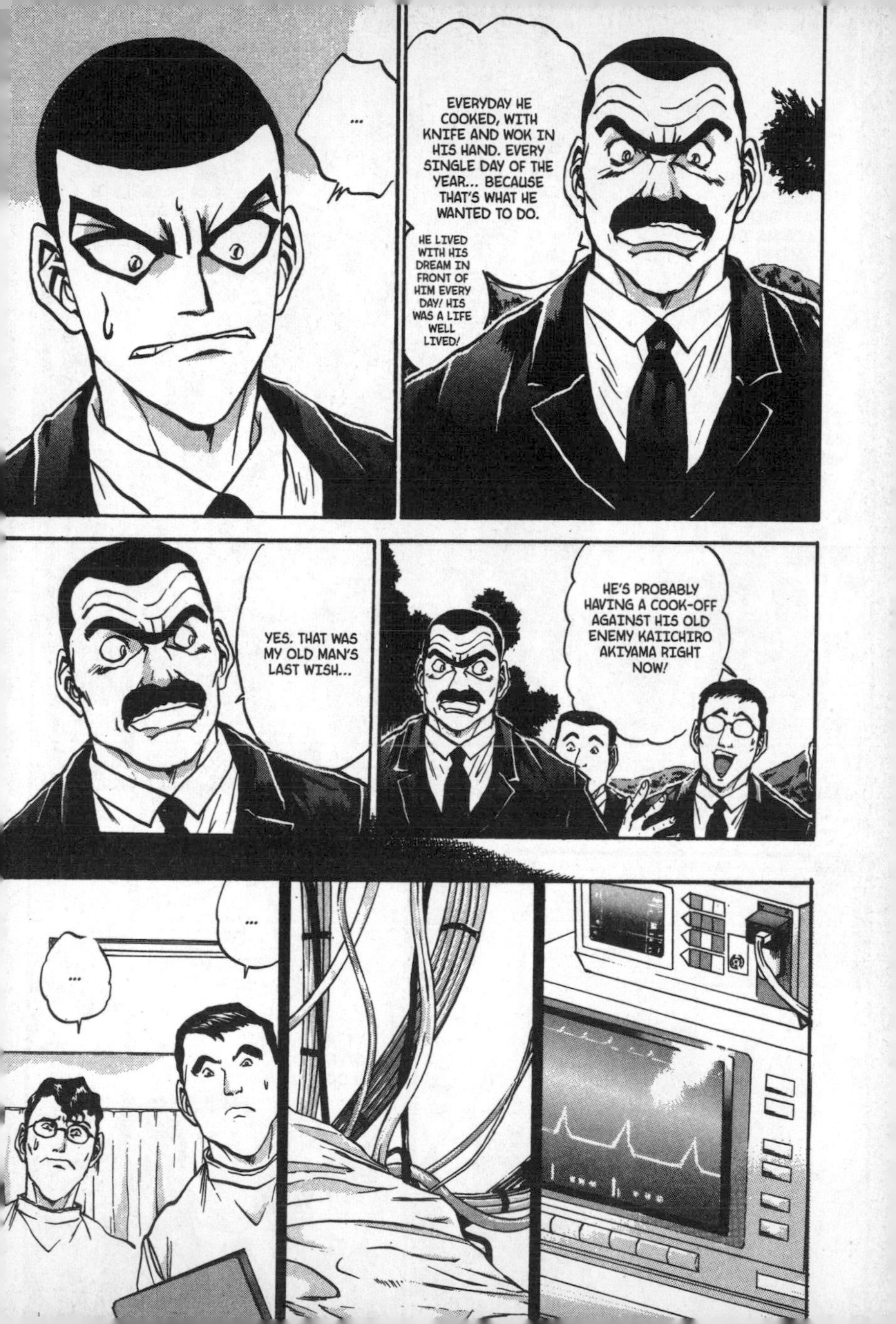
EVERYDAY HE COOKED, WITH KNIFE AND WOK IN HIS HAND. EVERY SINGLE DAY OF THE YEAR... BECAUSE THAT'S WHAT HE WANTED TO DO.
HE LIVED WITH HIS DREAM IN FRONT OF HIM EVERY DAY! HIS WAS A LIFE WELL LIVED!
...
HE'S PROBABLY HAVING A COOK-OFF AGAINST HIS OLD ENEMY KAIICHIRO AKIYAMA RIGHT NOW!
YES. THAT WAS MY OLD MAN'S LAST WISH...
...
...

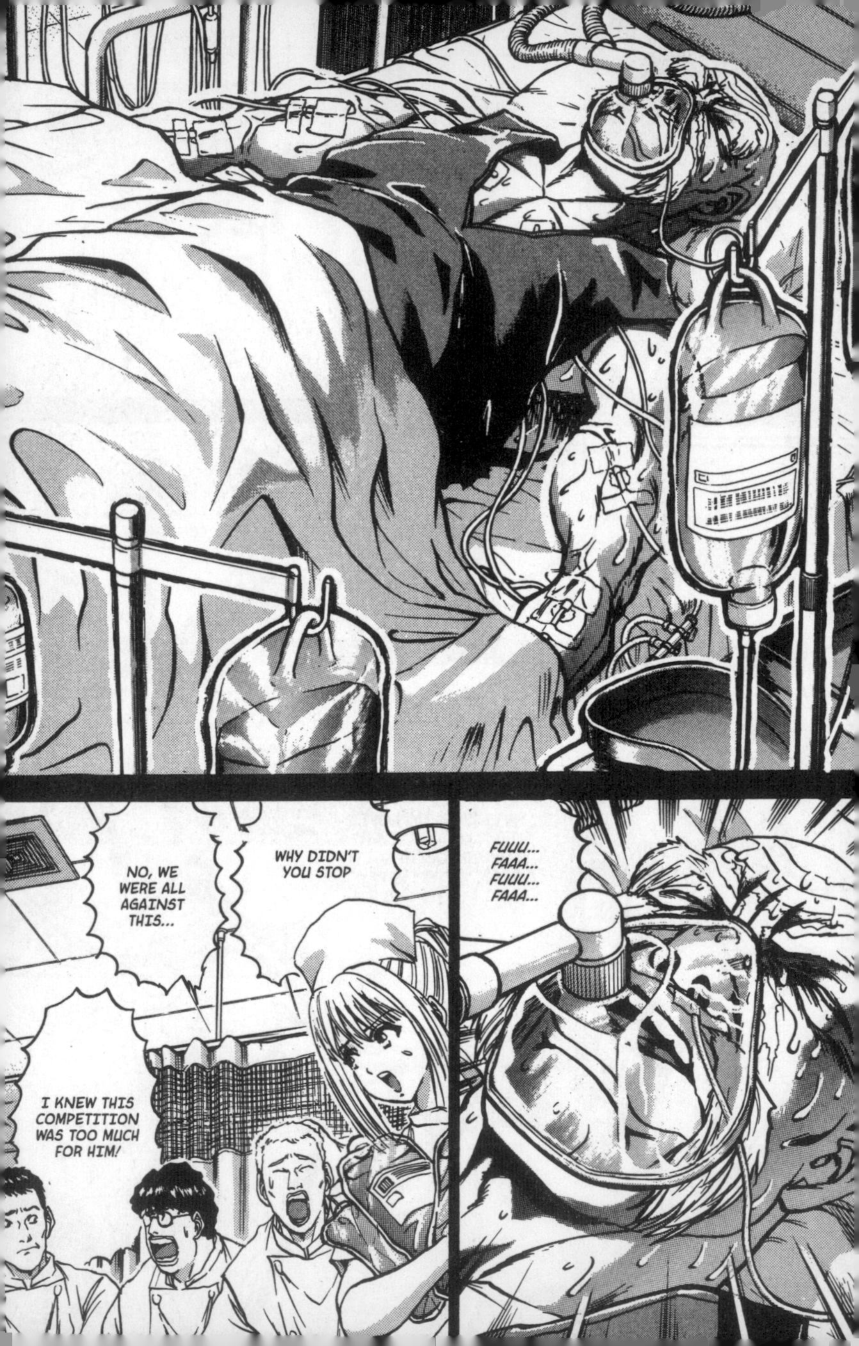
FUUU... FAAA... FUUU... FAAA...
WHY DIDN'T YOU STOP
NO, WE WERE ALL AGAINST THIS...
I KNEW THIS COMPETITION WAS TOO MUCH FOR HIM!

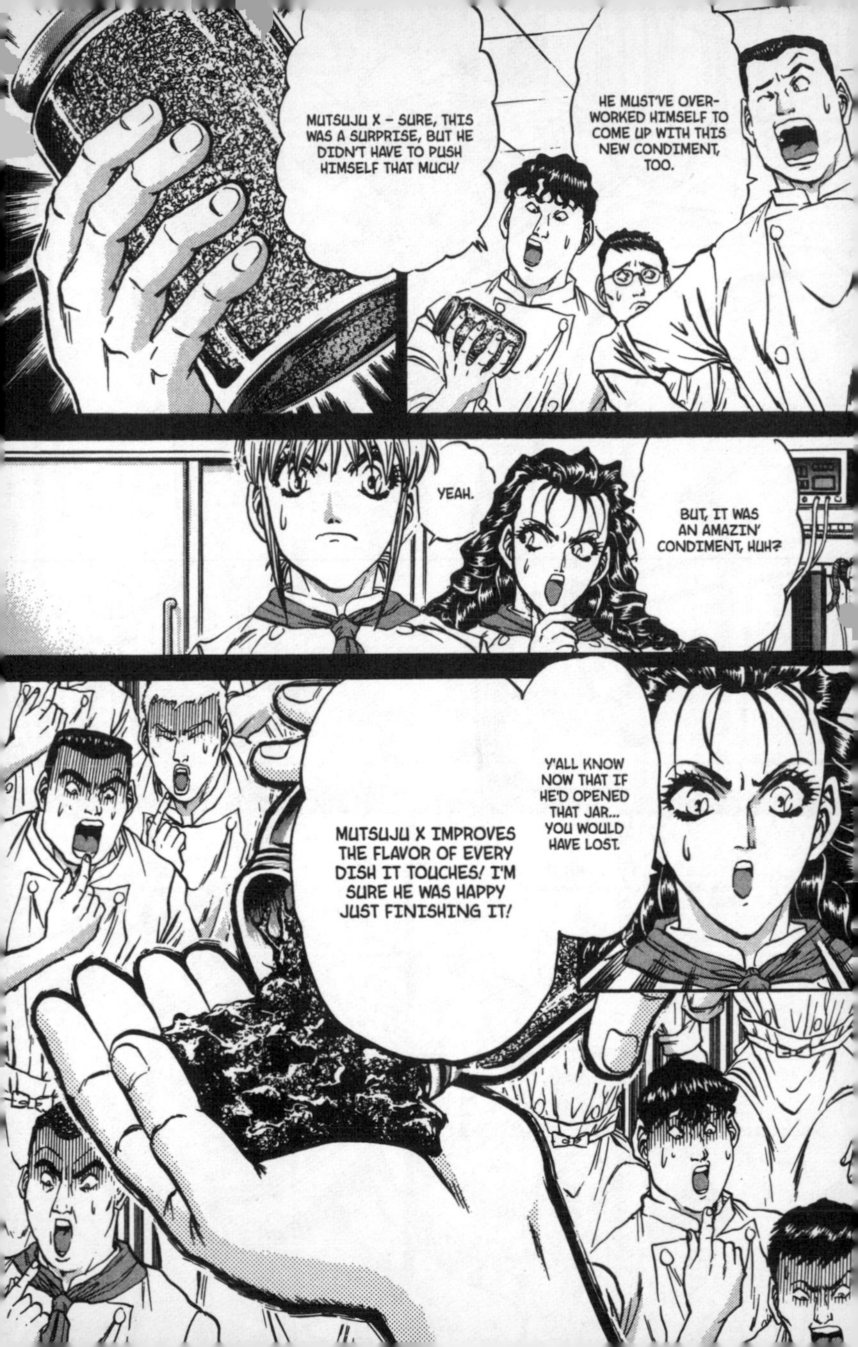
HE MUST'VE OVER-WORKED HIMSELF TO COME UP WITH THIS NEW CONDIMENT, TOO.
MUTSUJU X – SURE, THIS WAS A SURPRISE, BUT HE DIDN'T HAVE TO PUSH HIMSELF THAT MUCH!
BUT, IT WAS AN AMAZIN' CONDIMENT, HUH?
YEAH.
Y'ALL KNOW NOW THAT IF HE'D OPENED THAT JAR... YOU WOULD HAVE LOST.
MUTSUJU X IMPROVES THE FLAVOR OF EVERY DISH IT TOUCHES! I'M SURE HE WAS HAPPY JUST FINISHING IT!

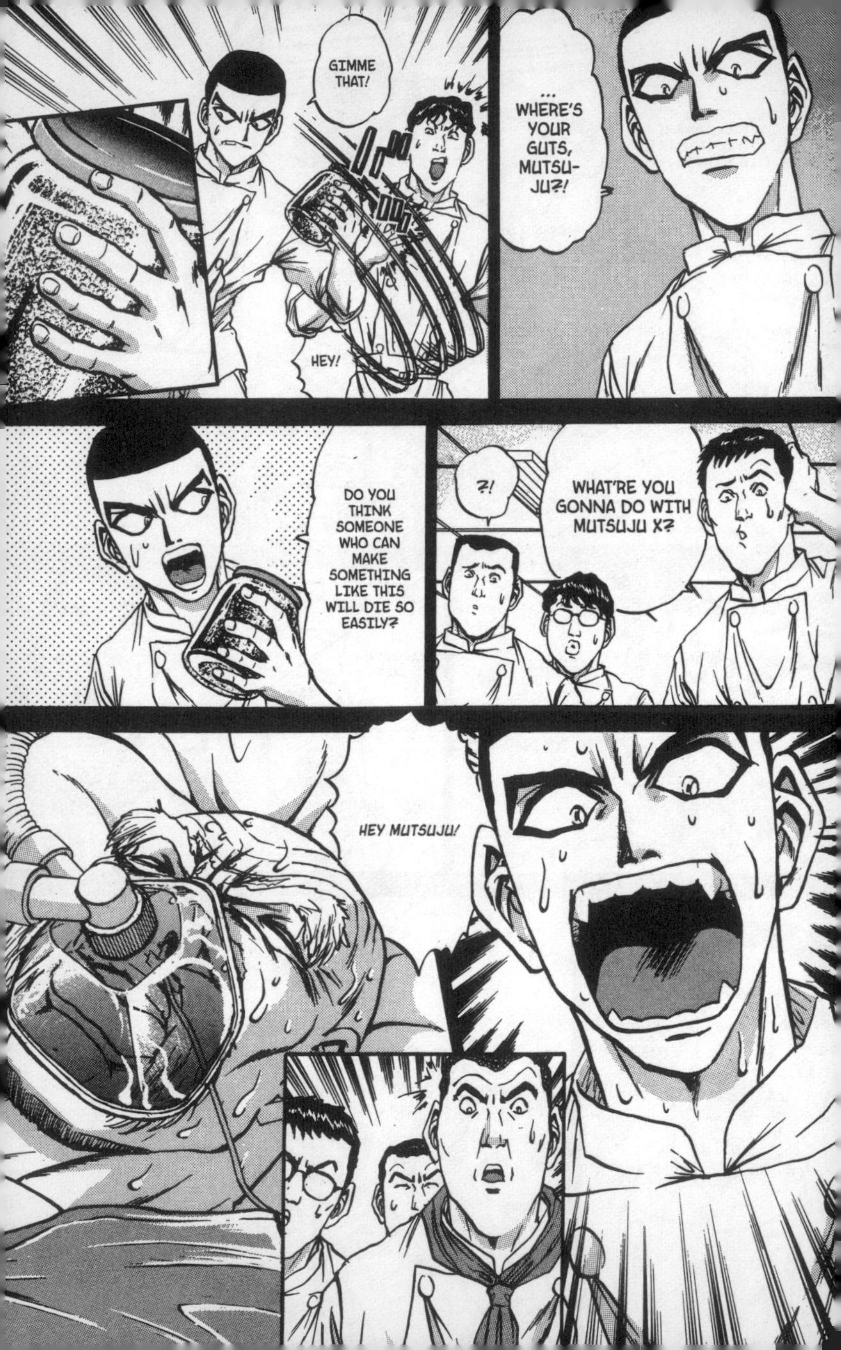

... WHERE'S YOUR GUTS, MUTSU-JU?!
GIMME THAT!
HEY!
WHAT'RE YOU GONNA DO WITH MUTSUJU X?
?!
DO YOU THINK SOMEONE WHO CAN MAKE SOMETHING LIKE THIS WILL DIE SO EASILY?
HEY MUTSUJU!

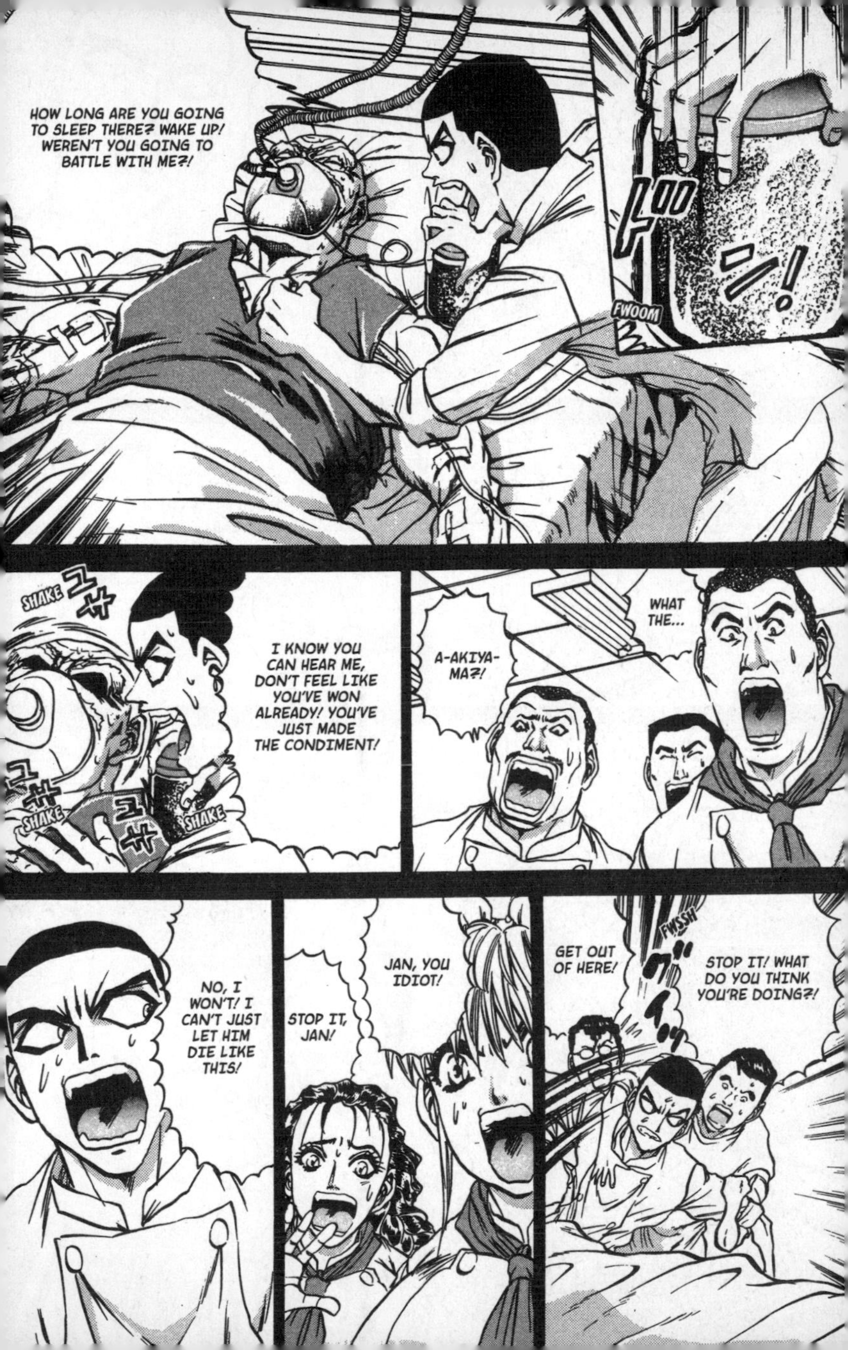
FWOOM
HOW LONG ARE YOU GOING TO SLEEP THERE? WAKE UP! WEREN'T YOU GOING TO BATTLE WITH ME?!
WHAT THE...
A-AKIYAMA?!
SHAKE
I KNOW YOU CAN HEAR ME, DON'T FEEL LIKE YOU'VE WON ALREADY! YOU'VE JUST MADE THE CONDIMENT!
SHAKE
SHAKE
FWSSH
STOP IT! WHAT DO YOU THINK YOU'RE DOING?!
GET OUT OF HERE!
JAN, YOU IDIOT!
STOP IT, JAN!
NO, I WON'T! I CAN'T JUST LET HIM DIE LIKE THIS!

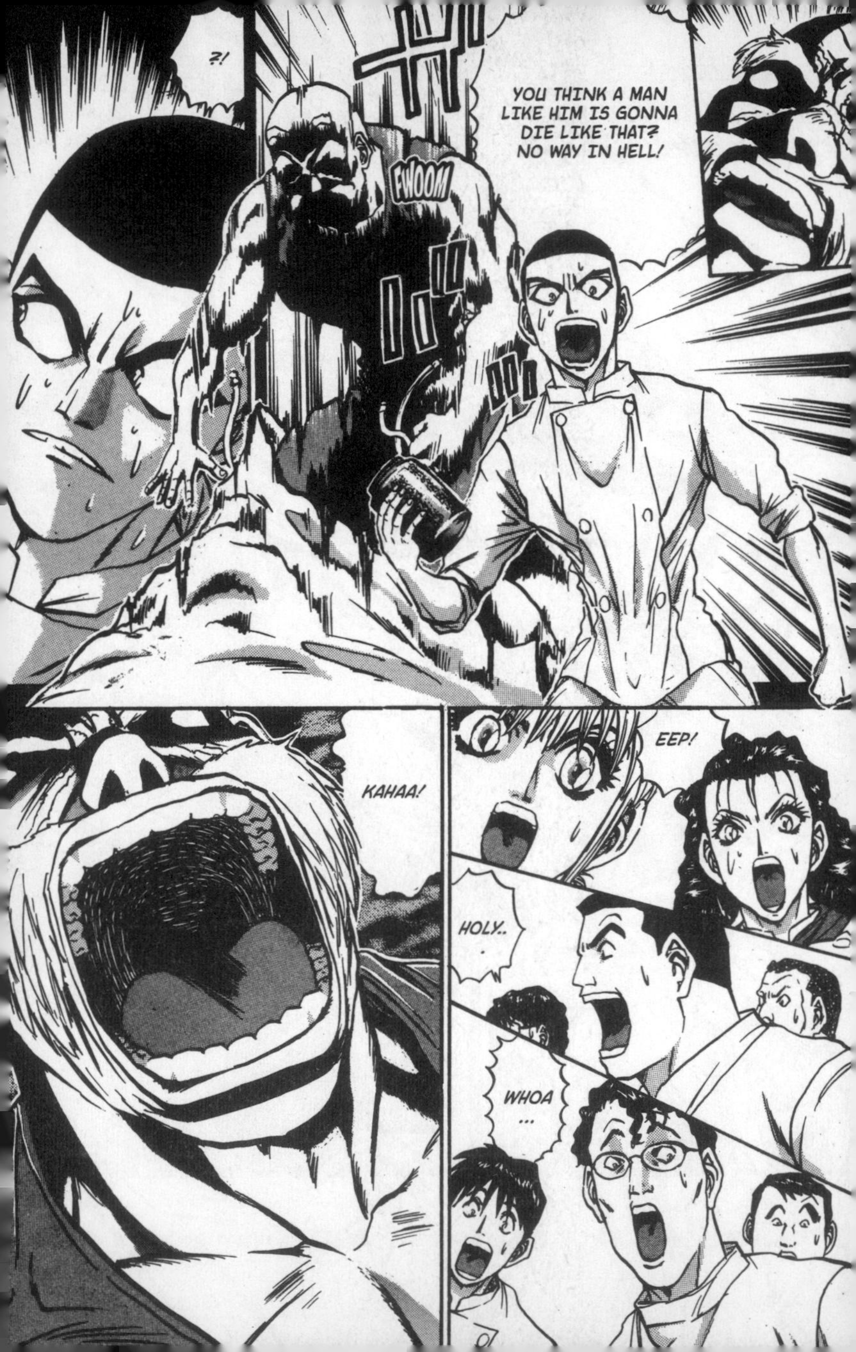
YOU THINK A MAN LIKE HIM IS GONNA DIE LIKE THAT? NO WAY IN HELL!
FWOOM
?!
EEP!
HOLY..
WHOA ...
KAHAA!

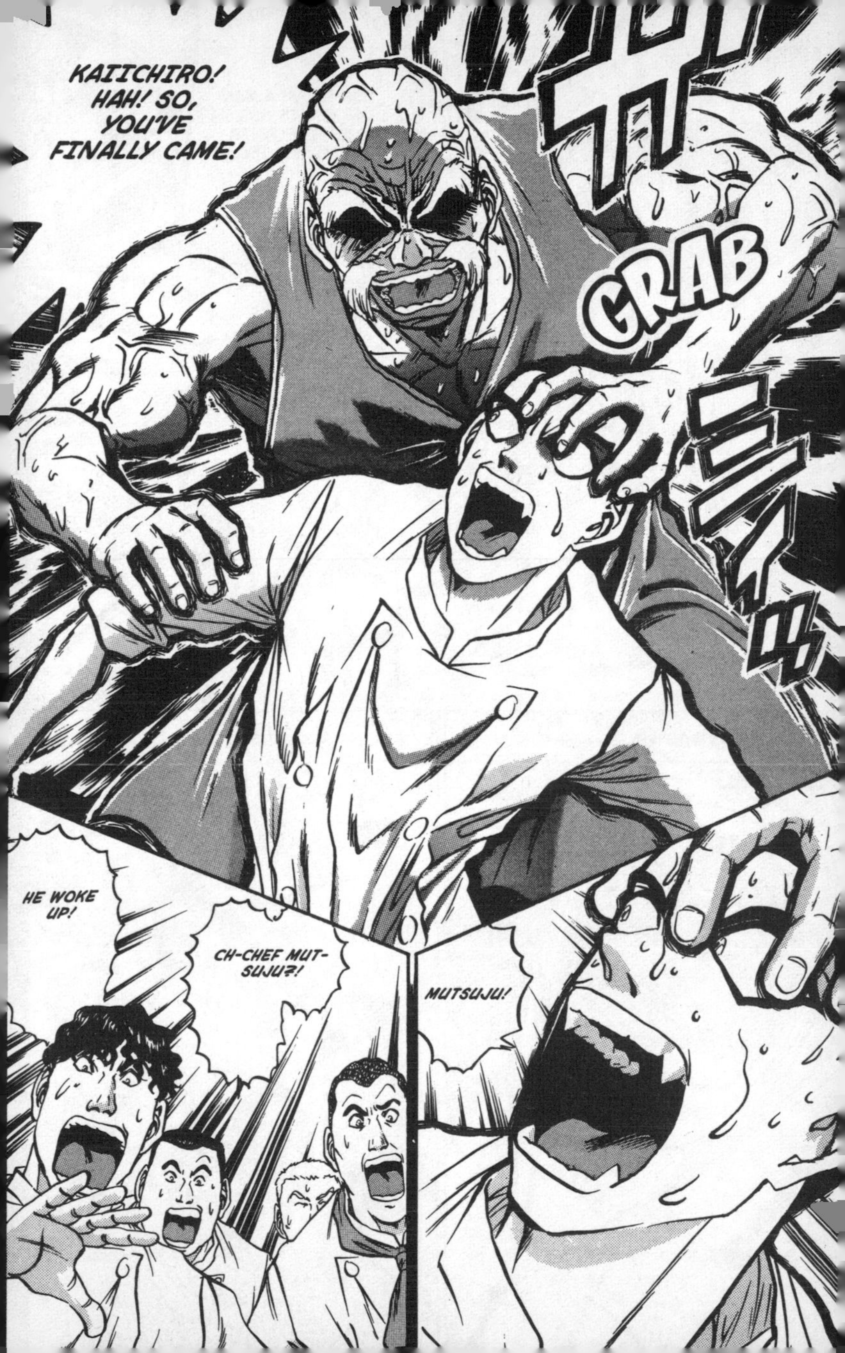
KAIICHIRO! HAH! SO, YOU'VE FINALLY CAME!
GRAB
GRAB
MUTSUJU!
CH-CHEF MUT-SUJU?!
HE WOKE UP!

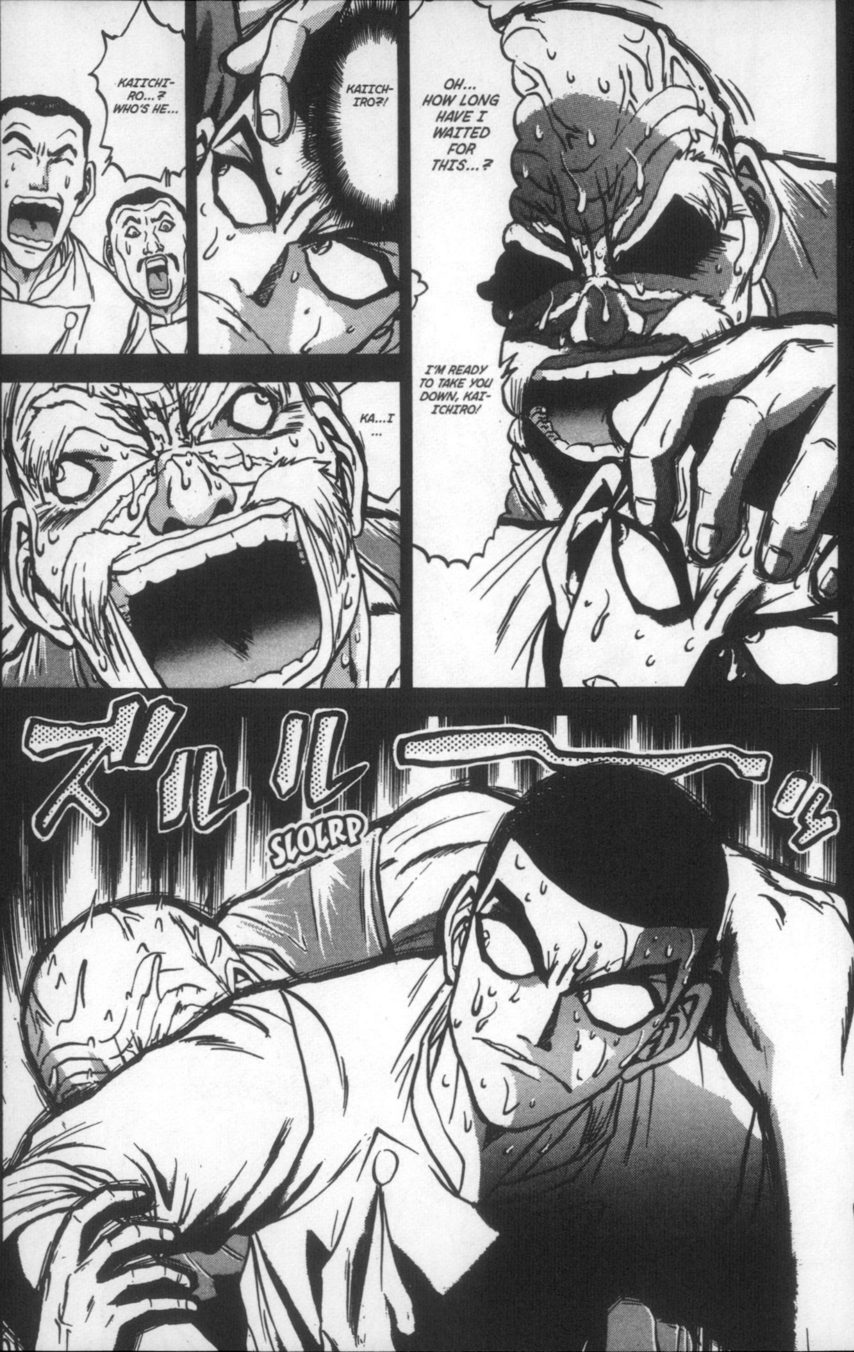
OH... HOW LONG HAVE I WAITED FOR THIS...?
I'M READY TO TAKE YOU DOWN, KAIICHIRO!
KAIICHIRO?!
KAIICHIRO...? WHO'S HE...
KA...I ...
ズルルーーッ
SLOLRP

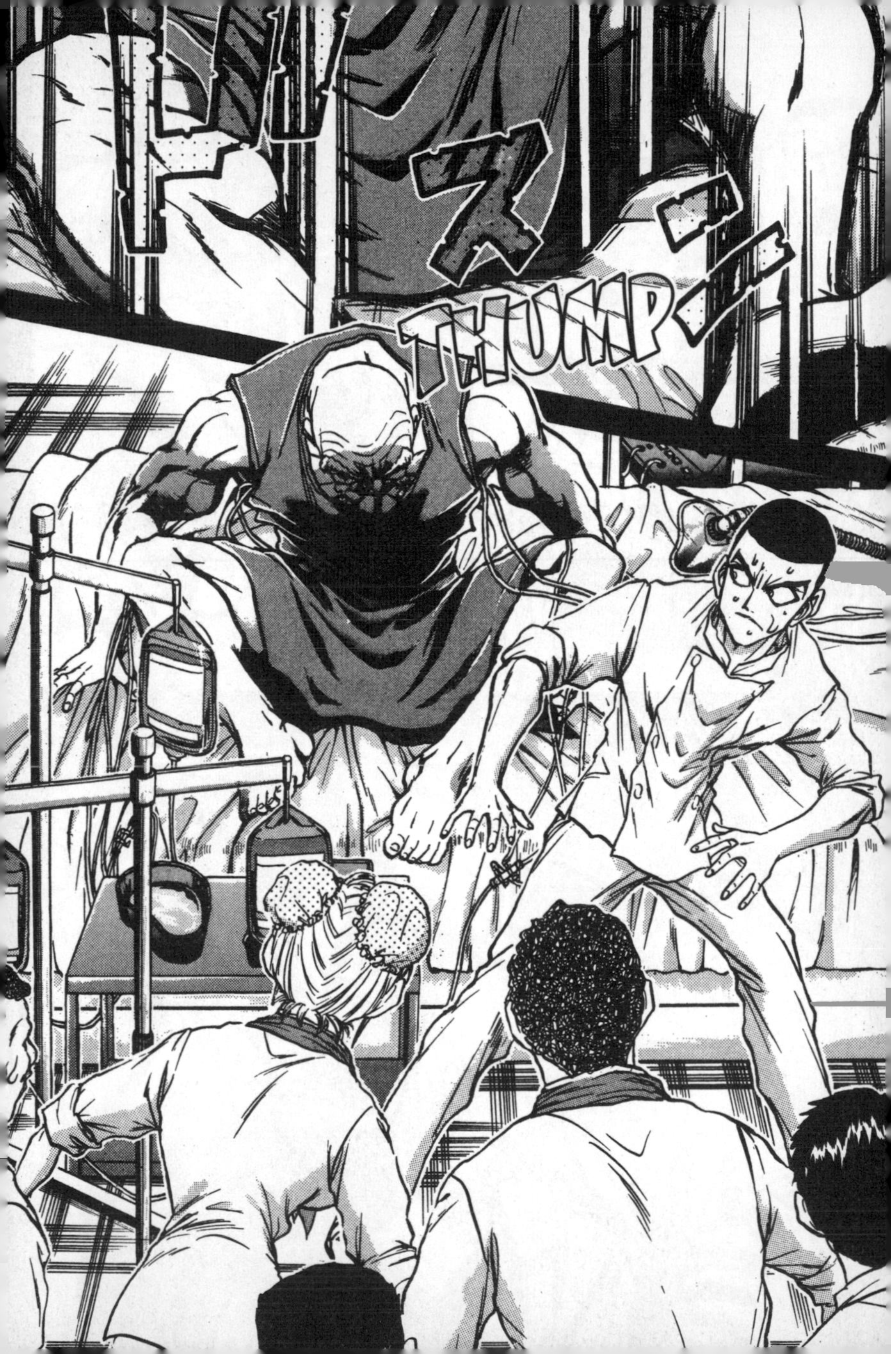
THUMP

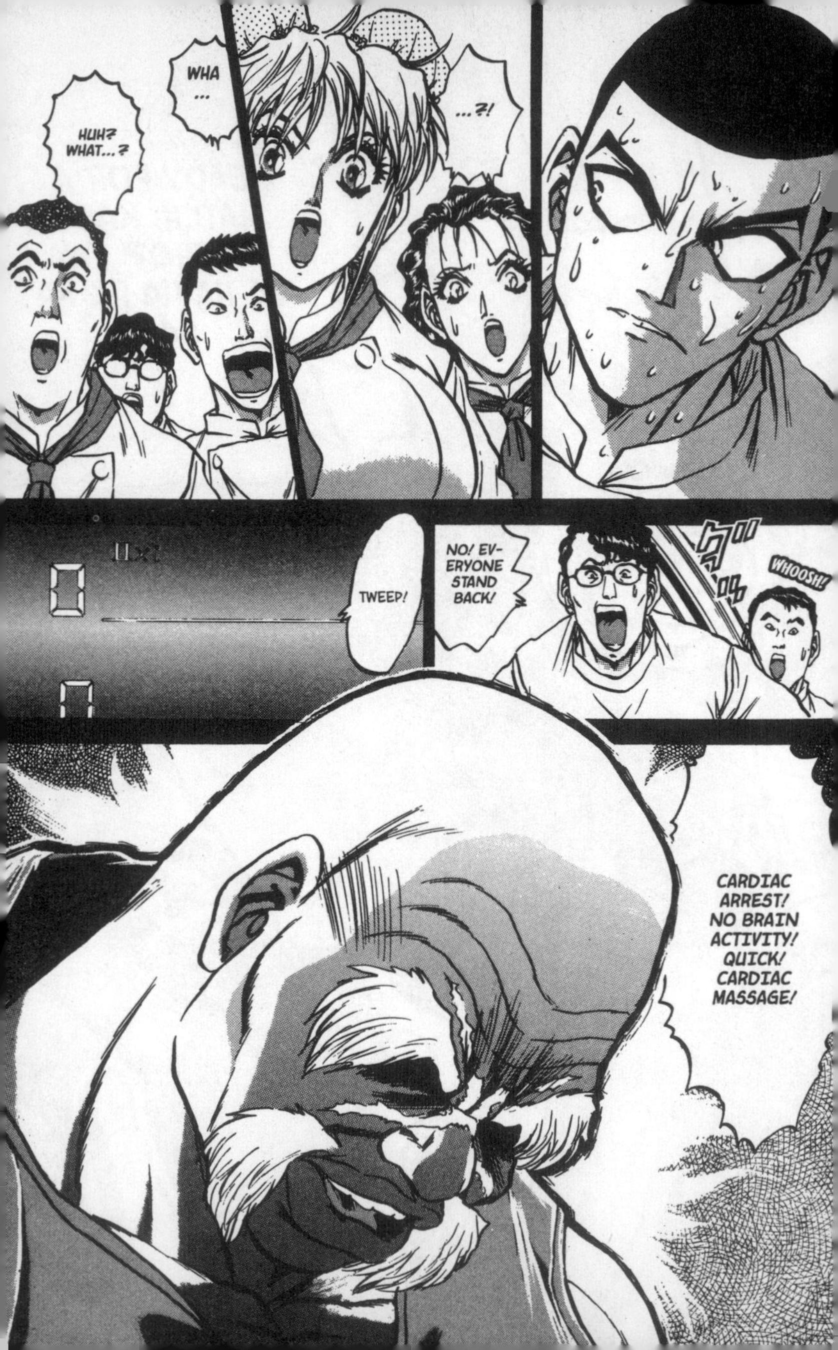
...?!
WHA ...
HUH? WHAT...?
WHOOSH!
NO! EV-ERYONE STAND BACK!
TWEEP!
CARDIAC ARREST! NO BRAIN ACTIVITY! QUICK! CARDIAC MASSAGE!

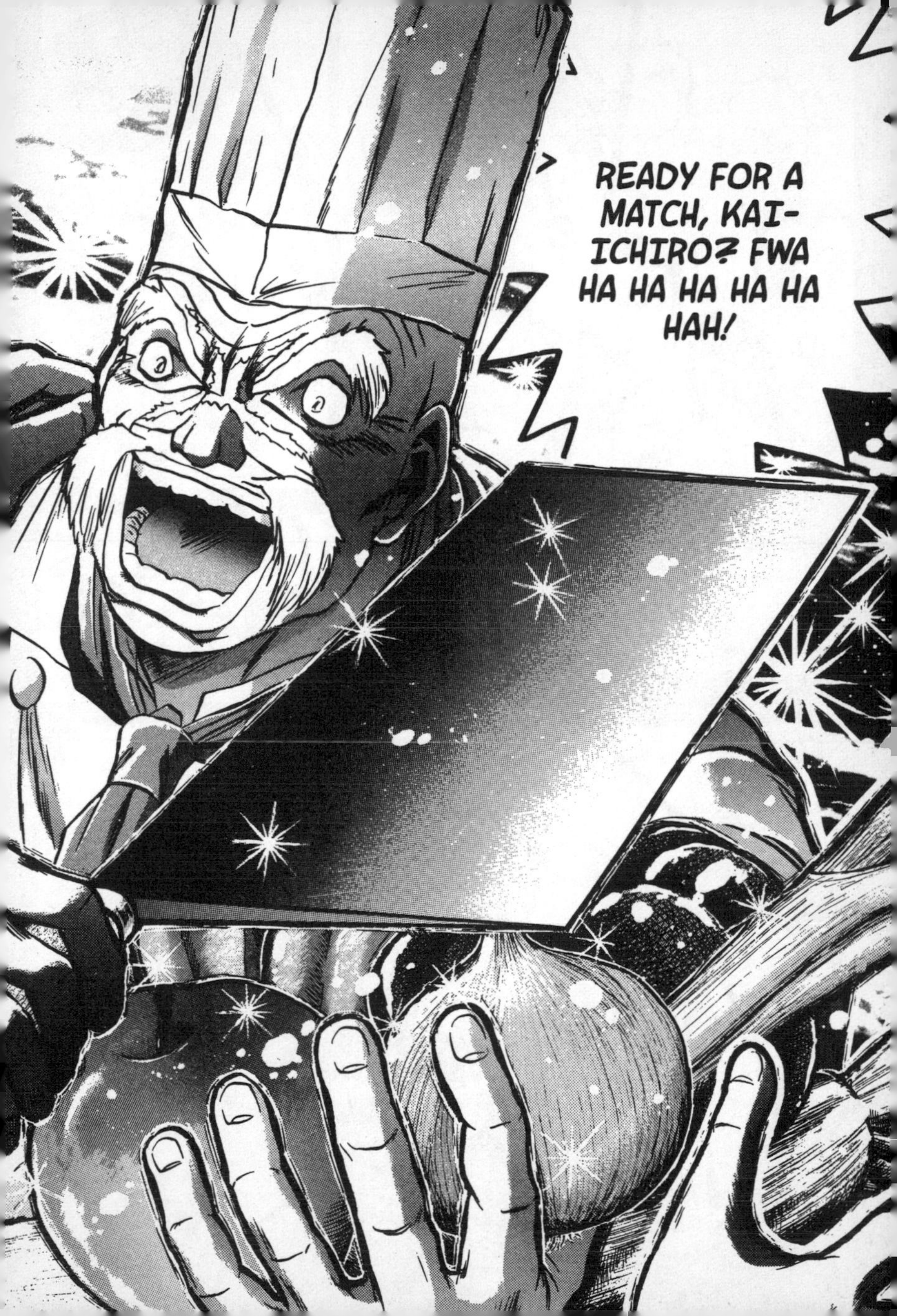
READY FOR A MATCH, KAI-ICHIRO? FWA HA HA HA HA HA HAH!

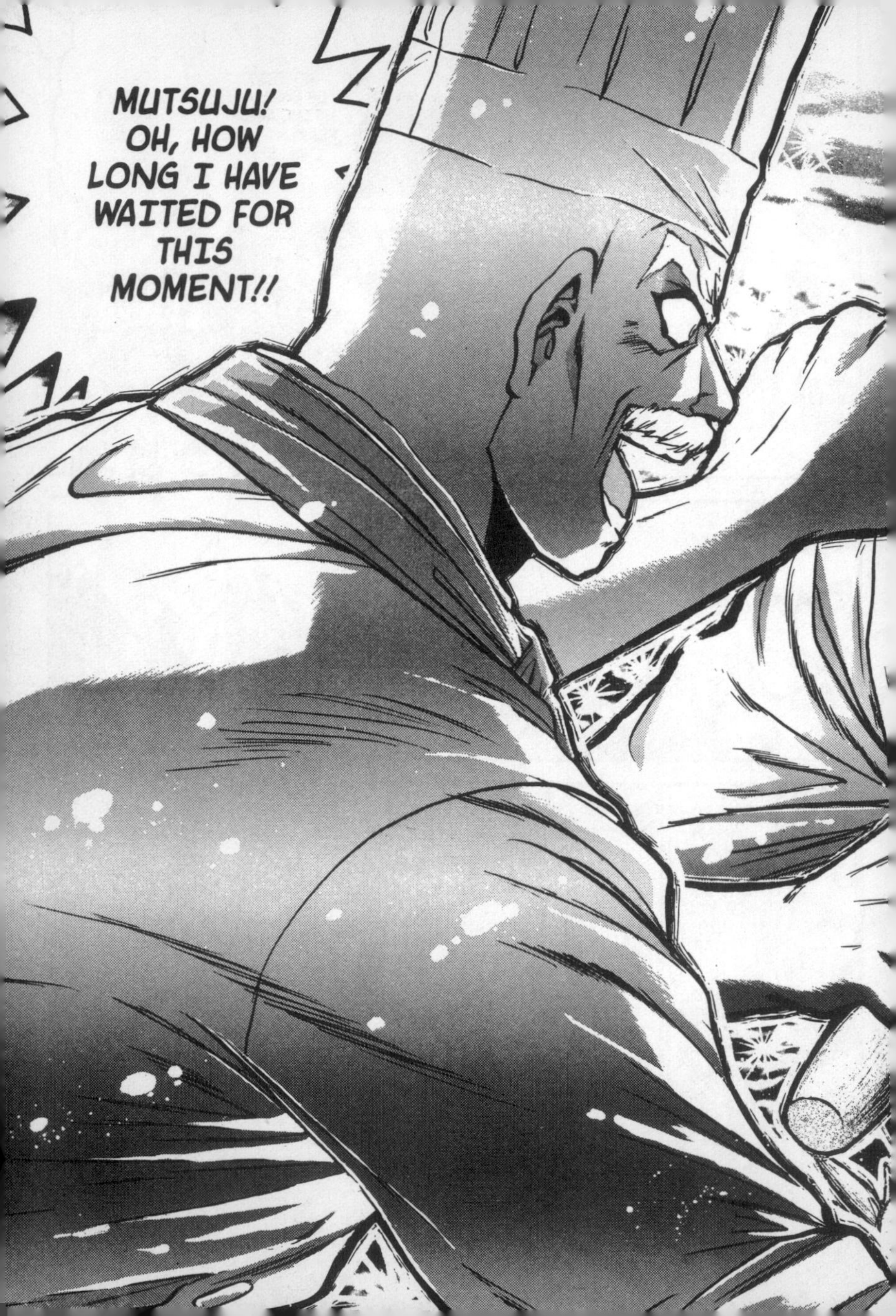
MUTSUJU! OH, HOW LONG I HAVE WAITED FOR THIS MOMENT!!

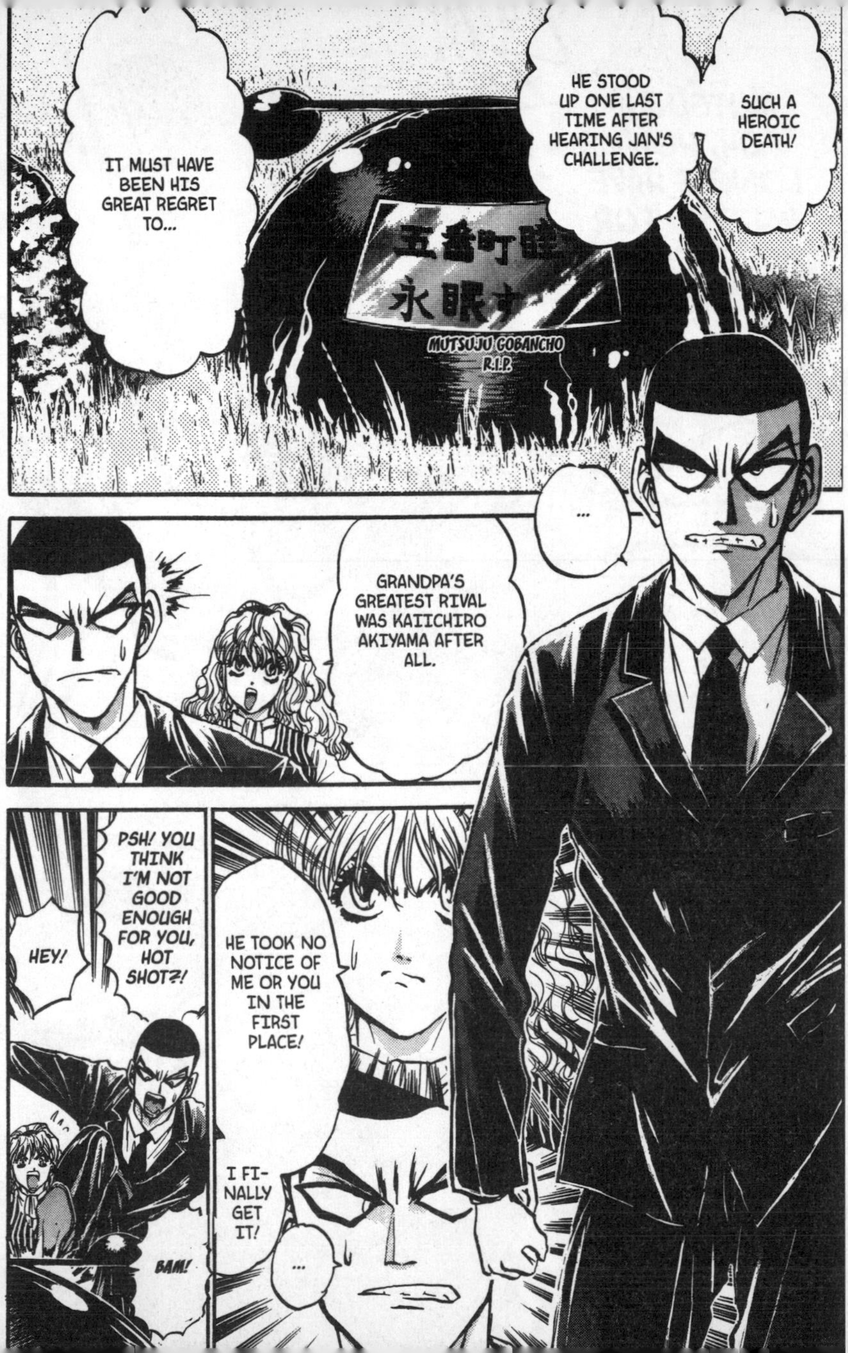
SUCH A HEROIC DEATH!
HE STOOD UP ONE LAST TIME AFTER HEARING JAN'S CHALLENGE.
IT MUST HAVE BEEN HIS GREAT REGRET TO...
五番町睦 永眠す
MUTSUJU GOBANCHO R.I.P.
...
GRANDPA'S GREATEST RIVAL WAS KAIICHIRO AKIYAMA AFTER ALL.
HE TOOK NO NOTICE OF ME OR YOU IN THE FIRST PLACE!
I FI-NALLY GET IT!
...
PSH! YOU THINK I'M NOT GOOD ENOUGH FOR YOU, HOT SHOT?!
HEY!
BAM!

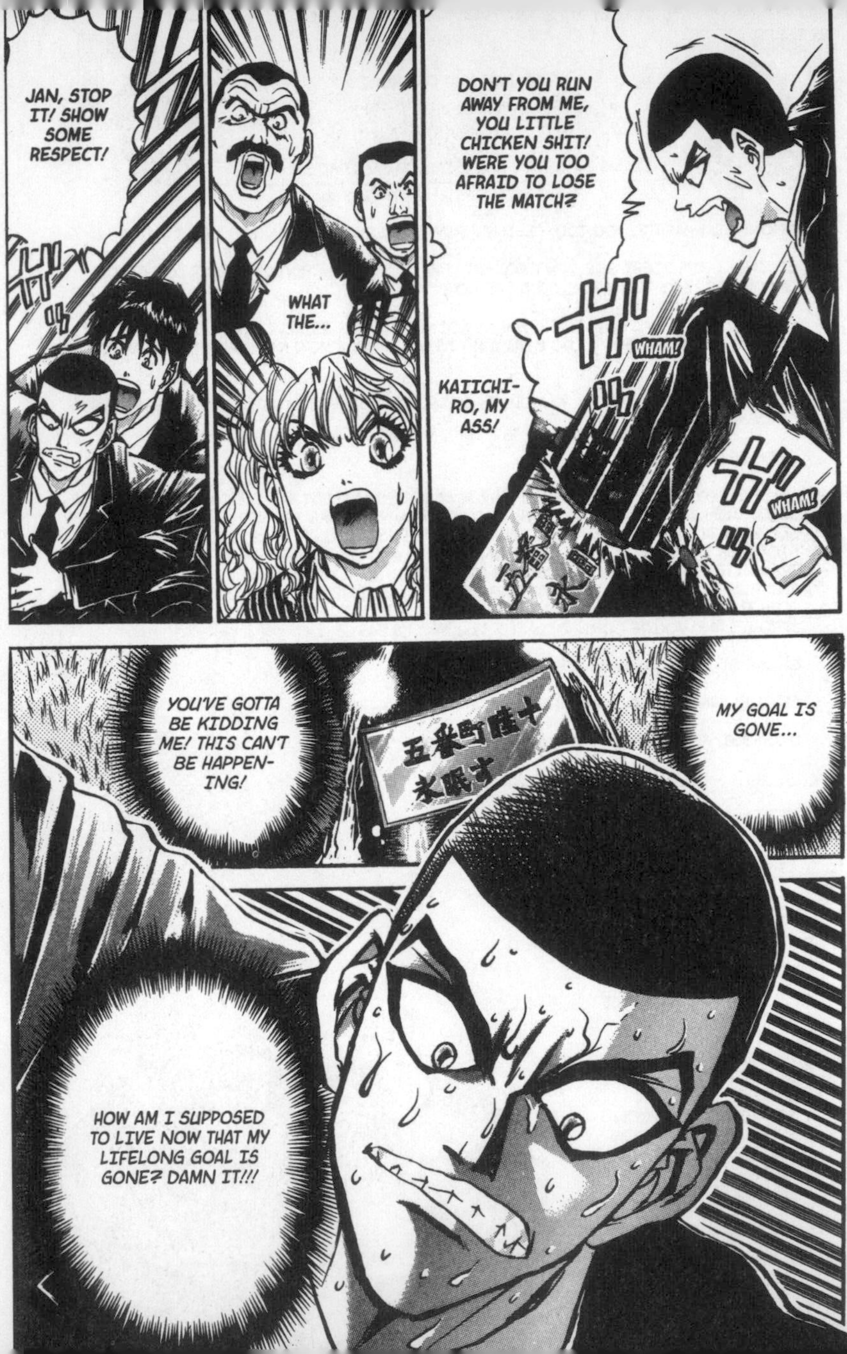
DON'T YOU RUN AWAY FROM ME, YOU LITTLE CHICKEN SHIT! WERE YOU TOO AFRAID TO LOSE THE MATCH?
WHAM!
KAIICHI-RO, MY ASS!
WHAM!
WHAT THE...
JAN, STOP IT! SHOW SOME RESPECT!
MY GOAL IS GONE...
YOU'VE GOTTA BE KIDDING ME! THIS CAN'T BE HAPPEN-ING!
HOW AM I SUPPOSED TO LIVE NOW THAT MY LIFELONG GOAL IS GONE? DAMN IT!!!

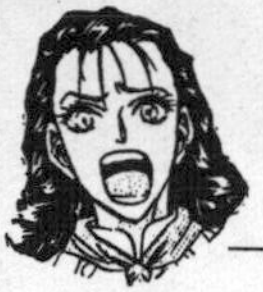

CELINE AND OKONOGI'S

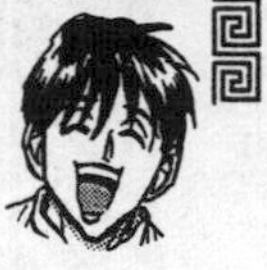

LIANG BAN XIAN BEI (SCALLOP SASHIMI SALAD)

OKONOGI: WHAAAT?! YOU TOO, CELINE? WHY IS EVERYONE TRYING TO TEACH ME?

CELINE: THAT'S RIGHT. YOU AIN'T GOT NO TIME TO WASTE WATCHIN' TV. THIS IS THE LAST OPPORTUNITY TO TEACH YOU, SO WE'RE GOIN' ALL OUT.

OKONOGI: I KNEW IT. SO, THAT'S WHAT'S GOING ON... ALL RIGHT, CELINE. I'M READY FOR ANYTHING. A MAN'S GOT TO DO WHAT A MAN'S GOTTA DO. C'MON NOW, SHOW ME WHAT YOU'VE GOT.

CELINE: THAT'S THE SPIRIT! MY DISH IS CALLED LIANG BAN XIAN BEI. IT'S REALLY SIMPLE, SO DON'T YOU FORGET IT!

OKONOGI: YOU BET!

CELINE: FIRST, GET SOME SASHIMI-GRADE SCALLOPS AND CUT OFF THE TOUGH PART AND SLICE THEM INTO THREE PIECES VERTICALLY. THEN YOU MAKE THE MARINADE AND PUT THE SLICED SCALLOPS IN. MARINATE THEM FOR 30 MINUTES TO AN HOUR, STIRRING OCCASIONALLY. IN THE MEANTIME, JULIENNE CARROT AND GREEN PEPPER AFTER TAKING OUT THE WHITE LINING INSIDE. WASH THE BEAN SPROUTS, REMOVE THE SEED AND THE ROOT, AND BLANCH THEM AND YOU'RE ALMOST DONE. ALL YOU NEED TO DO NOW IS PUT THE CARROTS IN THE MARINADE AND MIX WELL, AND THEN MIX IN THE GREEN PEPPER AND BEAN SPROUTS AND YOU'RE DONE! DIDN'T I TELL YA IT'S EASY?

OKONOGI: YOU SURE DID! AND IT'S DELISH!

CELINE: JAN, KIRIKO! I'M DONE, TOO!

OKONOGI: NOOOO! DON'T TELL ME THERE'S MORE!!

INGREDIENTS:
SCALLOPS (SASHIMI-GRADE): 10 PIECES
BEAN SPROUTS: 50 GRAMS
CARROT: 1/3
GREEN PEPPER: 3
MARINADE:
SOY SAUCE: 1 TABLESPOON
SUGAR: 1?2 TEASPOON
VINEGAR: 1?2 TEASPOON
SESAME OIL: 1 TEASPOON
GINGER EXTRACT: 1/2 TABLE SPOON
LAYU CHILI OIL TO TASTE

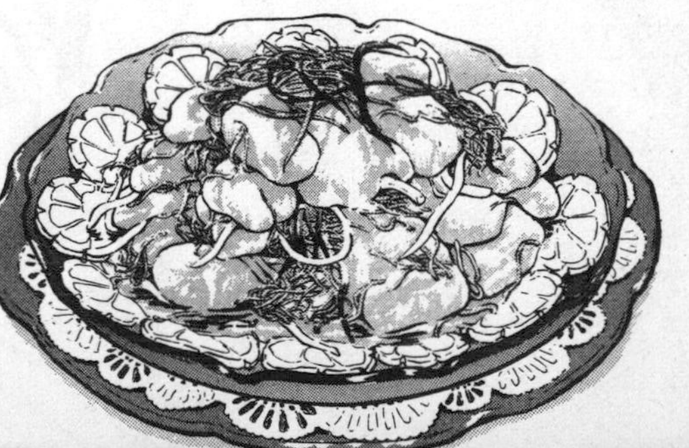

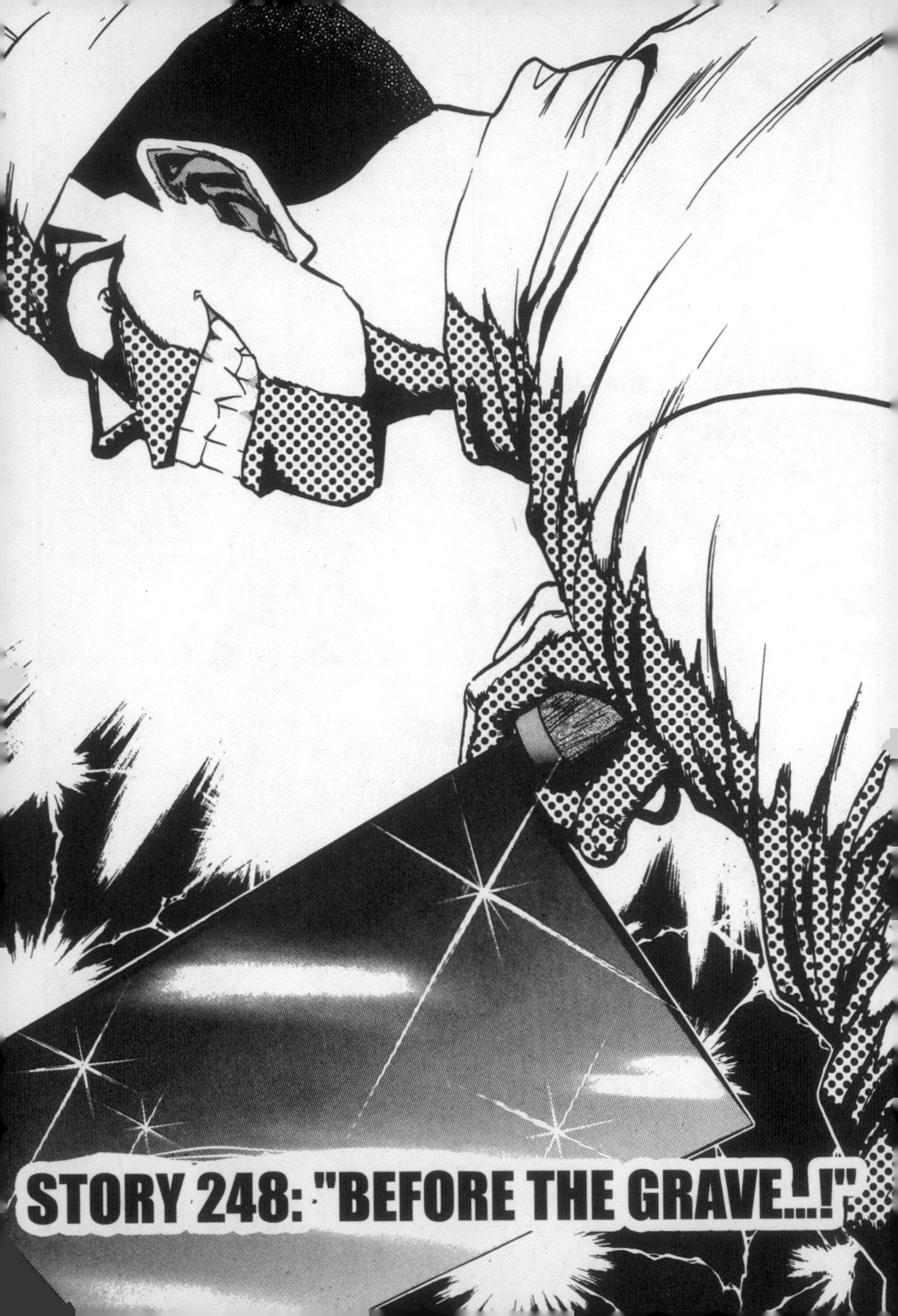
STORY 248: "BEFORE THE GRAVE...!"

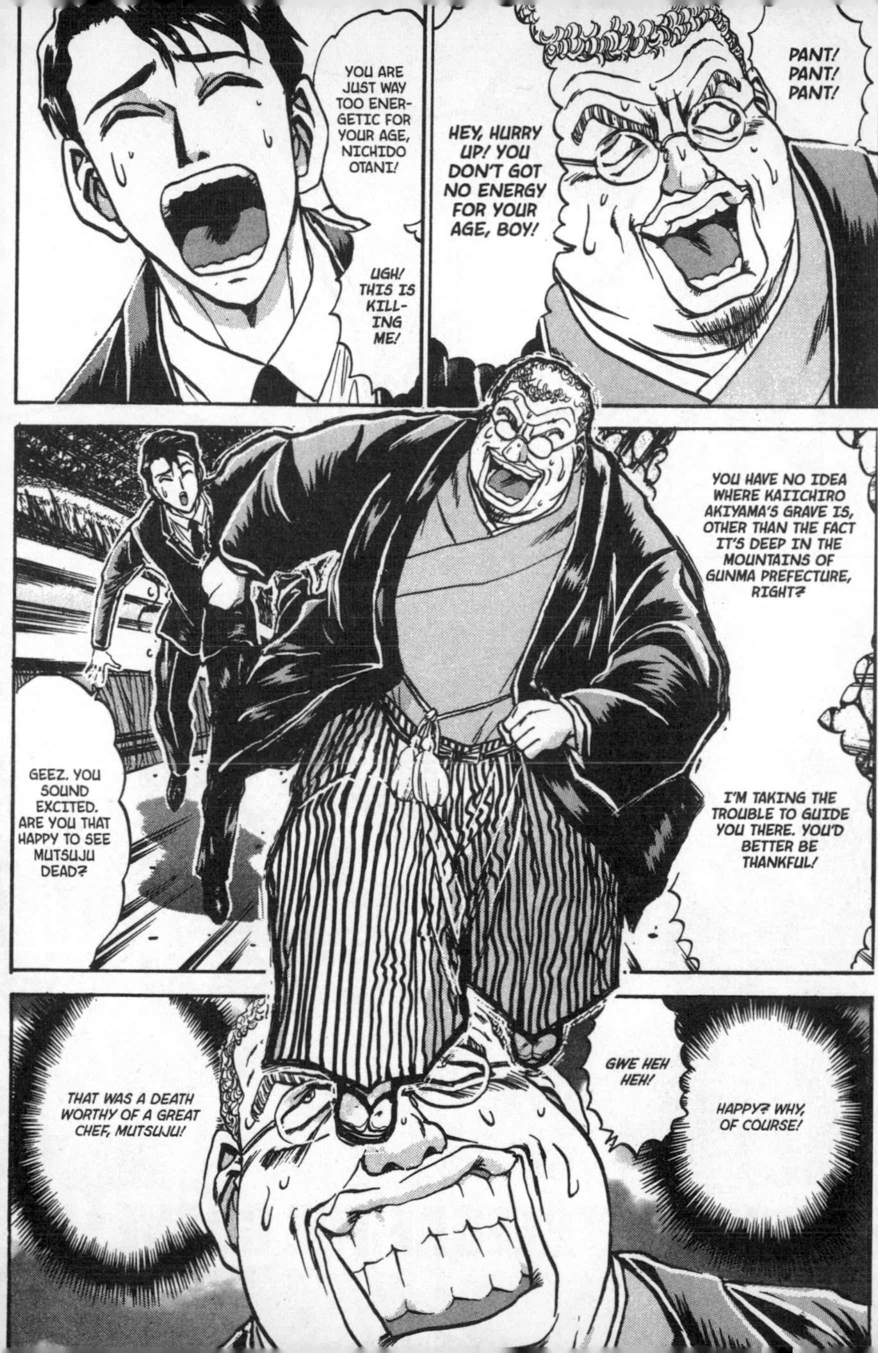
PANT! PANT! PANT!
HEY, HURRY UP! YOU DON'T GOT NO ENERGY FOR YOUR AGE, BOY!
YOU ARE JUST WAY TOO ENERGETIC FOR YOUR AGE, NICHIDO OTANI!
UGH! THIS IS KILLING ME!
YOU HAVE NO IDEA WHERE KAIICHIRO AKIYAMA'S GRAVE IS, OTHER THAN THE FACT IT'S DEEP IN THE MOUNTAINS OF GUNMA PREFECTURE, RIGHT?
I'M TAKING THE TROUBLE TO GUIDE YOU THERE. YOU'D BETTER BE THANKFUL!
GEEZ. YOU SOUND EXCITED. ARE YOU THAT HAPPY TO SEE MUTSUJU DEAD?
GWE HEH HEH!
HAPPY? WHY, OF COURSE!
THAT WAS A DEATH WORTHY OF A GREAT CHEF, MUTSUJU!

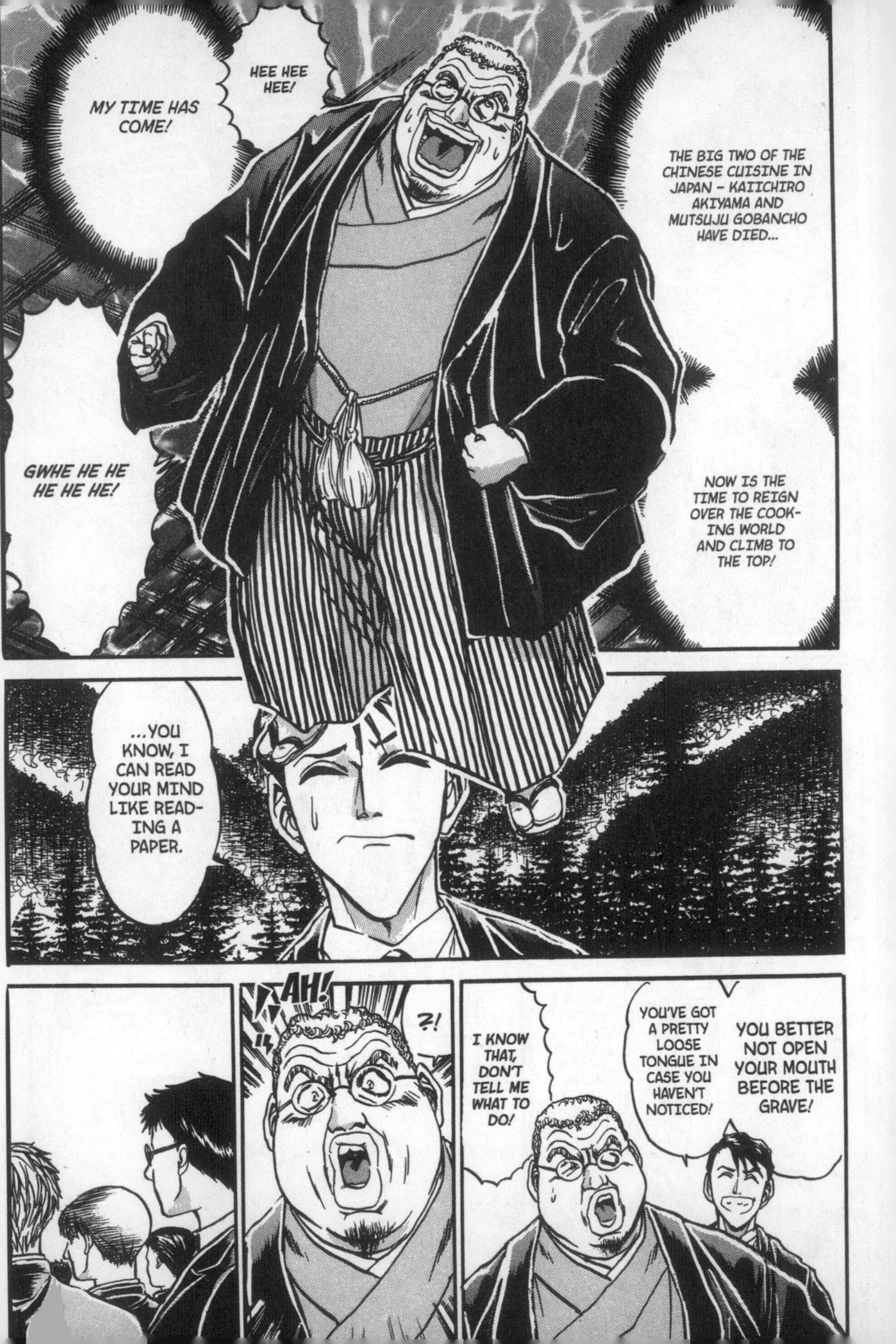
HEE HEE HEE!
MY TIME HAS COME!
THE BIG TWO OF THE CHINESE CUISINE IN JAPAN – KAIICHIRO AKIYAMA AND MUTSUJU GOBANCHO HAVE DIED...
NOW IS THE TIME TO REIGN OVER THE COOK-ING WORLD AND CLIMB TO THE TOP!
GWHE HE HE HE HE HE!
...YOU KNOW, I CAN READ YOUR MIND LIKE READ-ING A PAPER.
YOU BETTER NOT OPEN YOUR MOUTH BEFORE THE GRAVE!
YOU'VE GOT A PRETTY LOOSE TONGUE IN CASE YOU HAVEN'T NOTICED!
I KNOW THAT, DON'T TELL ME WHAT TO DO!
AH!
?!

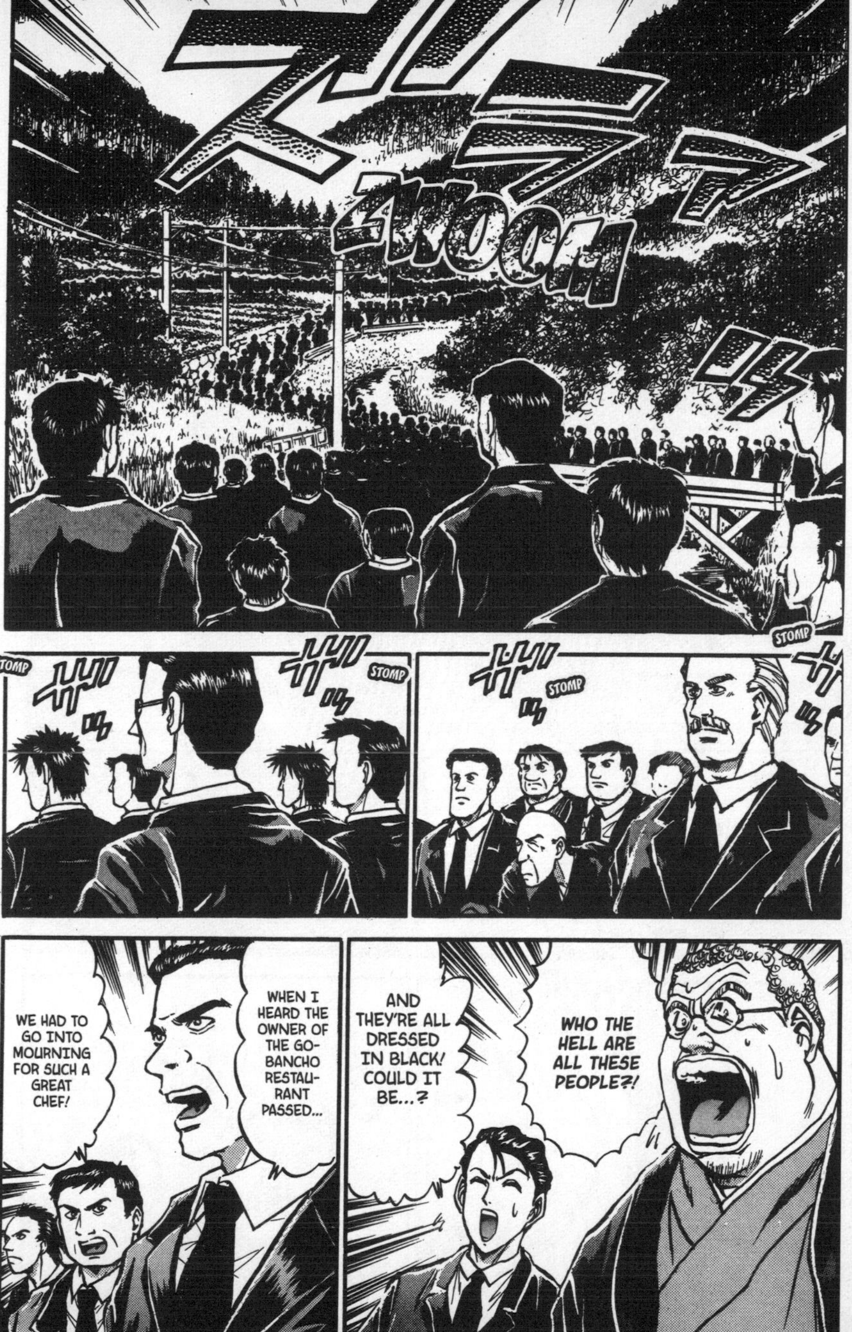

ZWOOM
STOMP
STOMP
STOMP
STOMP
WHO THE HELL ARE ALL THESE PEOPLE?!
AND THEY'RE ALL DRESSED IN BLACK! COULD IT BE...?
WHEN I HEARD THE OWNER OF THE GO-BANCHO RESTAU-RANT PASSED...
WE HAD TO GO INTO MOURNING FOR SUCH A GREAT CHEF!

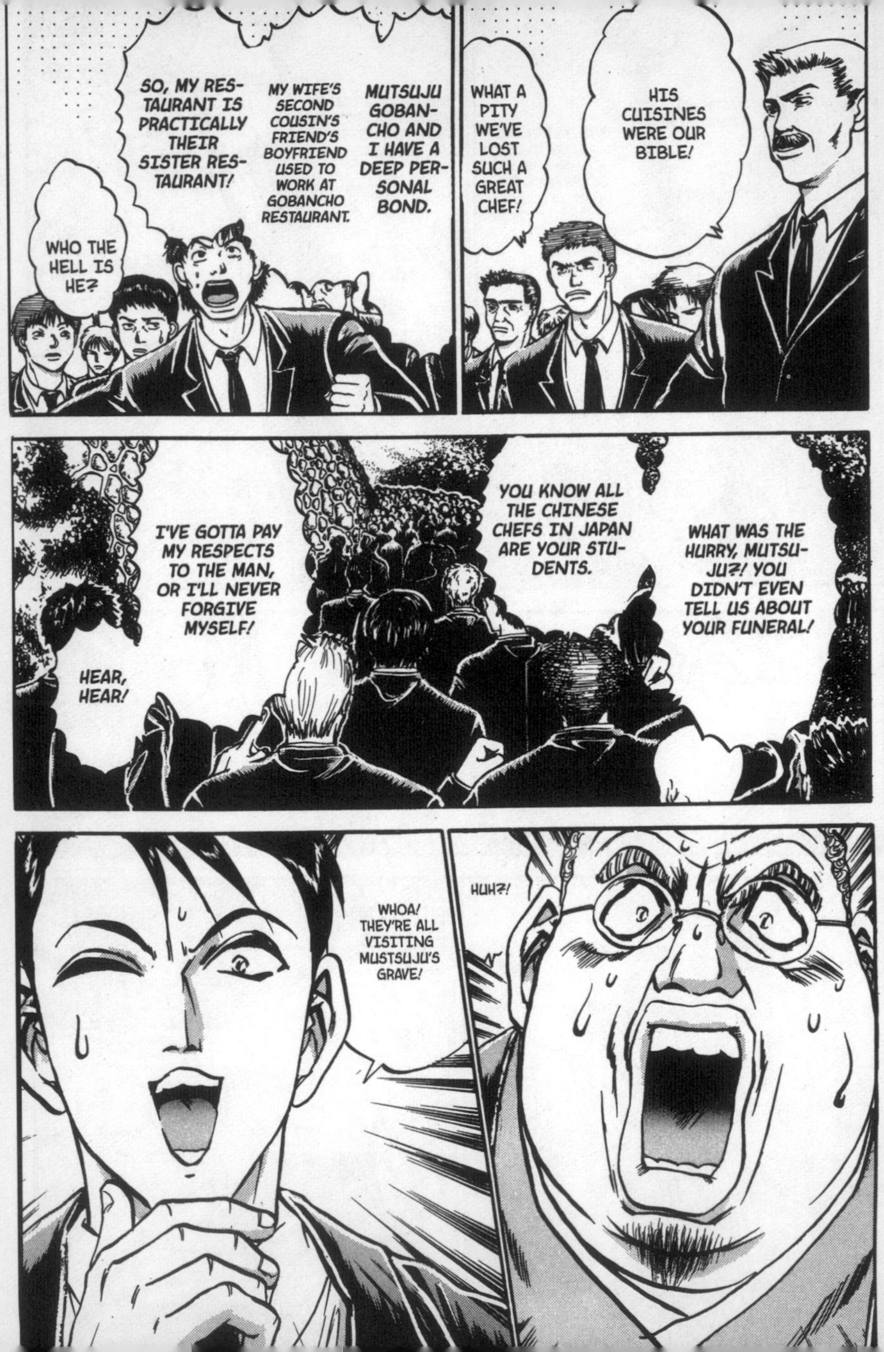

HIS CUISINES WERE OUR BIBLE!
WHAT A PITY WE'VE LOST SUCH A GREAT CHEF!
MUTSUJU GOBANCHO AND I HAVE A DEEP PERSONAL BOND.
MY WIFE'S SECOND COUSIN'S FRIEND'S BOYFRIEND USED TO WORK AT GOBANCHO RESTAURANT.
SO, MY RESTAURANT IS PRACTICALLY THEIR SISTER RESTAURANT!
WHO THE HELL IS HE?
WHAT WAS THE HURRY, MUTSUJU?! YOU DIDN'T EVEN TELL US ABOUT YOUR FUNERAL!
YOU KNOW ALL THE CHINESE CHEFS IN JAPAN ARE YOUR STUDENTS.
I'VE GOTTA PAY MY RESPECTS TO THE MAN, OR I'LL NEVER FORGIVE MYSELF!
HEAR, HEAR!
HUH?!
WHOA! THEY'RE ALL VISITING MUSTSUJU'S GRAVE!

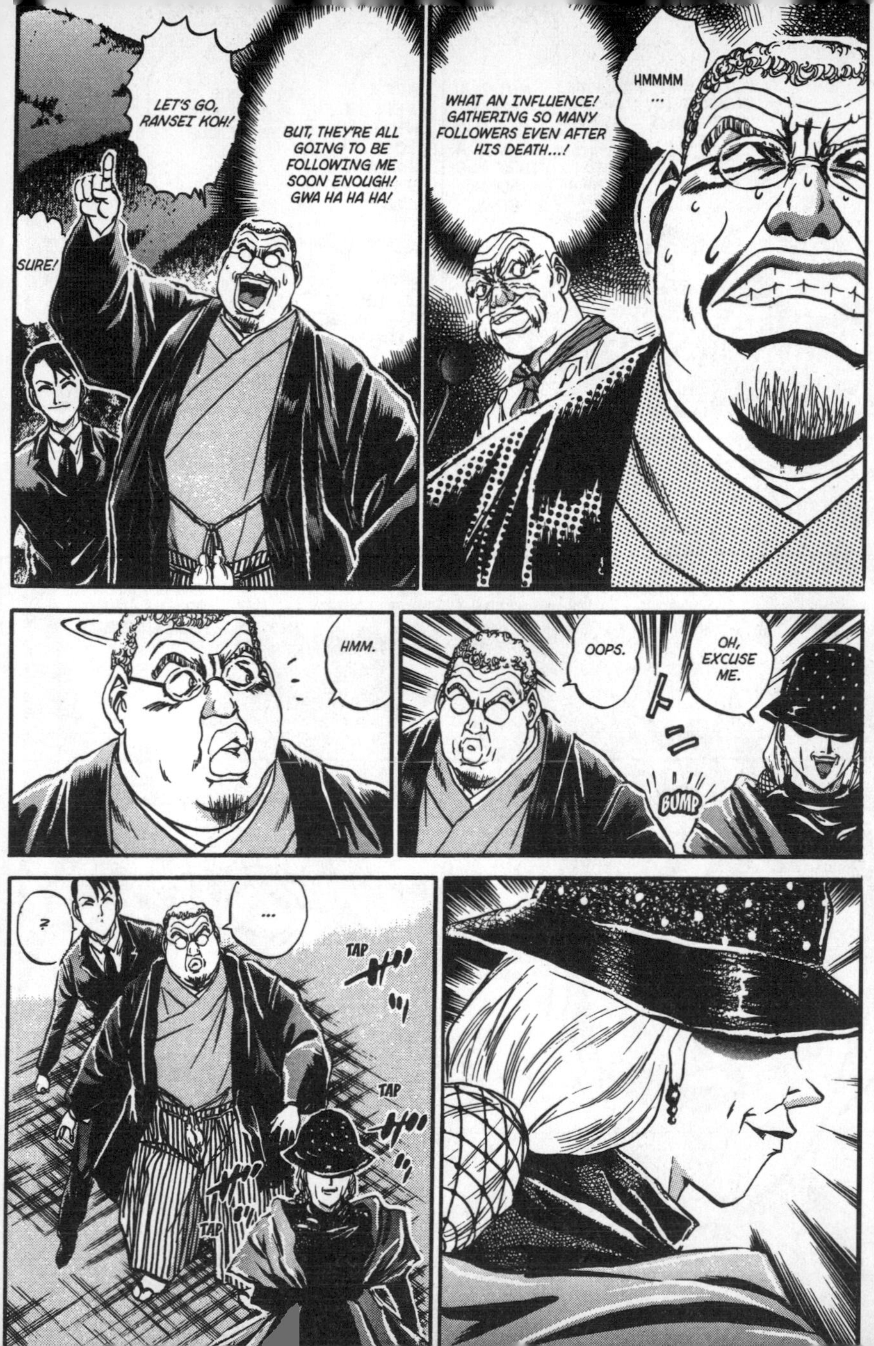
HMMMM ...
WHAT AN INFLUENCE! GATHERING SO MANY FOLLOWERS EVEN AFTER HIS DEATH...!
BUT, THEY'RE ALL GOING TO BE FOLLOWING ME SOON ENOUGH! GWA HA HA HA!
LET'S GO, RANSEI KOH!
SURE!
OH, EXCUSE ME.
OOPS.
BUMP
HMM.
...
?
TAP
TAP
TAP

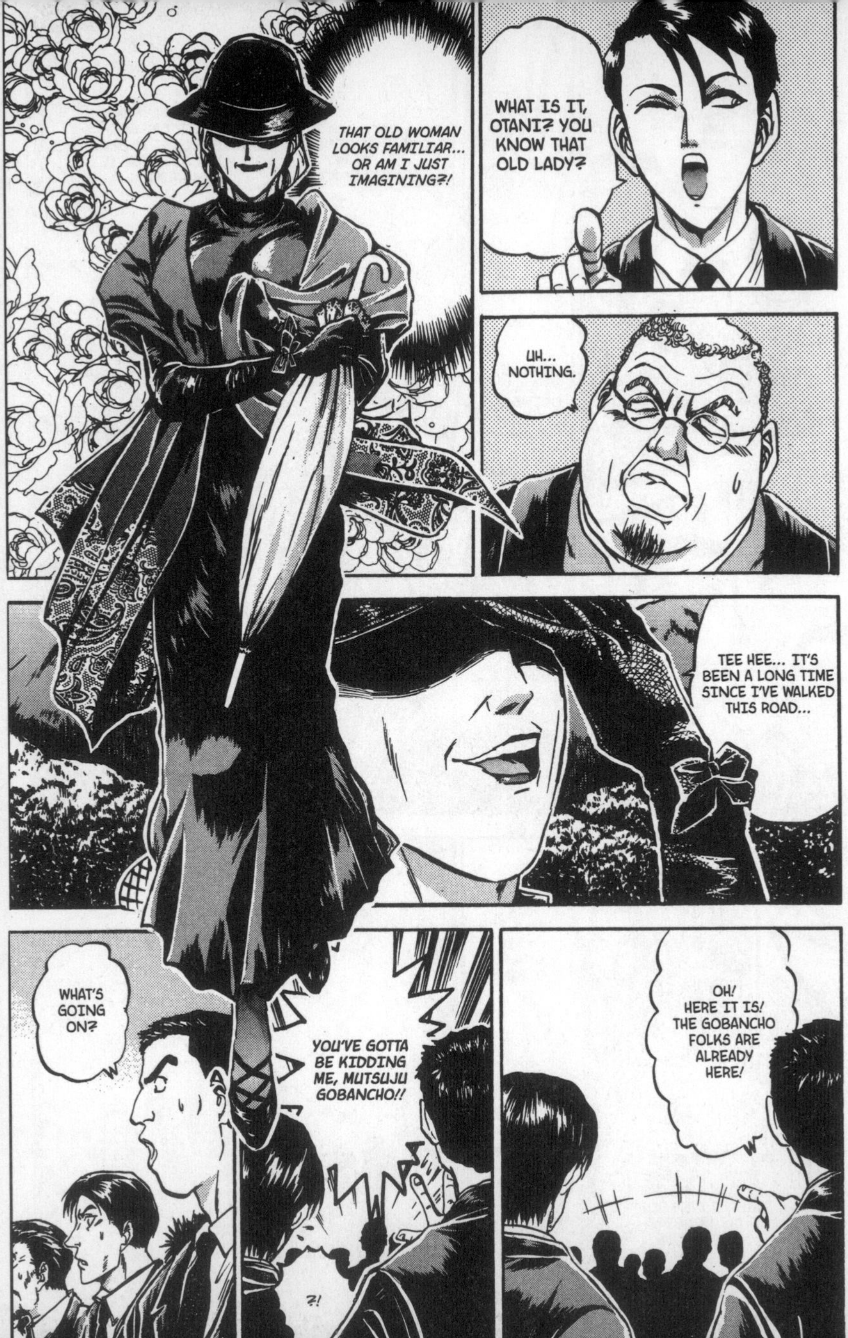

WHAT IS IT, OTANI? YOU KNOW THAT OLD LADY?
UH... NOTHING.
THAT OLD WOMAN LOOKS FAMILIAR... OR AM I JUST IMAGINING?!
TEE HEE... IT'S BEEN A LONG TIME SINCE I'VE WALKED THIS ROAD...
OH! HERE IT IS! THE GOBANCHO FOLKS ARE ALREADY HERE!
YOU'VE GOTTA BE KIDDING ME, MUTSUJU GOBANCHO!!
WHAT'S GOING ON?
?!

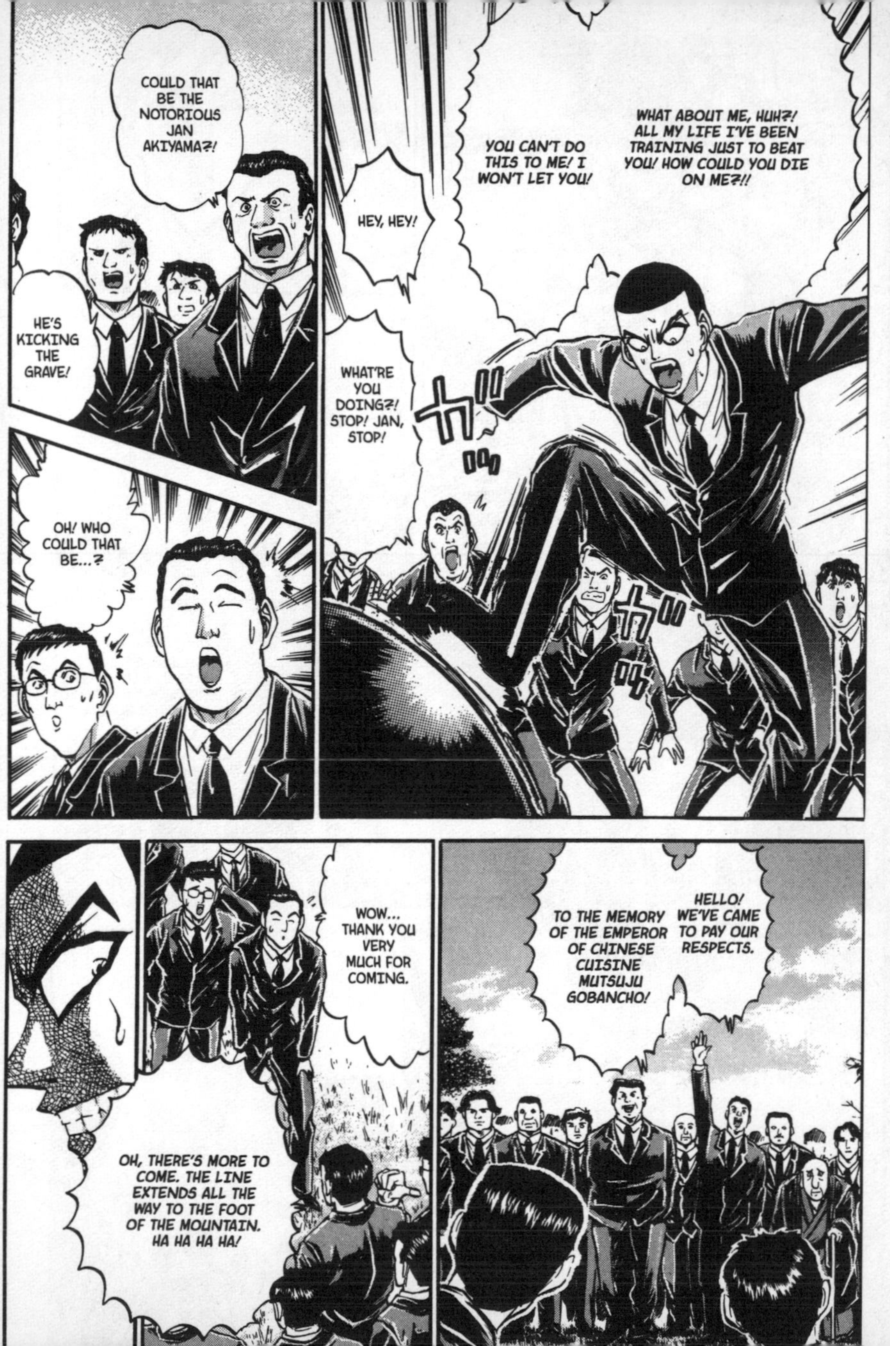
WHAT ABOUT ME, HUH?! ALL MY LIFE I'VE BEEN TRAINING JUST TO BEAT YOU! HOW COULD YOU DIE ON ME?!!
YOU CAN'T DO THIS TO ME! I WON'T LET YOU!
HEY, HEY!
WHAT'RE YOU DOING?! STOP! JAN, STOP!
COULD THAT BE THE NOTORIOUS JAN AKIYAMA?!
HE'S KICKING THE GRAVE!
OH! WHO COULD THAT BE...?
HELLO! WE'VE CAME TO PAY OUR RESPECTS.
TO THE MEMORY OF THE EMPEROR OF CHINESE CUISINE MUTSUJU GOBANCHO!
WOW... THANK YOU VERY MUCH FOR COMING.
OH, THERE'S MORE TO COME. THE LINE EXTENDS ALL THE WAY TO THE FOOT OF THE MOUNTAIN. HA HA HA HA!

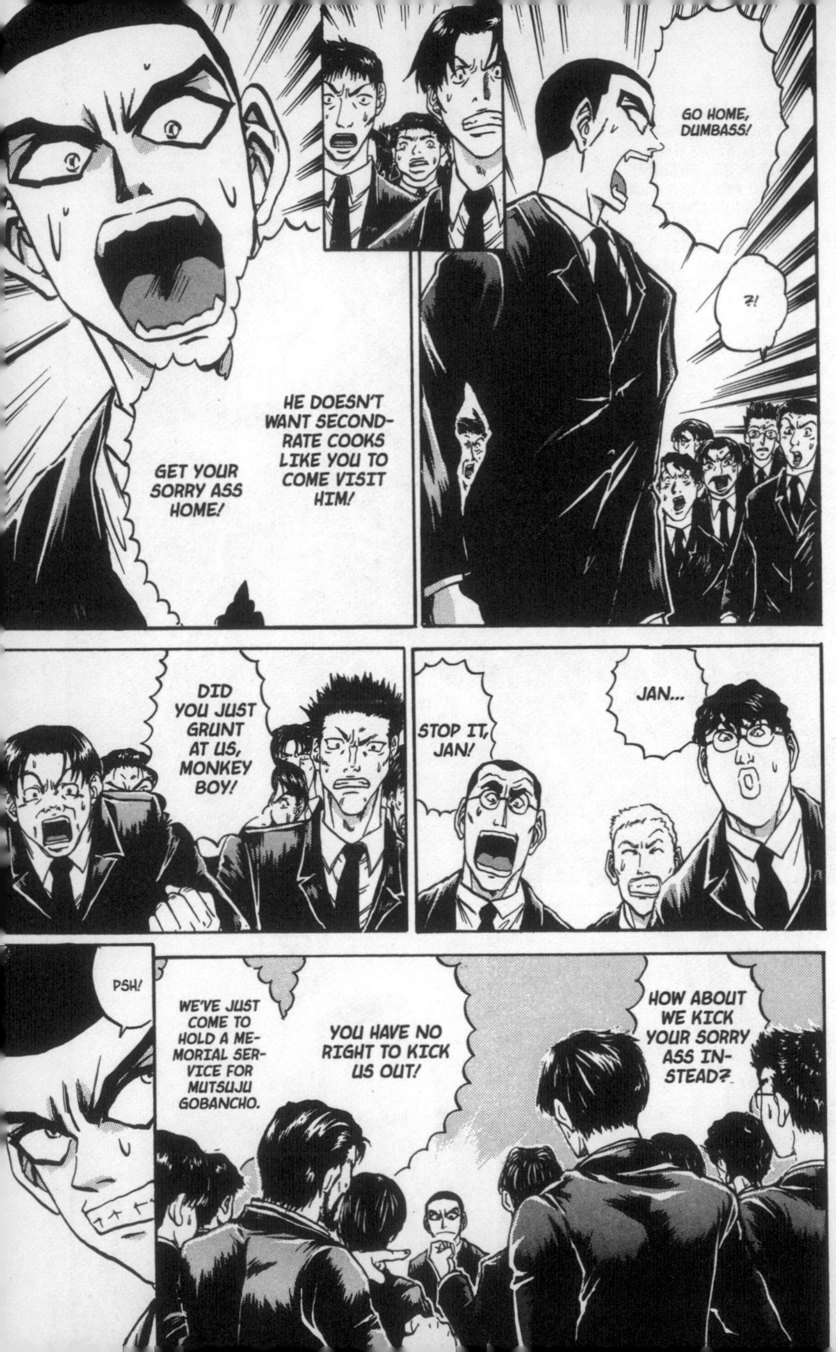
GO HOME, DUMBASS!
?!
HE DOESN'T WANT SECOND-RATE COOKS LIKE YOU TO COME VISIT HIM!
GET YOUR SORRY ASS HOME!
JAN...
STOP IT, JAN!
DID YOU JUST GRUNT AT US, MONKEY BOY!
HOW ABOUT WE KICK YOUR SORRY ASS INSTEAD?
YOU HAVE NO RIGHT TO KICK US OUT!
WE'VE JUST COME TO HOLD A MEMORIAL SERVICE FOR MUTSUJU GOBANCHO.
PSH!

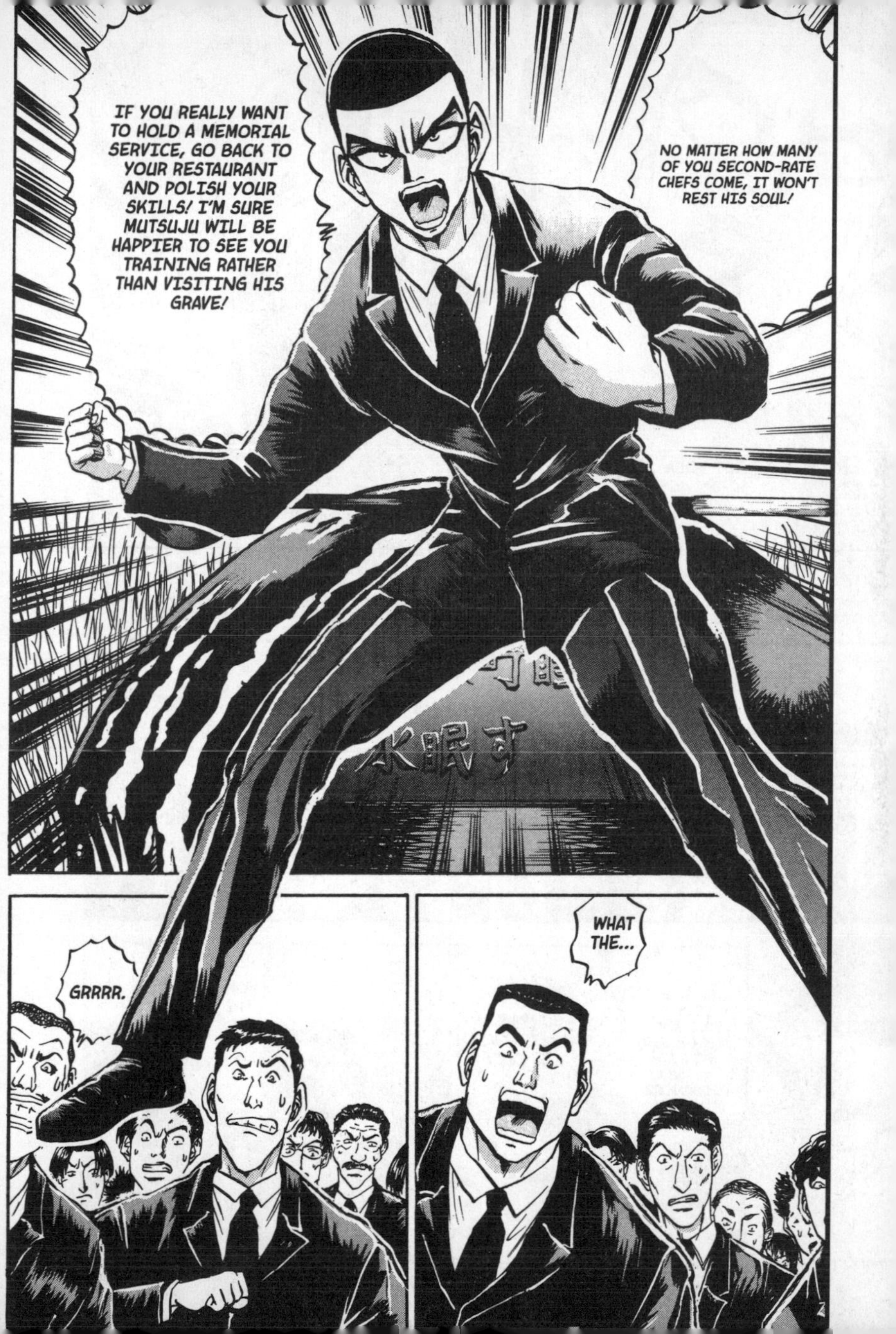
NO MATTER HOW MANY OF YOU SECOND-RATE CHEFS COME, IT WON'T REST HIS SOUL!
IF YOU REALLY WANT TO HOLD A MEMORIAL SERVICE, GO BACK TO YOUR RESTAURANT AND POLISH YOUR SKILLS! I'M SURE MUTSUJU WILL BE HAPPIER TO SEE YOU TRAINING RATHER THAN VISITING HIS GRAVE!
WHAT THE...
GRRRR.

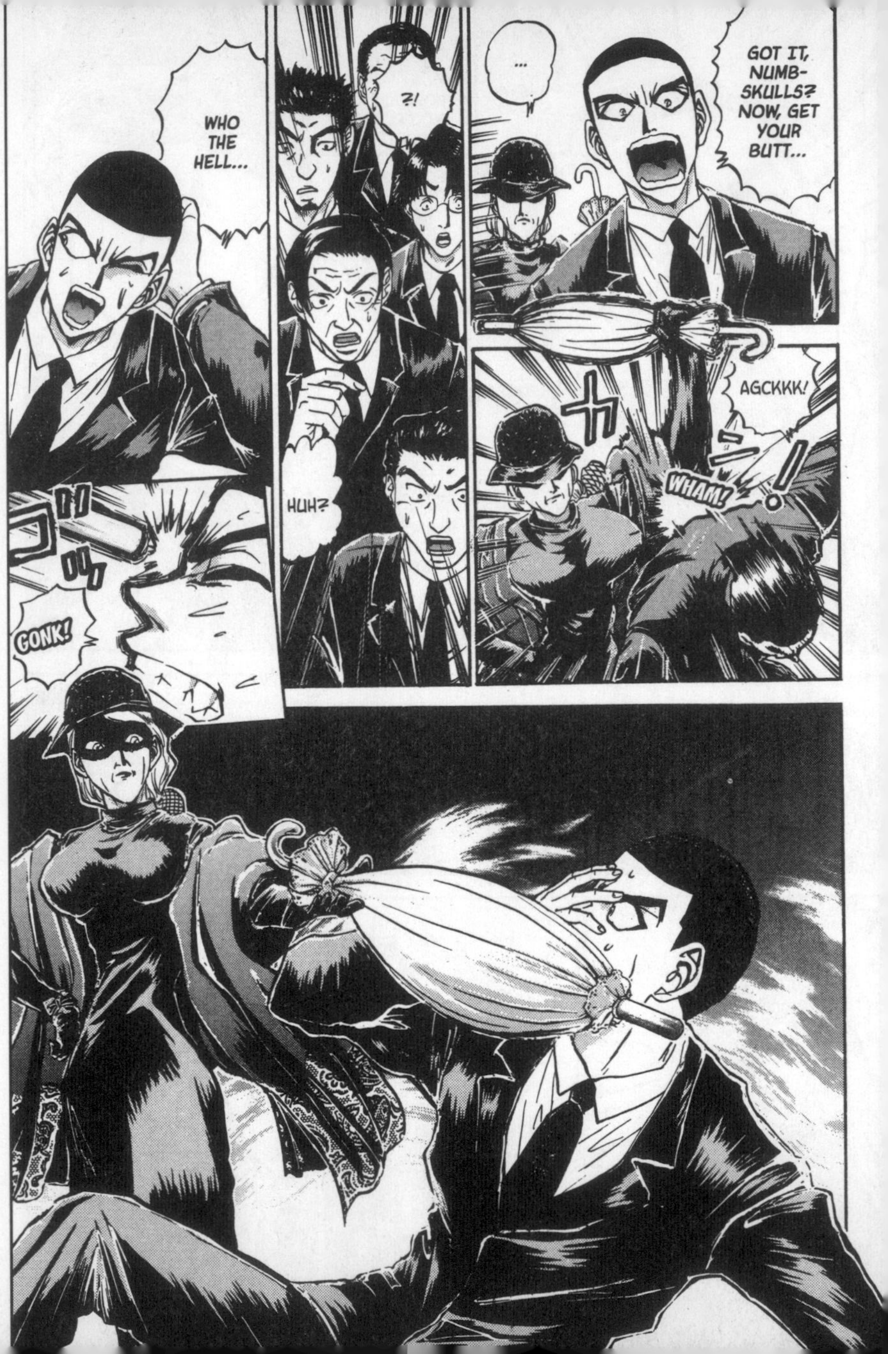

GOT IT, NUMB-SKULLS? NOW, GET YOUR BUTT...
...
AGCKKK!
WHAM!
?!
HUH?
WHO THE HELL...
GONK!

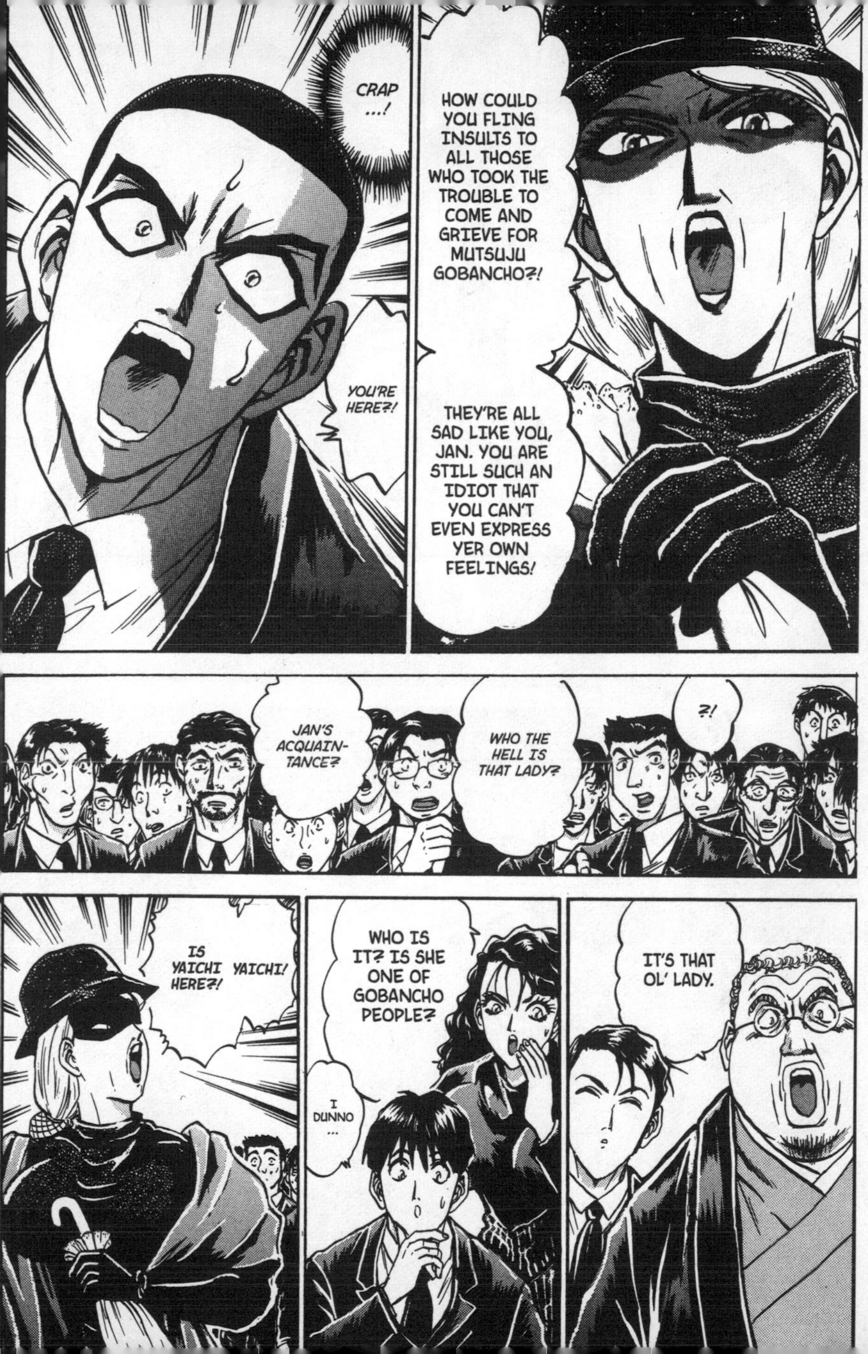

HOW COULD YOU FLING INSULTS TO ALL THOSE WHO TOOK THE TROUBLE TO COME AND GRIEVE FOR MUTSUJU GOBANCHO?!
THEY'RE ALL SAD LIKE YOU, JAN. YOU ARE STILL SUCH AN IDIOT THAT YOU CAN'T EVEN EXPRESS YER OWN FEELINGS!
CRAP ...!
YOU'RE HERE?!
?!
WHO THE HELL IS THAT LADY?
JAN'S ACQUAINTANCE?
IT'S THAT OL' LADY.
WHO IS IT? IS SHE ONE OF GOBANCHO PEOPLE?
I DUNNO ...
YAICHI!
IS YAICHI HERE?!

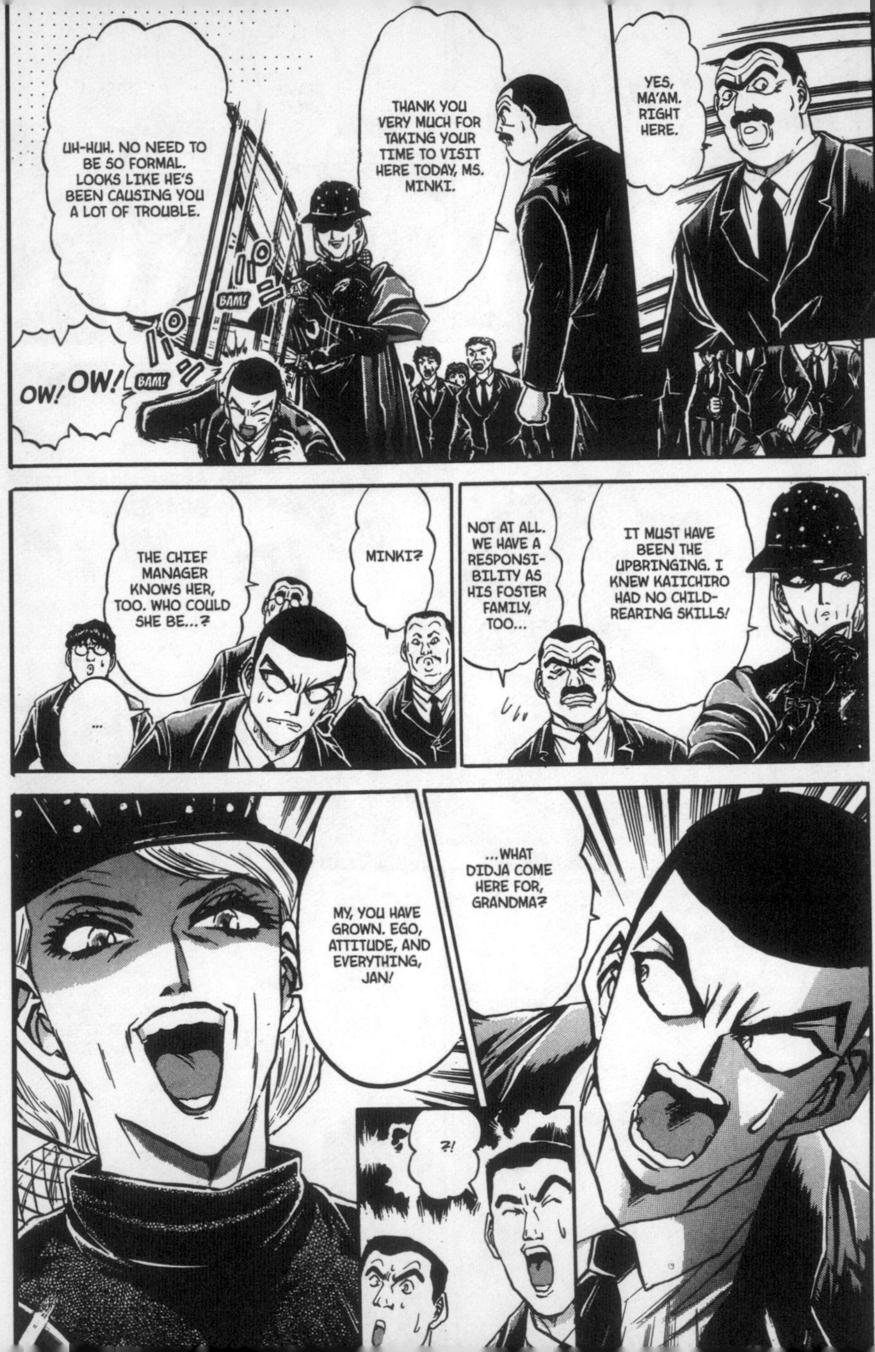
YES, MA'AM. RIGHT HERE.
THANK YOU VERY MUCH FOR TAKING YOUR TIME TO VISIT HERE TODAY, MS. MINKI.
UH-HUH. NO NEED TO BE SO FORMAL. LOOKS LIKE HE'S BEEN CAUSING YOU A LOT OF TROUBLE.
BAM!
BAM!
OW! OW!
IT MUST HAVE BEEN THE UPBRINGING. I KNEW KAIICHIRO HAD NO CHILD-REARING SKILLS!
NOT AT ALL. WE HAVE A RESPONSI-BILITY AS HIS FOSTER FAMILY, TOO...
MINKI?
THE CHIEF MANAGER KNOWS HER, TOO. WHO COULD SHE BE...?
...
...WHAT DIDJA COME HERE FOR, GRANDMA?
MY, YOU HAVE GROWN. EGO, ATTITUDE, AND EVERYTHING, JAN!
?!

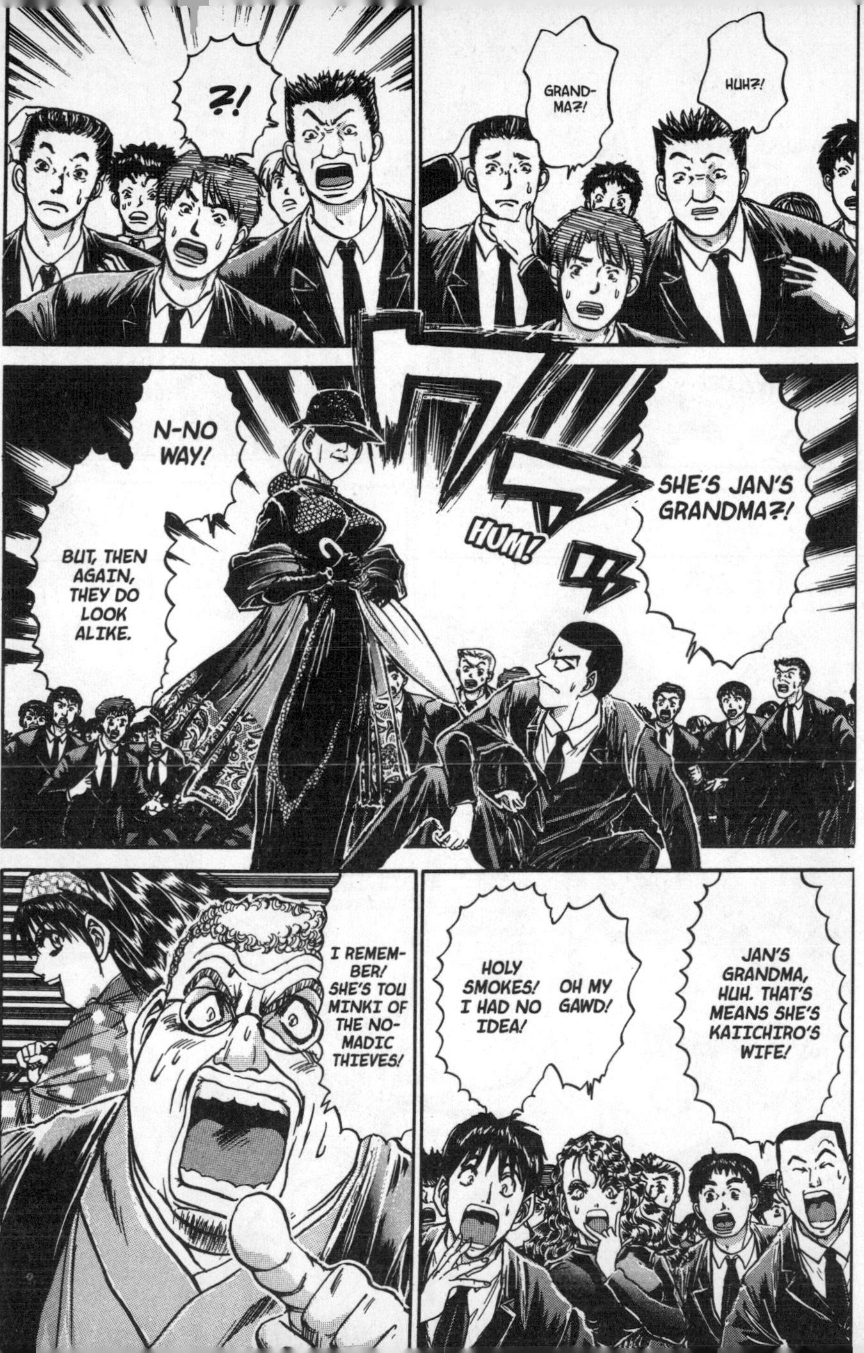
HUH?!
GRAND-MA?!
?!
SHE'S JAN'S GRANDMA?!
HUM!
N-NO WAY!
BUT, THEN AGAIN, THEY DO LOOK ALIKE.
JAN'S GRANDMA, HUH. THAT'S MEANS SHE'S KAIICHIRO'S WIFE!
OH MY GAWD!
HOLY SMOKES! I HAD NO IDEA!
I REMEM-BER! SHE'S TOU MINKI OF THE NO-MADIC THIEVES!

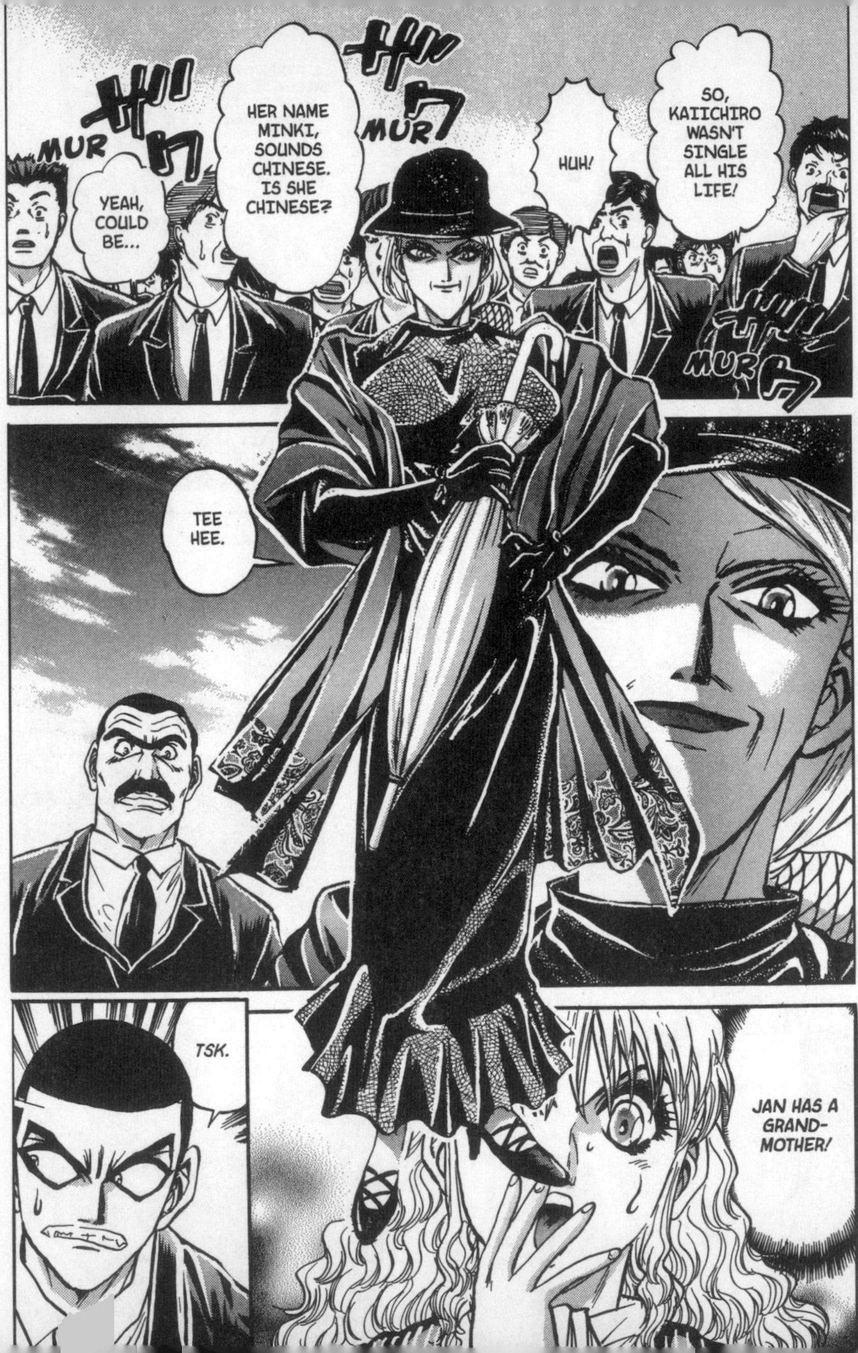
MUR
SO, KAIICHIRO WASN'T SINGLE ALL HIS LIFE!
HUH!
MUR
HER NAME MINKI, SOUNDS CHINESE. IS SHE CHINESE?
MUR
YEAH, COULD BE...
TEE HEE.
JAN HAS A GRAND-MOTHER!
TSK.

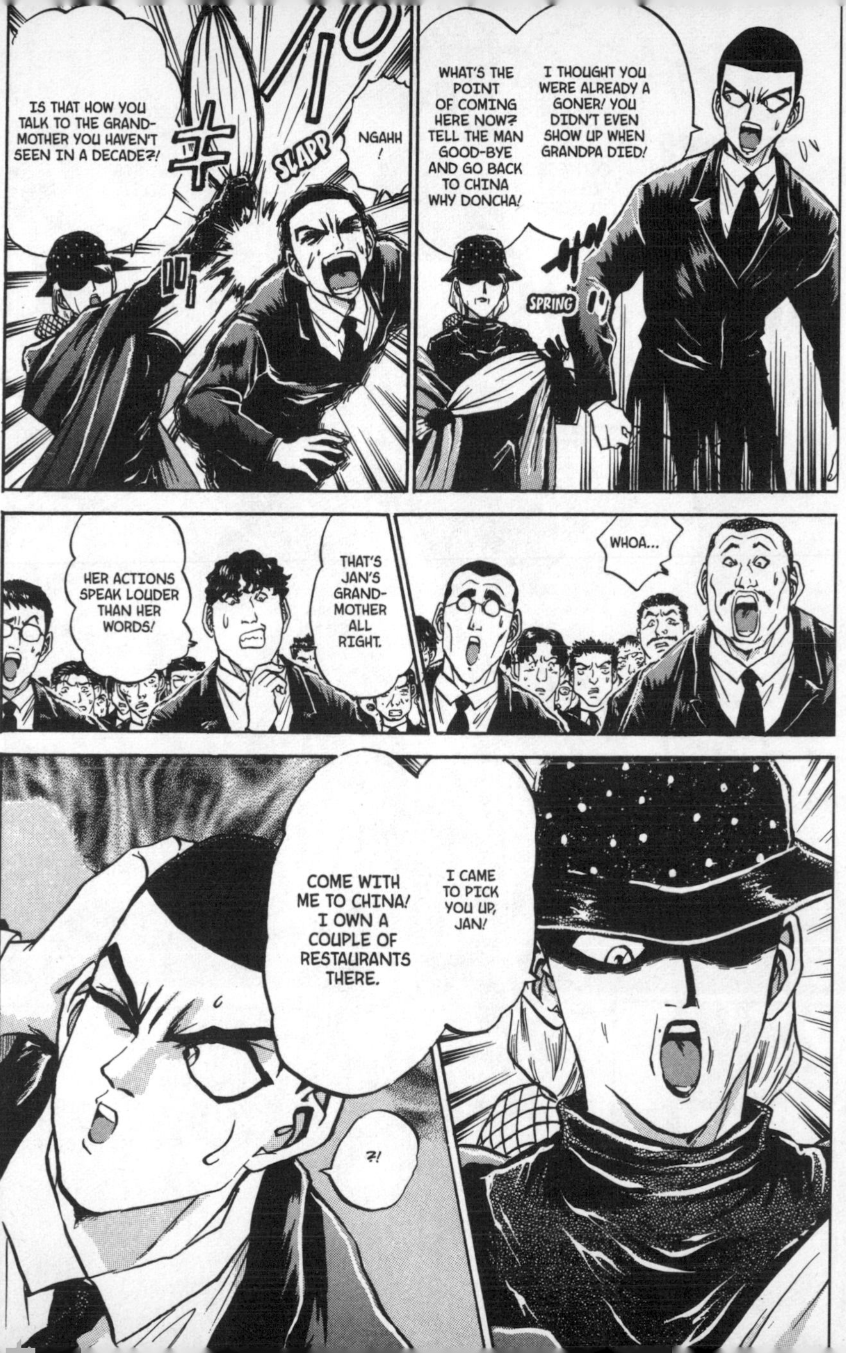
I THOUGHT YOU WERE ALREADY A GONER! YOU DIDN'T EVEN SHOW UP WHEN GRANDPA DIED!
WHAT'S THE POINT OF COMING HERE NOW? TELL THE MAN GOOD-BYE AND GO BACK TO CHINA WHY DONCHA!
SPRING
NGAHH!
SLAPP
IS THAT HOW YOU TALK TO THE GRAND-MOTHER YOU HAVEN'T SEEN IN A DECADE?!
WHOA...
THAT'S JAN'S GRAND-MOTHER ALL RIGHT.
HER ACTIONS SPEAK LOUDER THAN HER WORDS!
I CAME TO PICK YOU UP, JAN!
COME WITH ME TO CHINA! I OWN A COUPLE OF RESTAURANTS THERE.
?!

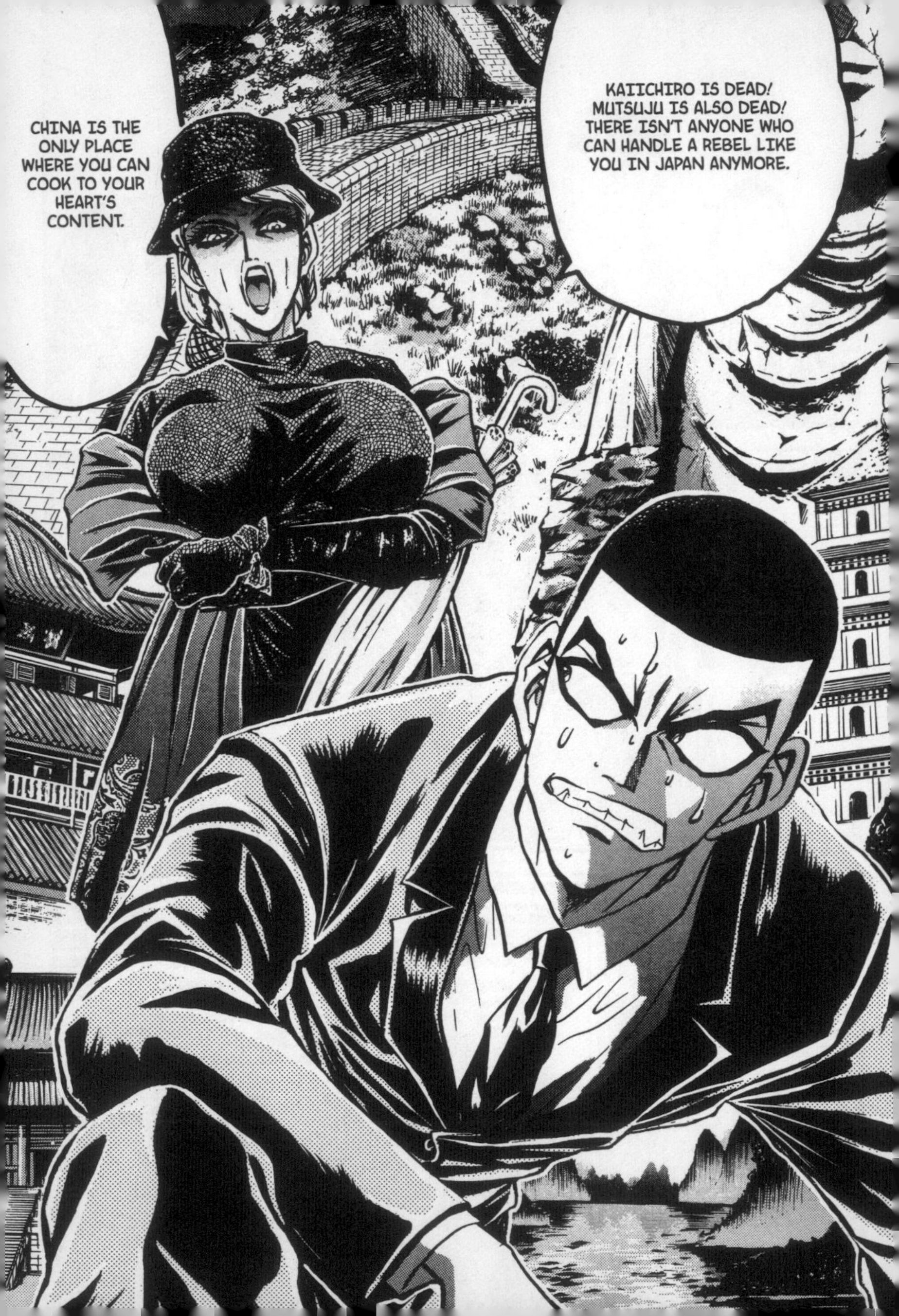
KAIICHIRO IS DEAD! MUTSUJU IS ALSO DEAD! THERE ISN'T ANYONE WHO CAN HANDLE A REBEL LIKE YOU IN JAPAN ANYMORE.
CHINA IS THE ONLY PLACE WHERE YOU CAN COOK TO YOUR HEART'S CONTENT.

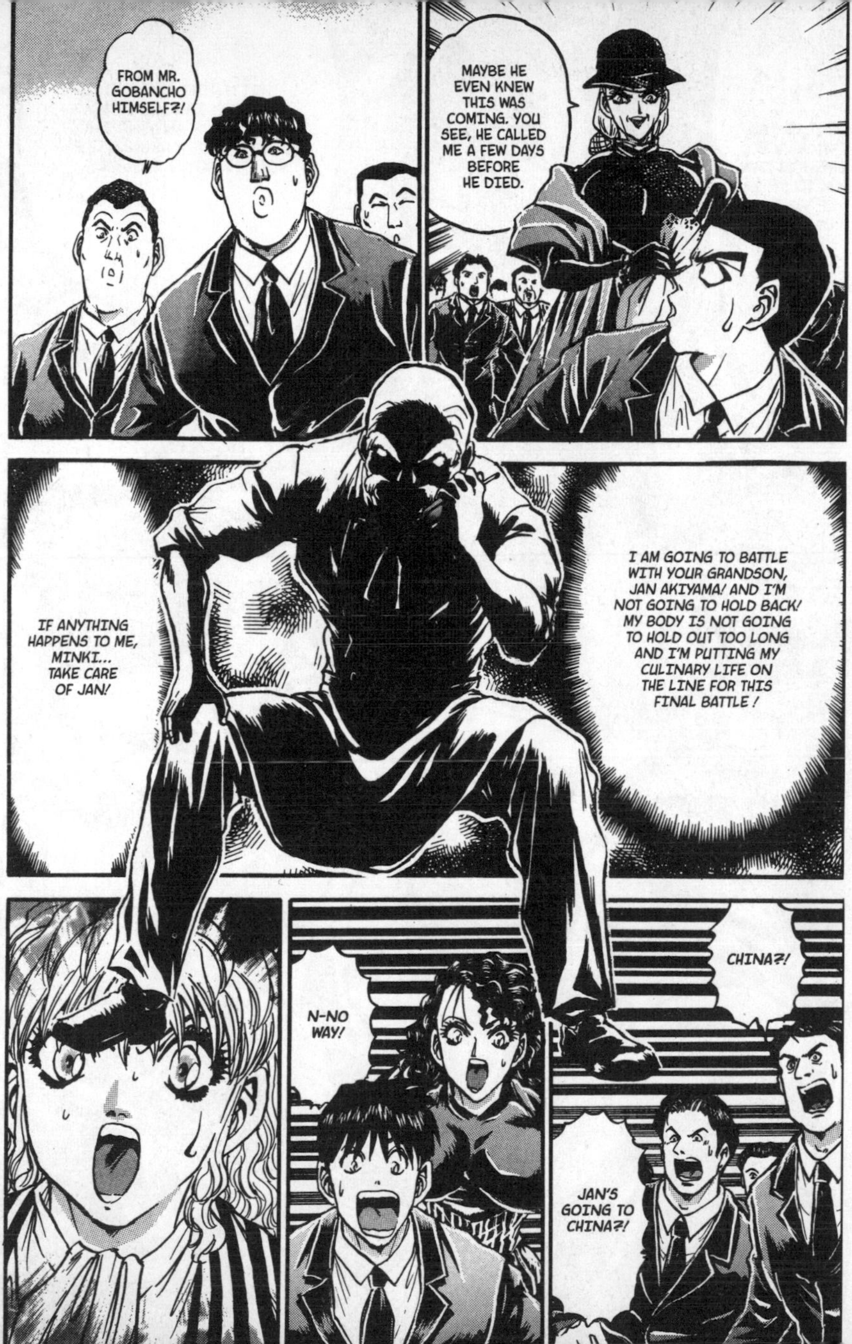
MAYBE HE EVEN KNEW THIS WAS COMING. YOU SEE, HE CALLED ME A FEW DAYS BEFORE HE DIED.
FROM MR. GOBANCHO HIMSELF?!
I AM GOING TO BATTLE WITH YOUR GRANDSON, JAN AKIYAMA! AND I'M NOT GOING TO HOLD BACK! MY BODY IS NOT GOING TO HOLD OUT TOO LONG AND I'M PUTTING MY CULINARY LIFE ON THE LINE FOR THIS FINAL BATTLE!
IF ANYTHING HAPPENS TO ME, MINKI... TAKE CARE OF JAN!
CHINA?!
JAN'S GOING TO CHINA?!
N-NO WAY!

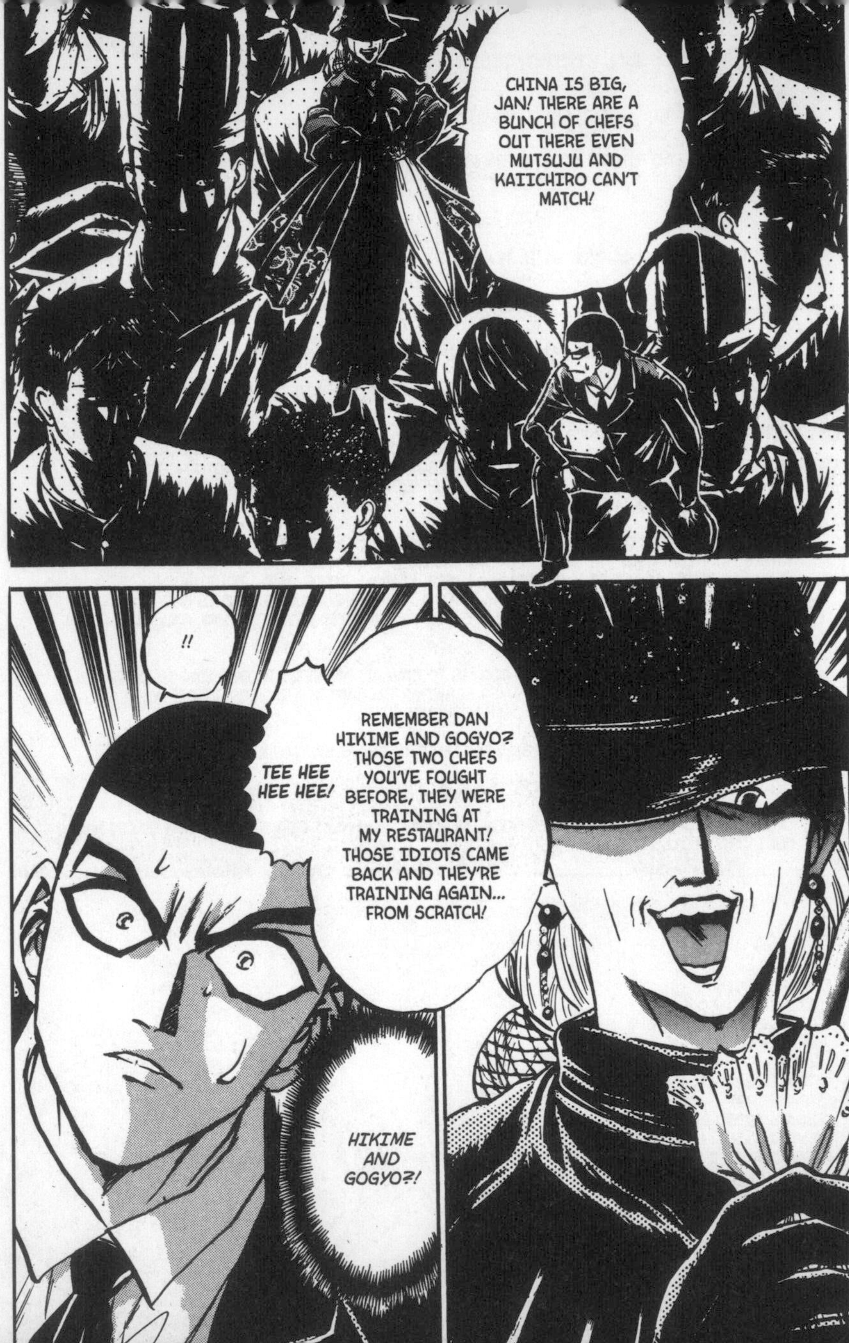
CHINA IS BIG, JAN! THERE ARE A BUNCH OF CHEFS OUT THERE EVEN MUTSUJU AND KAIICHIRO CAN'T MATCH!
REMEMBER DAN HIKIME AND GOGYO? THOSE TWO CHEFS YOU'VE FOUGHT BEFORE, THEY WERE TRAINING AT MY RESTAURANT! THOSE IDIOTS CAME BACK AND THEY'RE TRAINING AGAIN... FROM SCRATCH!
!!
TEE HEE HEE HEE!
HIKIME AND GOGYO?!

JAN, KIRIKO, CELINE, AND OKONOGI'S

CAO MEI XI MI LU (STRAWBERRY MILK WITH TAPIOCA)

JAN: THIS IS IT, OKONOGI! WE'LL TEACH YOU THE LAST DISH WHETHER YOU LIKE IT OR NOT!

KIRIKO: YUP. AND WHAT A WAY TO TOP OFF WITH A DESSERT!

CELINE: MMM-MMM! DON'T GET ME STARTED NOW! HERE WE GO, SUGAR!

OKONOGI: PLEASE, JUST SHOOT ME AND SUCK THE SPIRIT OUT OF MY LIMP DEAD BODY.

JAN: WE'RE MAKING CAO MEI XI MI LU. WE'RE GOING TO BOIL THE TAPIOCA UNTIL IT BECOMES TRANSLUCENT. ADD 3-5 TABLESPOONS OF SUGAR. YOU MIGHT NEED TO ADD MORE WATER, OR IF IT'S TOO SWEET, YOU MIGHT HAVE TO DUMP SOME OUT AND PUT BACK SOME WATER TO ADJUST THE SWEETNESS. THIS IS WHERE YOU NEED THE SKILLZ, OKO-NOGI. YOU KNOW WHAT I'M MEAN?

KIRIKO: WHEN THE TAPIOCA HAS BECOME COMPLETELY TRANSLUCENT, COOL IT IN WATER WHILE WASHING AWAY THE SLIME ON THE SURFACE. DRAIN AND PLACE THEM ON TO A SERVING PLATE. PLACE STRAWBERRIES, SUGAR, LEMON JUICE, AND LIQUEUR IN A BLENDER AND BLEND UNTIL IT TURNS INTO A PUREE. POUR INTO A BOWL AND ADD HEAVY CREAM AND MILK. MIX WELL AND CHILL IN THE FRIDGE. THAT'S HOW YOU MAKE STRAWBERRY MILK.

CELINE: HONEY, THERE AIN'T MUCH FOR ME TO SAY! ALL YA NEED TO DO NOW, IS POUR STRAWBERRY MILK INTO THE PLATE YER SERVING THE TAPIOCA IN, TOP IT OFF WITH A SCOOP OF ICE CREAM N' A SPRIG O' MINT. HOW'S IT?

OKONOGI: MM-MMM! UNBELIEVABLE! DEFINITELY BEATS WATCHING TV AT HOME!

CELINE: SHUT YO' MOUTH, OKONOGI. WHAT DIDJA REALLY WANT TO WATCH, REALLY?

OKONOGI: I WANTED TO WATCH A COOKING SHOW. YOU KNOW, SO I CAN BRUSH UP ON MY CULINARY SKILLS...

INGREDIENTS:
 TAPIOCA: 50-60 GRAM
 SUGAR: 3-5 TABLESPOON
 VANILLA ICE CREAM: AS
 NEEDED
 ⟨STRAWBERRY MILK⟩
 STRAWBERRY: 300 GRAM
 SUGAR: 40-50 GRAM
 LEMON JUICE: 1 TABLESPOON
 FRESH CREAM: 2 TABLESPOON
 MILK: 100 ML
 KUEI HUA CHEN CHIEW OR
 BRANDY: A LITTLE LESS THAN A
 TABLESPOON

* MAKE SURE TO ADJUST THE AMOUNT OF SUGAR ACCORDING TO THE SWEET-NESS OF THE BERRIES AND YOUR TASTE.
* ADDING ICE CREAM IS OPTIONAL. COCONUT FLAVOR WORKS THE BEST.

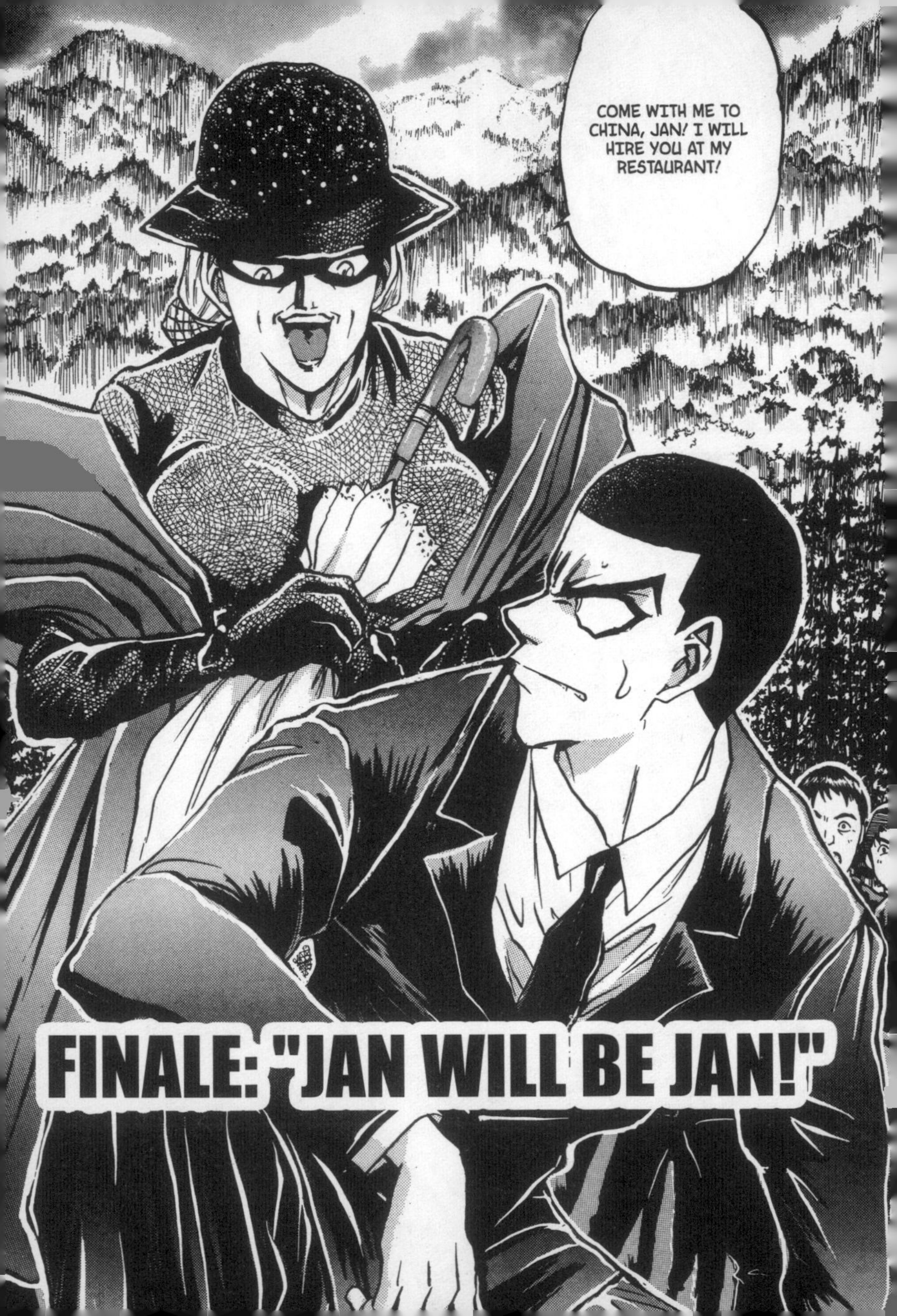
COME WITH ME TO CHINA, JAN! I WILL HIRE YOU AT MY RESTAURANT!
FINALE: "JAN WILL BE JAN!"

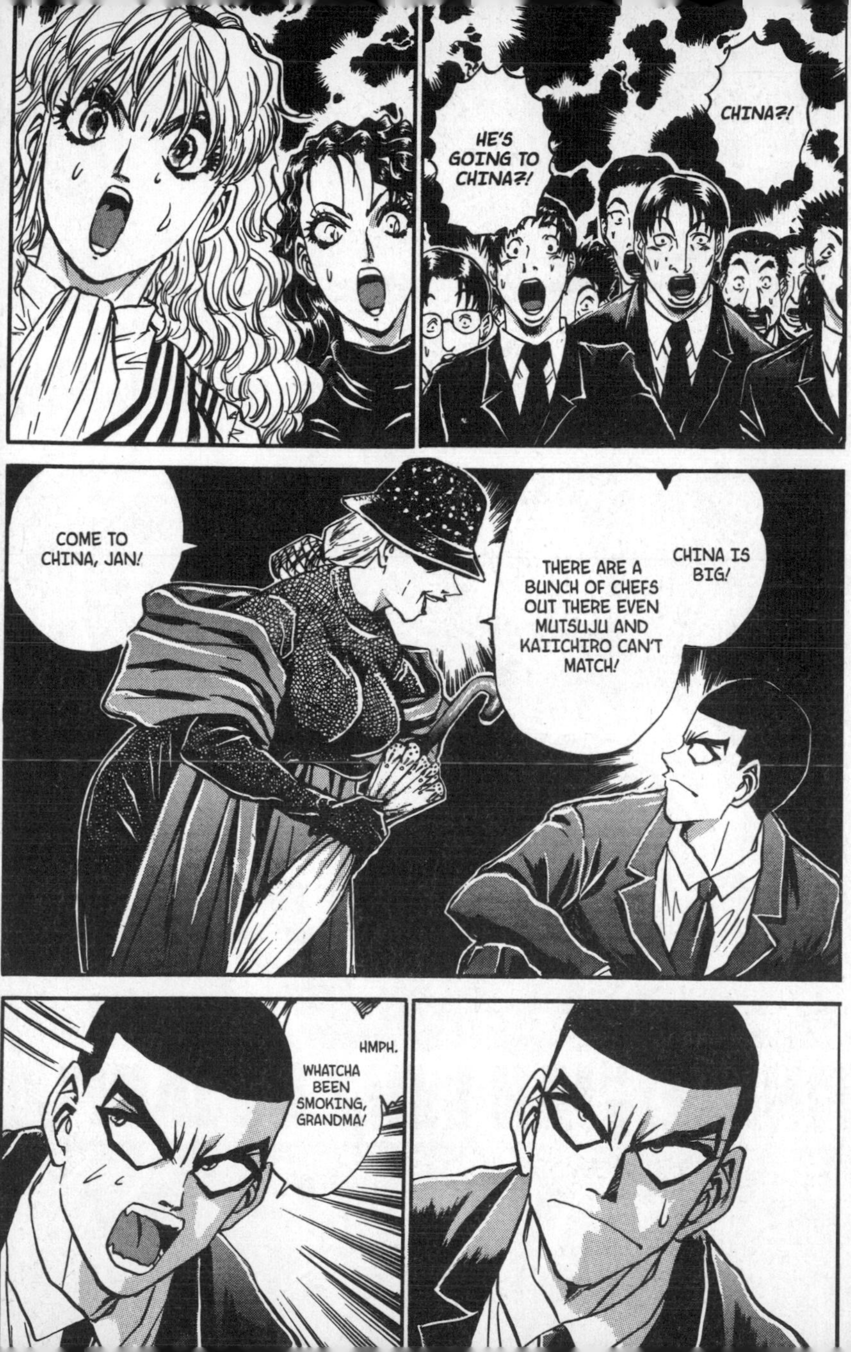
CHINA?!
HE'S GOING TO CHINA?!
CHINA IS BIG!
THERE ARE A BUNCH OF CHEFS OUT THERE EVEN MUTSUJU AND KAIICHIRO CAN'T MATCH!
COME TO CHINA, JAN!
HMPH.
WHATCHA BEEN SMOKING, GRANDMA!

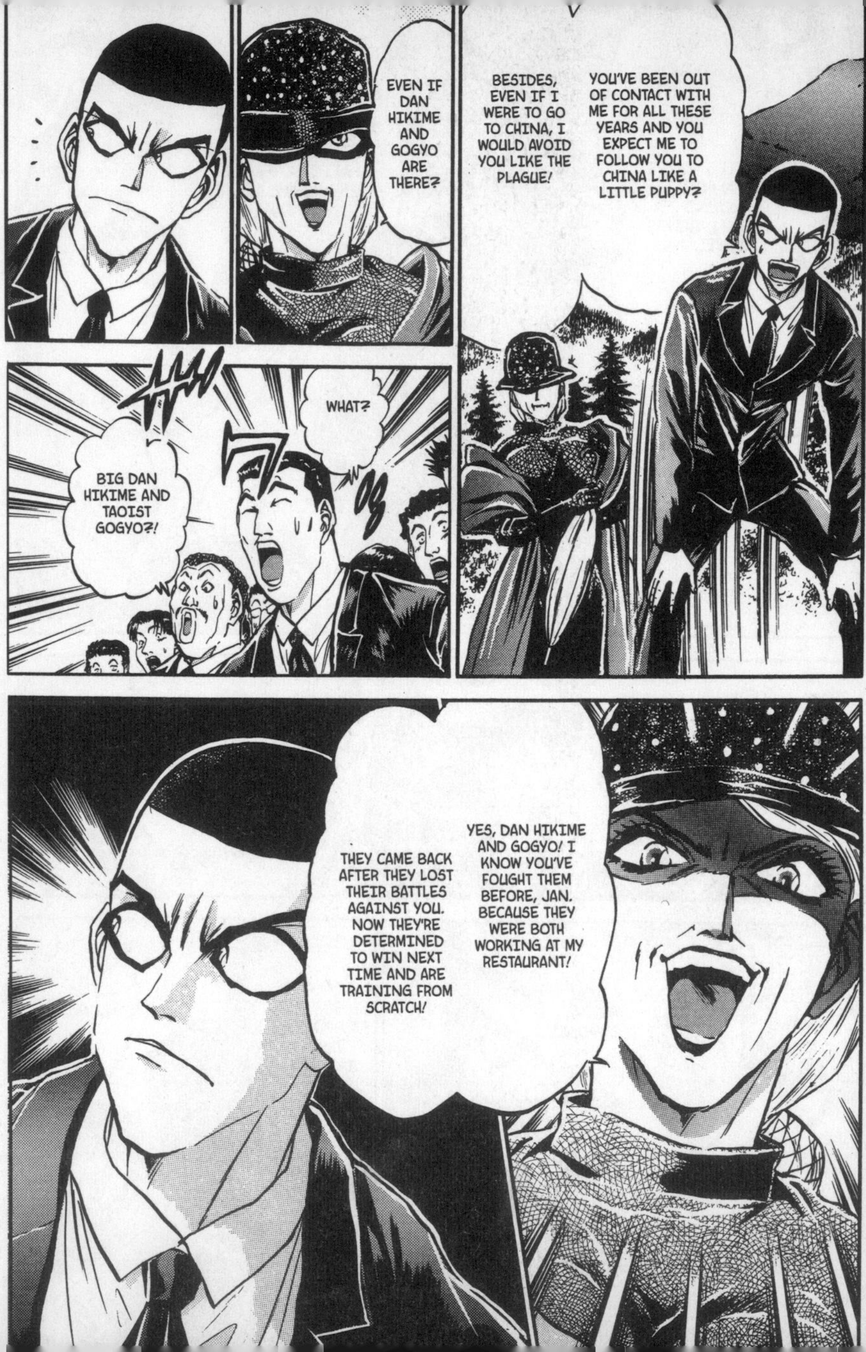
YOU'VE BEEN OUT OF CONTACT WITH ME FOR ALL THESE YEARS AND YOU EXPECT ME TO FOLLOW YOU TO CHINA LIKE A LITTLE PUPPY?
BESIDES, EVEN IF I WERE TO GO TO CHINA, I WOULD AVOID YOU LIKE THE PLAGUE!
EVEN IF DAN HIKIME AND GOGYO ARE THERE?
WHAT?
BIG DAN HIKIME AND TAOIST GOGYO?!
YES, DAN HIKIME AND GOGYO! I KNOW YOU'VE FOUGHT THEM BEFORE, JAN. BECAUSE THEY WERE BOTH WORKING AT MY RESTAURANT!
THEY CAME BACK AFTER THEY LOST THEIR BATTLES AGAINST YOU. NOW THEY'RE DETERMINED TO WIN NEXT TIME AND ARE TRAINING FROM SCRATCH!

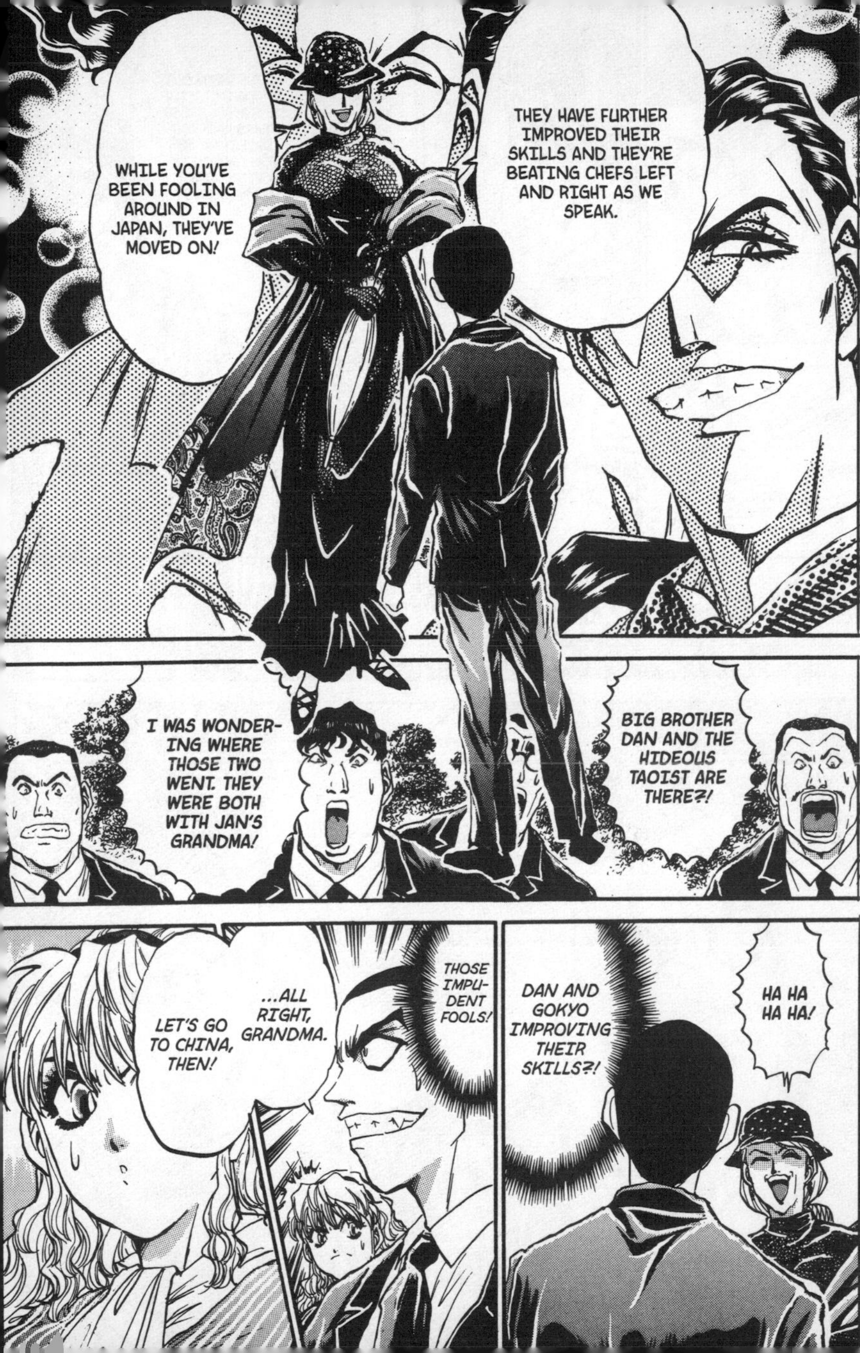
THEY HAVE FURTHER IMPROVED THEIR SKILLS AND THEY'RE BEATING CHEFS LEFT AND RIGHT AS WE SPEAK.
WHILE YOU'VE BEEN FOOLING AROUND IN JAPAN, THEY'VE MOVED ON!
BIG BROTHER DAN AND THE HIDEOUS TAOIST ARE THERE?!
I WAS WONDERING WHERE THOSE TWO WENT. THEY WERE BOTH WITH JAN'S GRANDMA!
HA HA HA HA!
DAN AND GOKYO IMPROVING THEIR SKILLS?!
THOSE IMPUDENT FOOLS!
...ALL RIGHT, GRANDMA.
LET'S GO TO CHINA, THEN!

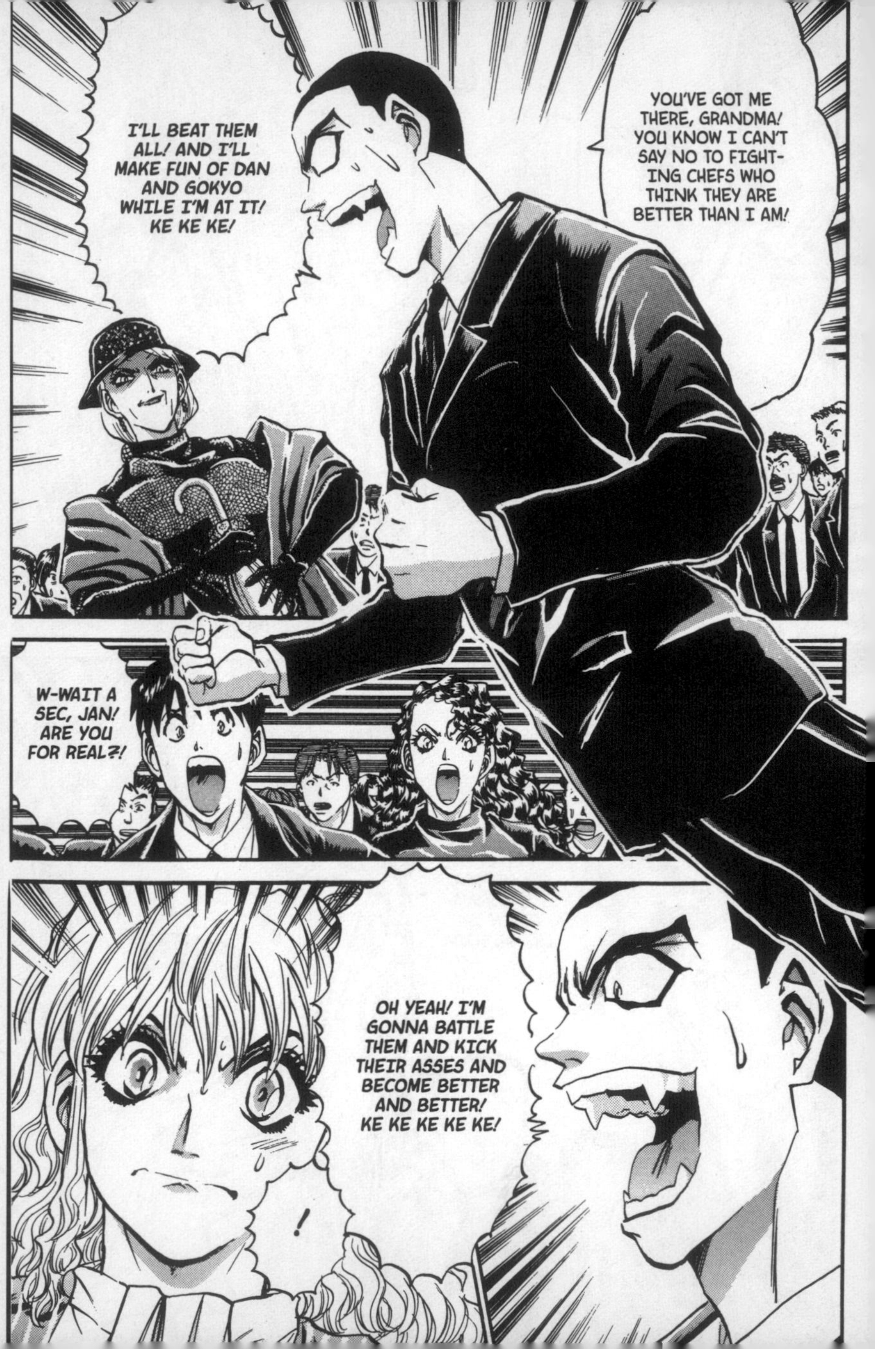
YOU'VE GOT ME THERE, GRANDMA! YOU KNOW I CAN'T SAY NO TO FIGHT-ING CHEFS WHO THINK THEY ARE BETTER THAN I AM!
I'LL BEAT THEM ALL! AND I'LL MAKE FUN OF DAN AND GOKYO WHILE I'M AT IT! KE KE KE!
W-WAIT A SEC, JAN! ARE YOU FOR REAL?!
OH YEAH! I'M GONNA BATTLE THEM AND KICK THEIR ASSES AND BECOME BETTER AND BETTER! KE KE KE KE KE!
!

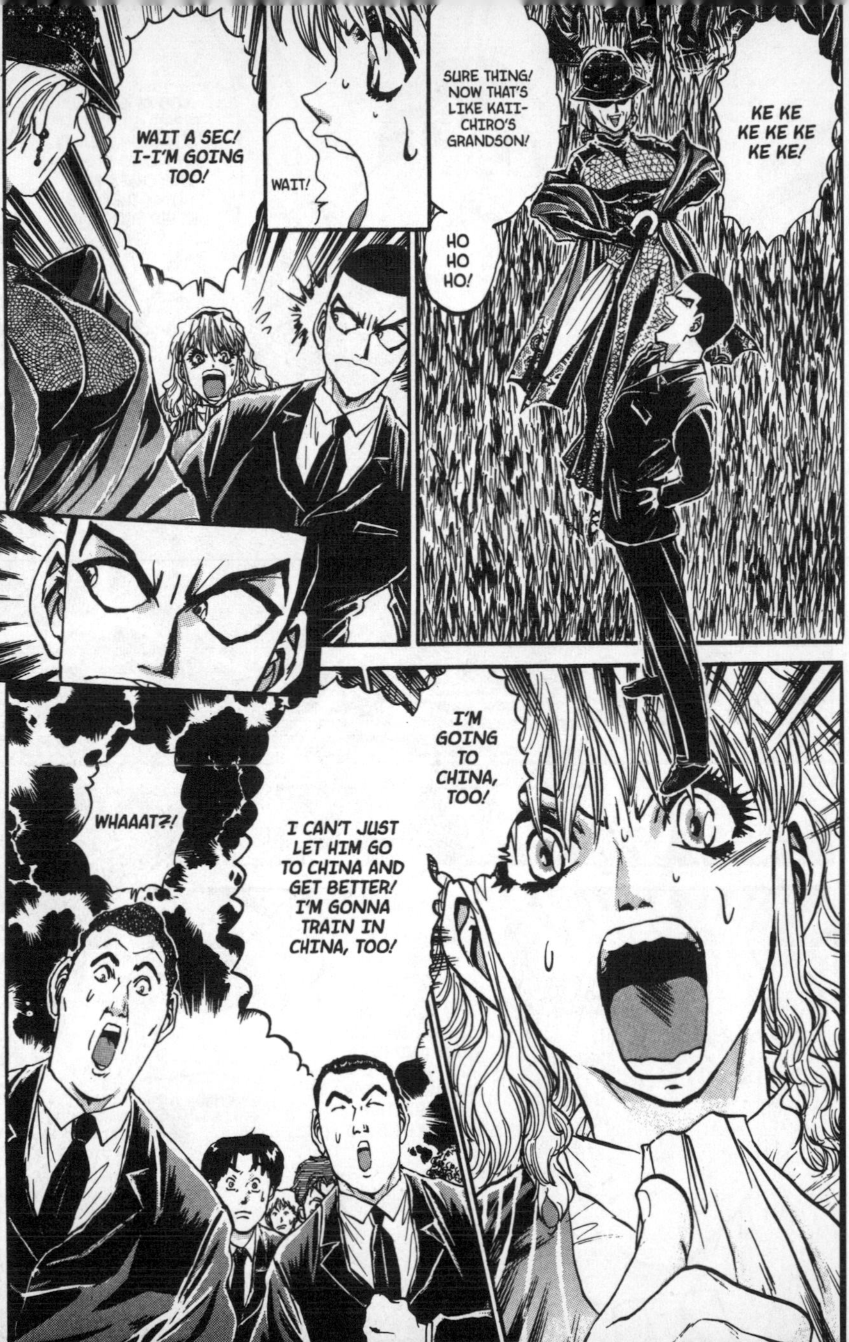
KE KE KE KE KE KE KE!
SURE THING! NOW THAT'S LIKE KAII-CHIRO'S GRANDSON!
HO HO HO!
WAIT!
WAIT A SEC! I-I'M GOING TOO!
I'M GOING TO CHINA, TOO!
I CAN'T JUST LET HIM GO TO CHINA AND GET BETTER! I'M GONNA TRAIN IN CHINA, TOO!
WHAAAT?!

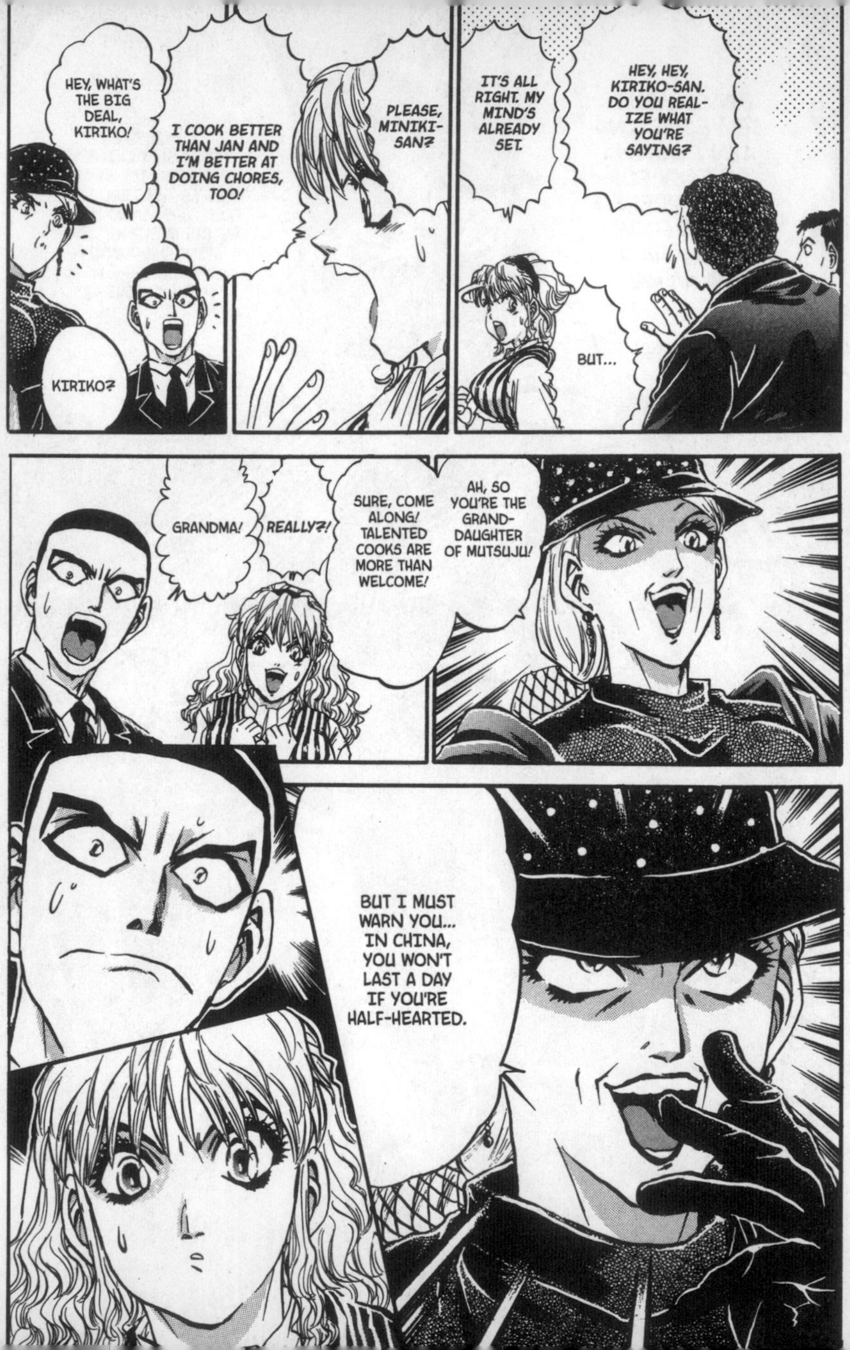
HEY, HEY, KIRIKO-SAN. DO YOU REAL-IZE WHAT YOU'RE SAYING?
IT'S ALL RIGHT. MY MIND'S ALREADY SET.
BUT...
PLEASE, MINIKI-SAN?
I COOK BETTER THAN JAN AND I'M BETTER AT DOING CHORES, TOO!
HEY, WHAT'S THE BIG DEAL, KIRIKO!
KIRIKO?
AH, SO YOU'RE THE GRAND-DAUGHTER OF MUTSUJU!
SURE, COME ALONG! TALENTED COOKS ARE MORE THAN WELCOME!
REALLY?!
GRANDMA!
BUT I MUST WARN YOU... IN CHINA, YOU WON'T LAST A DAY IF YOU'RE HALF-HEARTED.

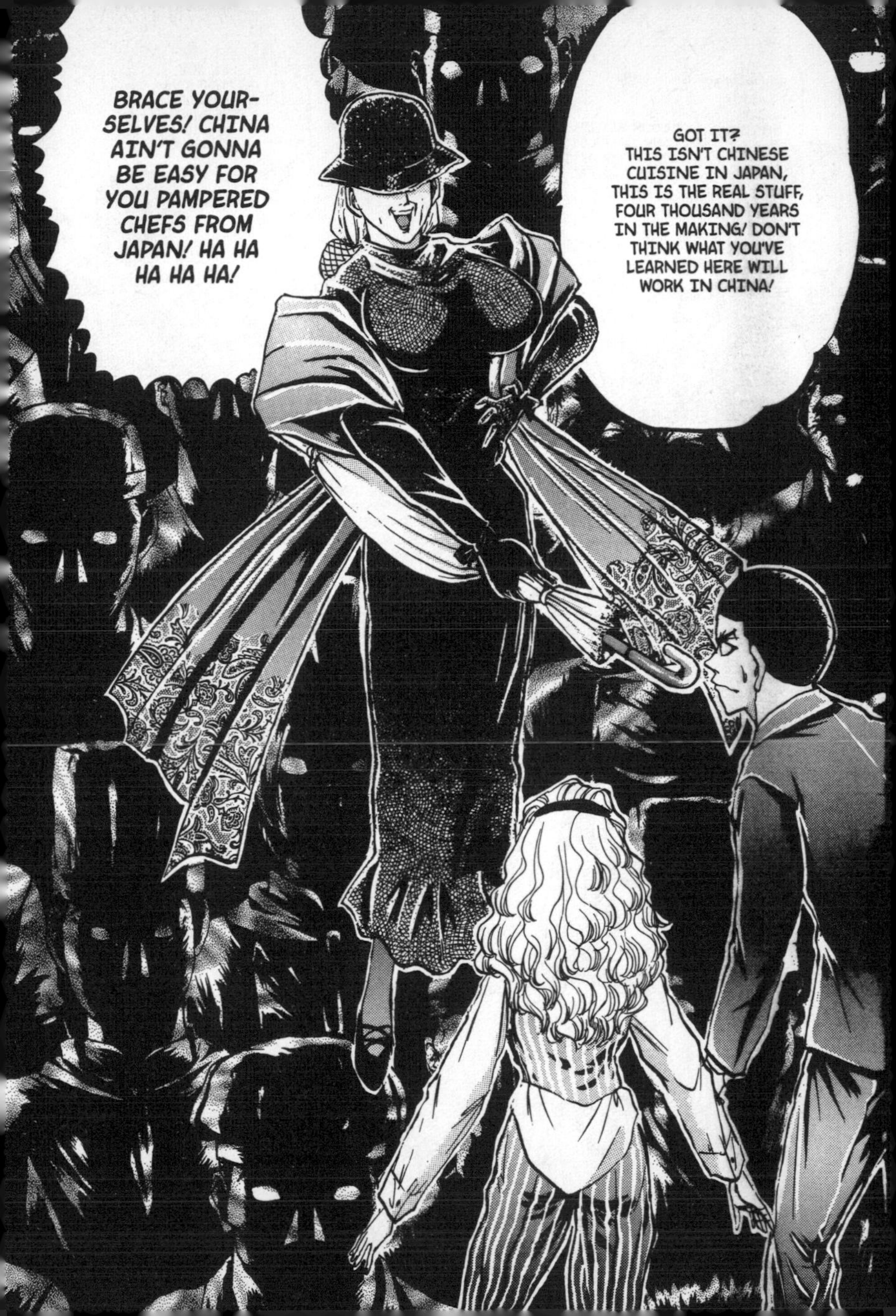
GOT IT? THIS ISN'T CHINESE CUISINE IN JAPAN, THIS IS THE REAL STUFF, FOUR THOUSAND YEARS IN THE MAKING! DON'T THINK WHAT YOU'VE LEARNED HERE WILL WORK IN CHINA!
BRACE YOUR-SELVES! CHINA AIN'T GONNA BE EASY FOR YOU PAMPERED CHEFS FROM JAPAN! HA HA HA HA HA!

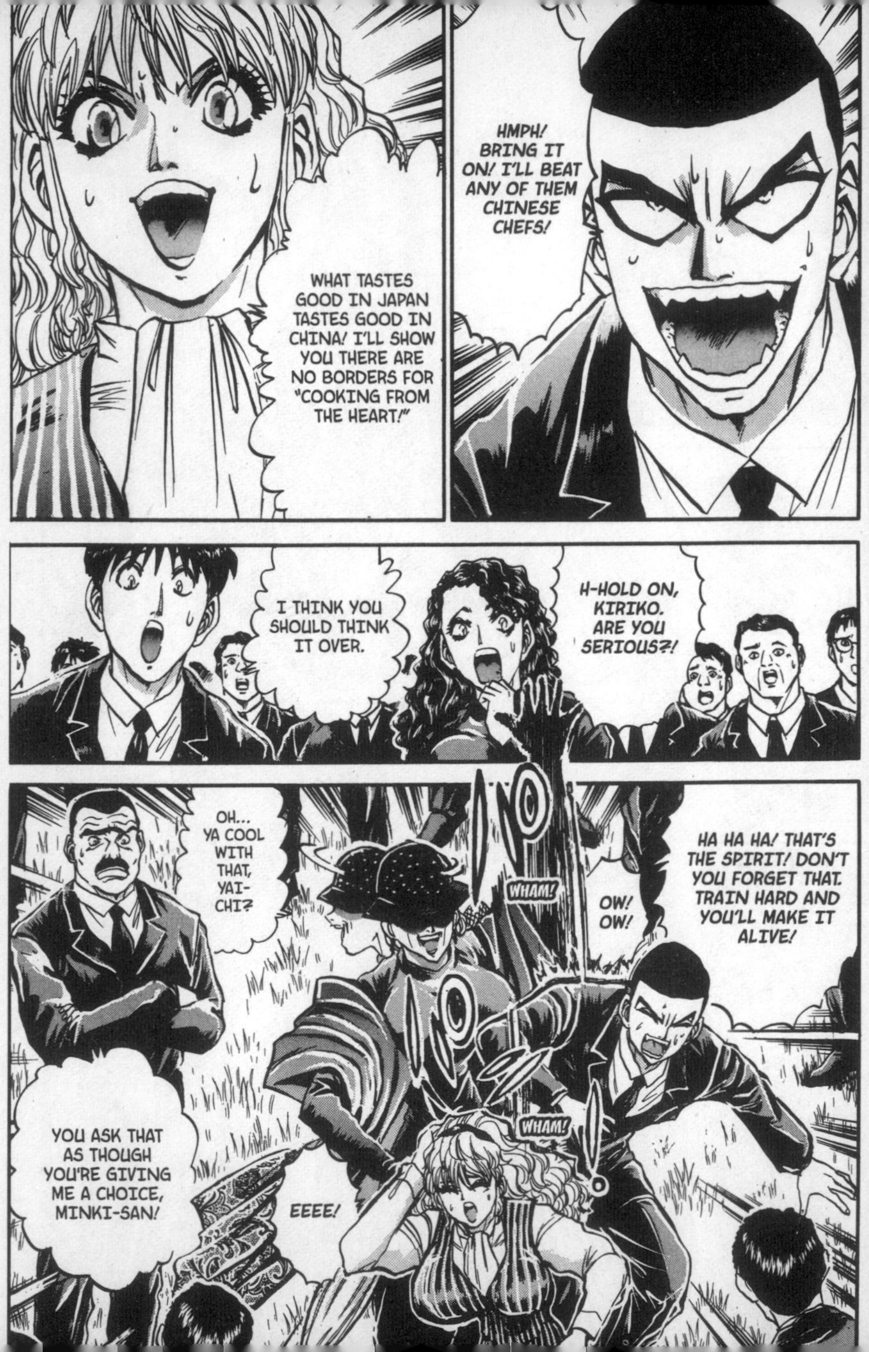
HMPH! BRING IT ON! I'LL BEAT ANY OF THEM CHINESE CHEFS!
WHAT TASTES GOOD IN JAPAN TASTES GOOD IN CHINA! I'LL SHOW YOU THERE ARE NO BORDERS FOR "COOKING FROM THE HEART!"
H-HOLD ON, KIRIKO. ARE YOU SERIOUS?!
I THINK YOU SHOULD THINK IT OVER.
HA HA HA! THAT'S THE SPIRIT! DON'T YOU FORGET THAT. TRAIN HARD AND YOU'LL MAKE IT ALIVE!
OW! OW!
WHAM!
OH... YA COOL WITH THAT, YAI-CHI?
WHAM!
EEEE!
YOU ASK THAT AS THOUGH YOU'RE GIVING ME A CHOICE, MINKI-SAN!

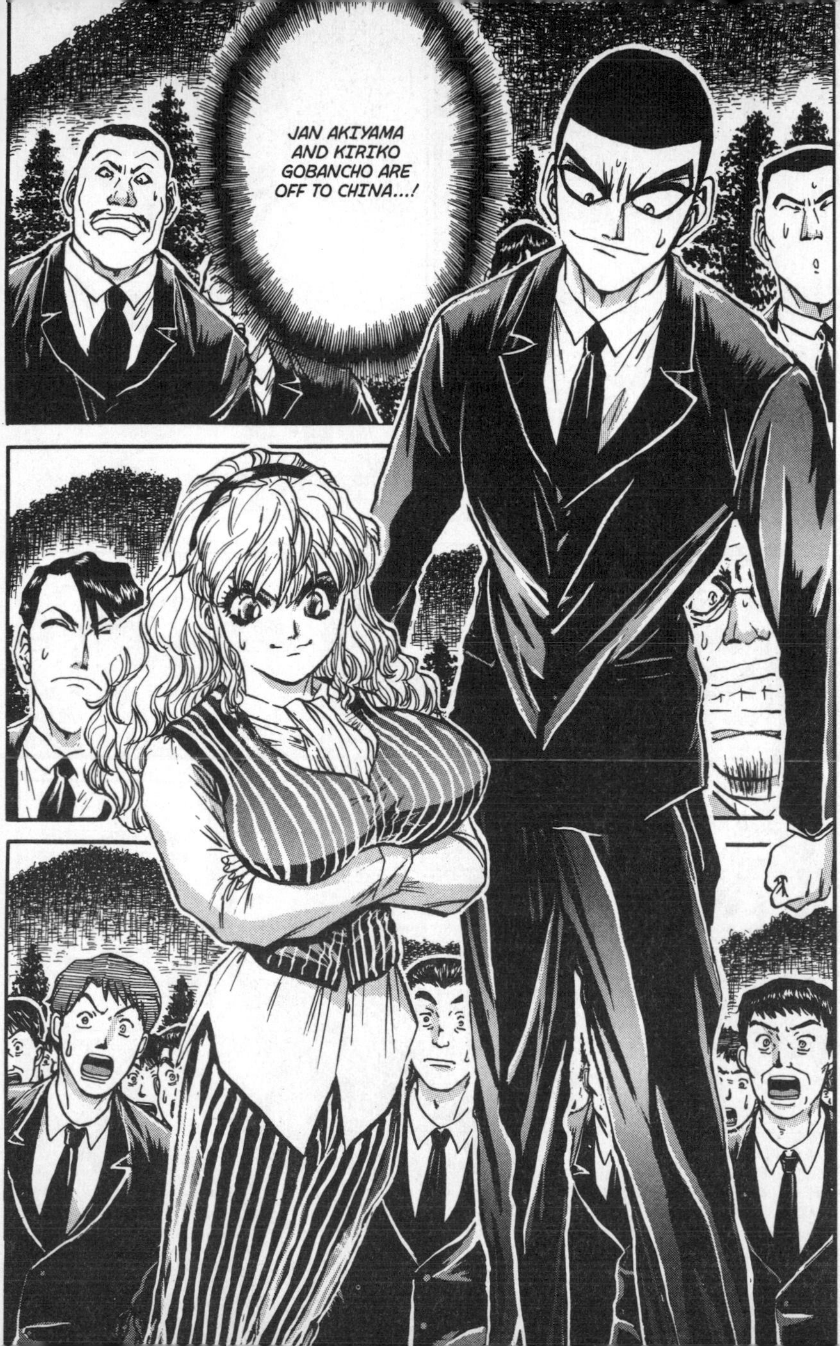
JAN AKIYAMA AND KIRIKO GOBANCHO ARE OFF TO CHINA...!

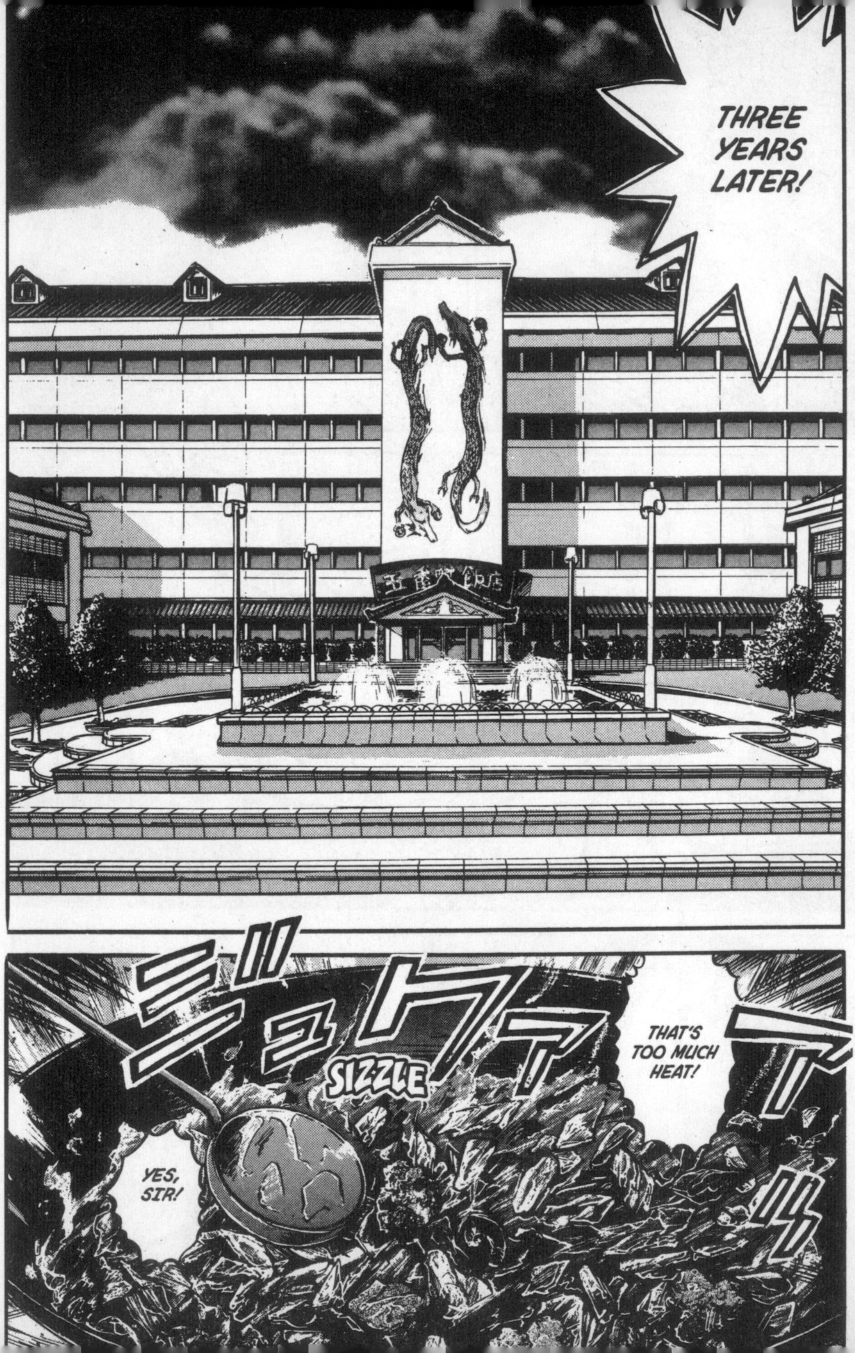
THREE YEARS LATER!
THAT'S TOO MUCH HEAT!
SIZZLE
YES, SIR!

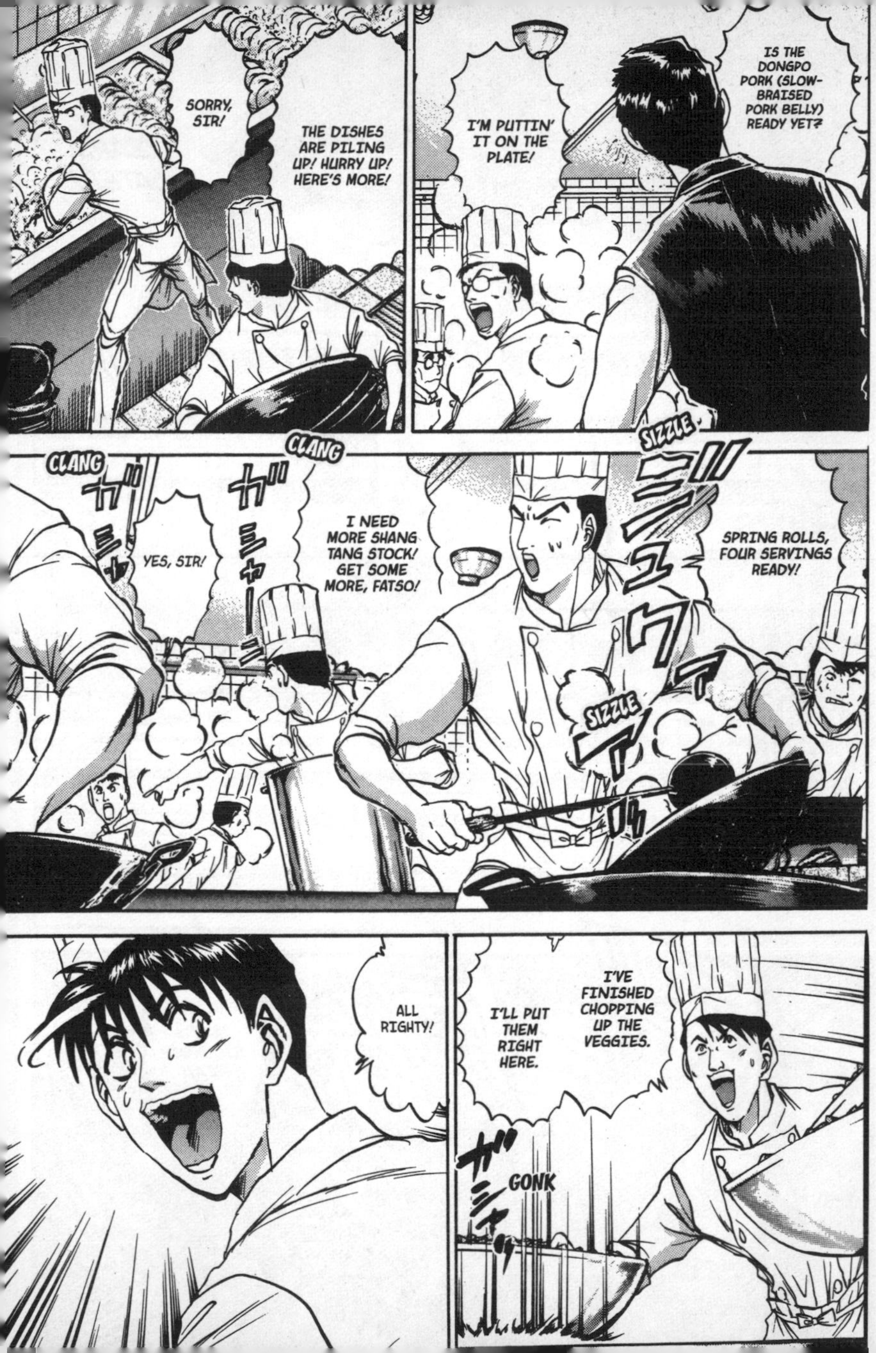
IS THE DONGPO PORK (SLOW-BRAISED PORK BELLY) READY YET?
I'M PUTTIN' IT ON THE PLATE!
THE DISHES ARE PILING UP! HURRY UP! HERE'S MORE!
SORRY, SIR!
SIZZLE
SPRING ROLLS, FOUR SERVINGS READY!
SIZZLE
I NEED MORE SHANG TANG STOCK! GET SOME MORE, FATSO!
CLANG
YES, SIR!
CLANG
I'VE FINISHED CHOPPING UP THE VEGGIES.
I'LL PUT THEM RIGHT HERE.
GONK
ALL RIGHTY!

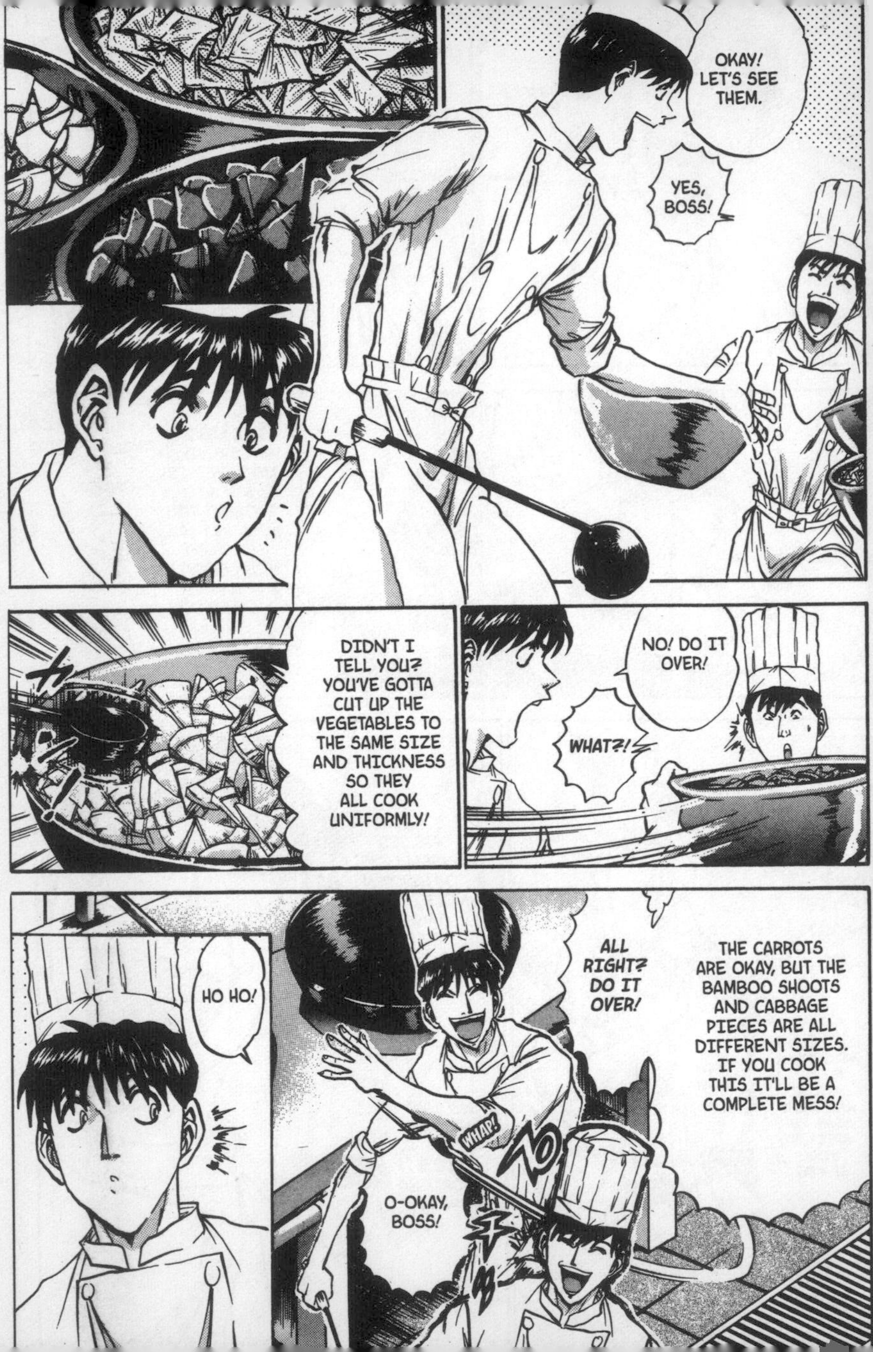
OKAY! LET'S SEE THEM.
YES, BOSS!
NO! DO IT OVER!
WHAT?!
DIDN'T I TELL YOU? YOU'VE GOTTA CUT UP THE VEGETABLES TO THE SAME SIZE AND THICKNESS SO THEY ALL COOK UNIFORMLY!
THE CARROTS ARE OKAY, BUT THE BAMBOO SHOOTS AND CABBAGE PIECES ARE ALL DIFFERENT SIZES. IF YOU COOK THIS IT'LL BE A COMPLETE MESS!
ALL RIGHT? DO IT OVER!
WHAP!
O-OKAY, BOSS!
HO HO!

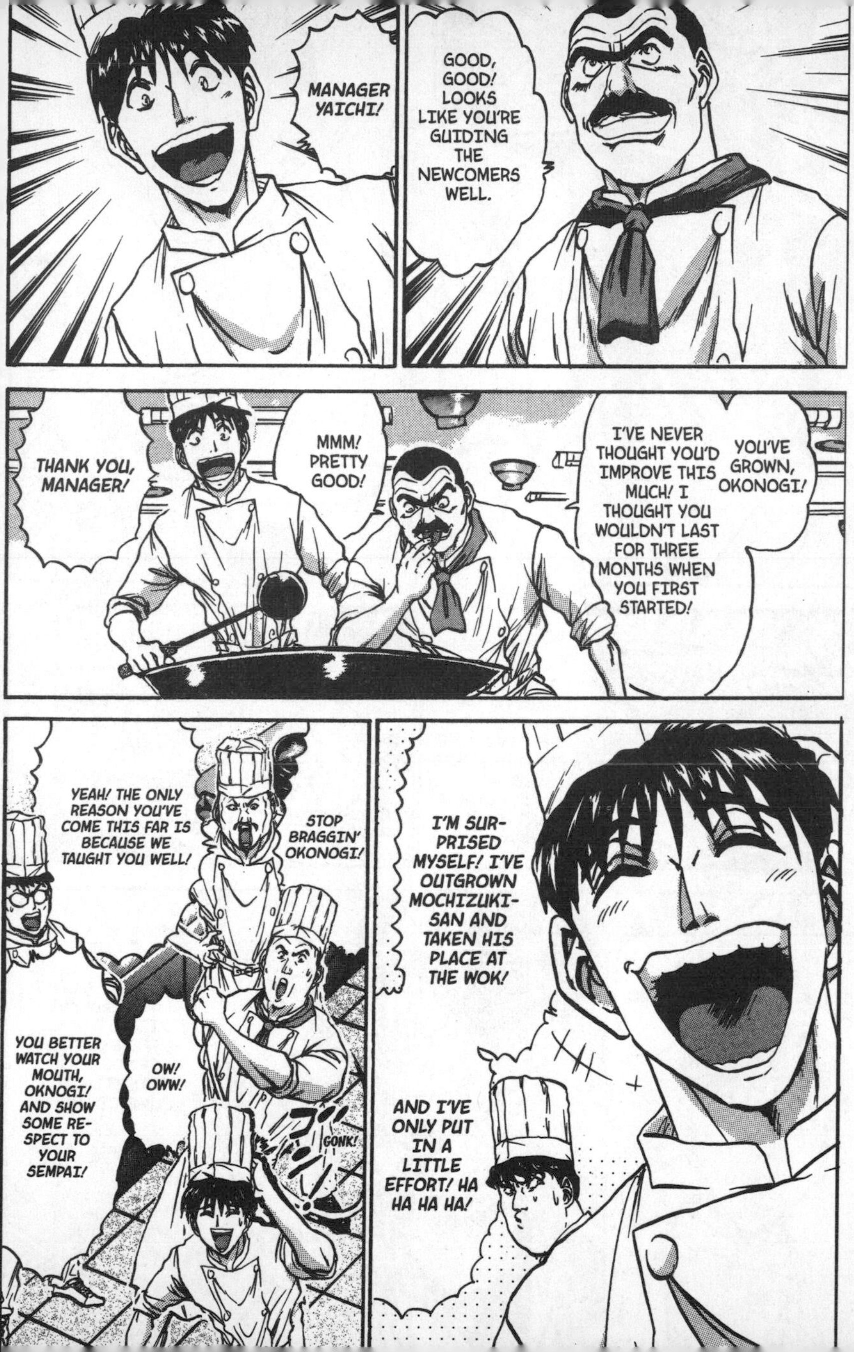
GOOD, GOOD! LOOKS LIKE YOU'RE GUIDING THE NEWCOMERS WELL.
MANAGER YAICHI!
YOU'VE GROWN, OKONOGI!
I'VE NEVER THOUGHT YOU'D IMPROVE THIS MUCH! I THOUGHT YOU WOULDN'T LAST FOR THREE MONTHS WHEN YOU FIRST STARTED!
MMM! PRETTY GOOD!
THANK YOU, MANAGER!
I'M SUR-PRISED MYSELF! I'VE OUTGROWN MOCHIZUKI-SAN AND TAKEN HIS PLACE AT THE WOK!
AND I'VE ONLY PUT IN A LITTLE EFFORT! HA HA HA HA!
STOP BRAGGIN' OKONOGI!
YEAH! THE ONLY REASON YOU'VE COME THIS FAR IS BECAUSE WE TAUGHT YOU WELL!
GONK!
OW! OWW!
YOU BETTER WATCH YOUR MOUTH, OKNOGI! AND SHOW SOME RE-SPECT TO YOUR SEMPAI!

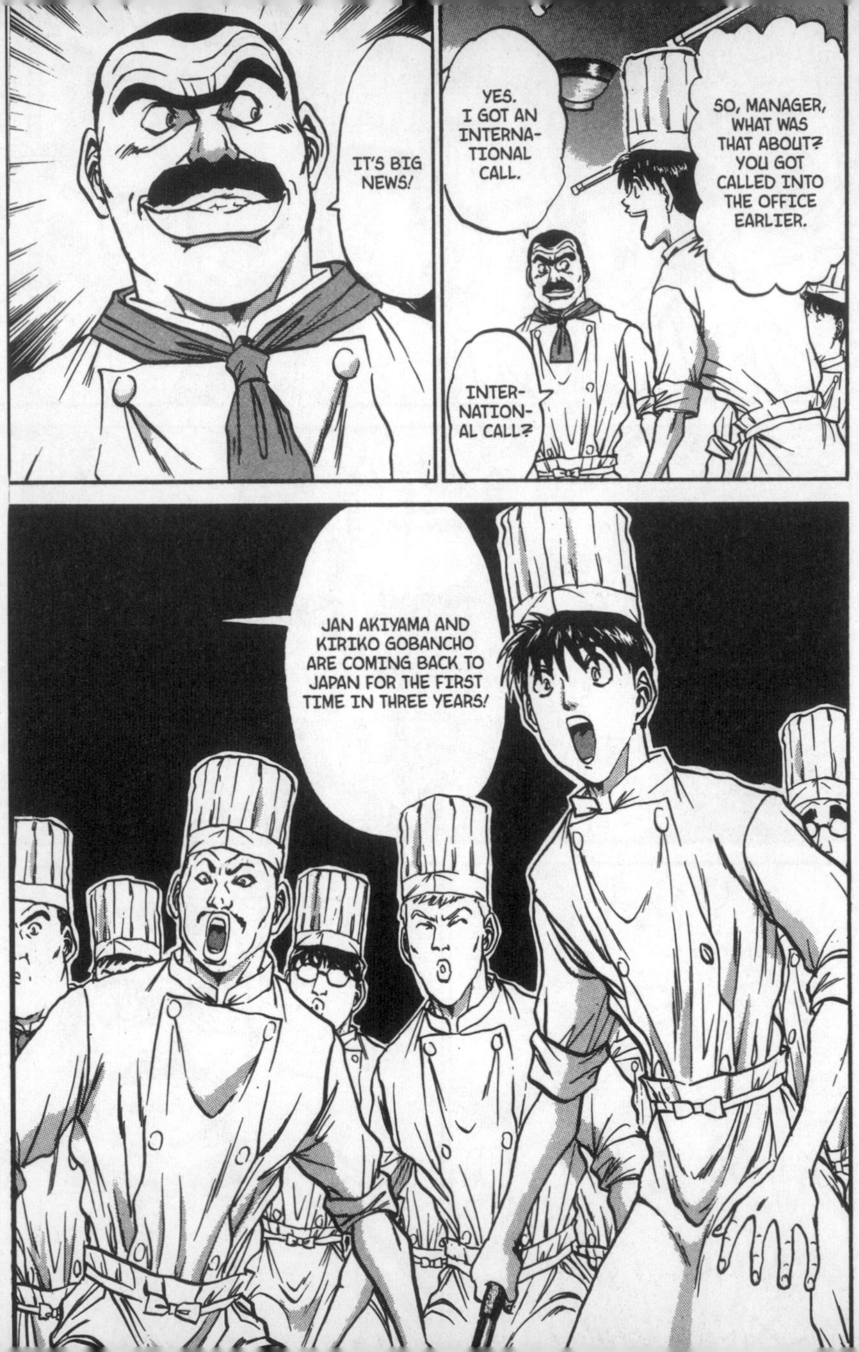
SO, MANAGER, WHAT WAS THAT ABOUT? YOU GOT CALLED INTO THE OFFICE EARLIER.
YES. I GOT AN INTERNATIONAL CALL.
INTERNATIONAL CALL?
IT'S BIG NEWS!
JAN AKIYAMA AND KIRIKO GOBANCHO ARE COMING BACK TO JAPAN FOR THE FIRST TIME IN THREE YEARS!

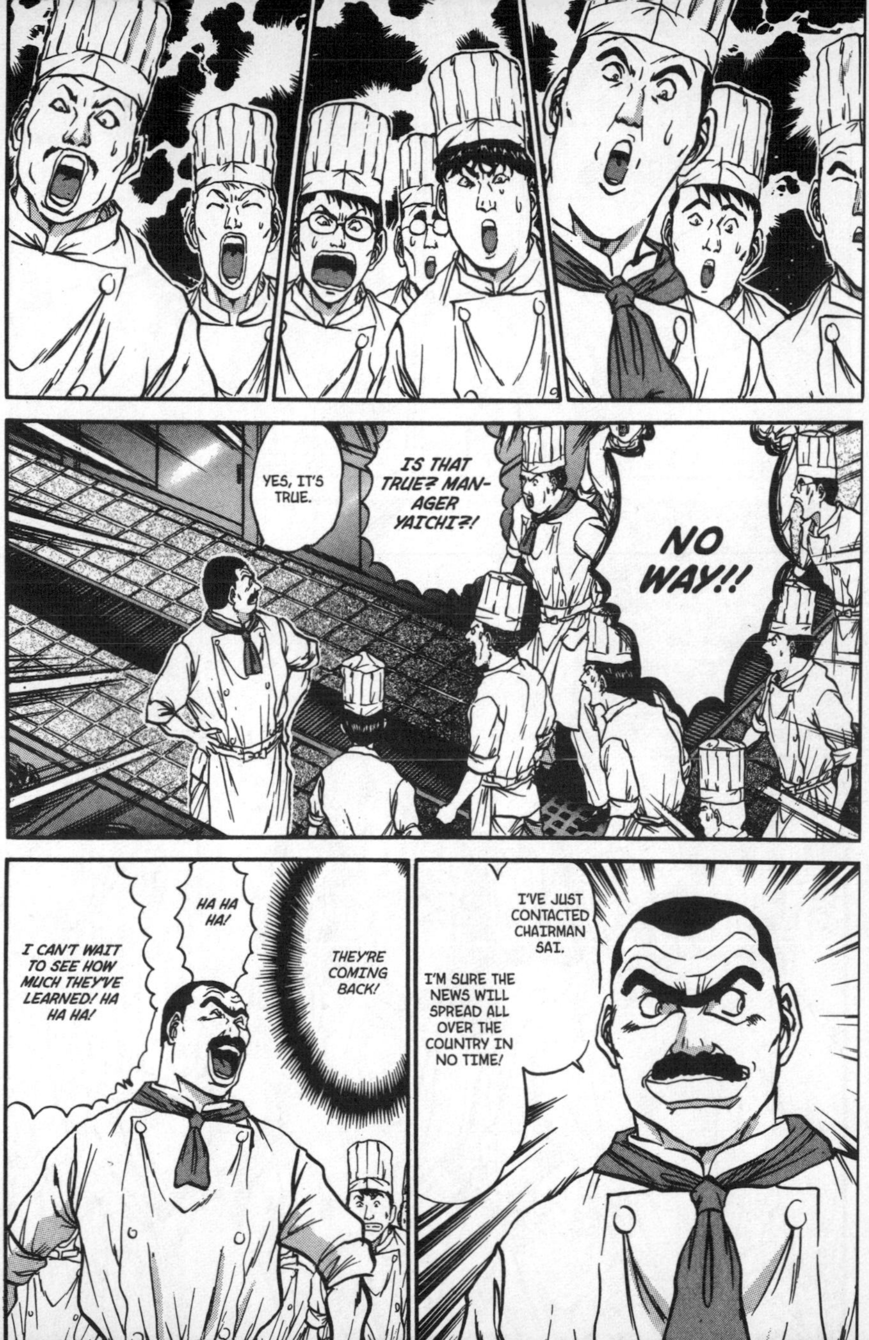
NO WAY!!
IS THAT TRUE? MAN-
AGER YAICHI?!
YES, IT'S TRUE.
I'VE JUST CONTACTED CHAIRMAN SAI.
I'M SURE THE NEWS WILL SPREAD ALL OVER THE COUNTRY IN NO TIME!
THEY'RE COMING BACK!
HA HA HA!
I CAN'T WAIT TO SEE HOW MUCH THEY'VE LEARNED! HA HA HA!

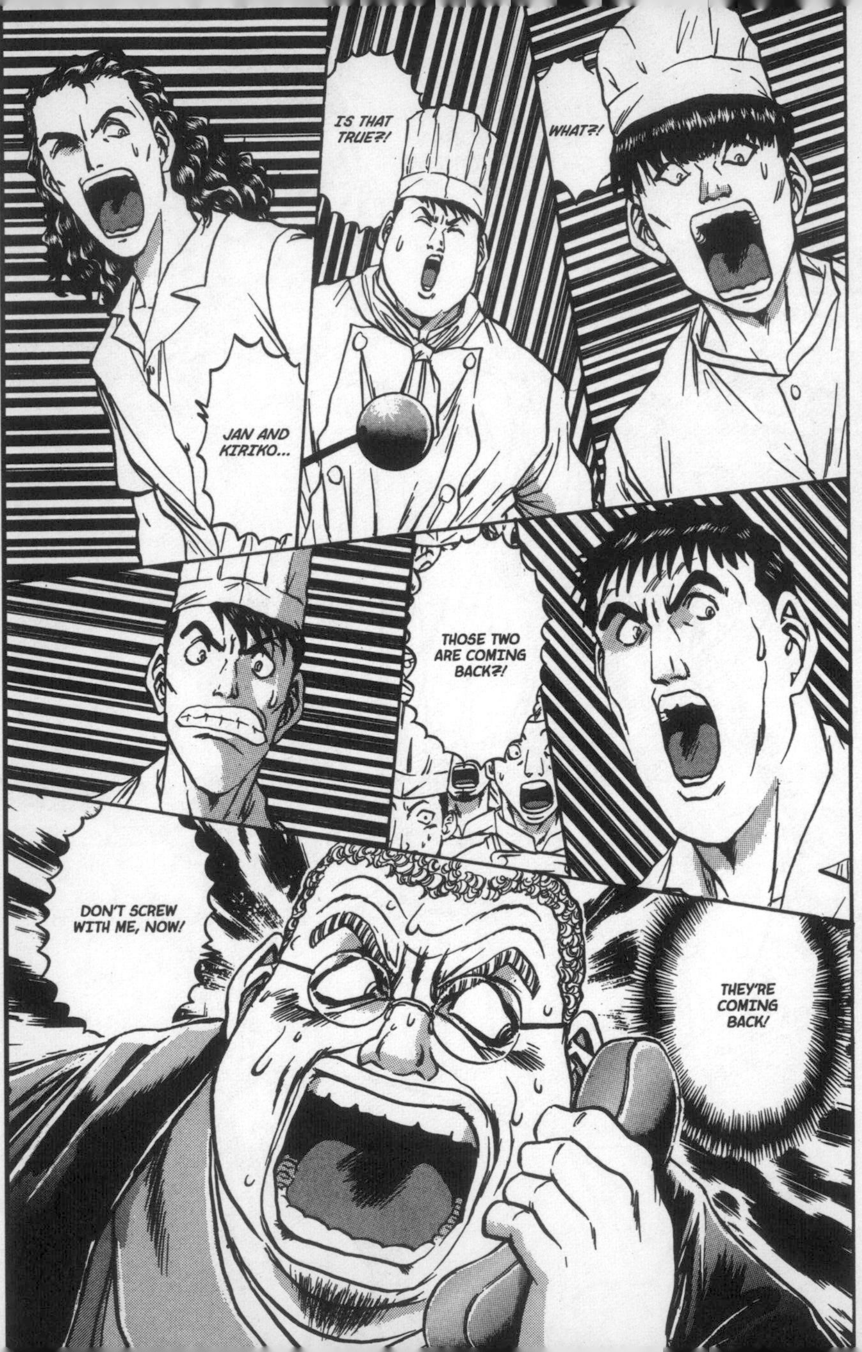
WHAT?!
IS THAT TRUE?!
JAN AND KIRIKO...
THOSE TWO ARE COMING BACK?!
THEY'RE COMING BACK!
DON'T SCREW WITH ME, NOW!

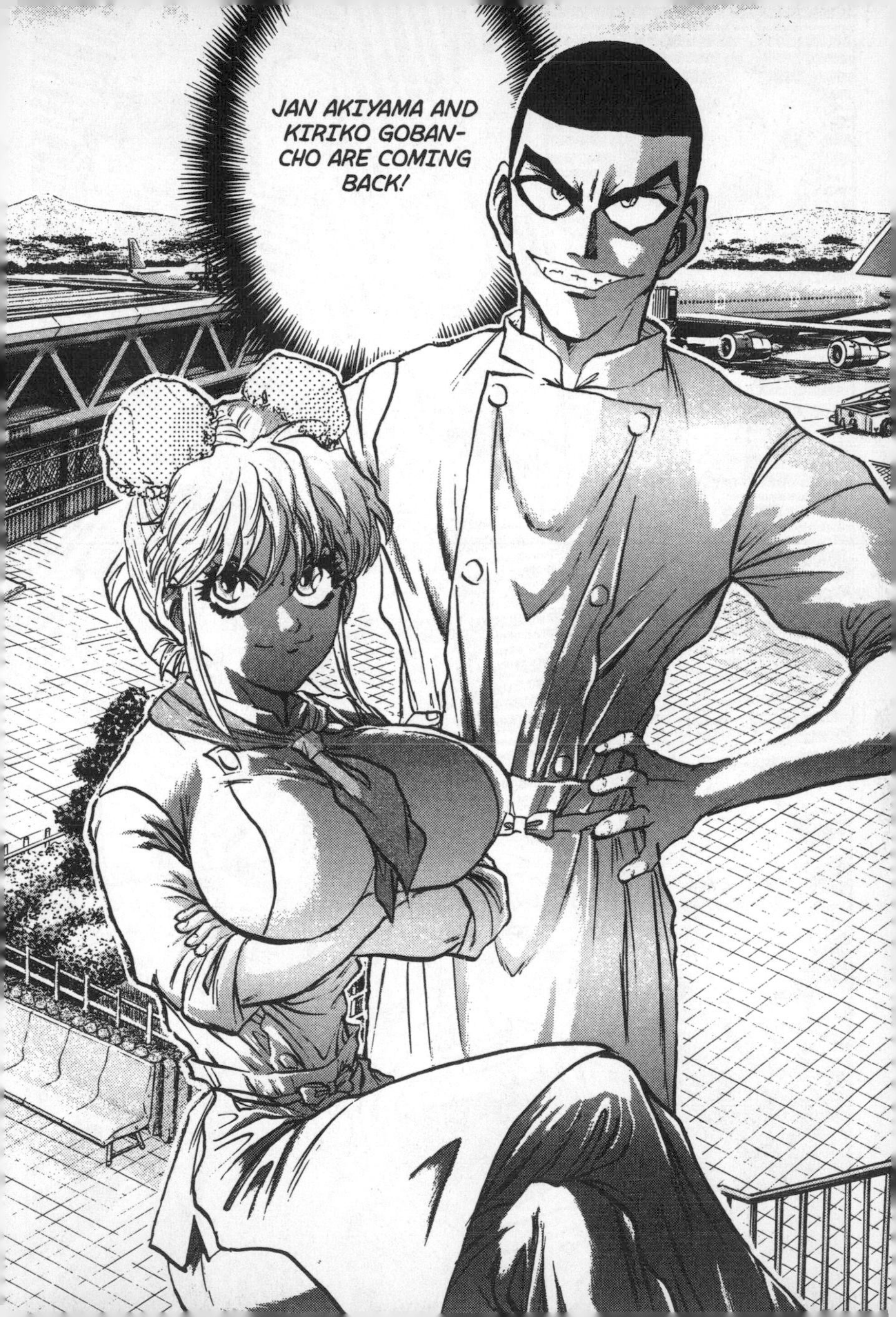
JAN AKIYAMA AND KIRIKO GOBAN-CHO ARE COMING BACK!

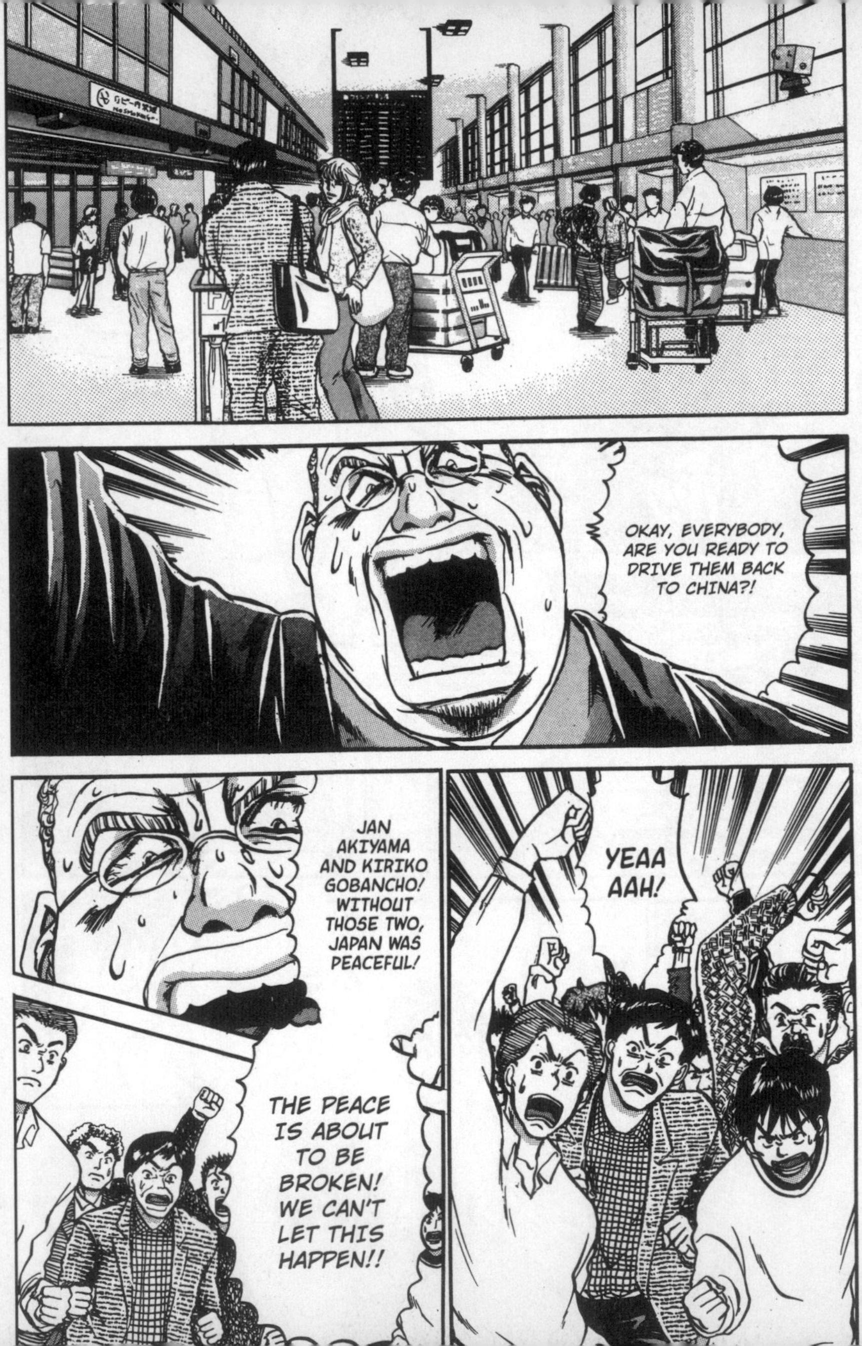
OKAY, EVERYBODY, ARE YOU READY TO DRIVE THEM BACK TO CHINA?!
YEAA AAH!
JAN AKIYAMA AND KIRIKO GOBANCHO! WITHOUT THOSE TWO, JAPAN WAS PEACEFUL!
THE PEACE IS ABOUT TO BE BROKEN! WE CAN'T LET THIS HAPPEN!!

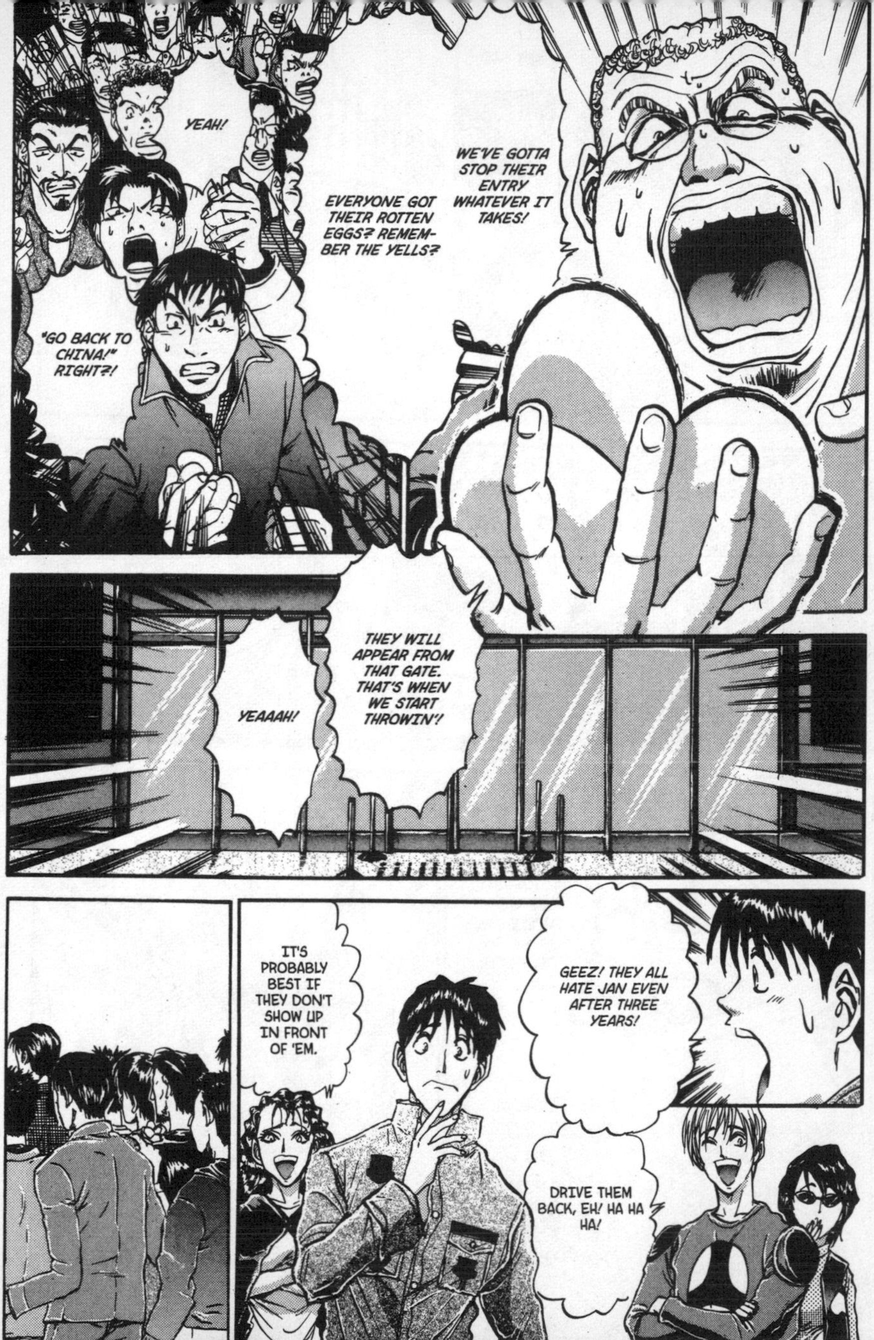
WE'VE GOTTA STOP THEIR ENTRY WHATEVER IT TAKES!
EVERYONE GOT THEIR ROTTEN EGGS? REMEMBER THE YELLS?
YEAH!
"GO BACK TO CHINA!" RIGHT?!
THEY WILL APPEAR FROM THAT GATE. THAT'S WHEN WE START THROWIN'!
YEAAAH!
GEEZ! THEY ALL HATE JAN EVEN AFTER THREE YEARS!
IT'S PROBABLY BEST IF THEY DON'T SHOW UP IN FRONT OF 'EM.
DRIVE THEM BACK, EH! HA HA HA!

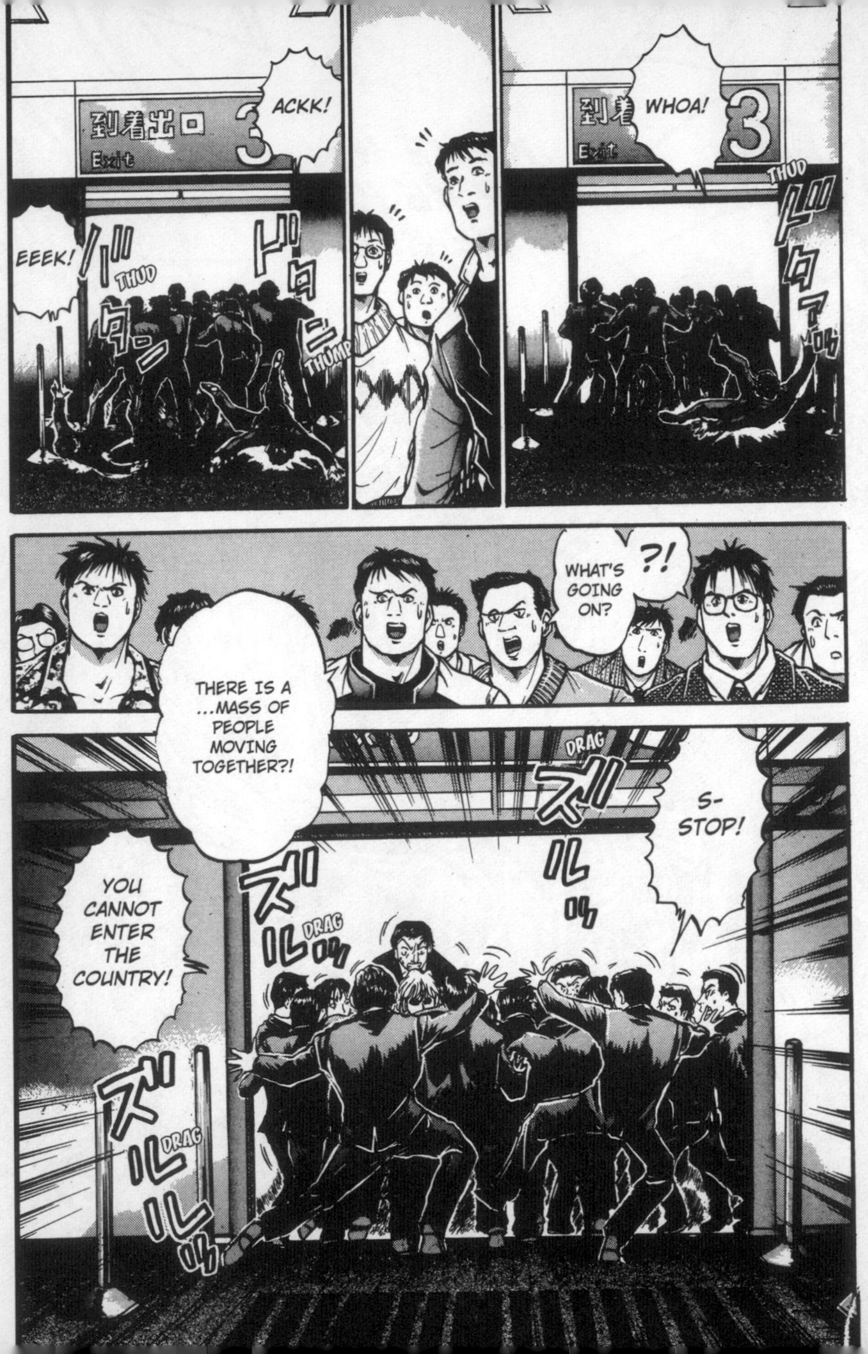
到着
3
Exit
WHOA!
THUD
到着出口
3
Exit
ACKK!
THUMP
EEEK!
THUD
?!
WHAT'S GOING ON?
THERE IS A ...MASS OF PEOPLE MOVING TOGETHER?!
S-STOP!
DRAG
YOU CANNOT ENTER THE COUNTRY!
DRAG
DRAG

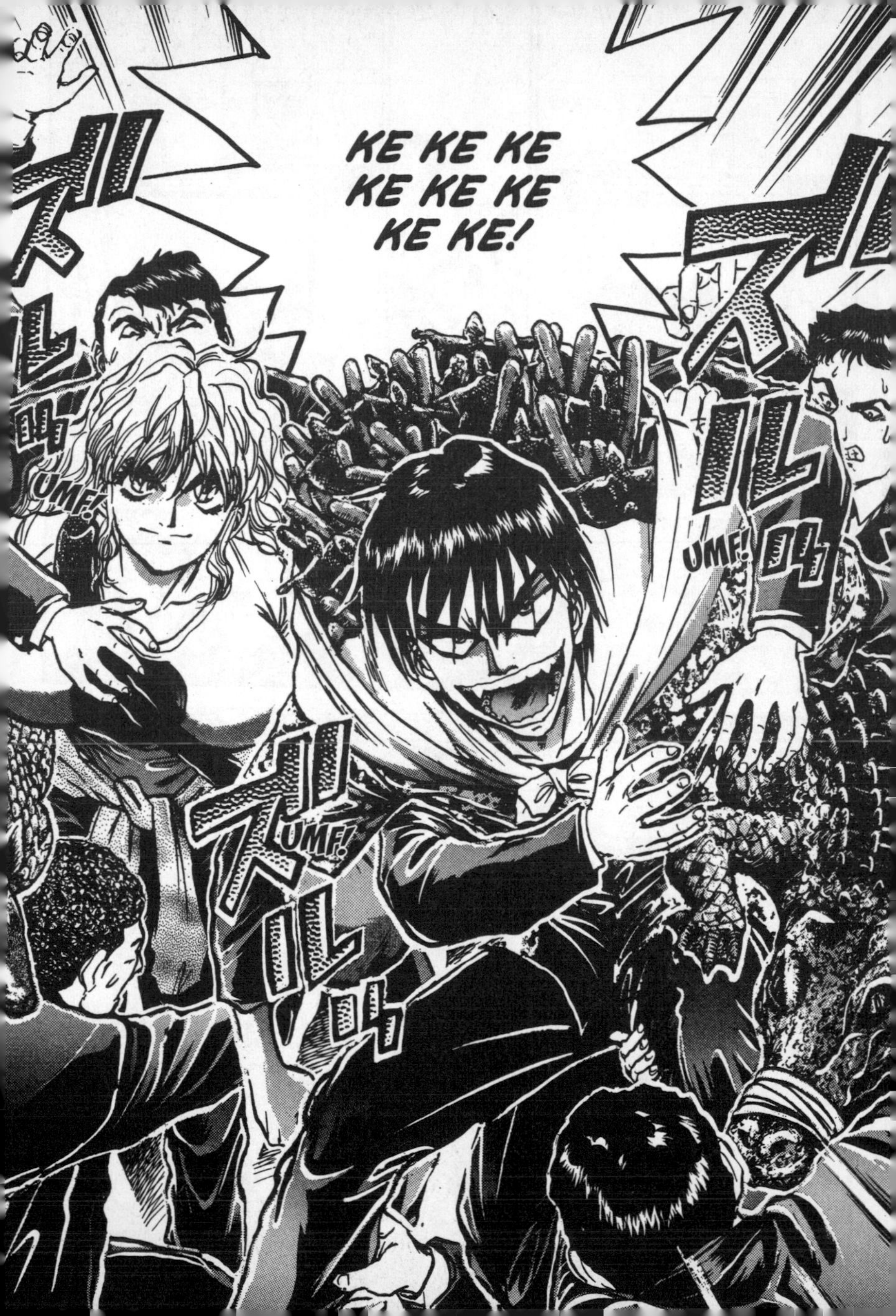
KE KE KE
KE KE KE
KE KE!
UMF!
UMF!
UMF!

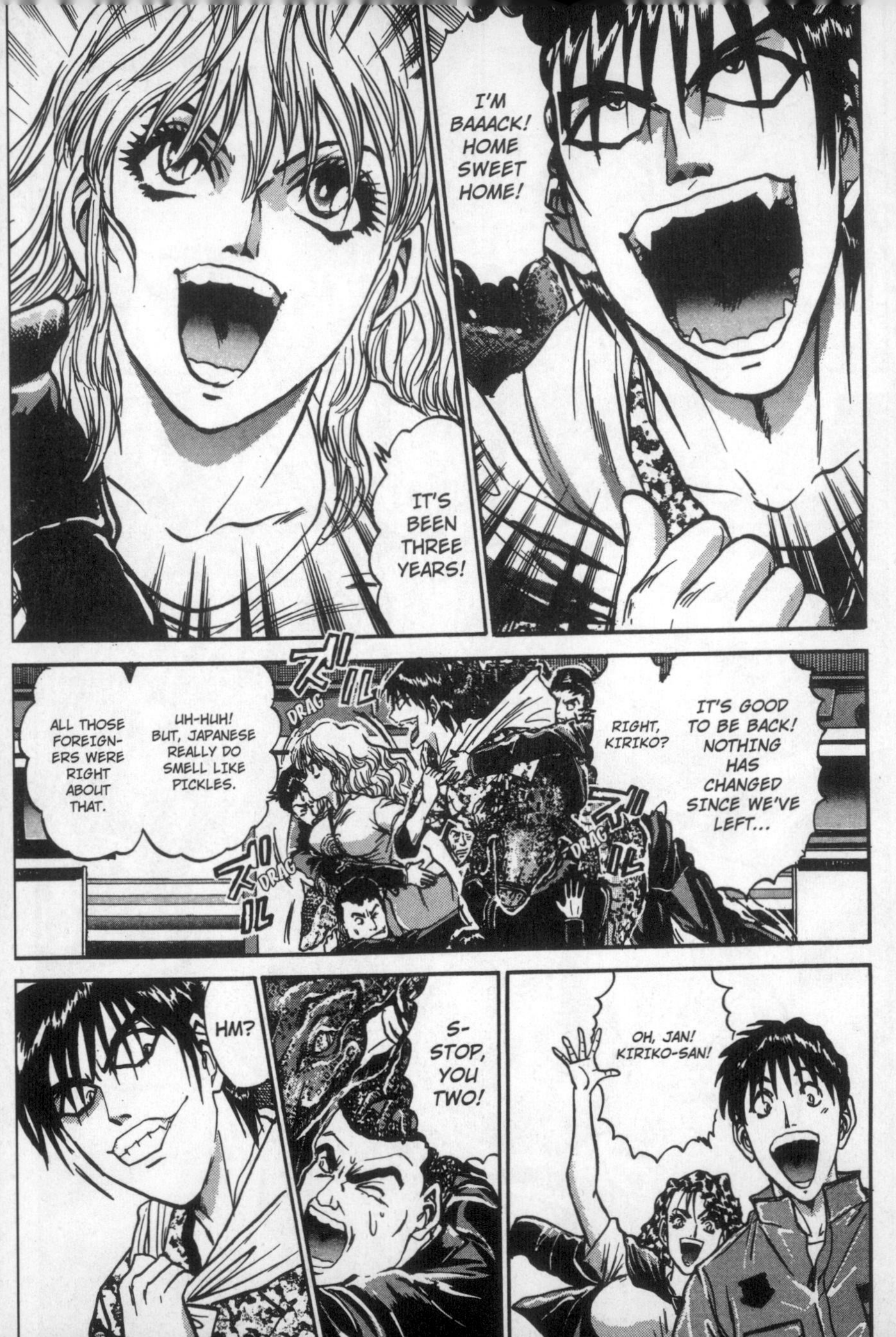
I'M BAAACK! HOME SWEET HOME!
IT'S BEEN THREE YEARS!
IT'S GOOD TO BE BACK! NOTHING HAS CHANGED SINCE WE'VE LEFT...
RIGHT, KIRIKO?
DRAG
DRAG
UH-HUH! BUT, JAPANESE REALLY DO SMELL LIKE PICKLES.
ALL THOSE FOREIGNERS WERE RIGHT ABOUT THAT.
DRAG
OH, JAN! KIRIKO-SAN!
S-STOP, YOU TWO!
HM?

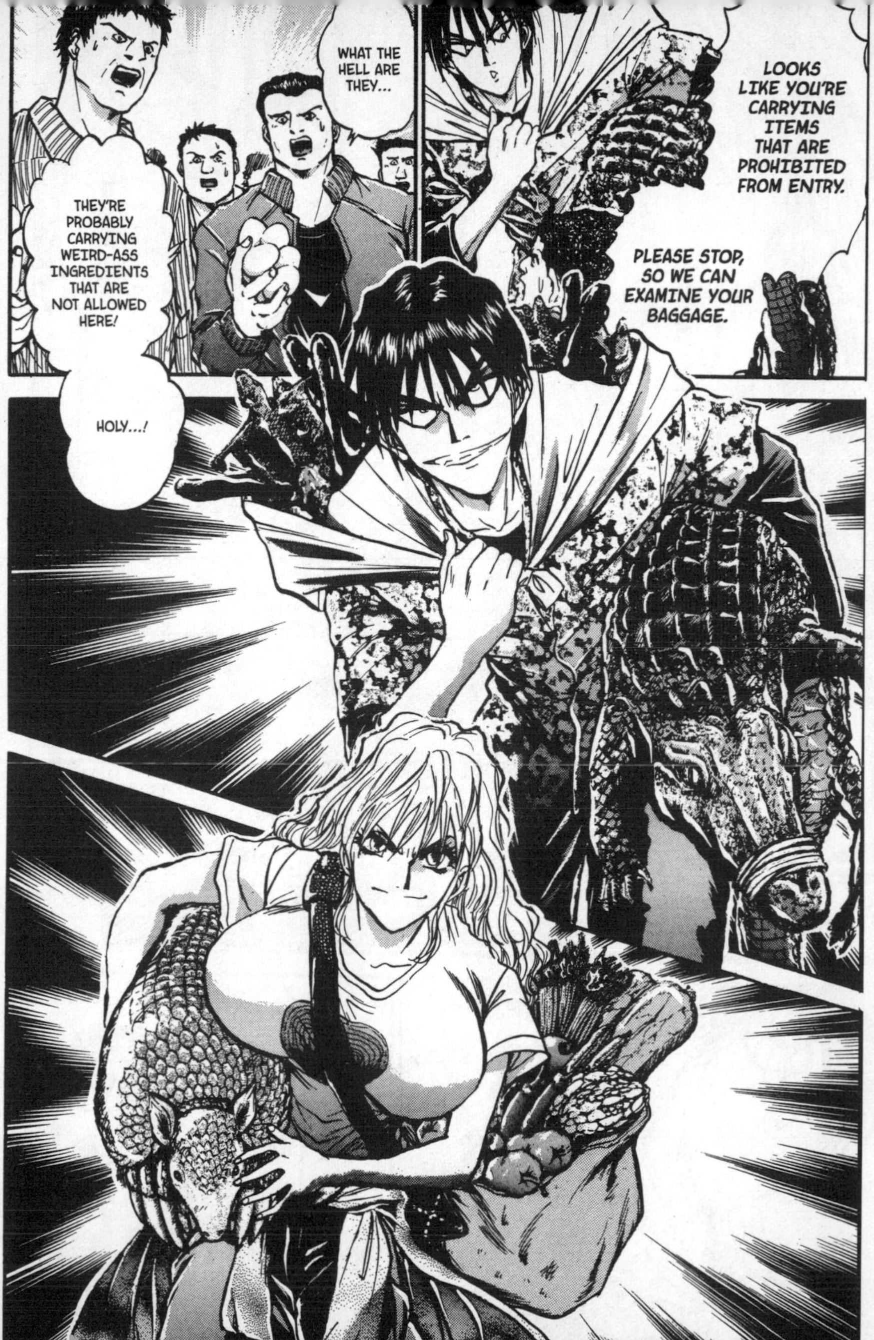
LOOKS LIKE YOU'RE CARRYING ITEMS THAT ARE PROHIBITED FROM ENTRY.
PLEASE STOP, SO WE CAN EXAMINE YOUR BAGGAGE.
WHAT THE HELL ARE THEY...
THEY'RE PROBABLY CARRYING WEIRD-ASS INGREDIENTS THAT ARE NOT ALLOWED HERE!
HOLY...!

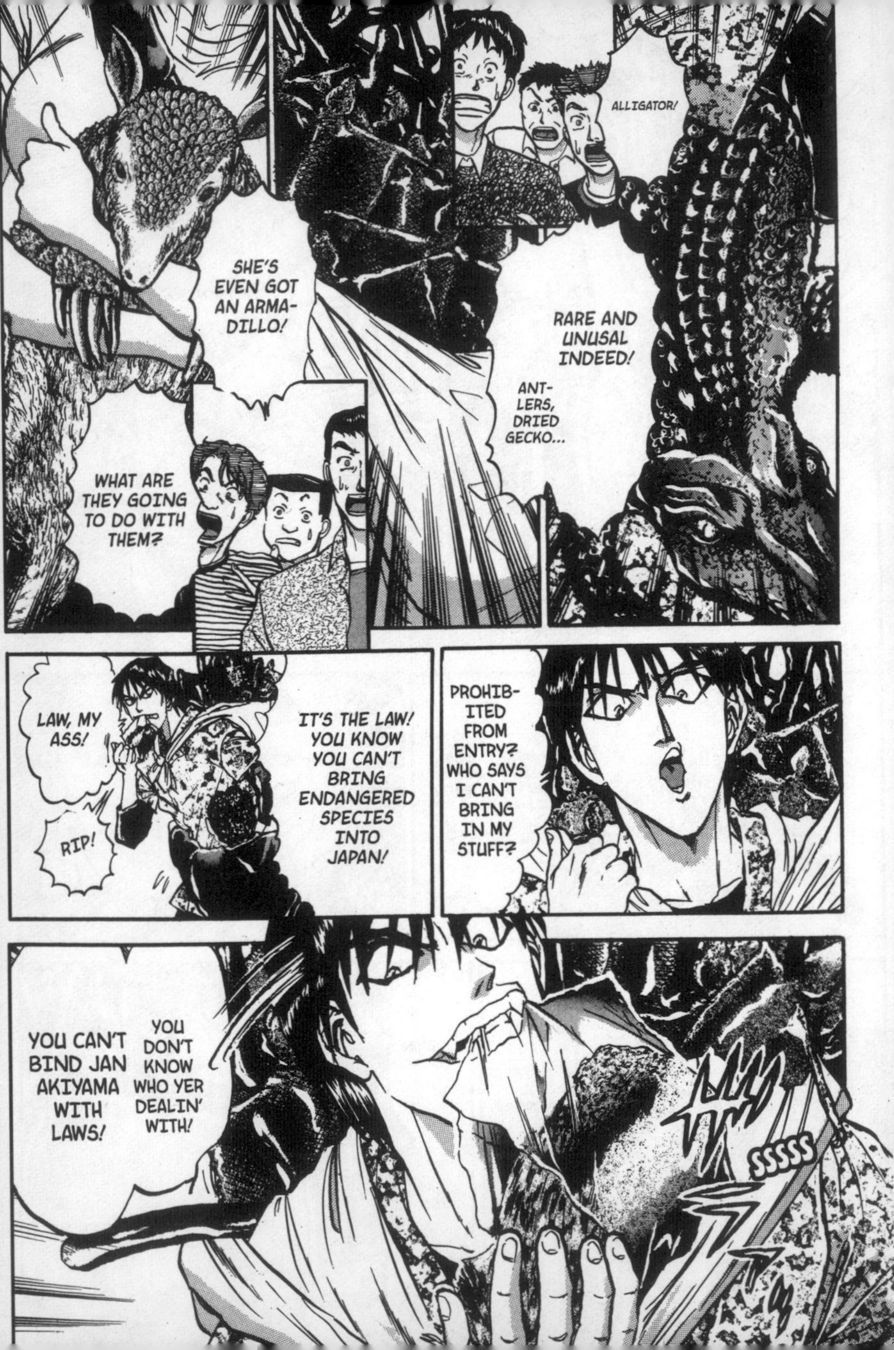
ALLIGATOR!
RARE AND UNUSAL INDEED!
ANT-LERS, DRIED GECKO...
SHE'S EVEN GOT AN ARMA-DILLO!
WHAT ARE THEY GOING TO DO WITH THEM?
PROHIB-ITED FROM ENTRY? WHO SAYS I CAN'T BRING IN MY STUFF?
IT'S THE LAW! YOU KNOW YOU CAN'T BRING ENDANGERED SPECIES INTO JAPAN!
LAW, MY ASS!
RIP!
YOU DON'T KNOW WHO YER DEALIN' WITH!
YOU CAN'T BIND JAN AKIYAMA WITH LAWS!
SSSSS

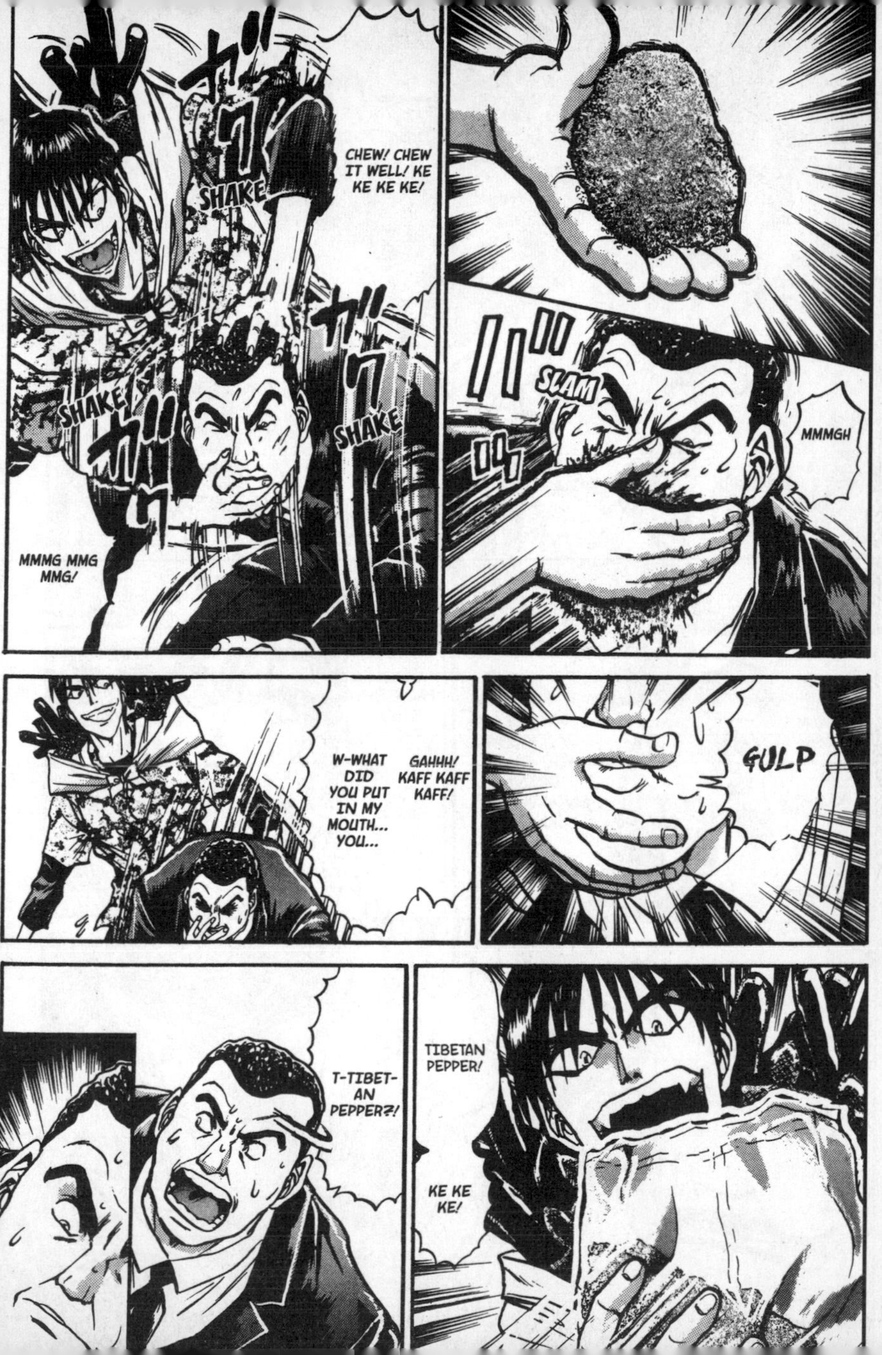
SLAM
MMMGH
CHEW! CHEW IT WELL! KE KE KE KE!
SHAKE
SHAKE
SHAKE
MMMG MMG MMG!
GULP
GAHHH! KAFF KAFF KAFF!
W-WHAT DID YOU PUT IN MY MOUTH... YOU...
TIBETAN PEPPER!
KE KE KE!
T-TIBET-AN PEPPER?!

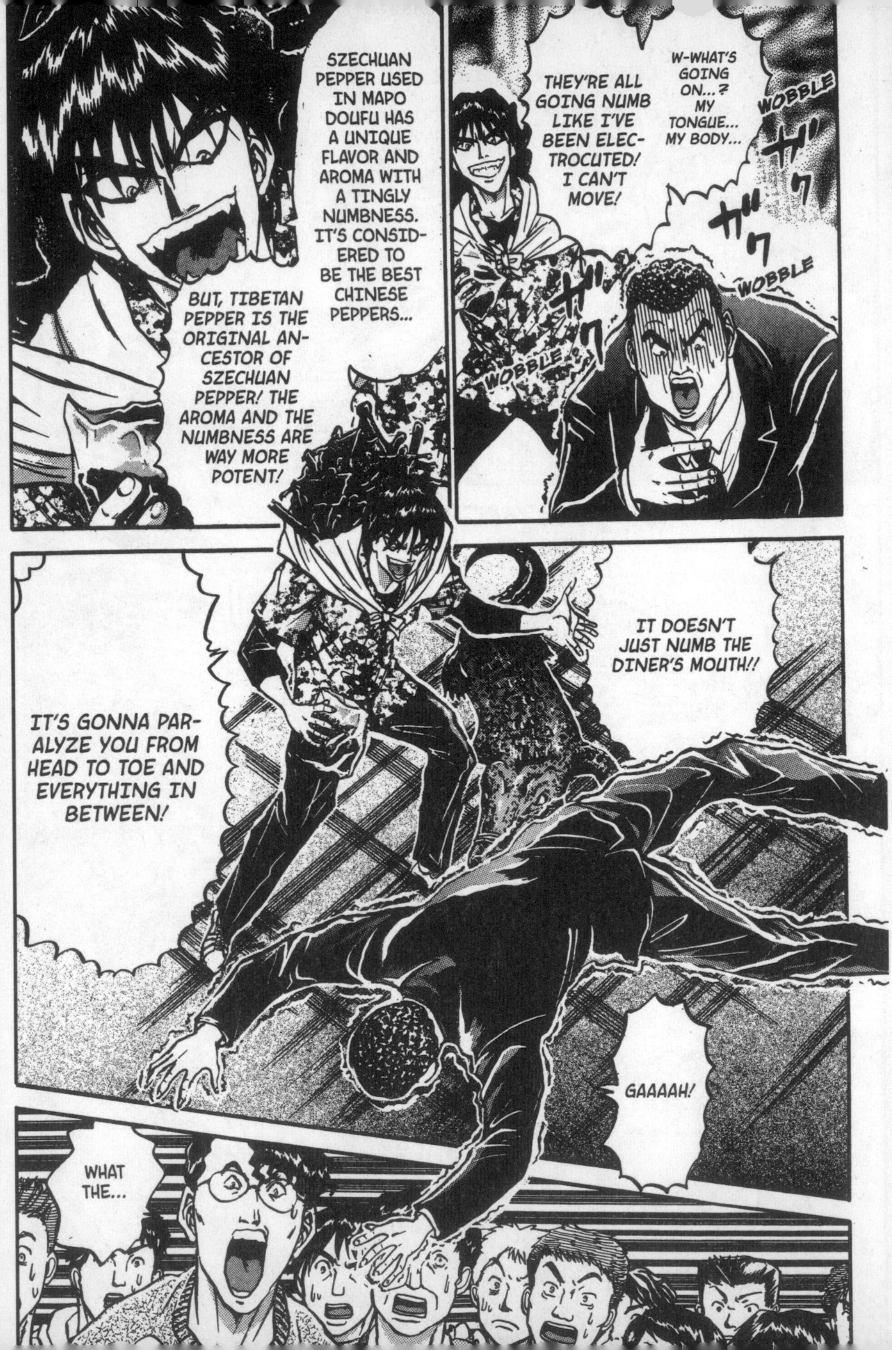
W-WHAT'S GOING ON...? MY TONGUE... MY BODY...
WOBBLE
WOBBLE
THEY'RE ALL GOING NUMB LIKE I'VE BEEN ELEC-TROCUTED! I CAN'T MOVE!
WOBBLE
SZECHUAN PEPPER USED IN MAPO DOUFU HAS A UNIQUE FLAVOR AND AROMA WITH A TINGLY NUMBNESS. IT'S CONSID-ERED TO BE THE BEST CHINESE PEPPERS...
BUT, TIBETAN PEPPER IS THE ORIGINAL AN-CESTOR OF SZECHUAN PEPPER! THE AROMA AND THE NUMBNESS ARE WAY MORE POTENT!
IT DOESN'T JUST NUMB THE DINER'S MOUTH!!
IT'S GONNA PAR-ALYZE YOU FROM HEAD TO TOE AND EVERYTHING IN BETWEEN!
GAAAAH!
WHAT THE...

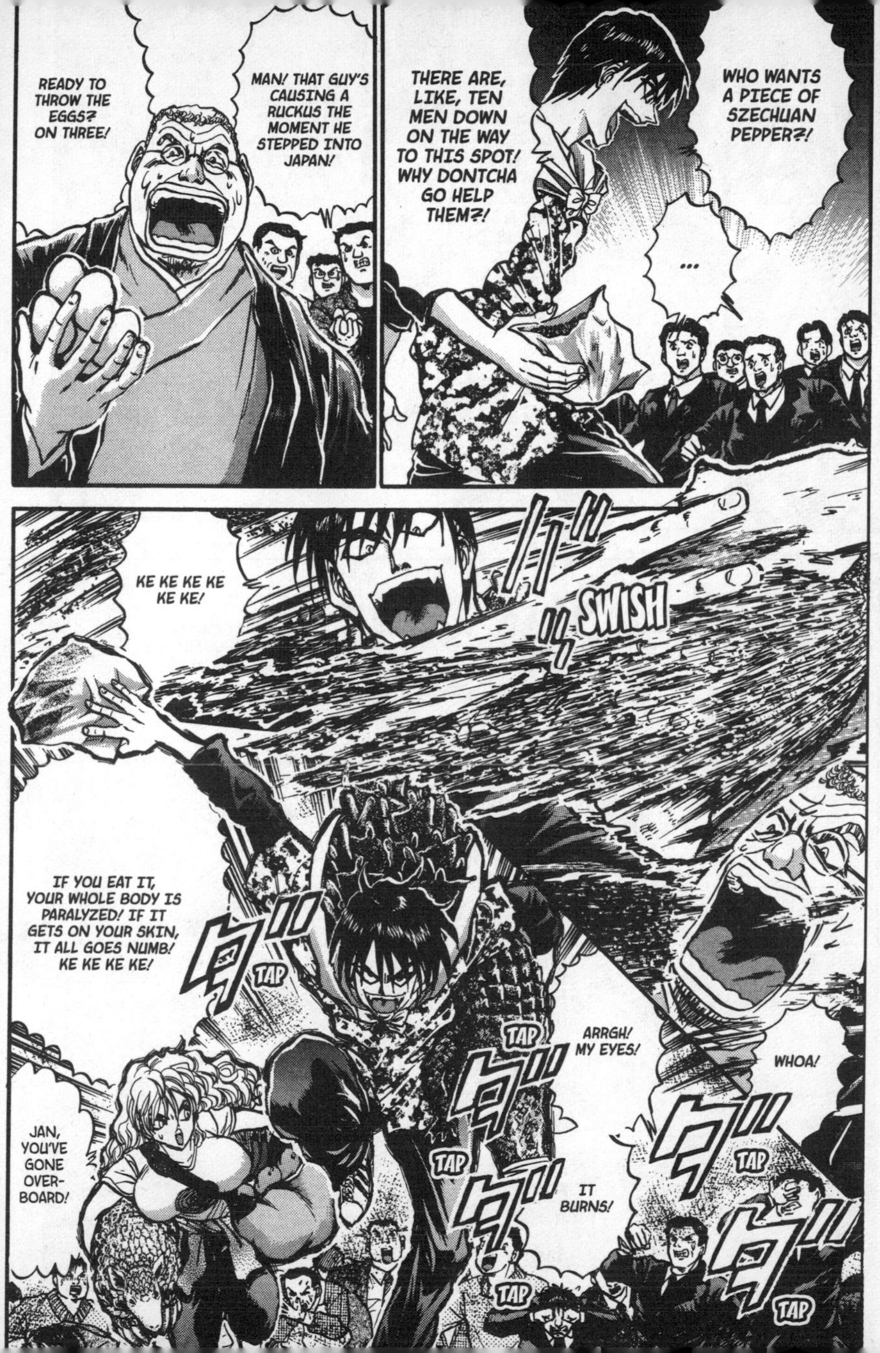
WHO WANTS A PIECE OF SZECHUAN PEPPER?!
THERE ARE, LIKE, TEN MEN DOWN ON THE WAY TO THIS SPOT! WHY DONTCHA GO HELP THEM?!
...
MAN! THAT GUY'S CAUSING A RUCKUS THE MOMENT HE STEPPED INTO JAPAN!
READY TO THROW THE EGGS? ON THREE!
SWISH
KE KE KE KE KE KE!
WHOA!
ARRGH! MY EYES!
TAP
IF YOU EAT IT, YOUR WHOLE BODY IS PARALYZED! IF IT GETS ON YOUR SKIN, IT ALL GOES NUMB! KE KE KE KE!
TAP
TAP
TAP
IT BURNS!
TAP
TAP
JAN, YOU'VE GONE OVER-BOARD!

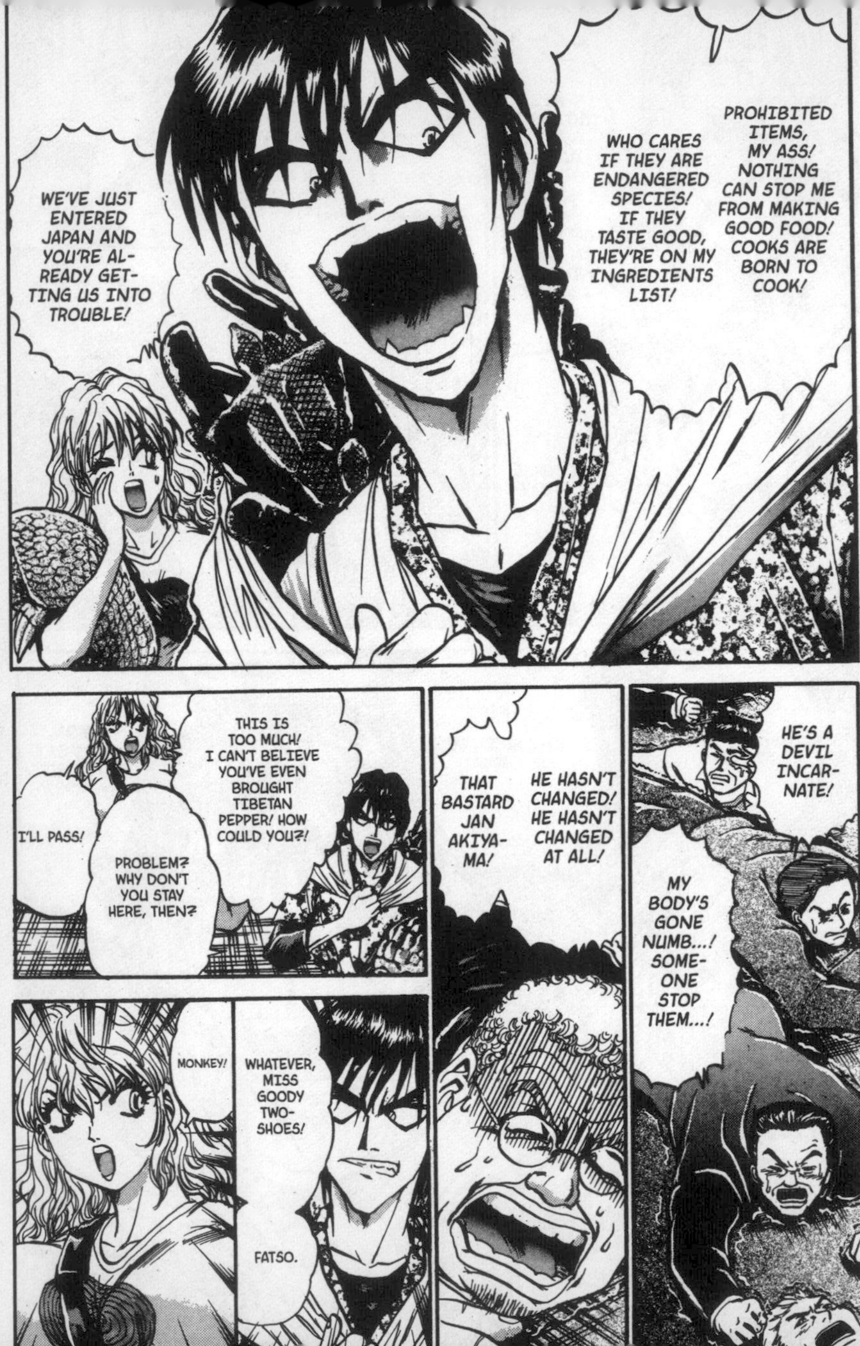
PROHIBITED ITEMS, MY ASS! NOTHING CAN STOP ME FROM MAKING GOOD FOOD! COOKS ARE BORN TO COOK!
WHO CARES IF THEY ARE ENDANGERED SPECIES! IF THEY TASTE GOOD, THEY'RE ON MY INGREDIENTS LIST!
WE'VE JUST ENTERED JAPAN AND YOU'RE AL-READY GET-TING US INTO TROUBLE!
HE'S A DEVIL INCAR-NATE!
MY BODY'S GONE NUMB...! SOME-ONE STOP THEM...!
HE HASN'T CHANGED! HE HASN'T CHANGED AT ALL!
THAT BASTARD JAN AKIYA-MA!
THIS IS TOO MUCH! I CAN'T BELIEVE YOU'VE EVEN BROUGHT TIBETAN PEPPER! HOW COULD YOU?!
PROBLEM? WHY DON'T YOU STAY HERE, THEN?
I'LL PASS!
WHATEVER, MISS GOODY TWO-SHOES!
MONKEY!
FATSO.

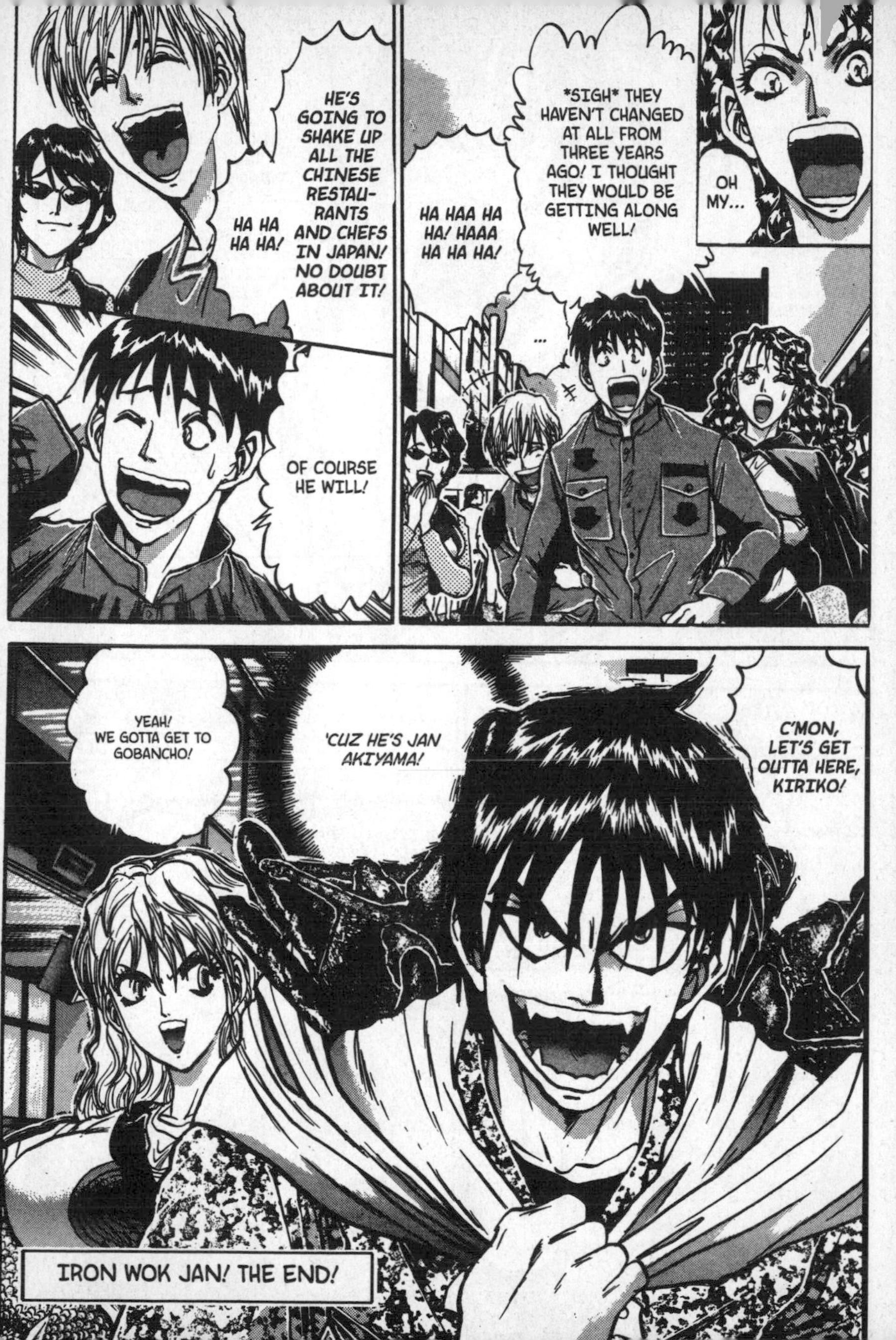
OH MY...
SIGH THEY HAVEN'T CHANGED AT ALL FROM THREE YEARS AGO! I THOUGHT THEY WOULD BE GETTING ALONG WELL!
HA HAA HA HA! HAAA HA HA HA!
...
HE'S GOING TO SHAKE UP ALL THE CHINESE RESTAU-RANTS AND CHEFS IN JAPAN! NO DOUBT ABOUT IT!
HA HA HA HA!
OF COURSE HE WILL!
C'MON, LET'S GET OUTTA HERE, KIRIKO!
'CUZ HE'S JAN AKIYAMA!
YEAH! WE GOTTA GET TO GOBANCHO!
IRON WOK JAN! THE END!

FRESH OFF THE PRESS

"SHOCKING ENDING"

FOREWARD...

THE SIX PAGES YOU'RE ABOUT TO READ WERE
NOT PUBLISHED IN THE PAGES OF THE SHONEN
CHAMPION MAGAZINE IN WHICH THE ORIGINAL
IRON WOK JAN WAS SERIALIZED. IRON WOK JAN
IS A COOKING MANGA, THEREFORE I COULDN'T
DRAW OR EVEN THINK ABOUT THIS ENDING,
BUT I COULD NOT LET GO OF THIS IDEA WHEN
I FIRST THOUGHT ABOUT THE ENDING.
BUT, THIS ENDING WILL TURN THE STORY INTO
SOMETHING OTHER THAN COOKING MANGA...
AFTER COUNTLESS SLEEPLESS NIGHTS OF
PONDERING AND COUNTING ROASTED SHEEP
JUMPING OVER THE GRILL, I'VE COME UP WITH
AN IDEA TO PUT IT IN THE GRAPHIC NOVEL AS A
SPECIAL ENDING. WHAT THE HELL WAS I THINK-
ING TO COME UP WITH THIS ENDING...?!
OF COURSE, I'M HAPPY WITH THE ENDING
SERIALIZED IN THE MAGAZINE, BUT BE SURE
TO CHECK OUT THIS ALTERNATE ENDING THAT'S
GUARANTEED TO BLOW YOU AWAY!

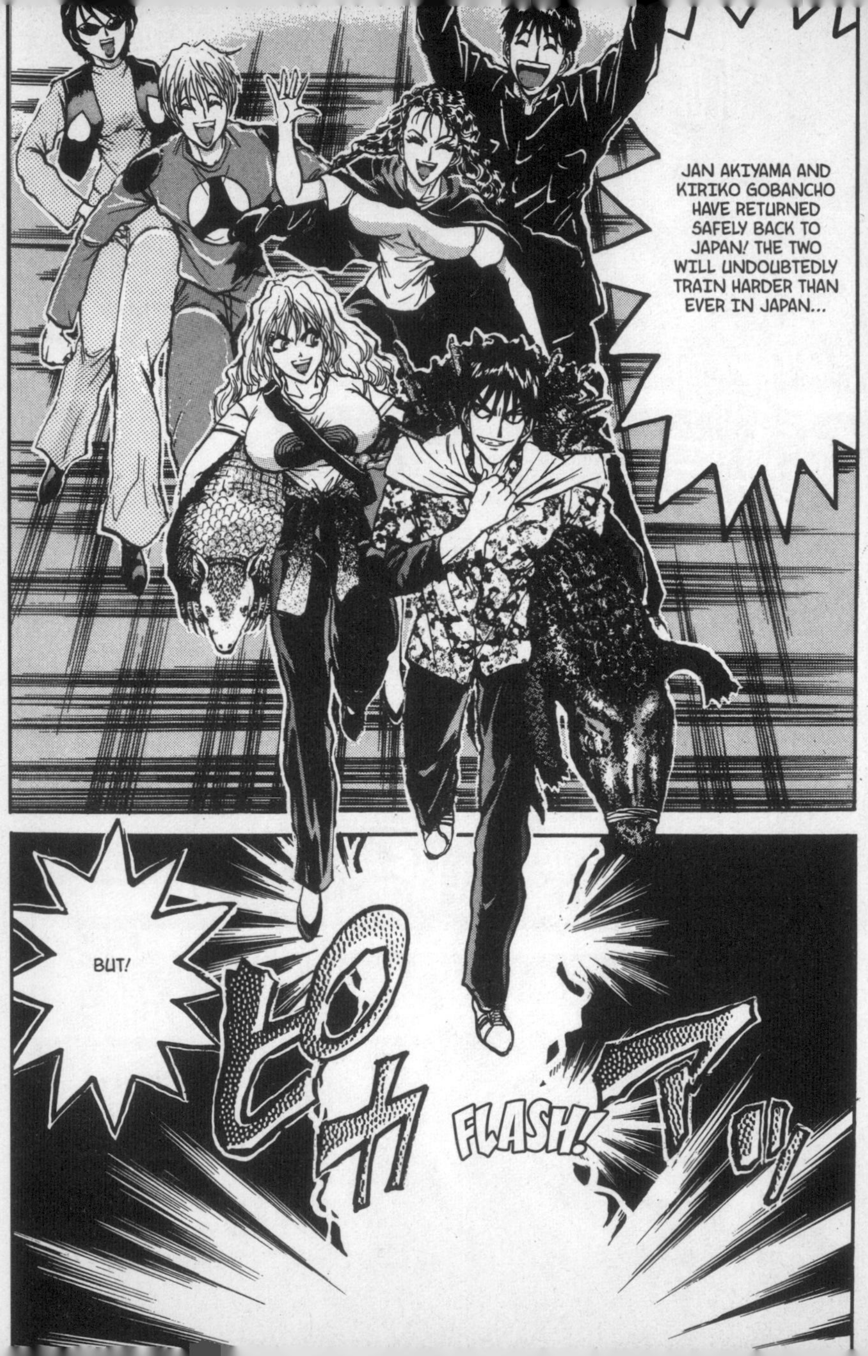
JAN AKIYAMA AND KIRIKO GOBANCHO HAVE RETURNED SAFELY BACK TO JAPAN! THE TWO WILL UNDOUBTEDLY TRAIN HARDER THAN EVER IN JAPAN...
BUT!
FLASH!

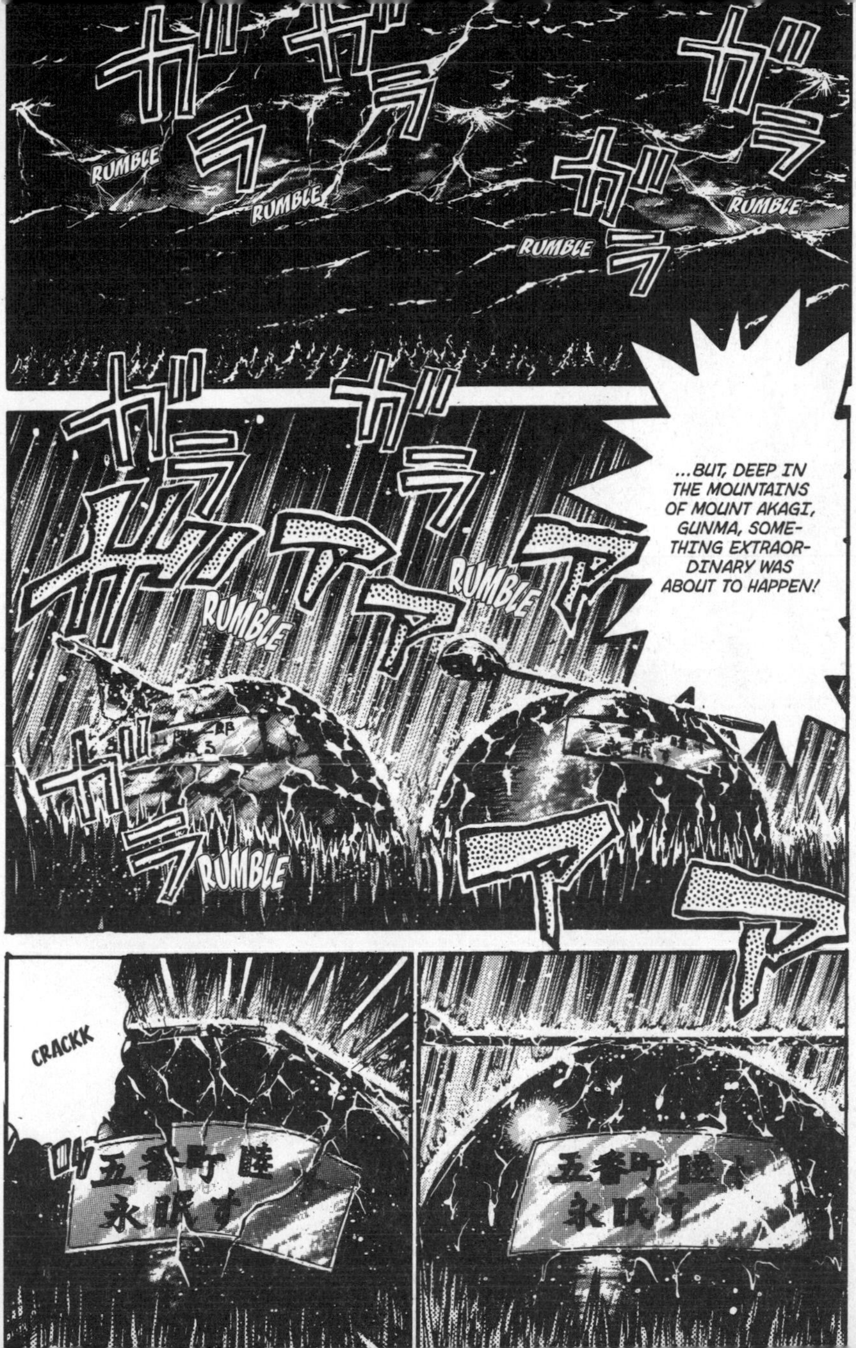

RUMBLE
RUMBLE
RUMBLE
RUMBLE
...BUT, DEEP IN THE MOUNTAINS OF MOUNT AKAGI, GUNMA, SOMETHING EXTRAORDINARY WAS ABOUT TO HAPPEN!
RUMBLE
RUMBLE
RUMBLE
五番町睦
永眠す
CRACKK
五番町睦
永眠す

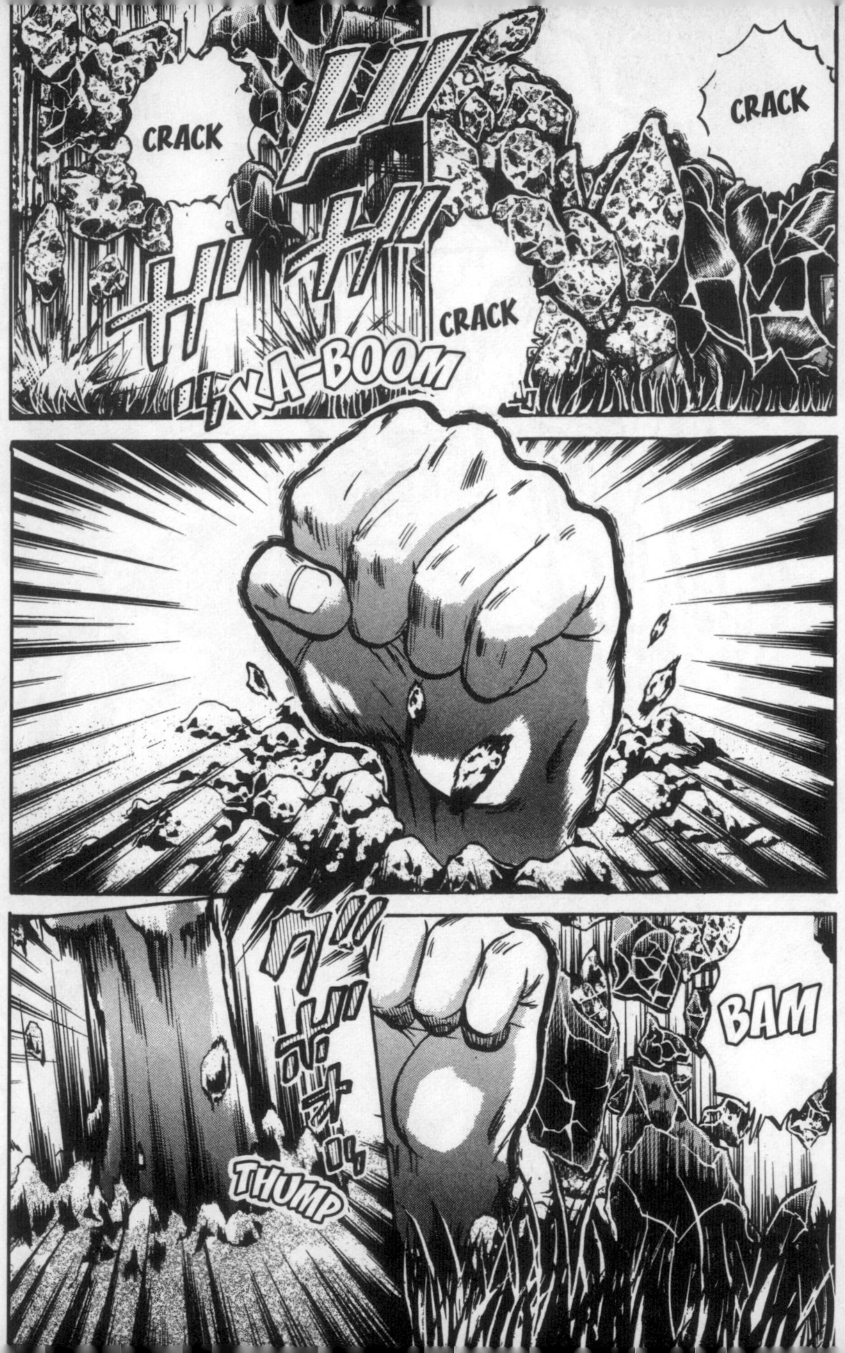
CRACK
CRACK
CRACK
KA-BOOM
BAM
THUMP

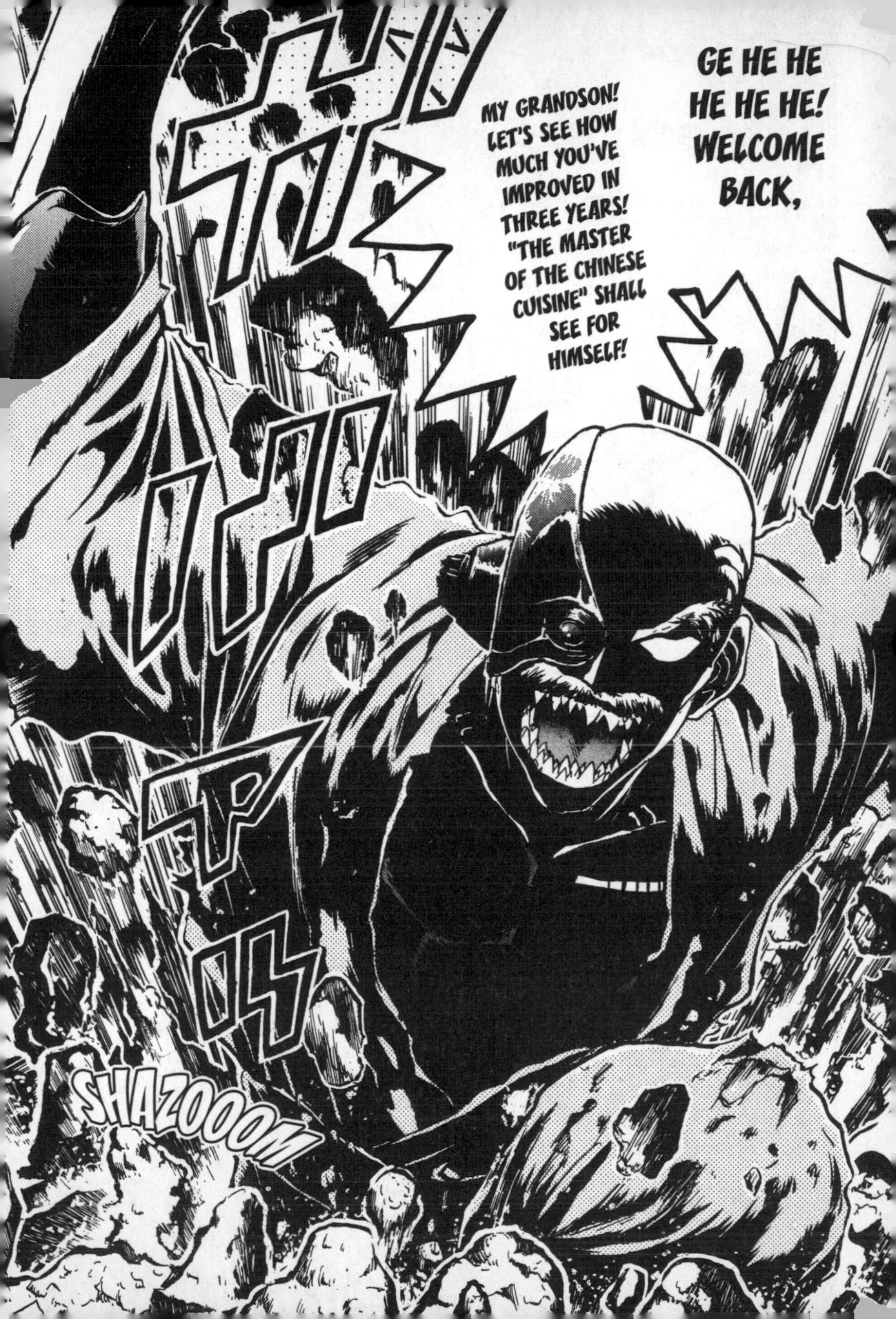
GE HE HE HE HE HE! WELCOME BACK,
MY GRANDSON! LET'S SEE HOW MUCH YOU'VE IMPROVED IN THREE YEARS! "THE MASTER OF THE CHINESE CUISINE" SHALL SEE FOR HIMSELF!
SHAZOOOM

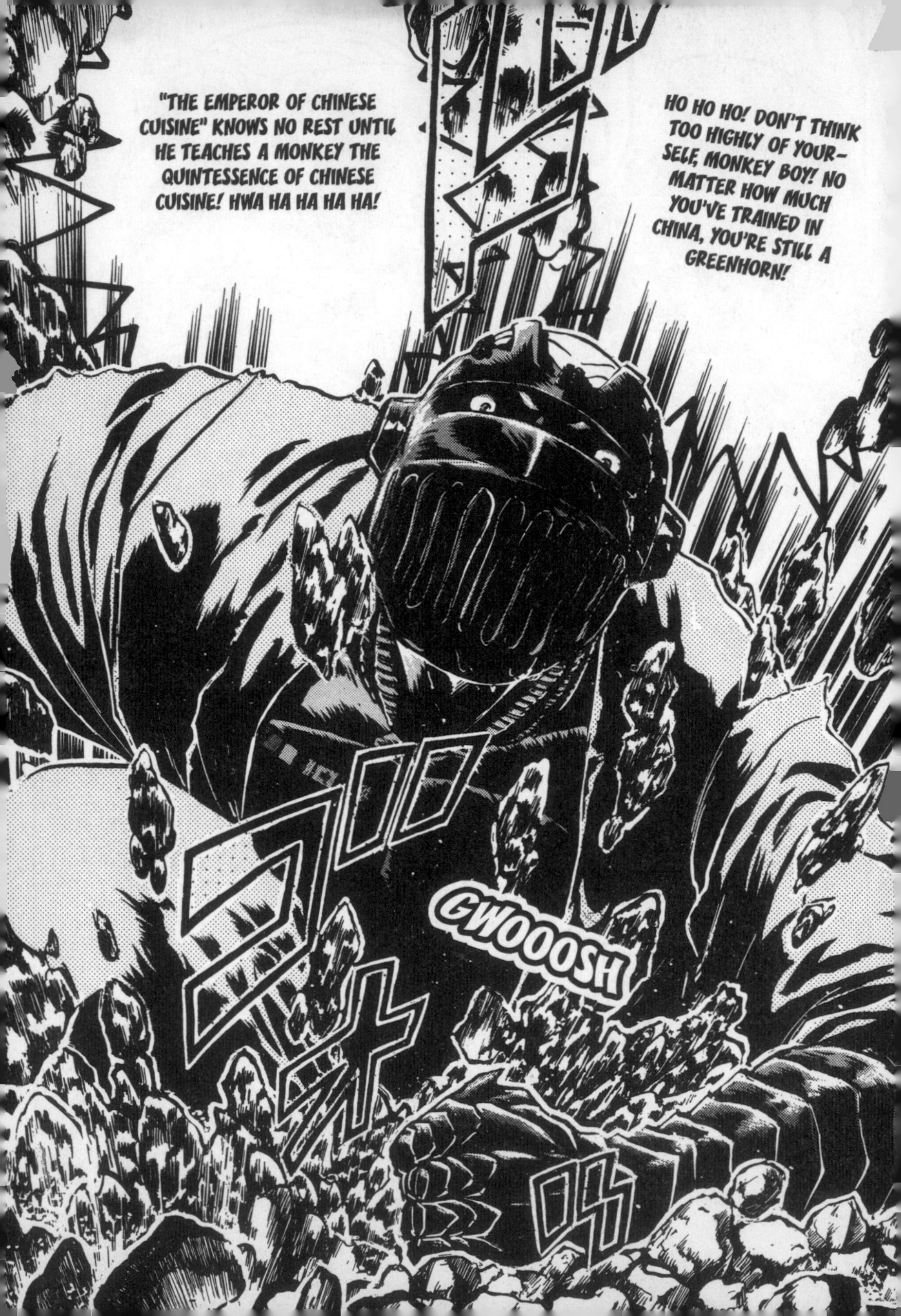
HO HO HO! DON'T THINK TOO HIGHLY OF YOUR-SELF, MONKEY BOY! NO MATTER HOW MUCH YOU'VE TRAINED IN CHINA, YOU'RE STILL A GREENHORN!
"THE EMPEROR OF CHINESE CUISINE" KNOWS NO REST UNTIL HE TEACHES A MONKEY THE QUINTESSENCE OF CHINESE CUISINE! HWA HA HA HA HA!
GWOOOSH

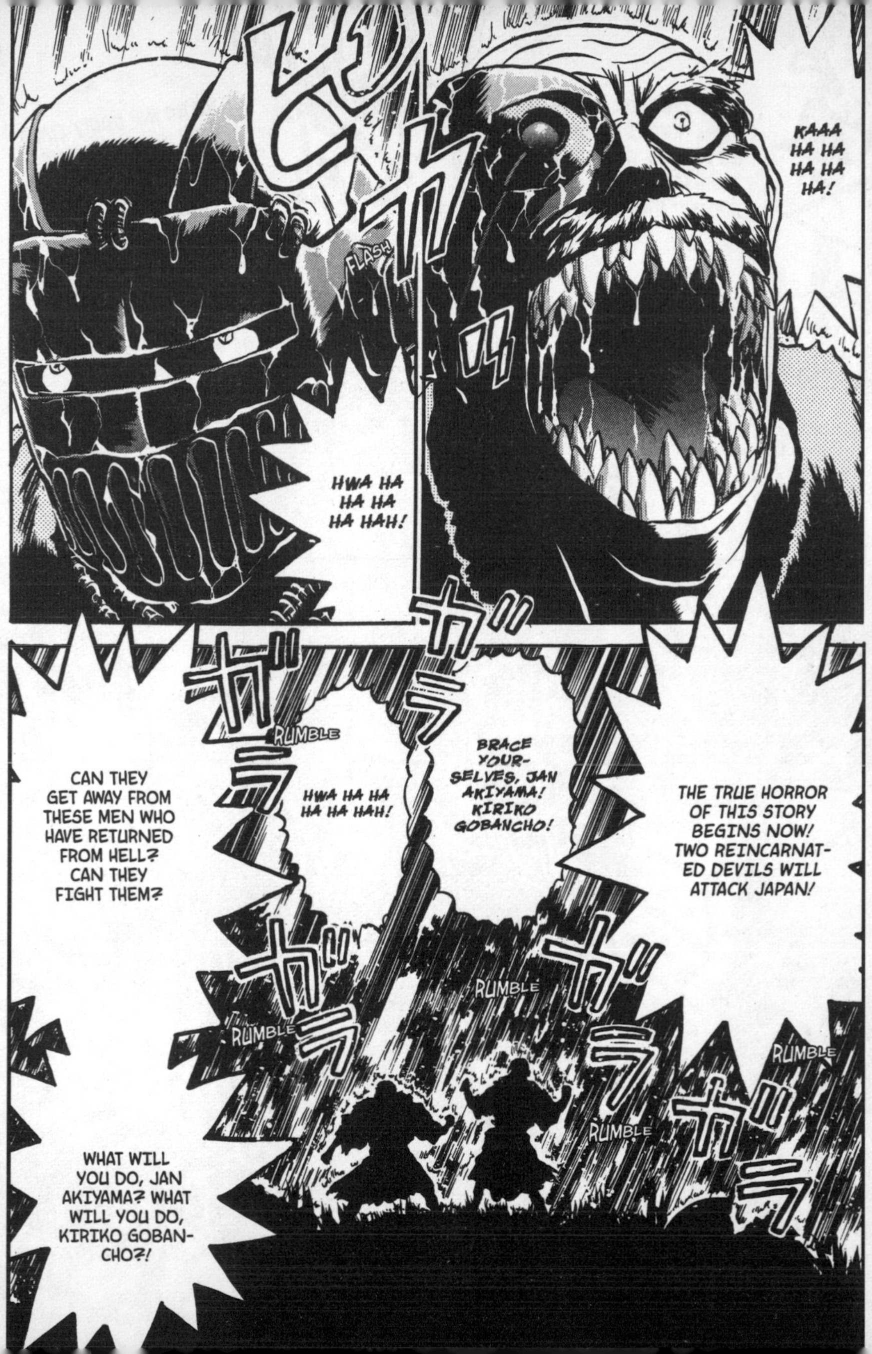
KAAA HA HA HA HA HA!
FLASH
HWA HA HA HA HA HAH!
ガラ
RUMBLE
THE TRUE HORROR OF THIS STORY BEGINS NOW! TWO REINCARNATED DEVILS WILL ATTACK JAPAN!
BRACE YOURSELVES, JAN AKIYAMA! KIRIKO GOBANCHO!
HWA HA HA HA HA HAH!
CAN THEY GET AWAY FROM THESE MEN WHO HAVE RETURNED FROM HELL? CAN THEY FIGHT THEM?
RUMBLE
RUMBLE
RUMBLE
RUMBLE
WHAT WILL YOU DO, JAN AKIYAMA? WHAT WILL YOU DO, KIRIKO GOBANCHO?!

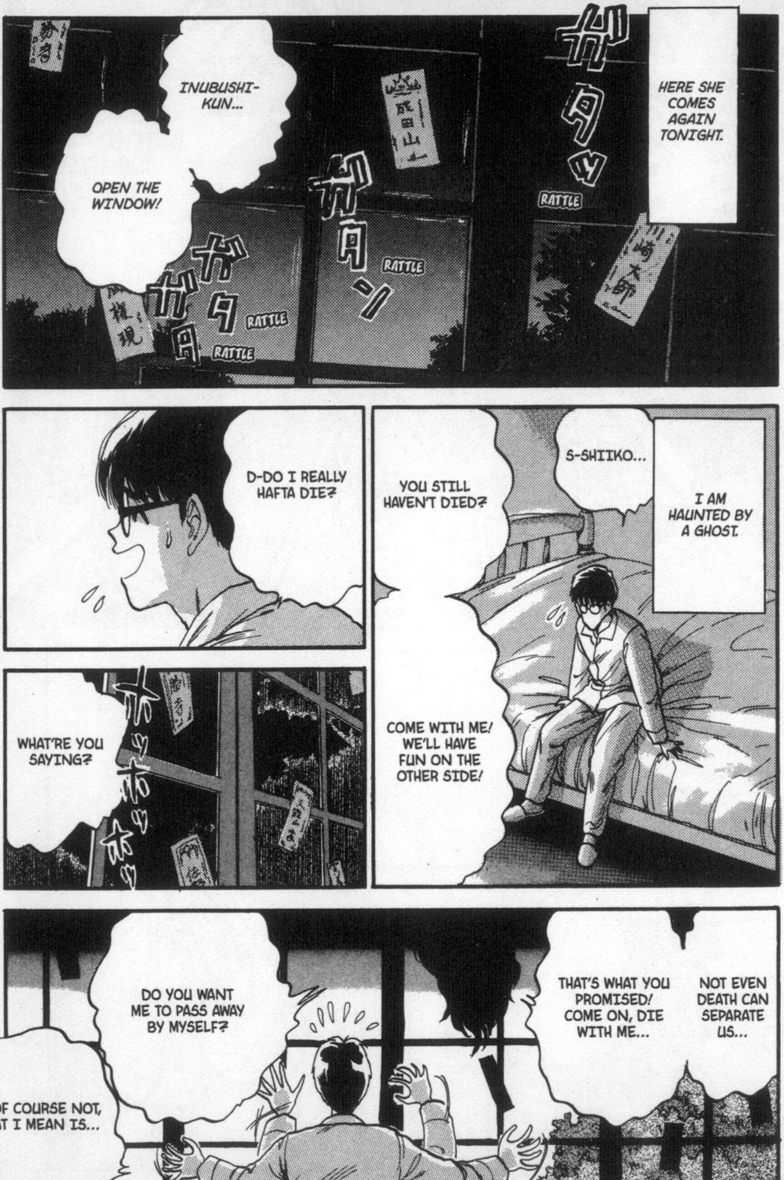
HERE SHE COMES AGAIN TONIGHT.
RATTLE
INUBUSHI-KUN...
OPEN THE WINDOW!
RATTLE
RATTLE
RATTLE
I AM HAUNTED BY A GHOST.
S-SHIIKO...
YOU STILL HAVEN'T DIED?
COME WITH ME! WE'LL HAVE FUN ON THE OTHER SIDE!
D-DO I REALLY HAFTA DIE?
WHAT'RE YOU SAYING?
NOT EVEN DEATH CAN SEPARATE US...
THAT'S WHAT YOU PROMISED! COME ON, DIE WITH ME...
DO YOU WANT ME TO PASS AWAY BY MYSELF?
O-OF COURSE NOT, WHAT I MEAN IS...

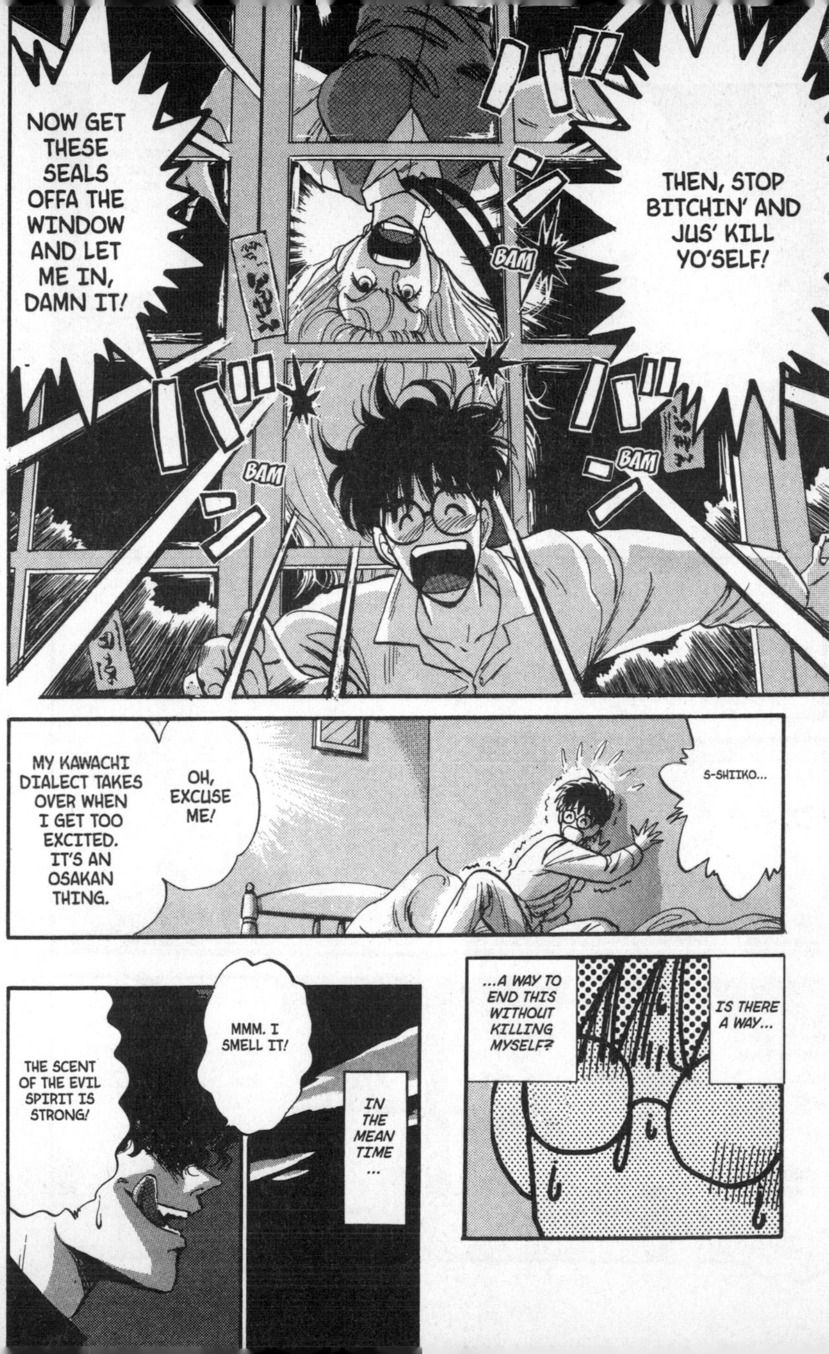
THEN, STOP BITCHIN' AND JUS' KILL YO'SELF!
NOW GET THESE SEALS OFFA THE WINDOW AND LET ME IN, DAMN IT!
BAM
BAM
BAM
S-SHIIKO...
OH, EXCUSE ME!
MY KAWACHI DIALECT TAKES OVER WHEN I GET TOO EXCITED. IT'S AN OSAKAN THING.
IS THERE A WAY...
...A WAY TO END THIS WITHOUT KILLING MYSELF?
IN THE MEAN TIME ...
MMM. I SMELL IT!
THE SCENT OF THE EVIL SPIRIT IS STRONG!

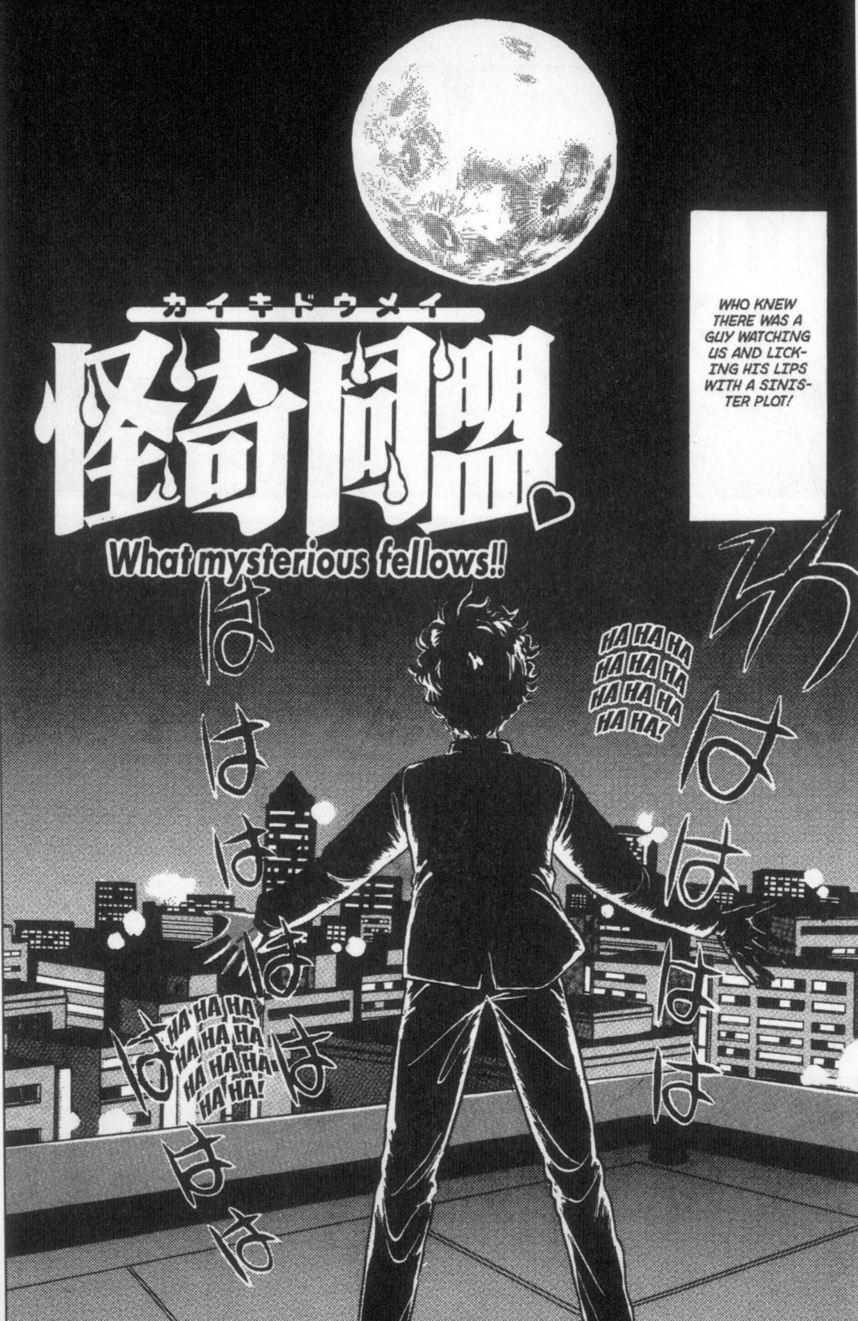
WHO KNEW THERE WAS A GUY WATCHING US AND LICK-ING HIS LIPS WITH A SINIS-TER PLOT!
カイキドウメイ
怪奇同盟
What mysterious fellows!!
はははは
HA HA HA HA HA HA HA HA HA HA HA!
はははははは
はははははは
HA HA HA HA HA HA HA HA HA HA HA!

THEY SAY SHIKO KIJITA LOOKED PEACEFUL WHEN SHE PASSED AWAY...

I'VE GOTTA TELL YOU, BUT THAT'S ONLY HOW SHE LOOKED ON THE OUTSIDE...

INUBUSHI-KUN, YOU LOOK GAUNT!

げっそり
HAGGARD

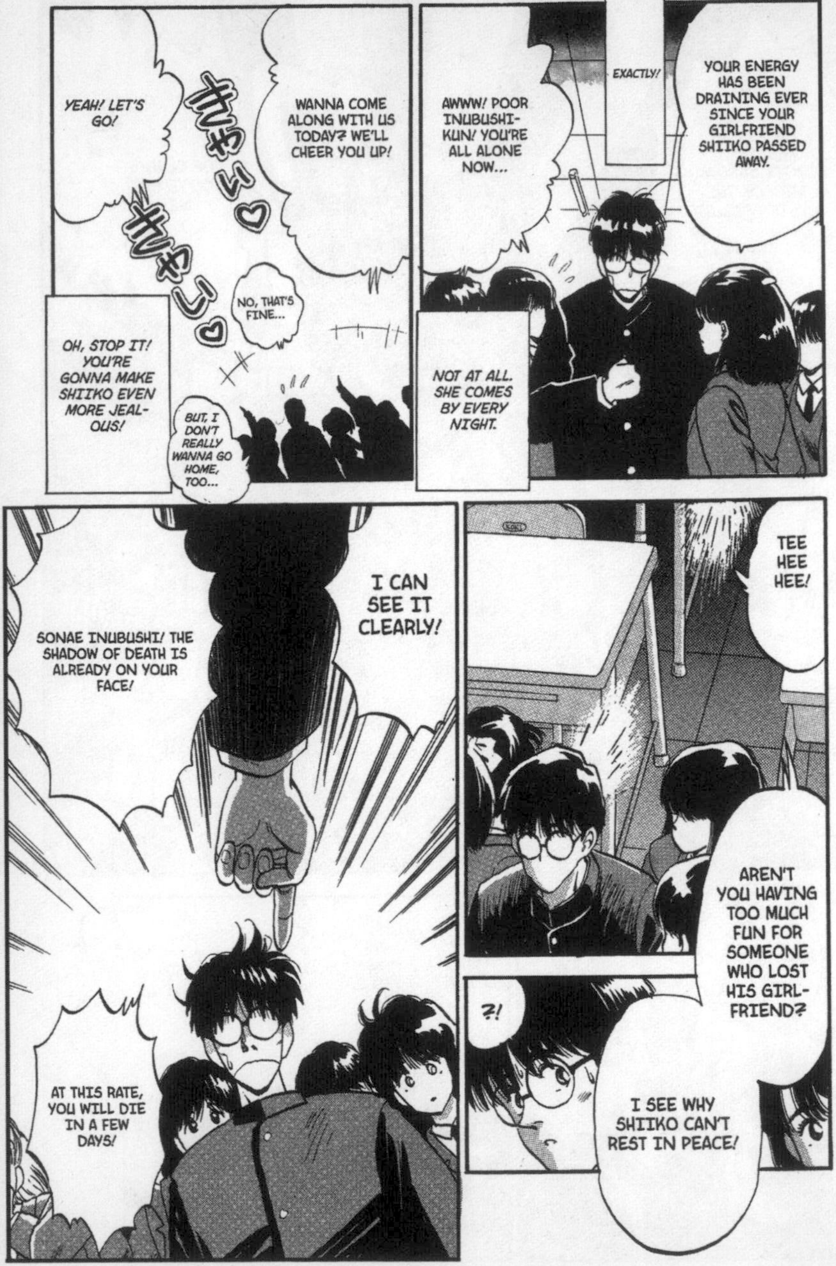
YOUR ENERGY HAS BEEN DRAINING EVER SINCE YOUR GIRLFRIEND SHIIKO PASSED AWAY.
EXACTLY!
AWWW! POOR INUBUSHI-KUN! YOU'RE ALL ALONE NOW...
NOT AT ALL. SHE COMES BY EVERY NIGHT.
WANNA COME ALONG WITH US TODAY? WE'LL CHEER YOU UP!
きゃい♡
きゃい♡
YEAH! LET'S GO!
NO, THAT'S FINE...
OH, STOP IT! YOU'RE GONNA MAKE SHIIKO EVEN MORE JEAL-OUS!
BUT, I DON'T REALLY WANNA GO HOME, TOO...
TEE HEE HEE!
AREN'T YOU HAVING TOO MUCH FUN FOR SOMEONE WHO LOST HIS GIRL-FRIEND?
?!
I SEE WHY SHIIKO CAN'T REST IN PEACE!
I CAN SEE IT CLEARLY!
SONAE INUBUSHI! THE SHADOW OF DEATH IS ALREADY ON YOUR FACE!
AT THIS RATE, YOU WILL DIE IN A FEW DAYS!

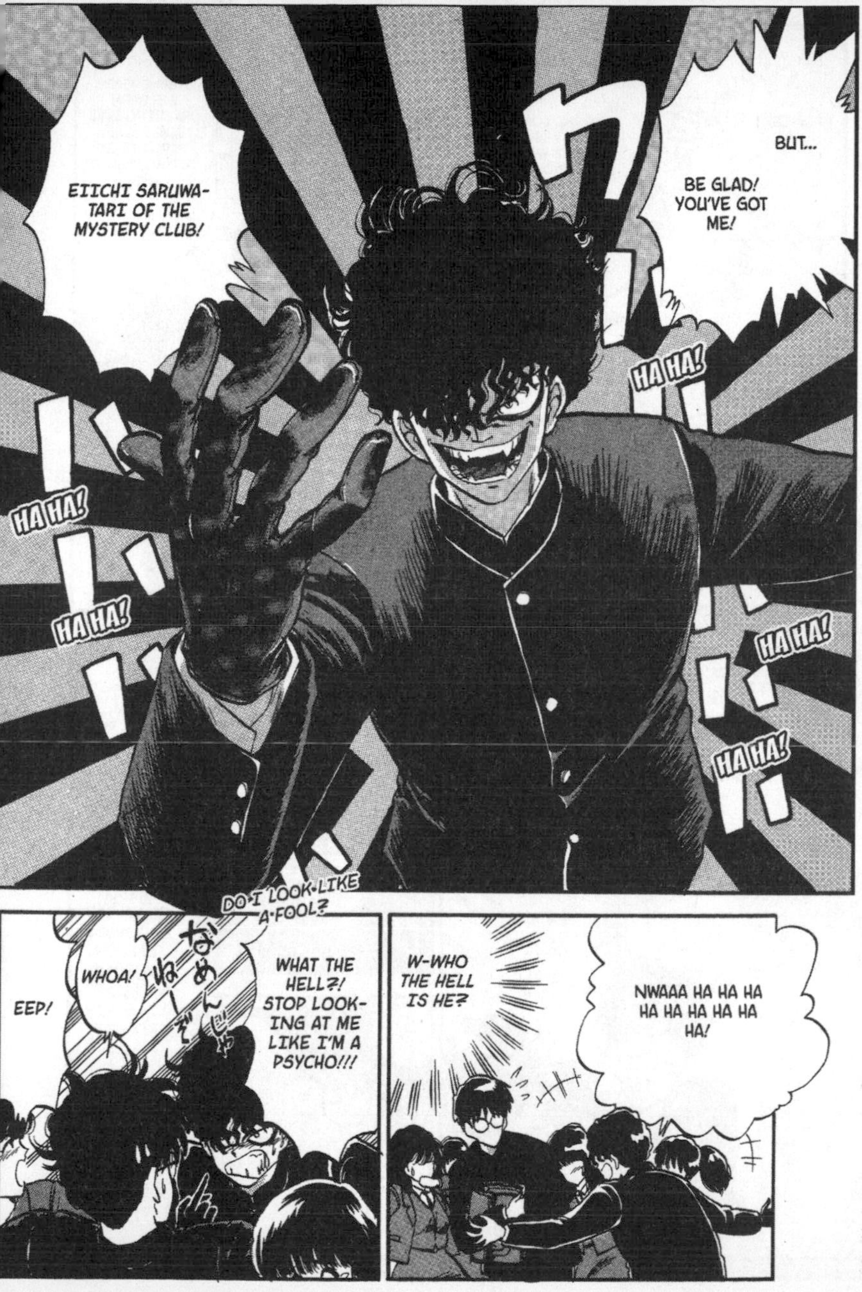
BUT...
BE GLAD! YOU'VE GOT ME!
EIICHI SARUWA-TARI OF THE MYSTERY CLUB!
HA HA!
HA HA!
HA HA!
HA HA!
HA HA!
NWAAA HA HA HA HA HA HA HA HA HA!
W-WHO THE HELL IS HE?
DO I LOOK LIKE A FOOL?
なめんじゃねーぞ
WHAT THE HELL?! STOP LOOK-ING AT ME LIKE I'M A PSYCHO!!!
WHOA!
EEP!

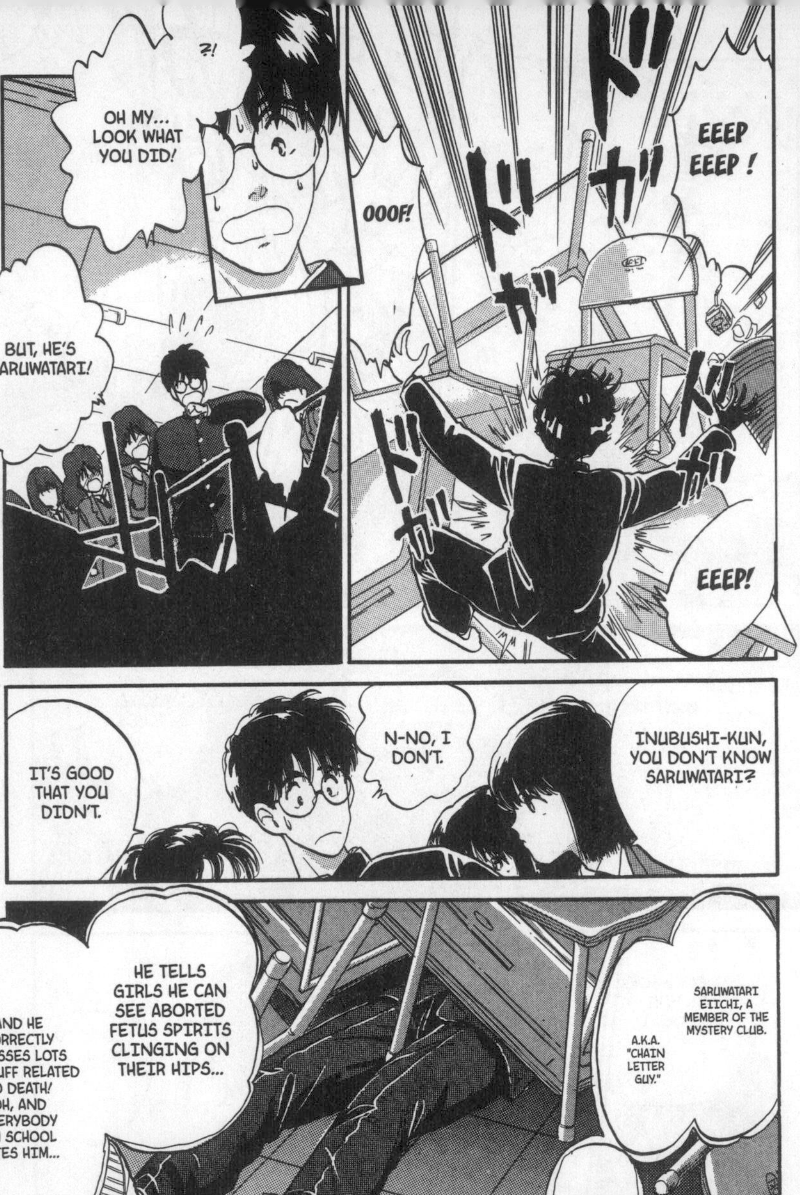
EEEP EEEP !
OOOF!
EEEP!
?!
OH MY... LOOK WHAT YOU DID!
BUT, HE'S SARUWATARI!
INUBUSHI-KUN, YOU DON'T KNOW SARUWATARI?
N-NO, I DON'T.
IT'S GOOD THAT YOU DIDN'T.
SARUWATARI EIICHI, A MEMBER OF THE MYSTERY CLUB.
A.K.A. "CHAIN LETTER GUY."
UH-HUH.!
HE TELLS GIRLS HE CAN SEE ABORTED FETUS SPIRITS CLINGING ON THEIR HIPS...
AND HE CORRECTLY GUESSES LOTS OF STUFF RELATED TO DEATH! OH, AND EVERYBODY IN SCHOOL HATES HIM...

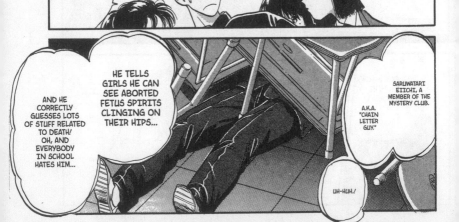

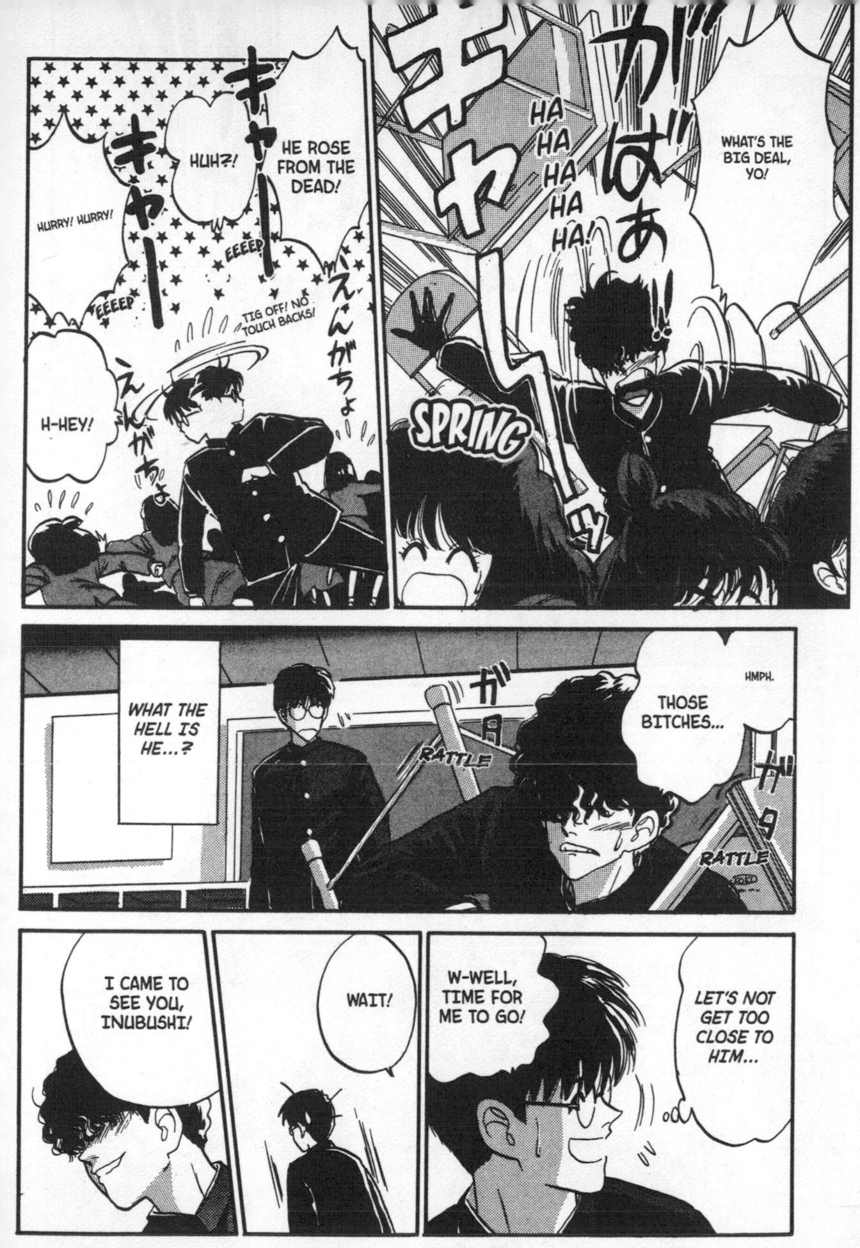
WHAT'S THE BIG DEAL, YO!
がばぁ!!
HA HA HA HA HA!
SPRING
えんがちょ
TIG OFF! NO TOUCH BACKS!
HE ROSE FROM THE DEAD!
キャーキャー
EEEEP
HUH?!
HURRY! HURRY!
EEEEP
H-HEY!
えんがちょ
HMPH.
THOSE BITCHES...
ガタ
RATTLE
ガタ
RATTLE
WHAT THE HELL IS HE...?
LET'S NOT GET TOO CLOSE TO HIM...
W-WELL, TIME FOR ME TO GO!
WAIT!
I CAME TO SEE YOU, INUBUSHI!

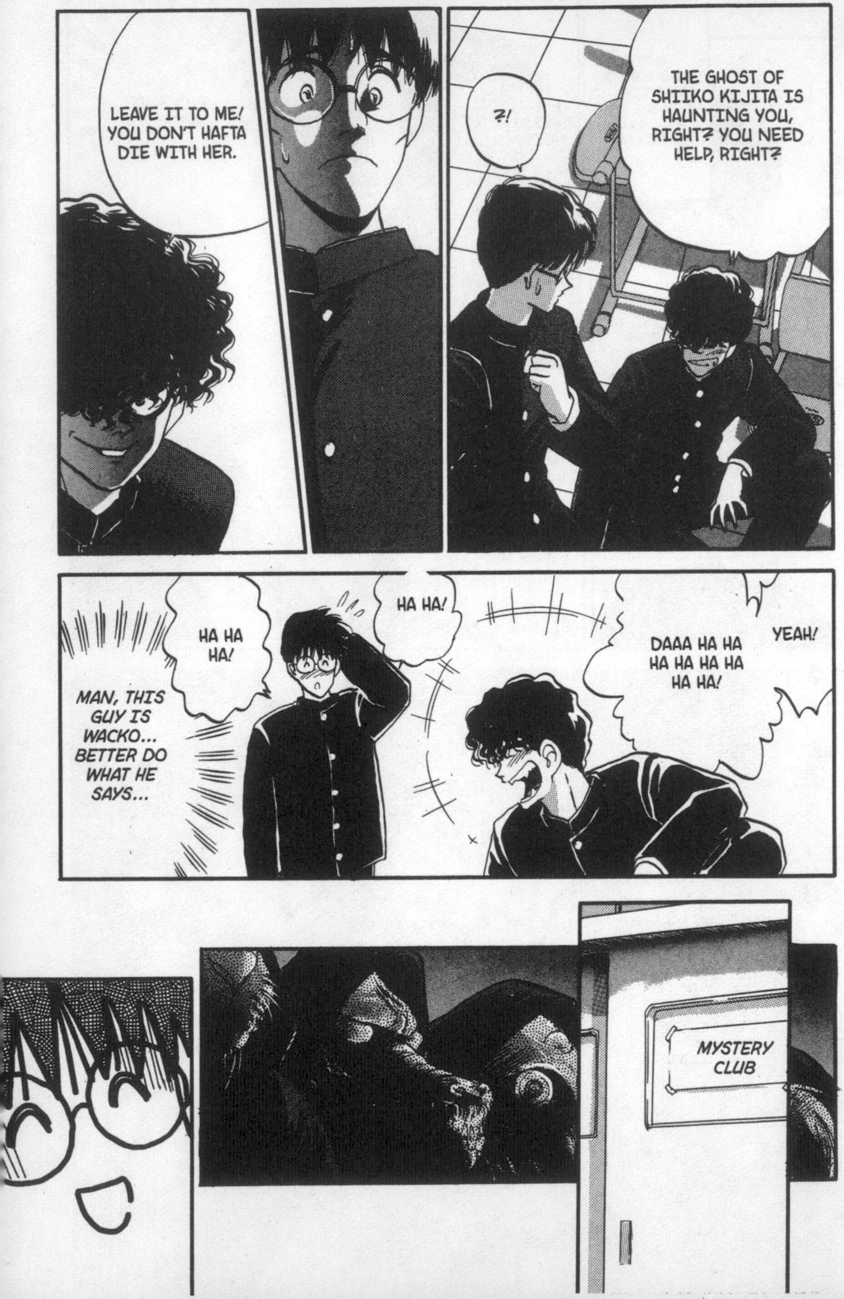
THE GHOST OF SHIIKO KIJITA IS HAUNTING YOU, RIGHT? YOU NEED HELP, RIGHT?
?!
LEAVE IT TO ME! YOU DON'T HAFTA DIE WITH HER.
YEAH!
DAAA HA HA HA HA HA HA HA HA!
HA HA!
HA HA HA!
MAN, THIS GUY IS WACKO... BETTER DO WHAT HE SAYS...
MYSTERY CLUB

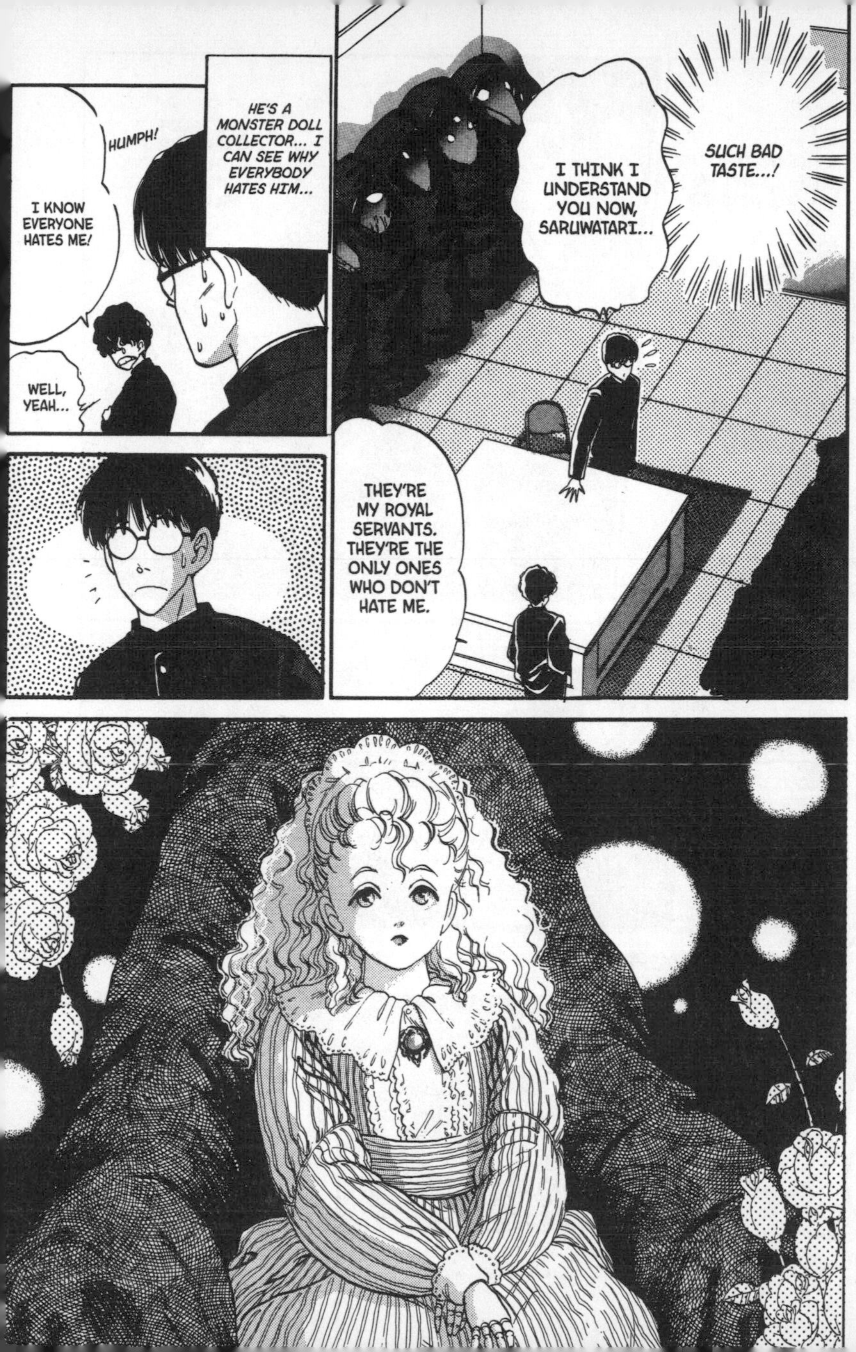
SUCH BAD TASTE...!
I THINK I UNDERSTAND YOU NOW, SARUWATARI...
THEY'RE MY ROYAL SERVANTS. THEY'RE THE ONLY ONES WHO DON'T HATE ME.
HE'S A MONSTER DOLL COLLECTOR... I CAN SEE WHY EVERYBODY HATES HIM...
HUMPH!
I KNOW EVERYONE HATES ME!
WELL, YEAH...

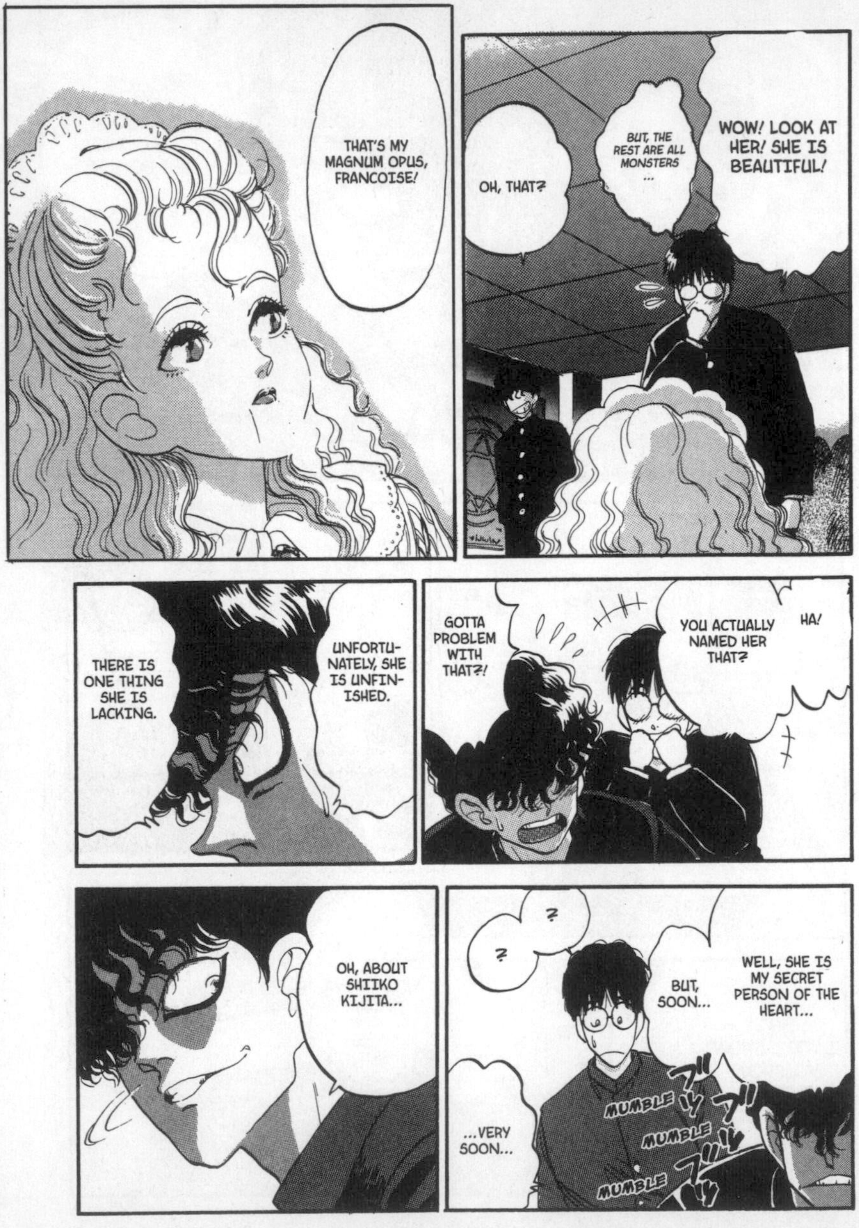
WOW! LOOK AT HER! SHE IS BEAUTIFUL!
BUT, THE REST ARE ALL MONSTERS ...
OH, THAT?
THAT'S MY MAGNUM OPUS, FRANCOISE!
HA!
YOU ACTUALLY NAMED HER THAT?
GOTTA PROBLEM WITH THAT?!
UNFORTUNATELY, SHE IS UNFINISHED.
THERE IS ONE THING SHE IS LACKING.
WELL, SHE IS MY SECRET PERSON OF THE HEART...
BUT, SOON...
?
?
MUMBLE
MUMBLE
MUMBLE
...VERY SOON...
OH, ABOUT SHIIKO KIJITA...

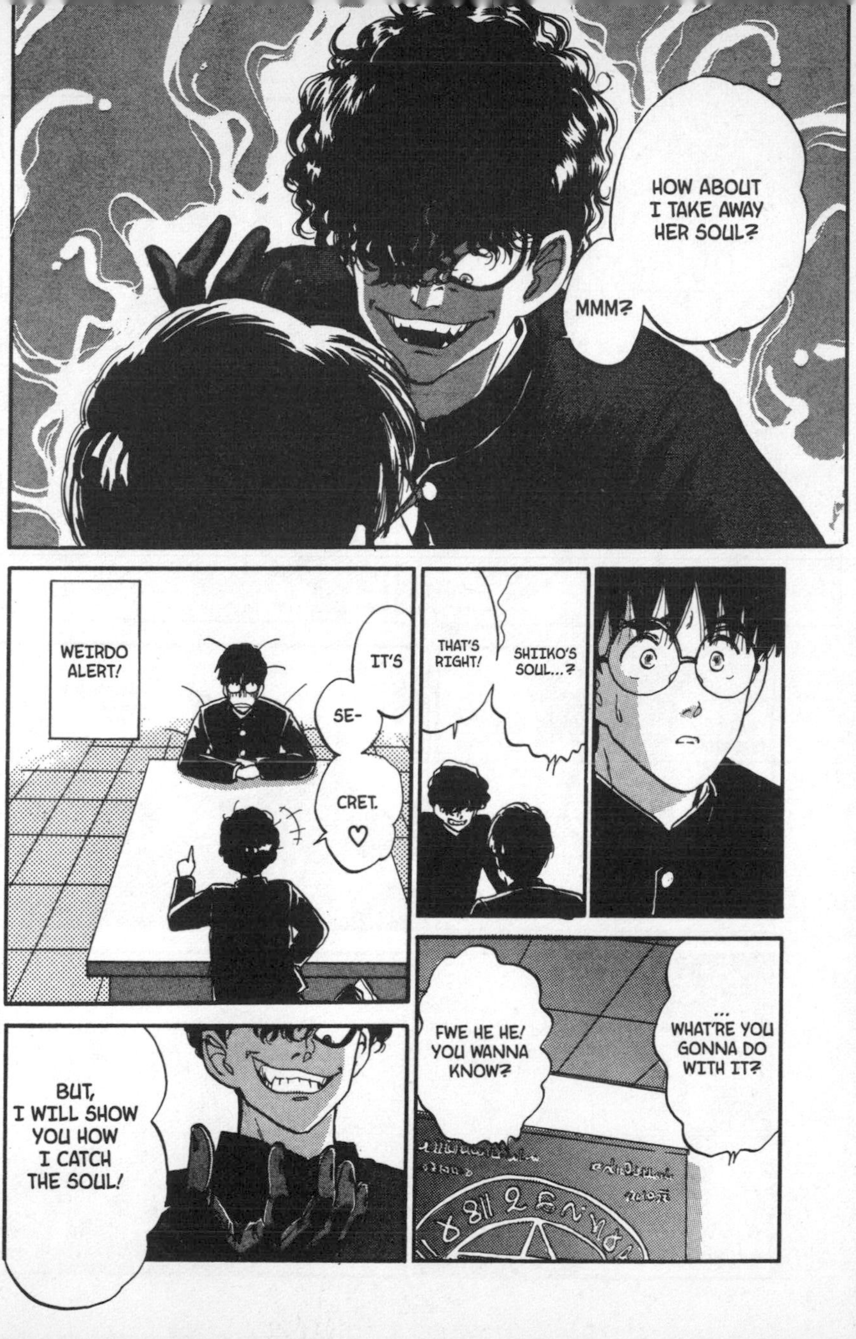
HOW ABOUT I TAKE AWAY HER SOUL?
MMM?
SHIIKO'S SOUL...?
THAT'S RIGHT!
IT'S SE- CRET. ♡
WEIRDO ALERT!
... WHAT'RE YOU GONNA DO WITH IT?
FWE HE HE! YOU WANNA KNOW?
BUT, I WILL SHOW YOU HOW I CATCH THE SOUL!

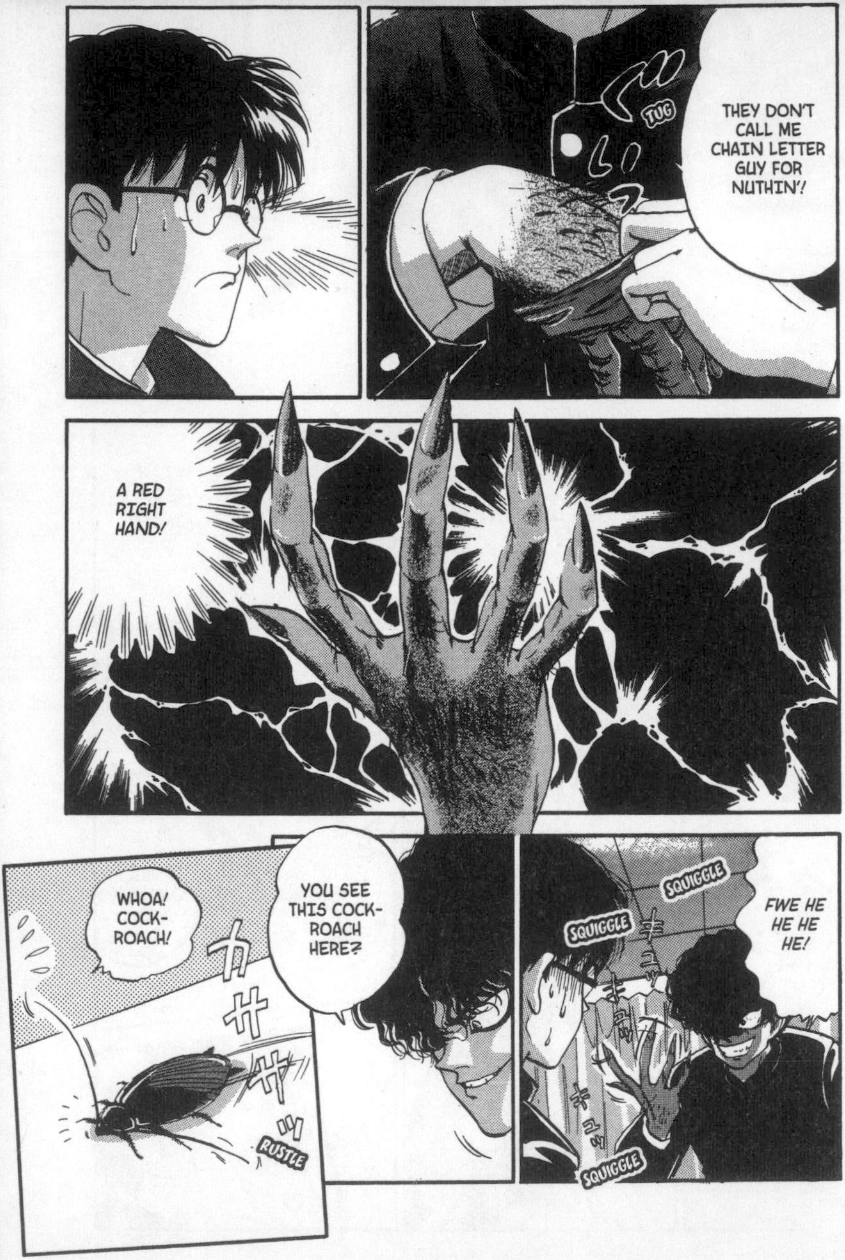
TUG
THEY DON'T CALL ME CHAIN LETTER GUY FOR NUTHIN'!
A RED RIGHT HAND!
SQUIGGLE
SQUIGGLE
FWE HE HE HE HE!
SQUIGGLE
SQUIGGLE
YOU SEE THIS COCK-ROACH HERE?
WHOA! COCK-ROACH!
RUSTLE

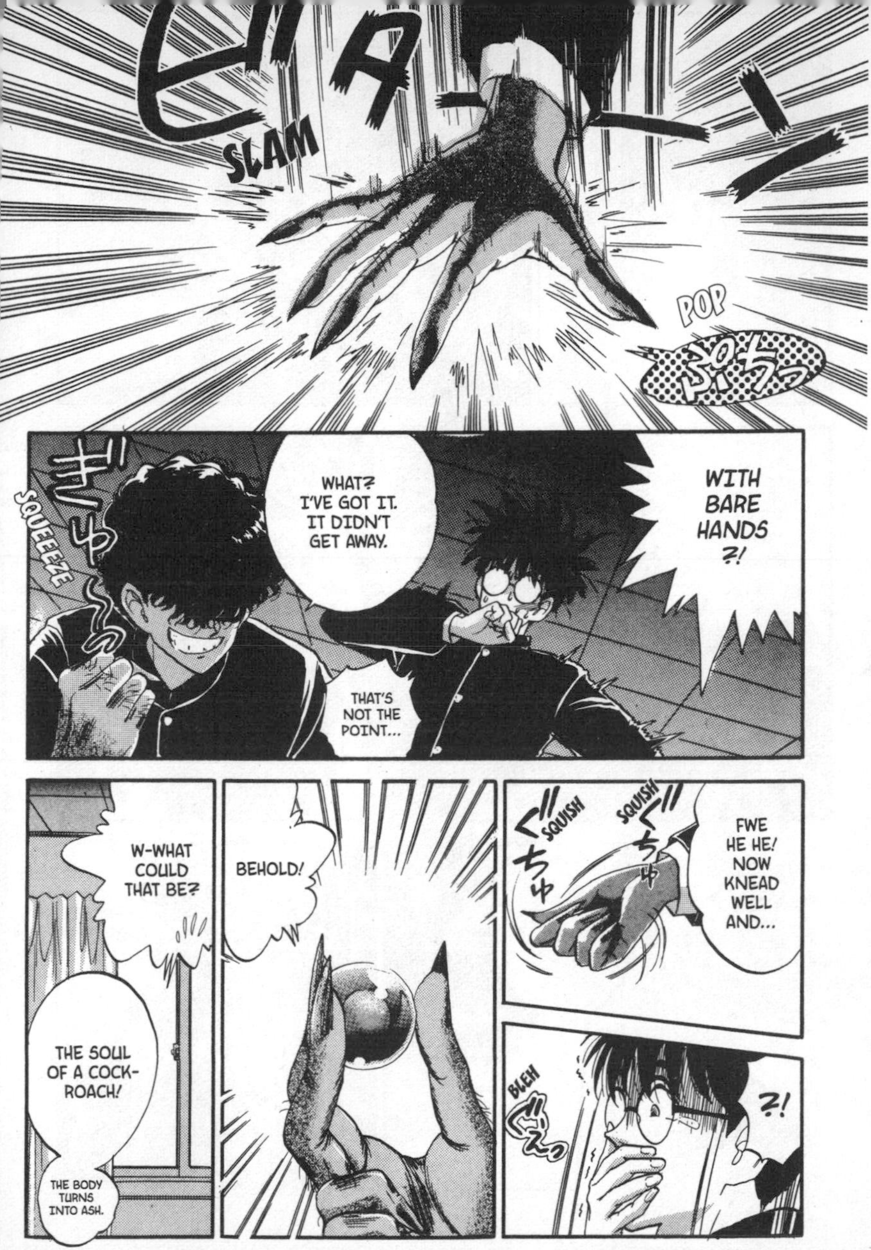
ビタ
SLAM
POP
ぷちっ
WITH BARE HANDS ?!
WHAT? I'VE GOT IT. IT DIDN'T GET AWAY.
THAT'S NOT THE POINT...
SQUEEEZE
FWE HE HE! NOW KNEAD WELL AND...
SQUISH
SQUISH
?!
BLEH
BEHOLD!
W-WHAT COULD THAT BE?
THE SOUL OF A COCK-ROACH!
THE BODY TURNS INTO ASH.

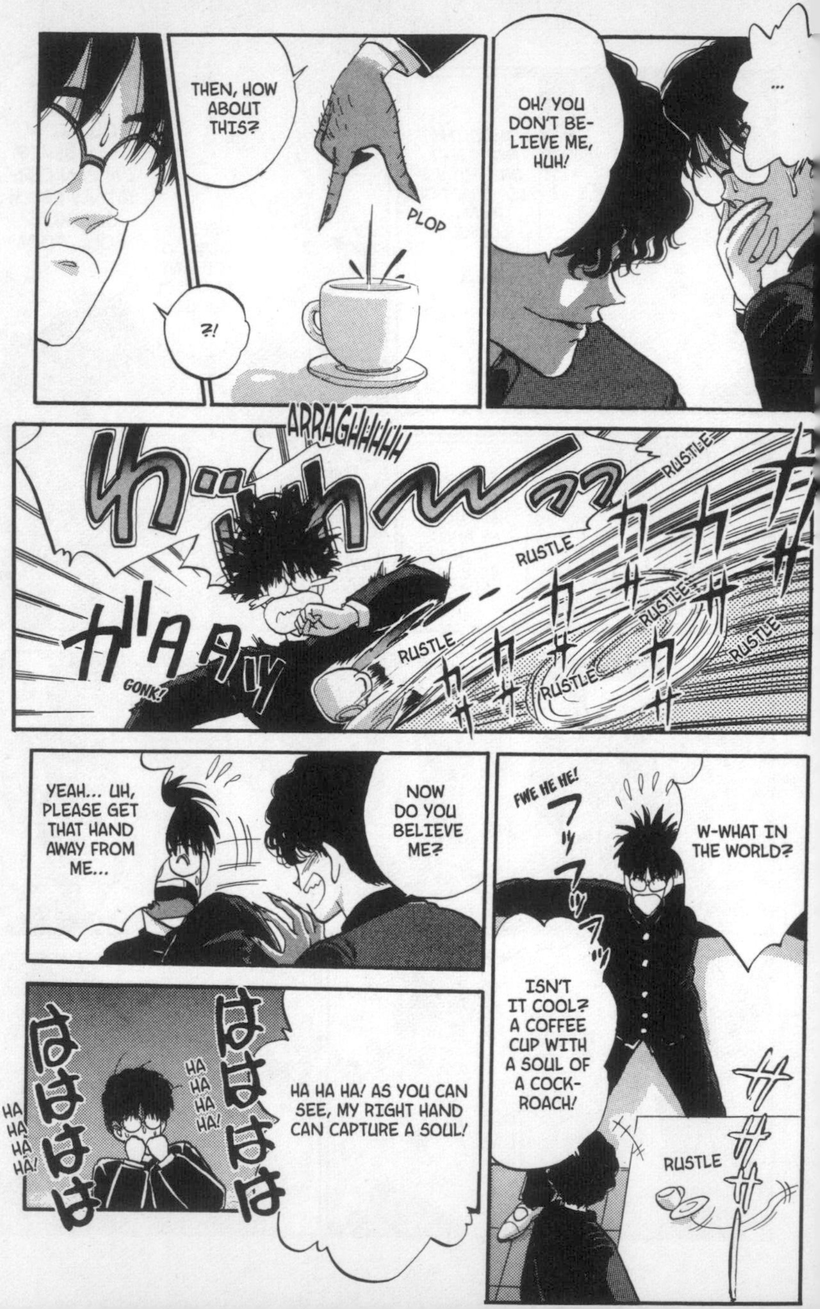
...
OH! YOU DON'T BE-LIEVE ME, HUH!
THEN, HOW ABOUT THIS?
PLOP
?!
ARRAGHHHHH
RUSTLE
RUSTLE
RUSTLE
RUSTLE
RUSTLE
RUSTLE
RUSTLE
GONK!
W-WHAT IN THE WORLD?
FWE HE HE!
ISN'T IT COOL? A COFFEE CUP WITH A SOUL OF A COCK-ROACH!
RUSTLE
NOW DO YOU BELIEVE ME?
YEAH... UH, PLEASE GET THAT HAND AWAY FROM ME...
HA HA HA! AS YOU CAN SEE, MY RIGHT HAND CAN CAPTURE A SOUL!
HA HA HA HA!
HA HA HA HA!

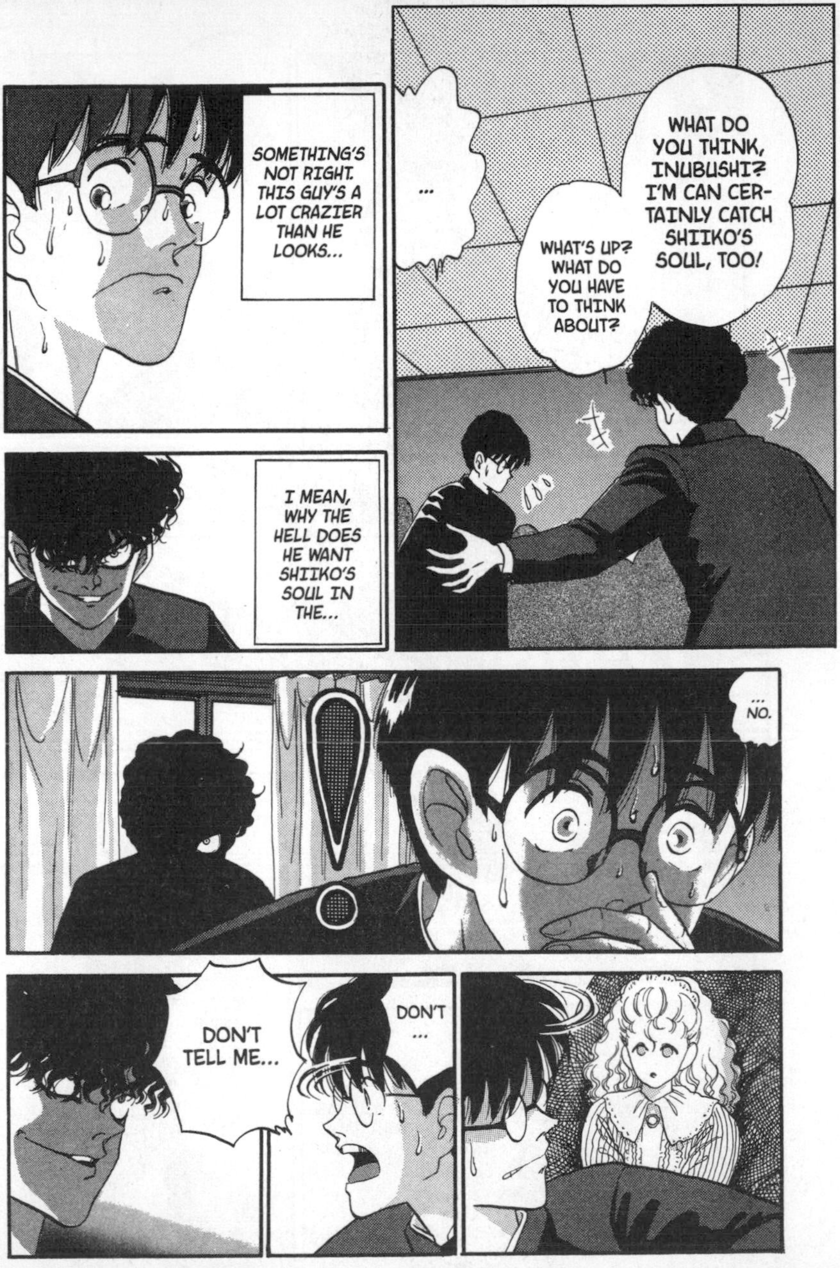
WHAT DO YOU THINK, INUBUSHI? I'M CAN CER-TAINLY CATCH SHIIKO'S SOUL, TOO!
...
WHAT'S UP? WHAT DO YOU HAVE TO THINK ABOUT?
SOMETHING'S NOT RIGHT. THIS GUY'S A LOT CRAZIER THAN HE LOOKS...
I MEAN, WHY THE HELL DOES HE WANT SHIIKO'S SOUL IN THE...
... NO.
DON'T ...
DON'T TELL ME...

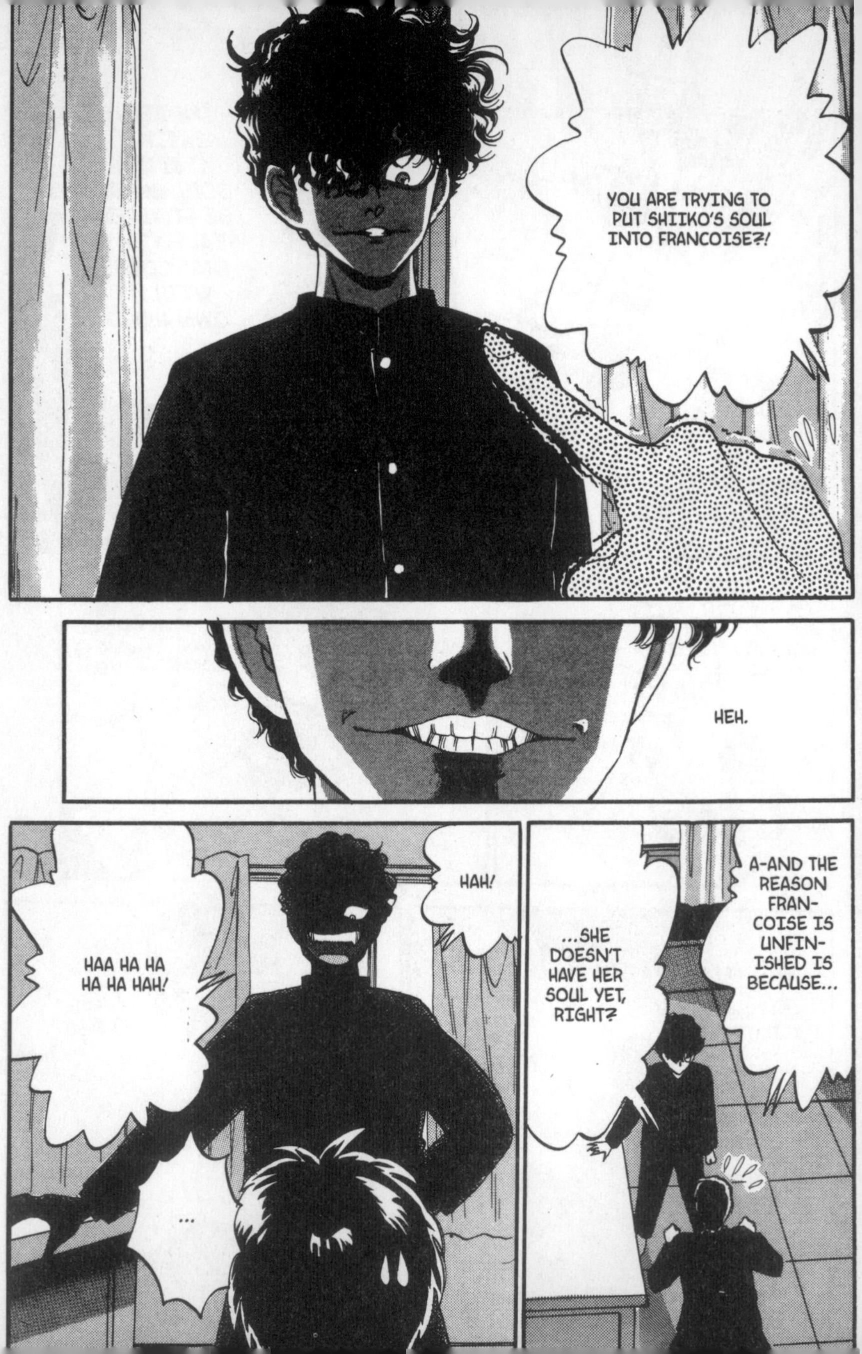
YOU ARE TRYING TO PUT SHIIKO'S SOUL INTO FRANCOISE?!
HEH.
A-AND THE REASON FRAN-COISE IS UNFIN-ISHED IS BECAUSE...
...SHE DOESN'T HAVE HER SOUL YET, RIGHT?
HAH!
HAA HA HA HA HA HAH!
...

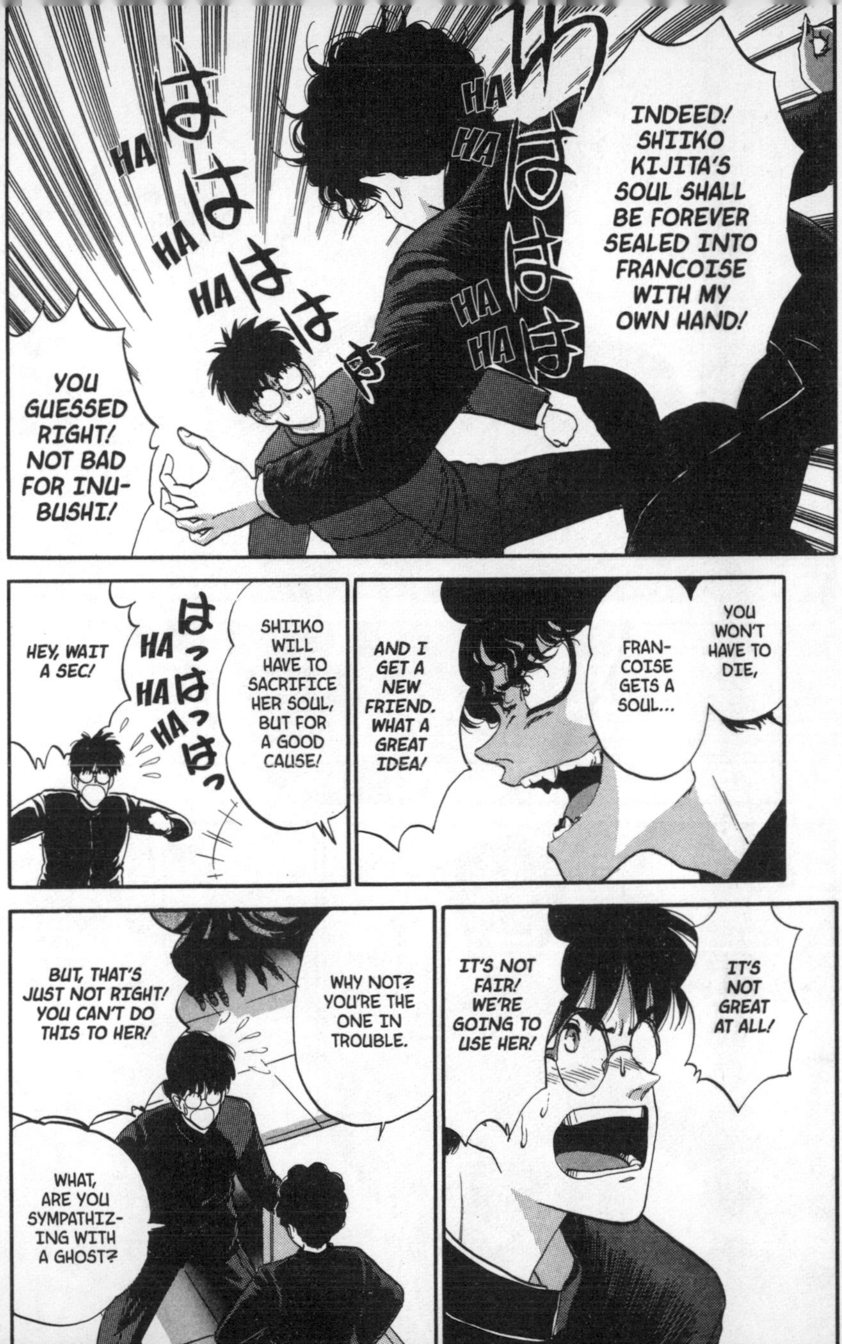
INDEED! SHIIKO KIJITA'S SOUL SHALL BE FOREVER SEALED INTO FRANCOISE WITH MY OWN HAND!
わははは
HA HA HA HA
ははは
HA HA HA HA
YOU GUESSED RIGHT! NOT BAD FOR INU-BUSHI!
YOU WON'T HAVE TO DIE,
FRAN-COISE GETS A SOUL...
AND I GET A NEW FRIEND. WHAT A GREAT IDEA!
SHIIKO WILL HAVE TO SACRIFICE HER SOUL, BUT FOR A GOOD CAUSE!
はっはっはっ
HA HA HA
HEY, WAIT A SEC!
IT'S NOT GREAT AT ALL!
IT'S NOT FAIR! WE'RE GOING TO USE HER!
WHY NOT? YOU'RE THE ONE IN TROUBLE.
BUT, THAT'S JUST NOT RIGHT! YOU CAN'T DO THIS TO HER!
WHAT, ARE YOU SYMPATHIZING WITH A GHOST?

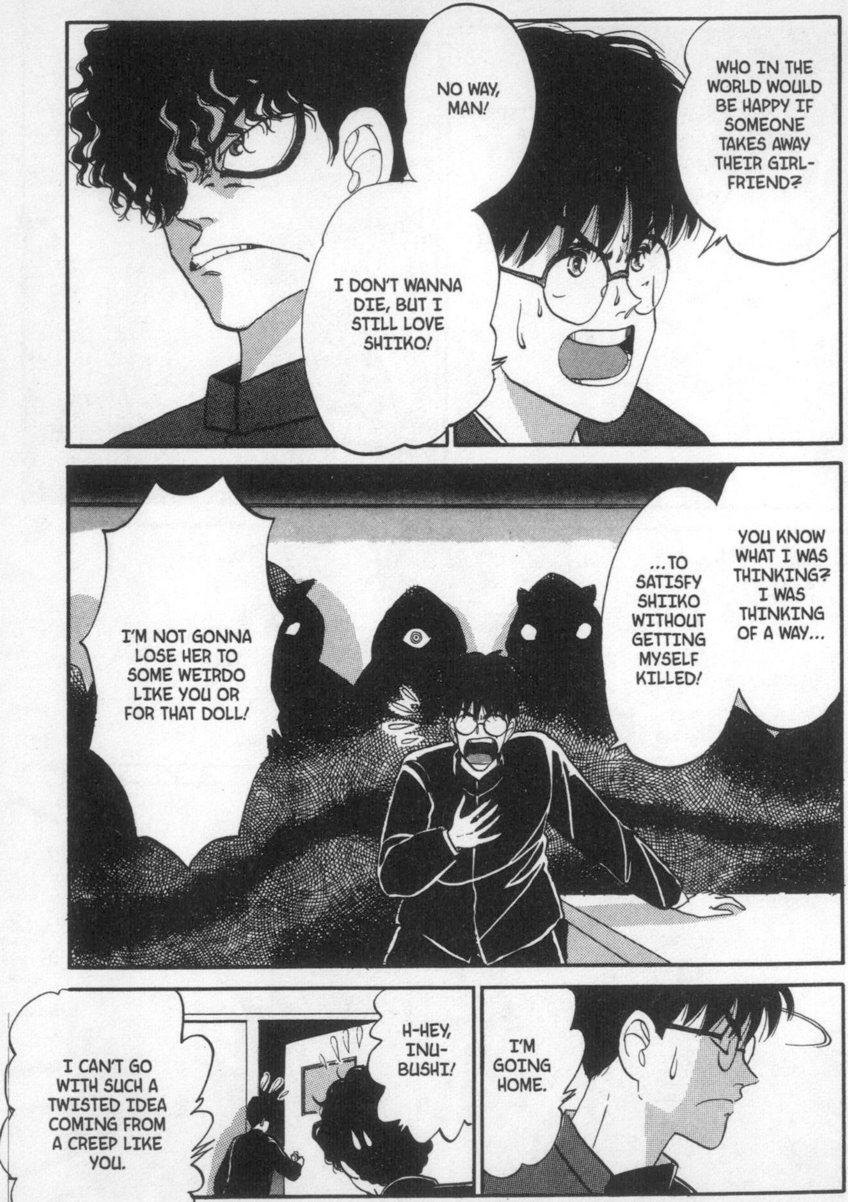
WHO IN THE WORLD WOULD BE HAPPY IF SOMEONE TAKES AWAY THEIR GIRL-FRIEND?
NO WAY, MAN!
I DON'T WANNA DIE, BUT I STILL LOVE SHIIKO!
YOU KNOW WHAT I WAS THINKING? I WAS THINKING OF A WAY...
...TO SATISFY SHIIKO WITHOUT GETTING MYSELF KILLED!
I'M NOT GONNA LOSE HER TO SOME WEIRDO LIKE YOU OR FOR THAT DOLL!
I'M GOING HOME.
H-HEY, INU-BUSHI!
I CAN'T GO WITH SUCH A TWISTED IDEA COMING FROM A CREEP LIKE YOU.

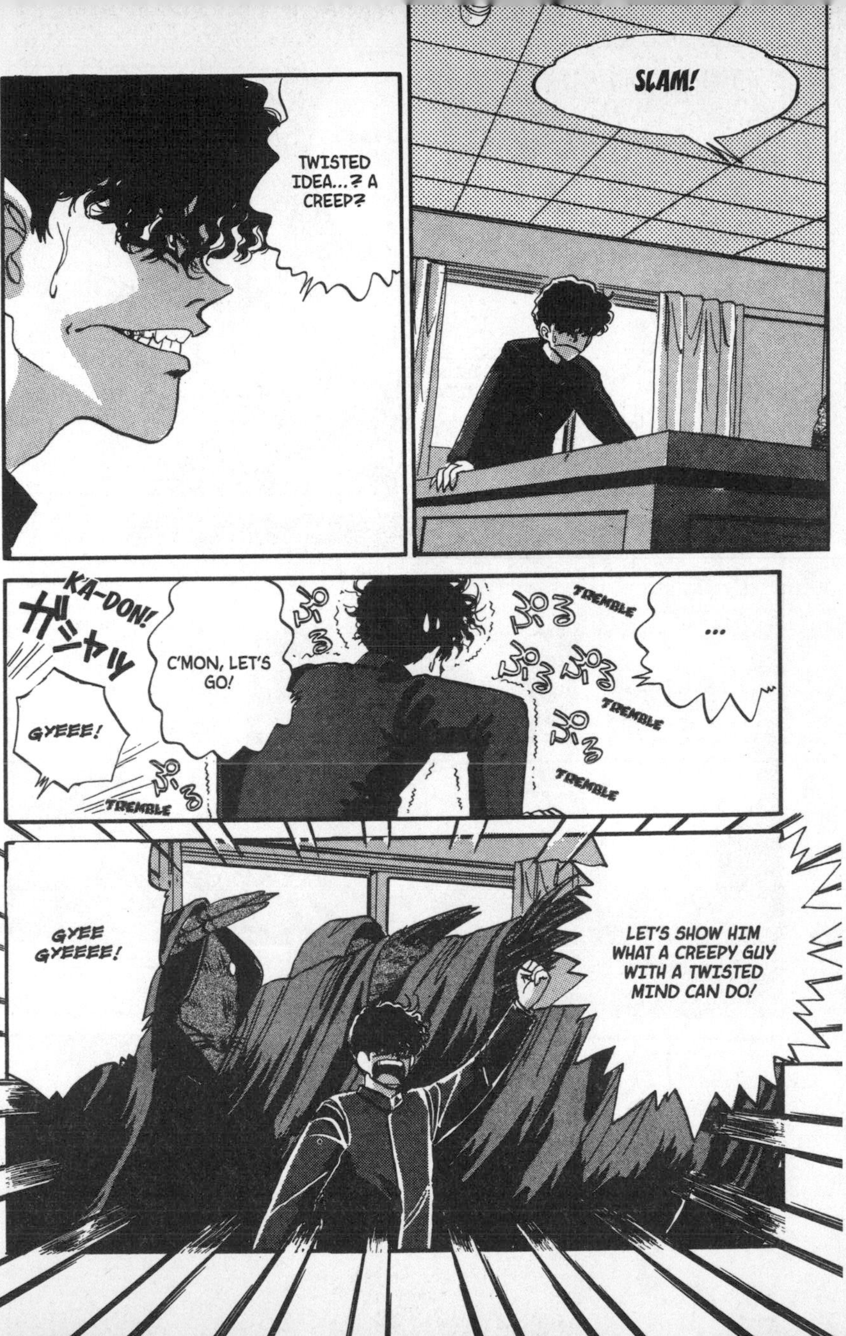
SLAM!
TWISTED IDEA...? A CREEP?
...
TREMBLE
ぷる
ぷる
ぷる
TREMBLE
ぷる
TREMBLE
ぷる
C'MON, LET'S GO!
KA-DON!
ガシャッ
GYEEE!
ぷる
TREMBLE
LET'S SHOW HIM WHAT A CREEPY GUY WITH A TWISTED MIND CAN DO!
GYEE GYEEEE!

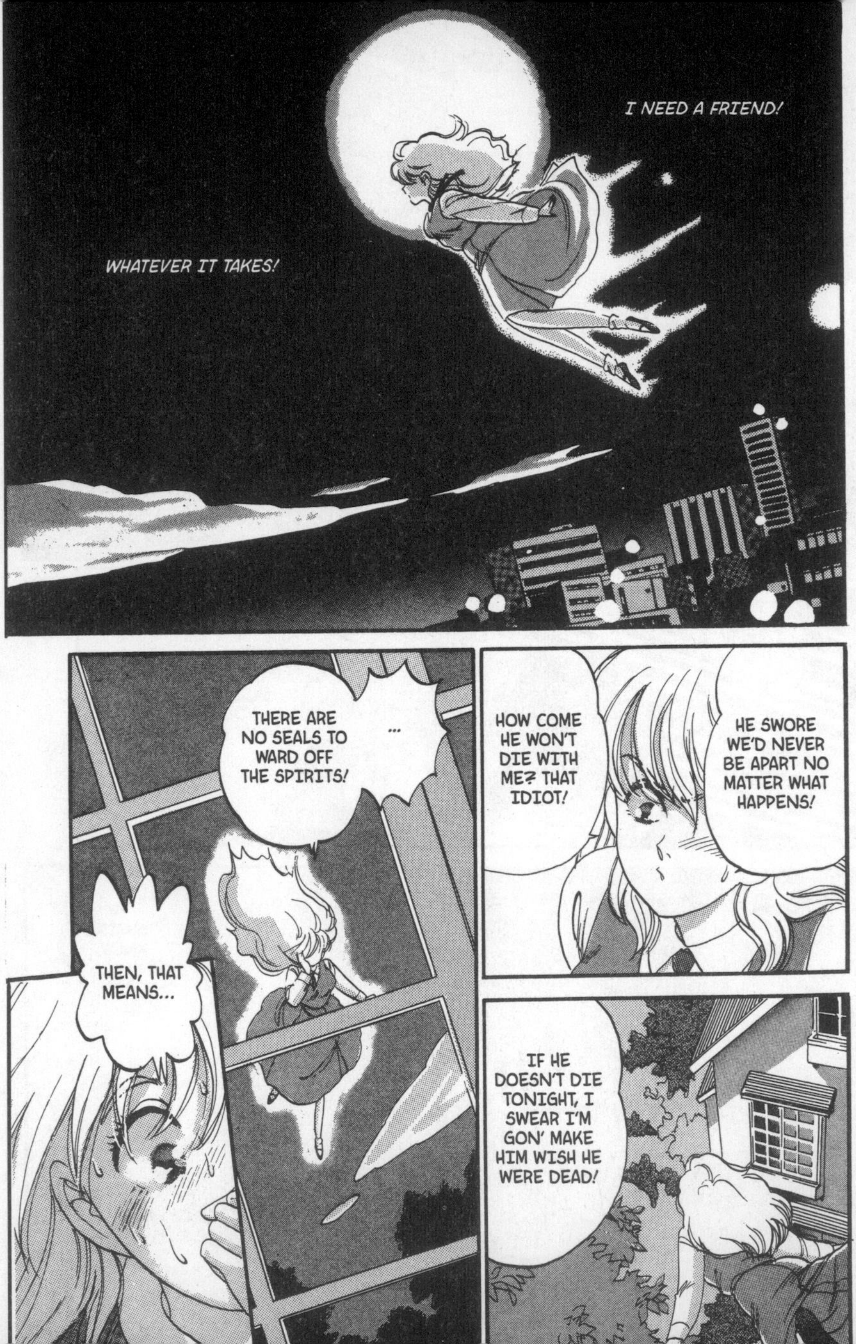
I NEED A FRIEND!
WHATEVER IT TAKES!
HE SWORE WE'D NEVER BE APART NO MATTER WHAT HAPPENS!
HOW COME HE WON'T DIE WITH ME? THAT IDIOT!
IF HE DOESN'T DIE TONIGHT, I SWEAR I'M GON' MAKE HIM WISH HE WERE DEAD!
...
THERE ARE NO SEALS TO WARD OFF THE SPIRITS!
THEN, THAT MEANS...

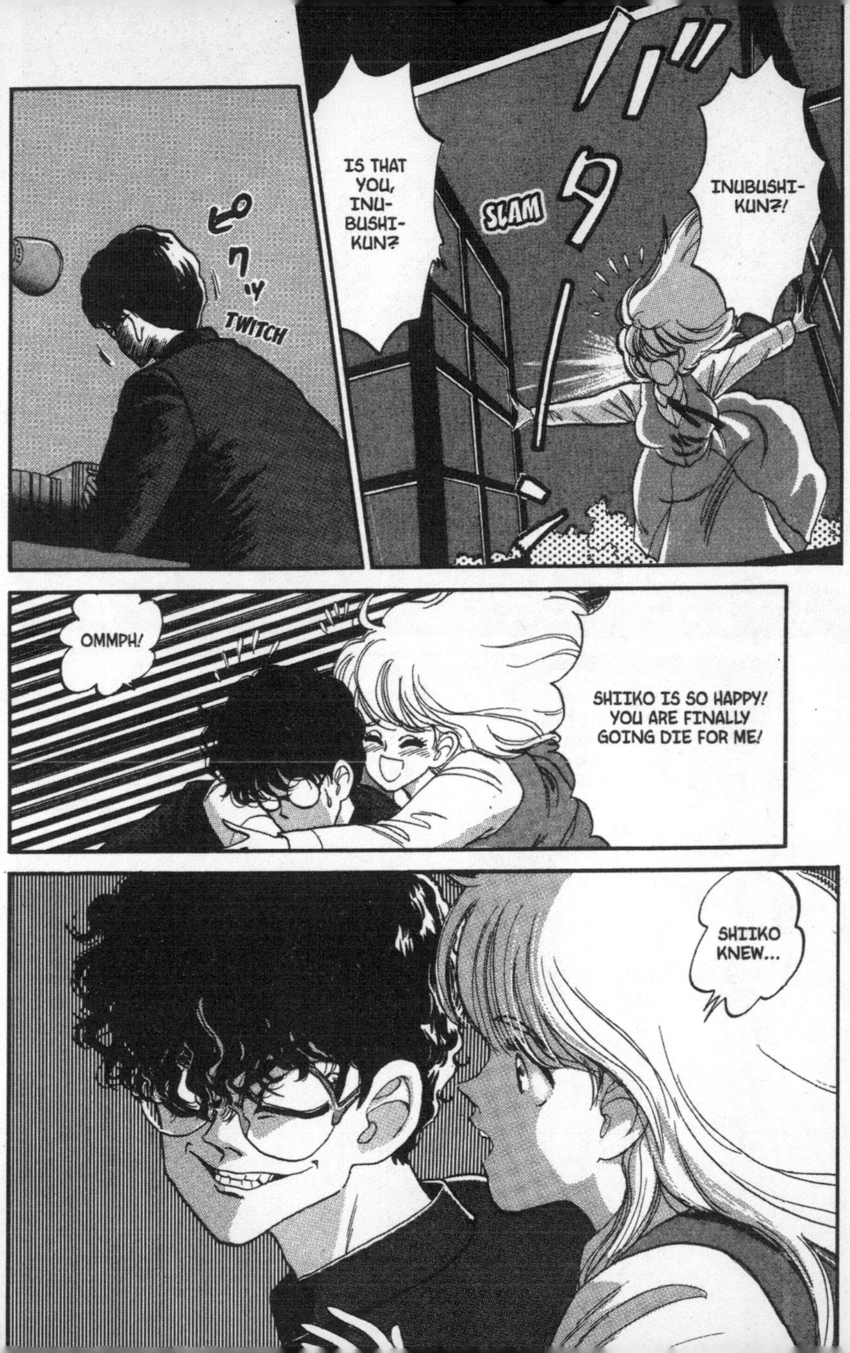
INUBUSHI-KUN?!
SLAM
IS THAT YOU, INU-BUSHI-KUN?
TWITCH
SHIIKO IS SO HAPPY! YOU ARE FINALLY GOING DIE FOR ME!
OMMPH!
SHIIKO KNEW...

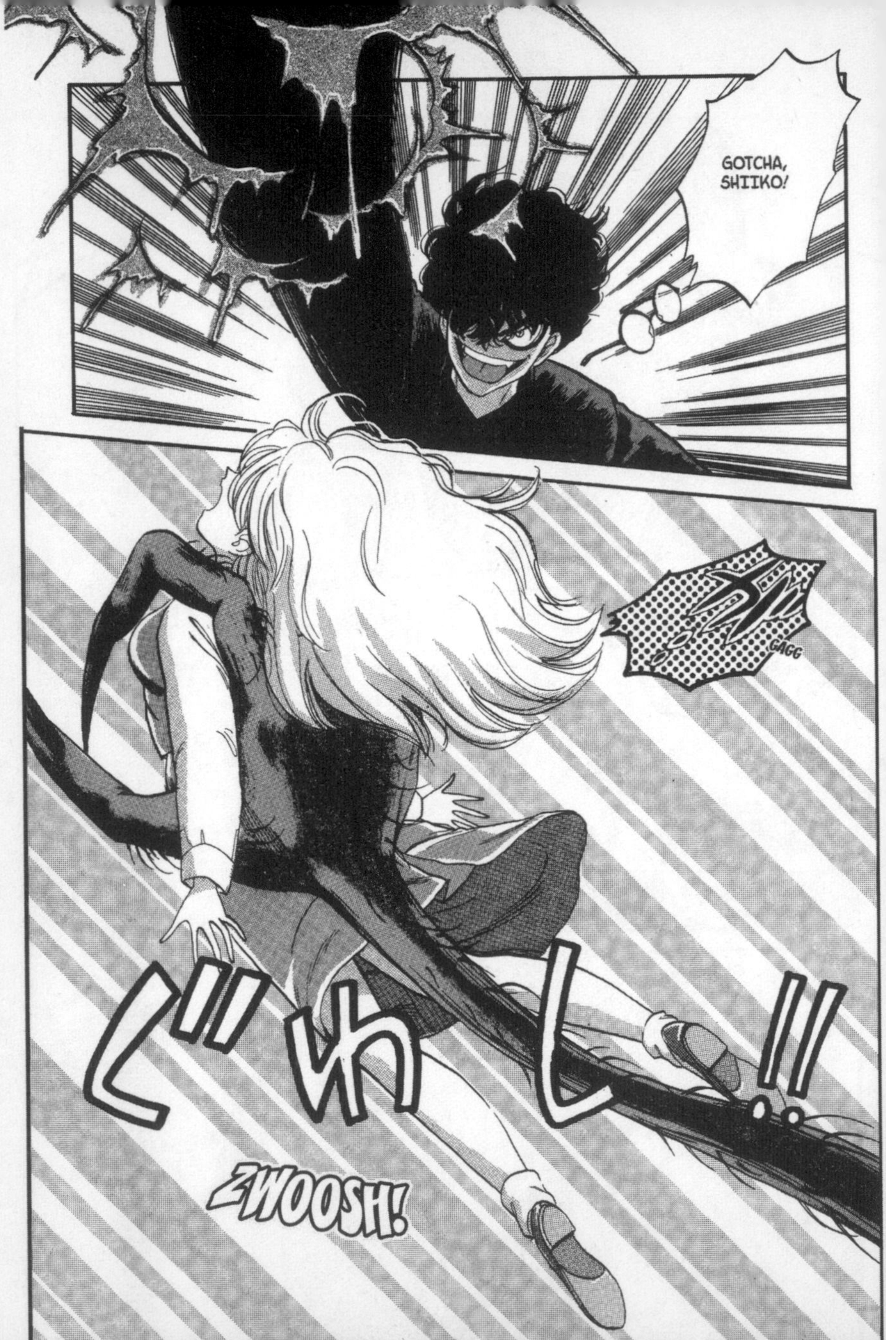
GOTCHA, SHIIKO!
GAGG
ぐわし!!
ZWOOSH!

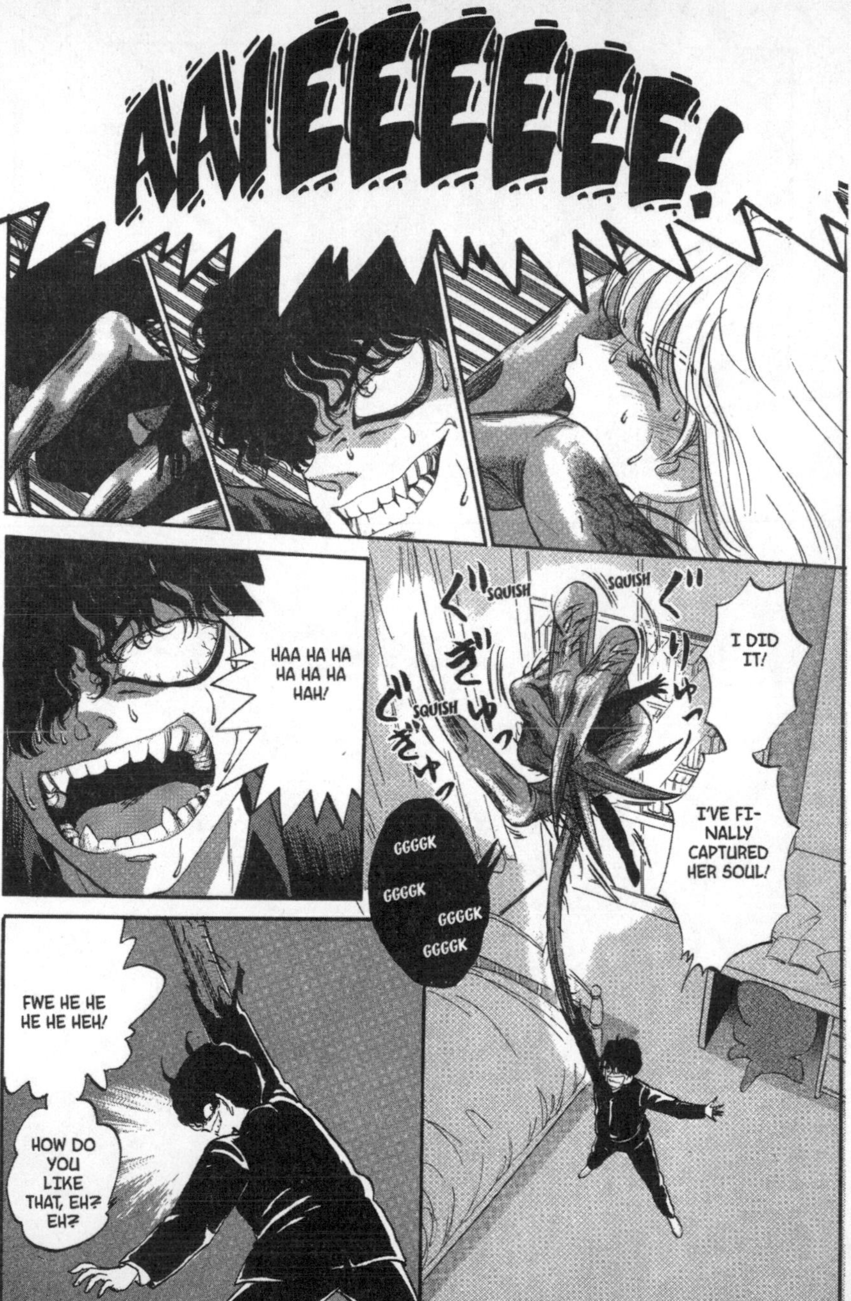
AAIEEEEEE!
SQUISH
SQUISH
SQUISH
I DID IT!
I'VE FI-NALLY CAPTURED HER SOUL!
GGGGK
GGGGK
GGGGK
GGGGK
HAA HA HA HA HA HA HAH!
FWE HE HE HE HE HEH!
HOW DO YOU LIKE THAT, EH? EH?

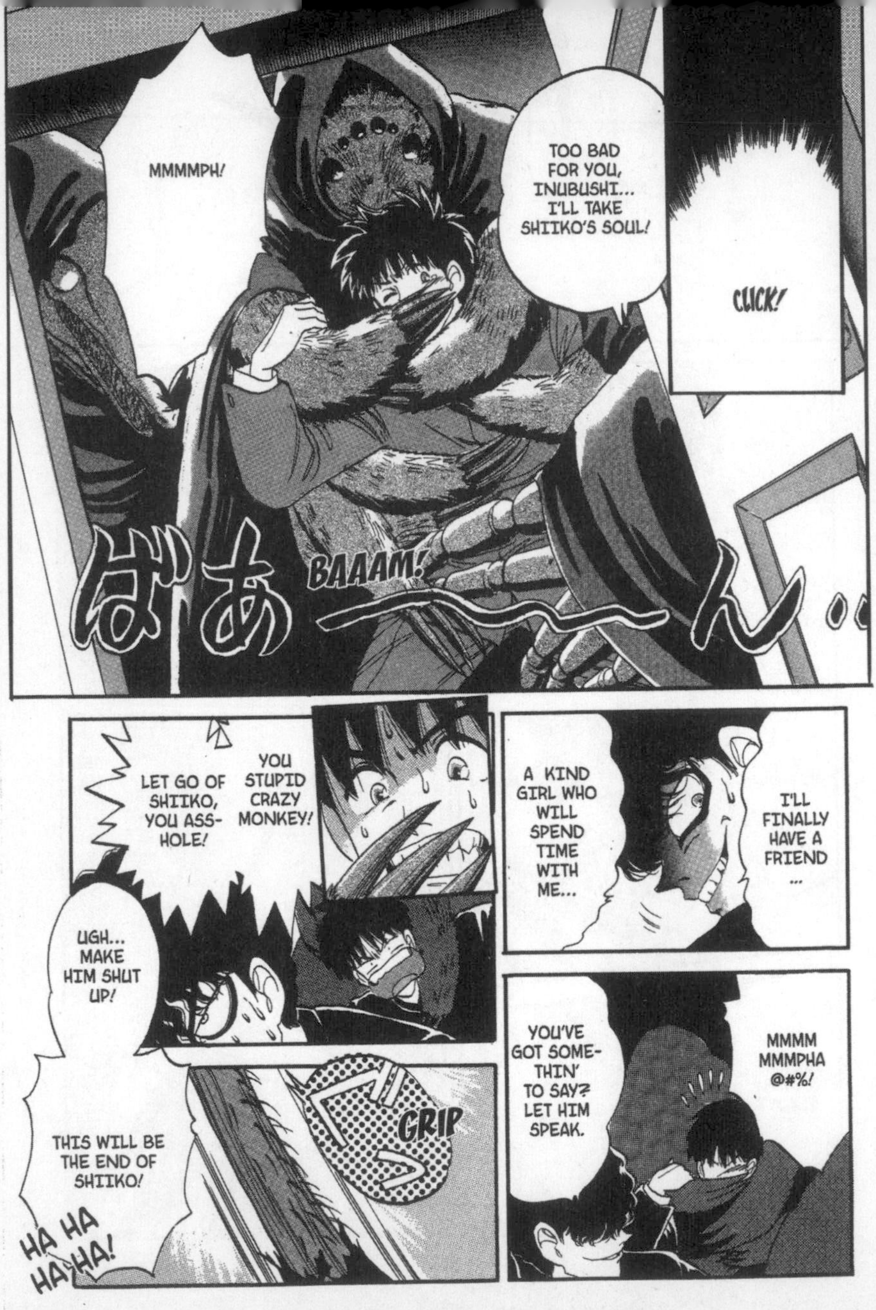
CLICK!
TOO BAD FOR YOU, INUBUSHI... I'LL TAKE SHIIKO'S SOUL!
MMMMPH!
ばあ〜〜ん…
BAAAM!
I'LL FINALLY HAVE A FRIEND ...
A KIND GIRL WHO WILL SPEND TIME WITH ME...
YOU STUPID CRAZY MONKEY!
LET GO OF SHIIKO, YOU ASS-HOLE!
UGH... MAKE HIM SHUT UP!
MMMM MMMPHA @#%!
YOU'VE GOT SOME-THIN' TO SAY? LET HIM SPEAK.
GRIP
THIS WILL BE THE END OF SHIIKO!
HA HA HA HA!

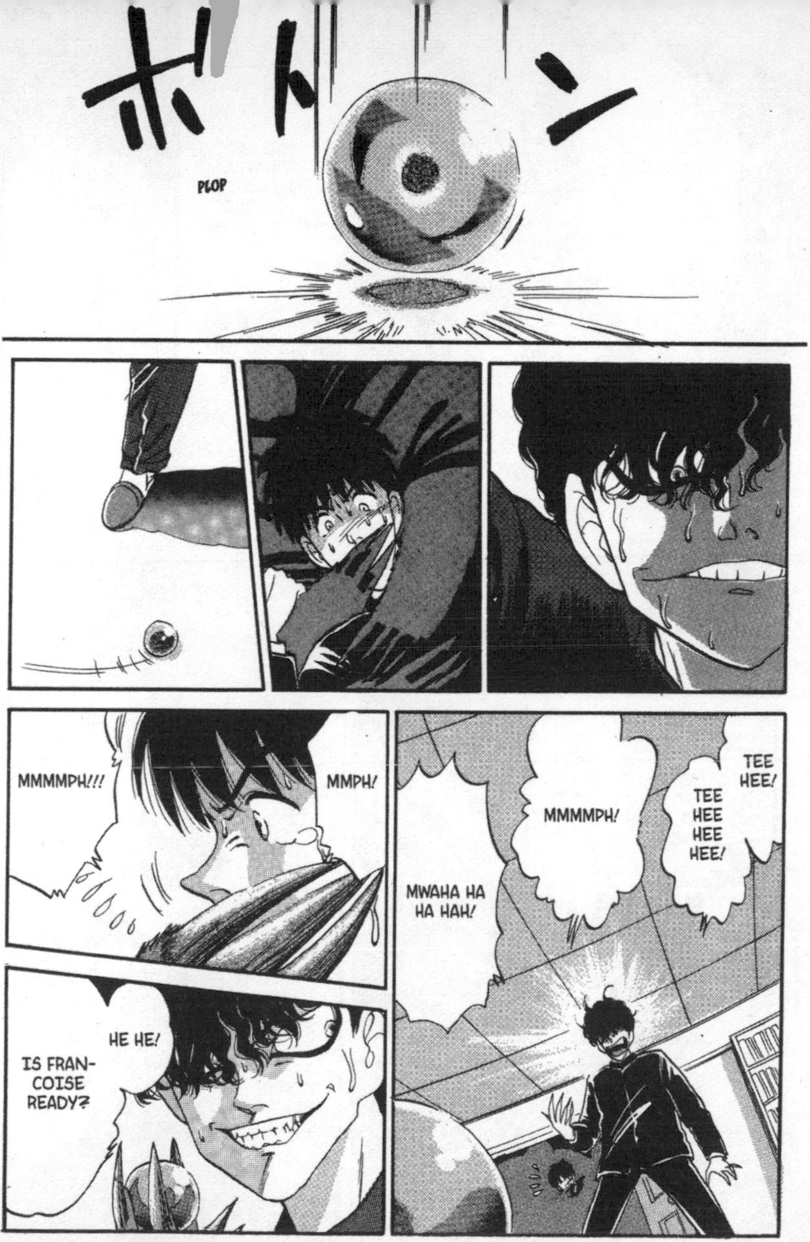
ボドン
PLOP
TEE HEE!
TEE HEE HEE HEE!
MMMMPH!
MWAHA HA HA HAH!
MMPH!
MMMMPH!!!
HE HE!
IS FRAN-COISE READY?

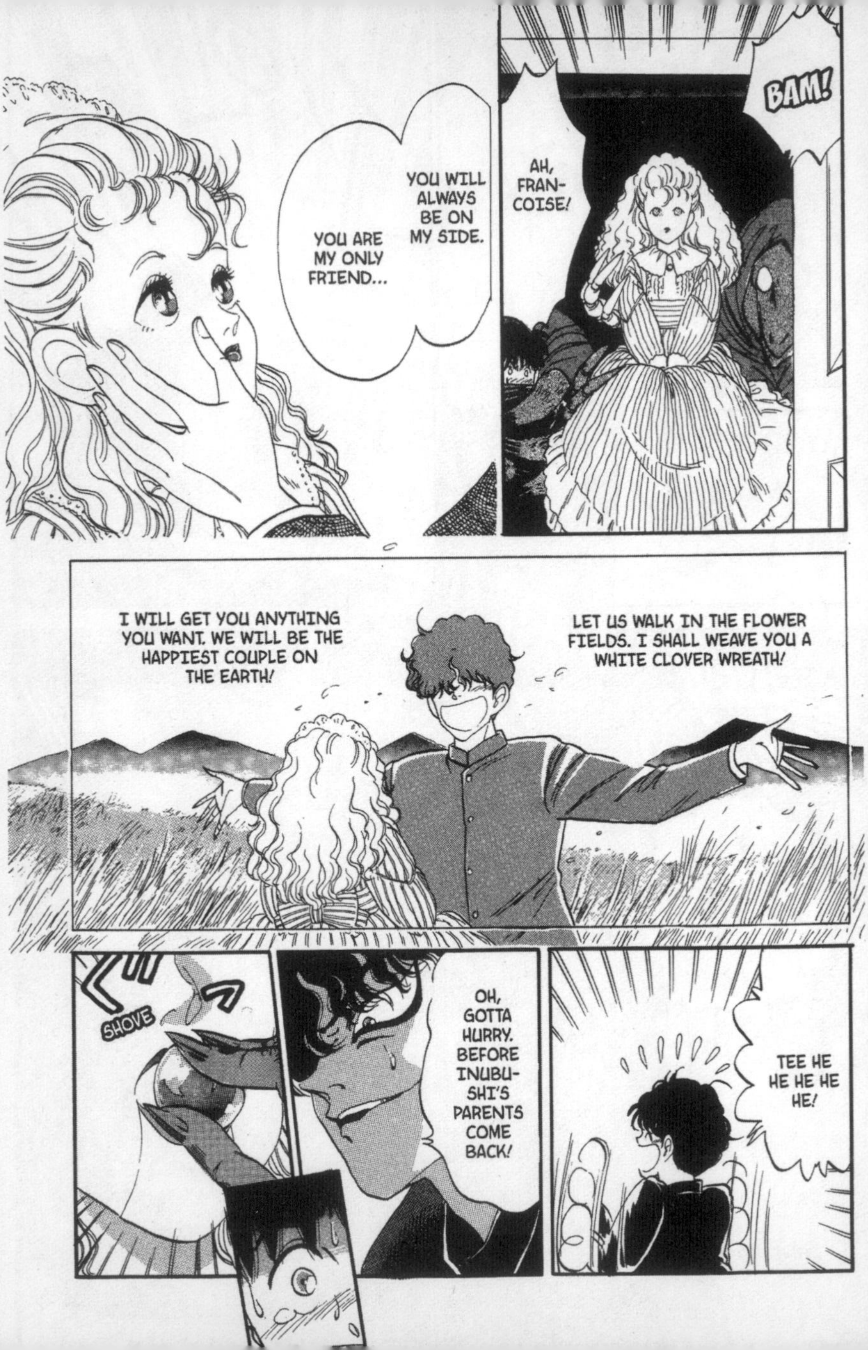
BAM!
AH, FRAN-COISE!
YOU ARE MY ONLY FRIEND... YOU WILL ALWAYS BE ON MY SIDE.
LET US WALK IN THE FLOWER FIELDS. I SHALL WEAVE YOU A WHITE CLOVER WREATH!
I WILL GET YOU ANYTHING YOU WANT. WE WILL BE THE HAPPIEST COUPLE ON THE EARTH!
TEE HE HE HE HE HE!
OH, GOTTA HURRY. BEFORE INUBU-SHI'S PARENTS COME BACK!
SHOVE

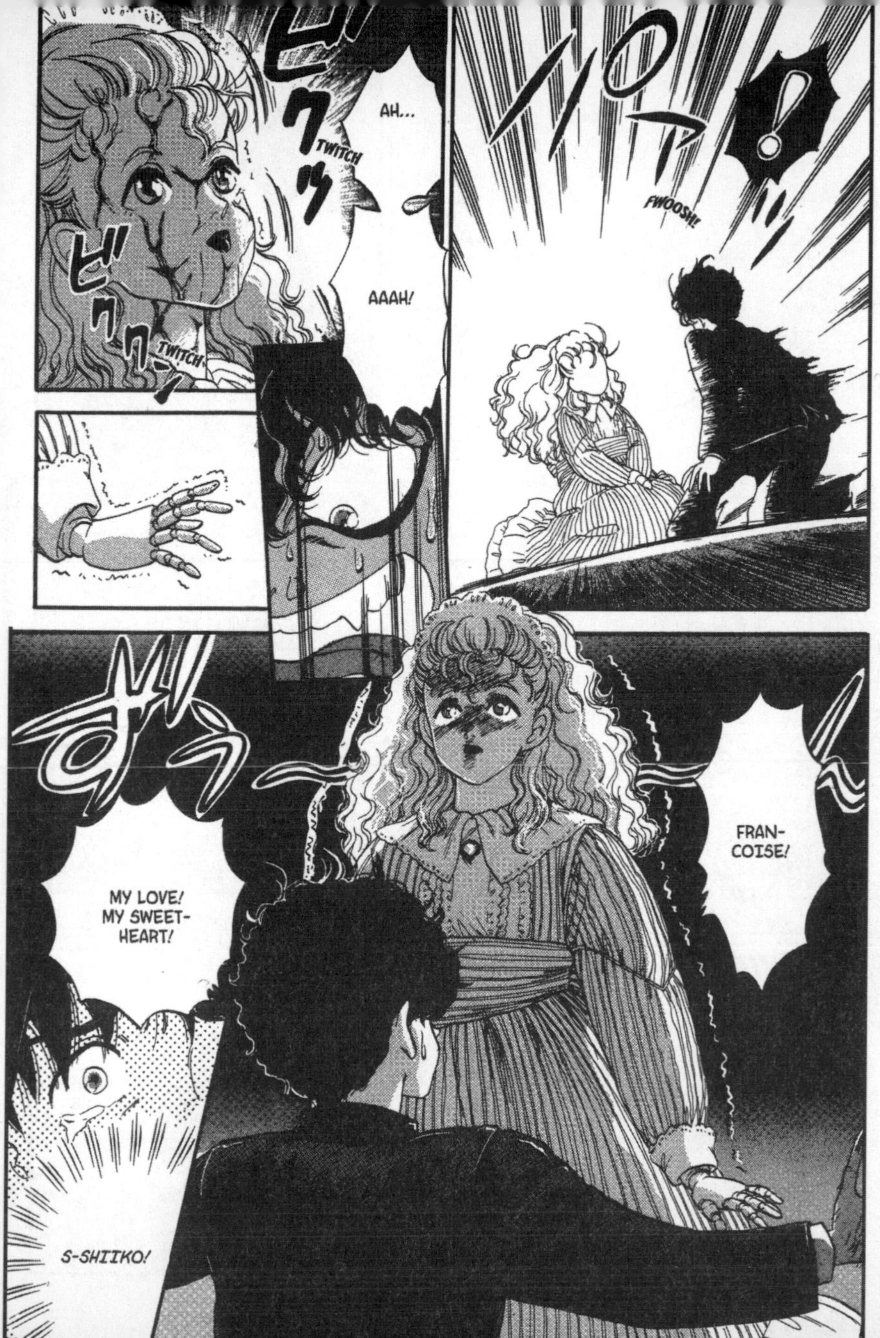

FWOOSH!
!
AH...
TWITCH
AAAH!
TWITCH
FRAN-
COISE!
MY LOVE!
MY SWEET-
HEART!
S-SHIIKO!

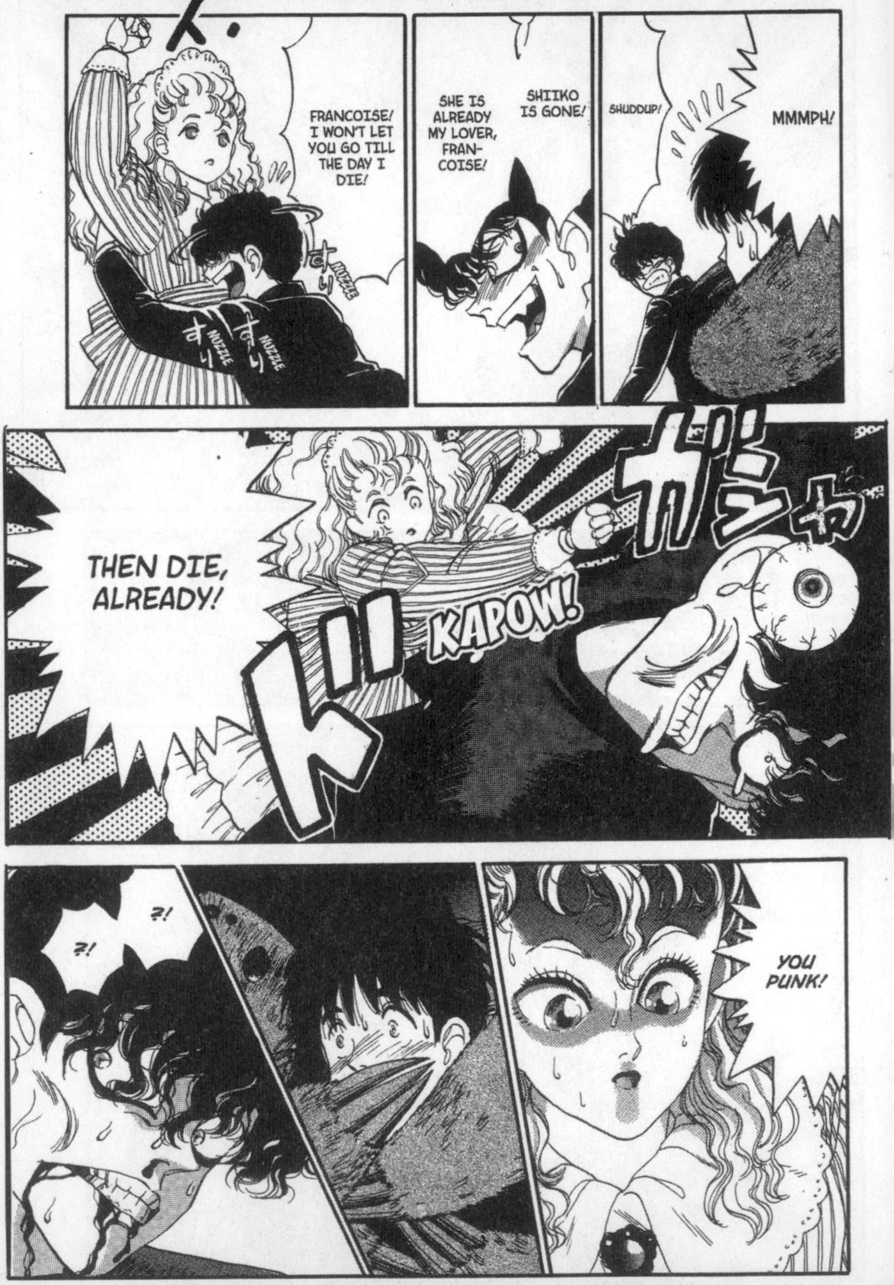
MMMPH!
SHUDDUP!
SHIIKO IS GONE!
SHE IS ALREADY MY LOVER, FRAN-COISE!
ス.
FRANCOISE! I WON'T LET YOU GO TILL THE DAY I DIE!
すり NUZZLE
すり NUZZLE
すり NUZZLE
ガシャ
KAPOW!
ドッ
THEN DIE, ALREADY!
YOU PUNK!
?!
?!

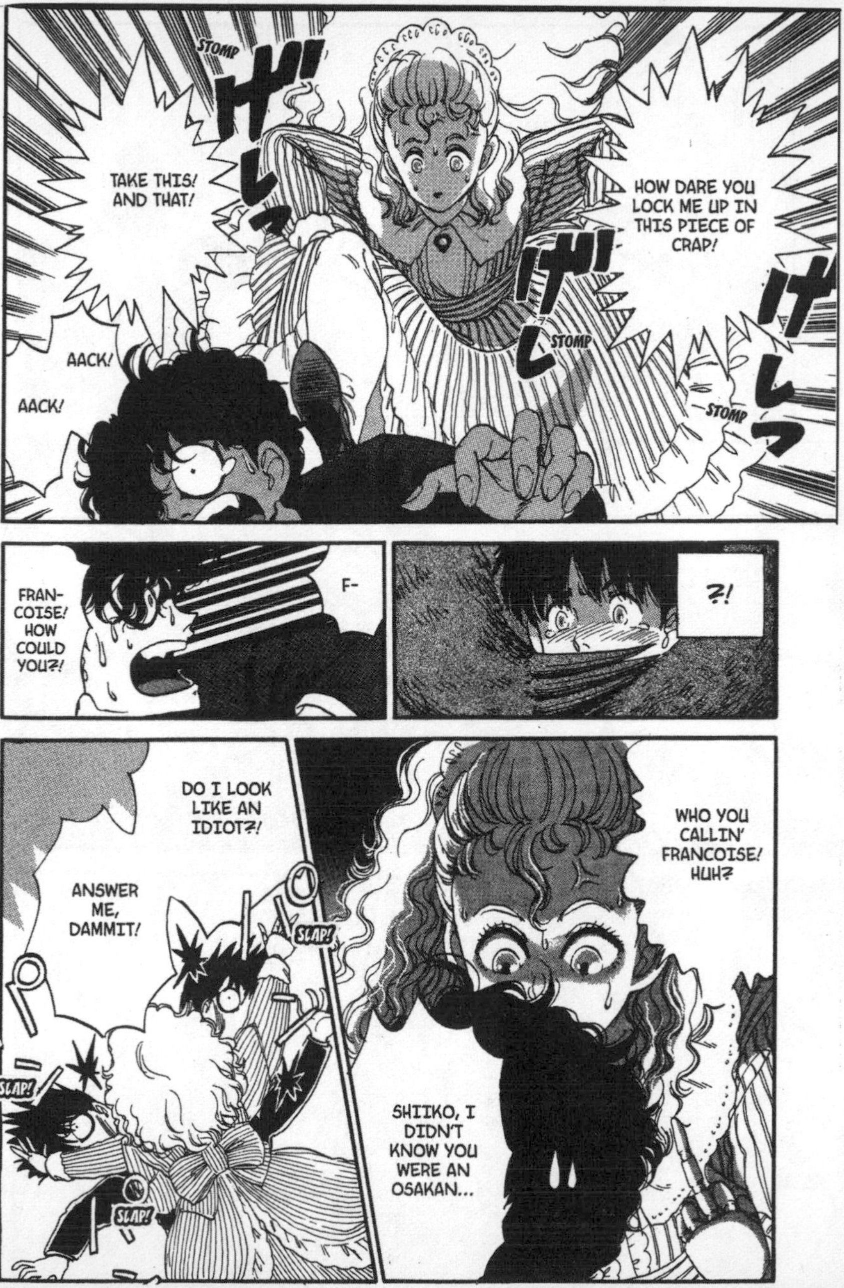

HOW DARE YOU LOCK ME UP IN THIS PIECE OF CRAP!
げしっ
STOMP
げしっ
STOMP
TAKE THIS! AND THAT!
げしっ
STOMP
AACK!
AACK!
?!
F-
FRAN-COISE! HOW COULD YOU?!
WHO YOU CALLIN' FRANCOISE! HUH?
SHIIKO, I DIDN'T KNOW YOU WERE AN OSAKAN...
DO I LOOK LIKE AN IDIOT?!
ANSWER ME, DAMMIT!
SLAP!
SLAP!
SLAP!

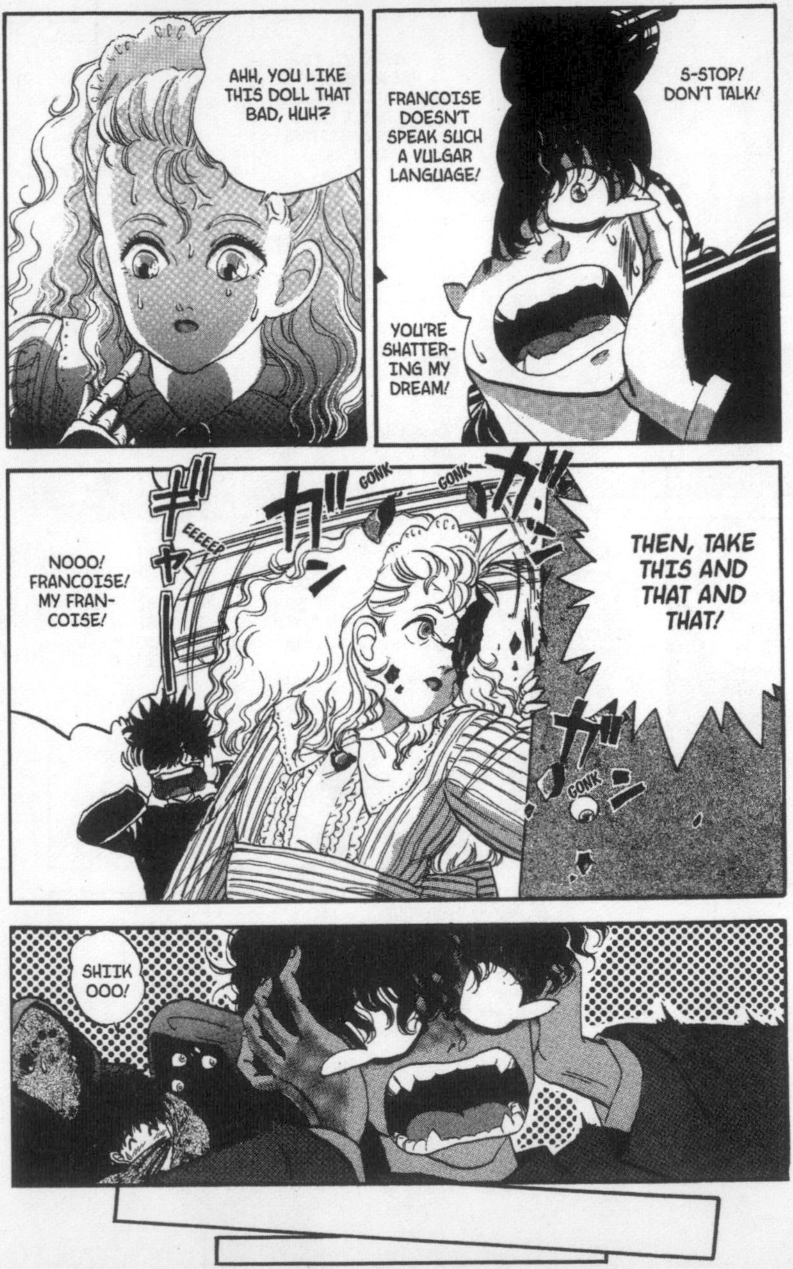
S-STOP! DON'T TALK!
FRANCOISE DOESN'T SPEAK SUCH A VULGAR LANGUAGE!
YOU'RE SHATTERING MY DREAM!
AHH, YOU LIKE THIS DOLL THAT BAD, HUH?
THEN, TAKE THIS AND THAT AND THAT!
GONK
GONK
EEEEEP
NOOO! FRANCOISE! MY FRANCOISE!
GONK
SHIIK OOO!

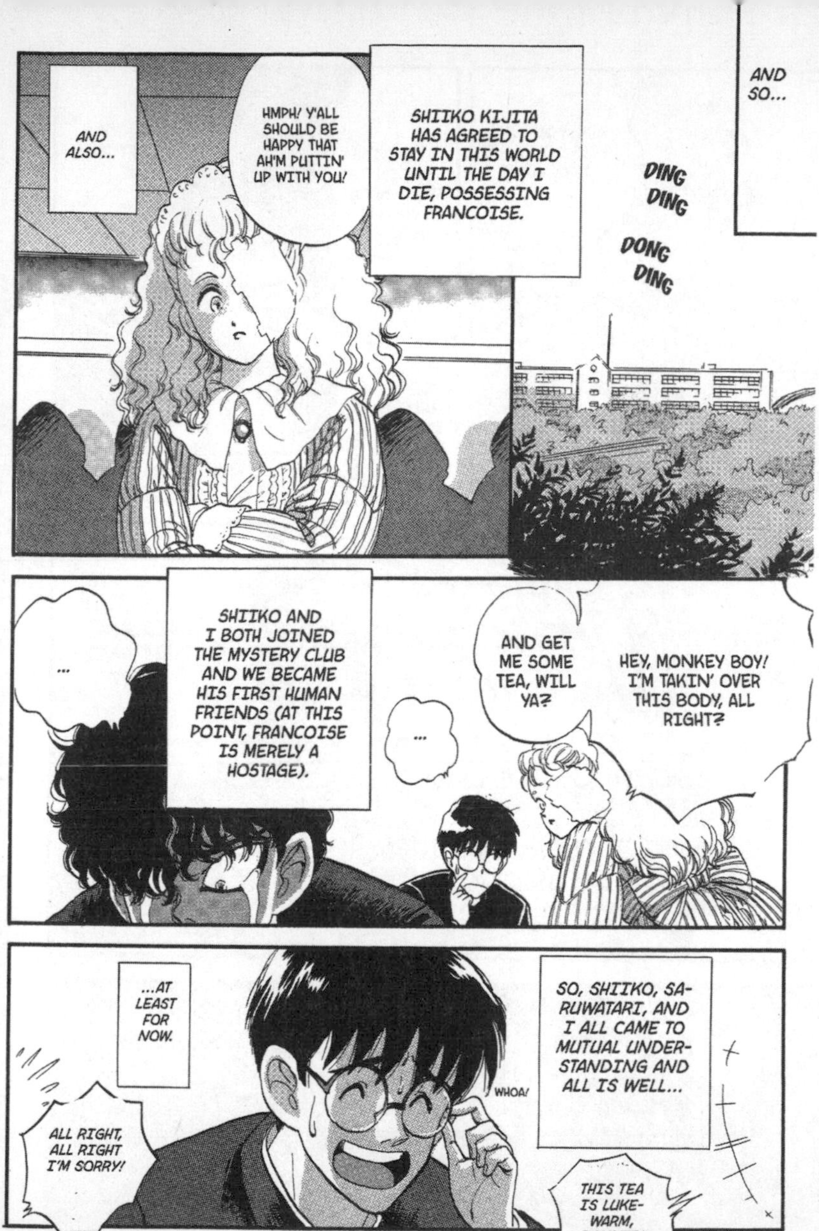
AND SO...
DING DING
DONG DING
SHIIKO KIJITA HAS AGREED TO STAY IN THIS WORLD UNTIL THE DAY I DIE, POSSESSING FRANCOISE.
HMPH! Y'ALL SHOULD BE HAPPY THAT AH'M PUTTIN' UP WITH YOU!
AND ALSO...
HEY, MONKEY BOY! I'M TAKIN' OVER THIS BODY, ALL RIGHT?
AND GET ME SOME TEA, WILL YA?
...
SHIIKO AND I BOTH JOINED THE MYSTERY CLUB AND WE BECAME HIS FIRST HUMAN FRIENDS (AT THIS POINT, FRANCOISE IS MERELY A HOSTAGE).
...
SO, SHIIKO, SA-RUWATARI, AND I ALL CAME TO MUTUAL UNDER-STANDING AND ALL IS WELL...
...AT LEAST FOR NOW.
WHOA!
THIS TEA IS LUKE-WARM, DAMMIT!
ALL RIGHT, ALL RIGHT I'M SORRY!

MYSTERY ALLIANCE THE END